<u>ERRATUM</u>

Pharmaceutical Autonomy and Public Health in Latin America: State, Society and Industry in Brazil's AIDS Program. 1st Edition.

ISBN: 9781138832534 (hbk)

Matthew Flynn

The publishers would like to apologize for the following error in this book:

In the above book, the date for when China changed its national legislation on the patenting of pharmaceuticals is wrong. Instead of the stated year of 2005 in the book, China became fully compliant with the Agreement on Trade-Related Aspects of Intellectual Property (TRIPS), a key part of the World Trade Organization (WTO), by 2001. Patents for drugs and new chemical entities were first introduced in revisions to the patent law in 1992. Additional revisions to the law in 2000 that took affect the following year confirmed the patenting of pharmaceuticals in accordance with TRIPS.

Pharmaceutical Autonomy and Public Health in Latin America

Brazil has occupied a central role in the access to medicines movement, especially with respect to drugs used to treat those with the human immunodeficiency virus (HIV) that causes the acquired immune deficiency syndrome (AIDS). How and why Brazil succeeded in overcoming powerful political and economic interests, both at home and abroad, to roll out and sustain treatment represents an intellectual puzzle.

In this book, Matthew Flynn traces the numerous challenges Brazil faced in its efforts to provide essential medicines to all of its citizens. Using dependency theory, state theory, and moral underpinnings of markets, Flynn delves deeper into the salient factors contributing to Brazil's successes and weaknesses, including control over technology, creation of political alliances, and instrumental use of normative frameworks, and effectively explains the ability of countries to fulfill the prescription drug needs of its population versus the interests and operations of the global pharmaceutical industry.

Pharmaceutical Autonomy and Public Health in Latin America is one of the only books to provide an in-depth account of the challenges that a developing country, like Brazil, faces to fulfill public health objectives amidst increasing global economic integration and new international trade agreements. Scholars interested in public health issues, HIV/AIDS, and human rights, but also social scientists interested in Latin America and international political economy, will find this an original and thought-provoking read.

Matthew Flynn is an Assistant Professor of Sociology and International Studies at Georgia Southern University in Statesboro, Georgia. His interests include political economy, health, and development with a focus on Latin America.

Routledge Studies in Latin American Politics

1 **Research and International Trade Policy Negotiations**
Knowledge and Power in Latin America
Edited by Mercedes Botto

2 **The United Nations in Latin America**
Aiding Development
Francis Adams

3 **Fear and Crime in Latin America**
Redefining State-Society Relations
Lucía Dammert

4 **Populism in Venezuela**
Ryan K. Brading

5 **Civil Society and Participatory Governance**
Municipal Councils and Social Housing Programs in Brazil
Maureen M. Donaghy

6 **Representation and Effectiveness in Latin American Democracies**
Congress, Judiciary and Civil Society
Edited by Moira B. MacKinnon and Ludovico Feoli

7 **Lula, the Workers' Party and the Governability Dilemma in Brazil**
Hernán F. Gómez Bruera

8 **Transnational Activism and National Movements in Latin America**
Bridging the Divide
Edited by Eduardo Silva

9 **Democracy, Revolution and Geopolitics in Latin America**
Venezuela and the International Politics of Discontent
Edited by Luis Fernando Angosto-Ferrández

10 **Transforming Brazil**
A History of National Development in the Postwar Era
Rafael R. Ioris

11 **Pharmaceutical Autonomy and Public Health in Latin America**
State, Society, and Industry in Brazil's AIDS Program
Matthew Flynn

Pharmaceutical Autonomy and Public Health in Latin America
State, Society, and Industry in Brazil's AIDS Program

Matthew Flynn

NEW YORK AND LONDON

First published 2015
by Routledge
711 Third Avenue, New York, NY 10017

and by Routledge
2 Park Square, Milton Park, Abingdon, Oxon, OX14 4RN

*Routledge is an imprint of the Taylor & Francis Group,
an informa business*

© 2015 Taylor & Francis

The right of Matthew Flynn to be identified as author of this work has
been asserted by him in accordance with sections 77 and 78 of the Copyright,
Designs and Patents Act 1988.

All rights reserved. No part of this book may be reprinted or reproduced or
utilized in any form or by any electronic, mechanical, or other means, now
known or hereafter invented, including photocopying and recording, or in any
information storage or retrieval system, without permission in writing from
the publishers.

Trademark Notice: Product or corporate names may be trademarks or
registered trademarks, and are used only for identification and explanation
without intent to infringe.

Library of Congress Cataloging-in-Publication Data

Flynn, Matthew (Matthew B.), author.
  Pharmaceutical autonomy and public health in Latin America : state,
society, and industry in Brazil's AIDS program / Matthew Flynn.
    p. ; cm. — (Routledge studies in Latin American politics ; 11)
  Includes bibliographical references and index.
  I. Title. II. Series: Routledge studies in Latin American politics ; 11.
[DNLM: 1. Acquired Immunodeficiency Syndrome—drug therapy—
Brazil.   2. Anti-Retroviral Agents—economics—Brazil.   3. Anti-Retroviral
Agents—therapeutic use—Brazil.   4. Drug Industry—economics—
Brazil.   5. Health Policy—Brazil. WC 503.2]
  RA643.86.B6
  362.19697'9200981—dc23
  2014034871

ISBN: 978-1-138-83253-4 (hbk)
ISBN: 978-1-315-73598-6 (ebk)

Typeset in Sabon
by Apex CoVantage, LLC

Printed and bound in the United States of America by Publishers Graphics,
LLC on sustainably sourced paper.

To my parents, Jim and Kathy Flynn

Contents

List of Abbreviations	ix
Timeline	xiii
Foreword	xv
Acknowledgements	xix
Introduction: Access to AIDS Medicines, Public Health, and the Brazilian Solution	1
1 Pharmaceutical Autonomy: Technology, Alliances, and Norms	7
2 Elements of Global Pharmaceutical Power	28
3 The Brazilian Context: Contradictions between Democracy and Neoliberalism	67
4 Asserting Antiretroviral Autonomy (1990–2001)	95
5 Patent Power and the Limits of Treatment Activism (2002–2006)	124
6 Consolidating the Pharmaceutical Alliance (2007–2013)	150
Conclusion	185
Appendices	205
Index	223

Abbreviations

ABIA	Brazilian Interdisciplinary Association for AIDS
ABIFINA	Brazilian Fine Chemicals Producers Association
ABIQUIF	Brazilian Pharmochemicals Producers Association
ACTPN	US President's Advisory Committee on Trade Policy and Negotiations
ADAPs	AIDS Drug Assistance Programs
AIDS	Acquired Immune Deficiency Syndrome
ALFOB	Brazilian Association of Public Labs
ANVISA	National Health Vigilance Agency (Brazil's drug regulatory agency)
API	Active Pharmaceutical Ingredient
ARV	Antiretroviral drug
AZT	Zidovudine, an antiretroviral drug
BMS	Bristol-Myers Squibb
BNDES	Brazilian National Development Bank
CEME	Central Medicines Agency
CL	Compulsory license
ENSP	Sergio Arouca National School of Public Health (*Escola Nacional de Saúde Pública Sergio Arouca*)
FDA	Food and Drug Administration
FDC	Fixed-dose combinations
FEBRAFARMA	Brazilian Pharmaceutical Industry Federation
FHC	Fernando Henrique Cardoso, President of Brazil from 1995–2002
FIOCRUZ	Oswaldo Cruz Foundation
FM	Farmanguinhos (*Instituto de Tecnologia em Fármacos*—Medicines and Drugs Technology Institute)
FOIA	Freedom of Information Act
FURP	Foundation for Public Drugs, Pharmaceutical Laboratory of São Paulo State
GATT	General Agreement on Tariffs and Trade
GECIS	Executive Group of the Industrial Health Complex

x *Abbreviations*

GSK	GlaxoSmithKline
INPI	Brazilian Patent Office
INTERFARMA	Brazilian Research-based Pharmaceutical Manufacturers Association
IP	Intellectual property
IPRs	Intellectual property rights
IQUEGO	Pharmaceutical Laboratory of Goania State
IVB	Vital Brazil Institute, Pharmaceutical Laboratory of Rio de Janeiro State
LAFEPE	Pharmaceutical Laboratory of Pernambuco State
LULA	Luiz Inácio Lula da Silva, President of Brazil from 2003–2010
MSD	Merck Sharpe & Dohme
MSF	Medicins Sans Frontiers (Doctors without Borders)
NGO	Nongovernmental organization
NIH	National Institutes of Health
PDPs	Productive Development Partnerships
PPPY	Per patient per year
PhRMA	Pharmaceutical Research and Manufacturers Association
PROGENERICOS	Brazilian Generic Medicines Industry Association
PSDB	The Brazilian Social Democratic Party
PT	The Workers' Party
UN	United Nations
US	United States
USTR	United States Trade Representative
SUS	Unified Health System (Brazil's federal health system)
TRIPS	Trade-Related Aspects of Intellectual Property Rights
UNAIDS	United Nations Joint Program on AIDS
UNCTAD	United Nations Conference on Trade and Development
UNGASS	United Nations General Assembly Special Session
WHO	World Health Organization
WIPO	World Intellectual Property Office
WTO	World Trade Organization

Timeline

1980	First case of HIV in São Paulo, later classified as HIV in 1982
1984	São Paulo State establishes first AIDS program in the country
1985	Brazil's federal government establishes first programs to fight the epidemic
1985	The first AIDS NGO, Prevention Support Group (*Grupo de Apoio à Prevenção à Aids*—GAPA), founded
1986	Ministry of Health establishes National STD/AIDS Program
1988	Brazil establishes new Constitution incorporating the right to health
1989	São Paulo State Health Department initiates limited distribution of AZT
1990	Unified Health System (*Sistema Única da Saúde*—SUS) established
1991	Federal government begins to distribute ARVs on a limited basis
1992	Microbiologica launches "Brazilian AZT" (zidovudine)
1994	Fernando Henrique Cardoso from the Brazilian Social Democratic Party assumes the presidency of Brazil
1994	Brazil signs first agreement with the World Bank to fight AIDS
1995	Member countries establish the World Trade Organization (WTO) along with the Agreement on Trade-Related Aspects of Intellectual Property (TRIPS)
1996	Brazil passes *Lei Sarney,* which stipulates that the state must offer universal free antiretroviral treatment to people living with HIV/AIDS
1996	Brazil passes Industrial Property Law No. 9.279 that provides patents for pharmaceutical processes and products, coming into force the following year
1998	Thirty-nine mostly transnational pharmaceutical companies file suit against the government of South Africa, alleging new legislation violates the TRIPS accord
2000	US initiates WTO-panel against Brazil concerning its patent legislation

xiv *Timeline*

2001 (Nov)	WTO members adopt the Doha Declaration on TRIPS and Public Health
2002 (Jan)	President Luiz Inacio "Lula" da Silva from the Workers' Party becomes the president of Brazil
2002	The United Nations establishes the Global Fund to Fight AIDS, Tuberculosis and Malaria
2003	The United States kicks off the President's Emergency Plan for AIDS Relief (PEPFAR)
2005	India and China introduce pharmaceutical product patents in accordance with the TRIPS Agreement
2006	Thailand issues a compulsory license for the AIDS drug efavirenz.
2007 (Jan)	Thailand issues compulsory license for the AIDS drug lopinavir/ritonavir (Kaletra) and the heart disease drug clopidogrel
2007 (May)	Brazil issues a compulsory license for efavirenz marketed by Merck Sharpe & Dohme
2010	Dilma Rouseff from the Workers' Party succeeds Lula as Brazil's president

Foreword

To start, I want to welcome and acknowledge the publication of *Pharmaceutical Autonomy and Public Health in Latin America*, which was carefully prepared and comprehensively studied by Matthew Flynn. As a member of what we can call a new generation of policy researchers, Matthew has analyzed how Brazil was at the center of the discussion regarding access to medicines and intellectual property issues in recent years. At a time when the world was skeptical about the ability of middle-income countries to adequately address this issue, Brazil responded to the broad social movement that sought a comprehensive policy on access to HIV-related medicines and other health technologies. Time proved how the world was wrong and how Brazil was right, despite being a "lone ranger" in a fight that many other countries later followed in striking down the costs of antiretroviral medicines (ARVs).

Matthew carefully describes the conflicts of interests between global health and the operations of the pharmaceutical industry by outlining both aspects of dependency and autonomy, as well as the State's role in fostering the division and control of markets. The range of interested stakeholders and people interviewed in preparation for this book provides a comprehensive assessment of the conflicting interests in order to narrate an evidence-based account of Brazil's challenges and successes. The illustration of a young person coming from Florida and moving to Brazil but, at the same time, having in Brazil access to treatment denied to her in her homeland, illustrates the challenges and successes the developing world has faced in addressing access to medicines.

The neoliberalism assumed by the Brazilian Government under Fernando Henrique Cardoso—a former and worldwide famous writer and sociologist recognized for his work on economic and social development through his critique of capitalism and his formulation of dependency theory—included privatization policies. This is not the only neoliberal act associated with this period of governance, as it was also during Cardoso's term of government that the Patent Law (Industrial Property Law or Law 9.279) was approved in spite of all the criticism that it trumped foreign over national interests and conceded to the Agreement on Trade-Related Aspects of Intellectual

xvi *Foreword*

Property (TRIPS) of the World Trade Organization (WTO) without using the flexibilities and special conditions that other countries not bound to the interests of Big Pharma adopted. In other words, this policy made Brazil bend to the demands of the United States Trade Representative.

Revisiting Gary Gereffi, who wrote in 1983, Matthew redefines dependency theory and proposes an analytical framework for understanding pharmaceutical autonomy, which he defines as "a country's ability to fulfill the prescription drug needs of its populations especially in the face of structural constraints." Research, production—including the manufacturing of APIs—and final formulation processes are described eloquently and discussed comprehensively, as two extremes between pharmaceutical autonomy and pharmaceutical dependency.

Historical conjunctures and short-term processes in Brazil give rise to the relationships between different government periods and landmarks in Brazilian policy, especially the use of the only compulsory license for an ARV product, efavirenz, in 2007. It is important to highlight that the preparation that took place prior to issuing this compulsory license, during the first mandate of President Lula, with Jose Gomes Temporão as the Minister of Health, involved complex discussions at all levels of the Brazilian government, and included support from international media and United Nations (UN) organizations, which I witnessed closely and supported from inside the World Health Organization's Regional Office for the Americas.

The book's outline progresses along a methodological and conceptual framework that traces the Brazilian response to HIV/AIDS. The global political economy, the growing power of global pharmaceutical companies, the establishment of the World Trade Organization (WTO) after the Uruguay Round of the General Agreement on Trade and Tariffs (GATT), encompass the so-called pendulum between autonomy and dependency.

Brazil's pharmaceutical capabilities, despite problems related to importation and the weakening of the installed pharmaceutical and raw material manufacturing capacity, are linked to an underfunded National Health System. The issue of local manufacturing of ARVs places Brazil in direct conflict with global efforts that empower global pharmaceutical manufacturers. The WTO panel between Brazil and the United States over the use of TRIPS flexibilities and the ongoing impact of patent protection on extending monopolies and oligopolies not only in Brazil but other dependent countries lead up to recent industrial policies in Brazil that seek to bridge industrial policies with health policies.

The end of the book addresses and highlights recent policies that Brazil is implementing. A political decision has been stated very clearly that seeks to link access to essential medical technologies with strengthening of local production, including the manufacturing of active principal ingredients and final formulation for products. More recently, this approach also expanded to the growing biotechnological industry, so it still is to be assessed what the impact of this new approach will be for local manufacturing efforts in Brazil.

Finally, I must say that this book correctly addresses crucial issues through an evidence-based approach, all the time comprising a normative framework based on human rights and calling for urgent state and government actions that may really enhance access to medicines and public health.

I really am very glad to highlight and welcome the contribution this book brings to issues related to global health! Congratulations to the author.

Jorge Bermudez
Vice-President for Health Production and Innovation
Fundação Oswaldo Cruz, Ministry of Health, Brazil

Acknowledgements

This book would not have been possible without the guidance and support of several people and institutions. I must first thank my doctoral co-supervisors Bryan Roberts and Cynthia Buckley who dedicated their time and knowledge in guiding me through field research and theory development. The rest of my committee, comprised of Peter Ward, Antonio Ugalde, Mounira Charrad, and Robert Wilson, also provided valuable insights and feedback during my doctoral years and beyond.

A special thanks goes to the Center for Pharmaceutical Policy Studies (*Nucleu de Assistência Farmaceûtica*—NAF), a research center at the National School of Public Health *(Escola Nacional da Saúde Pública)*, which is part of the Oswaldo Cruz Foundation *(Fundação Oswaldo Cruz)* in Rio de Janeiro, Brazil. NAF's institutional support was essential to carrying out my field research in Brazil. *Nafinhos* also provided the care of a family, the laughter of friends, support against bureaucracies, and insight into the Brazilian reality that no other Brazilian institution could provide. I want to give special mention to my host supervisors Egléubia Andrade de Oliveira and Vera Lucia Luiza.

Various other friends and colleagues also provided important support. In São Paulo, I want to thank José Ruben de Alcântara Bonfim at Sobrevime for office space and research support. Developing my ideas and questions would not have been possible without the many informal conversations I had with colleagues. In the United States, I would like to thank Daniel Ritter, Joshua Busby, Nicole Angotti, and Sam Cohn for feedback and support. In Brazil, I want to thank Hayne Felipe, Lia Hasenclever, Jessica Rich, Monica Samrsla, Marilena Correa, Orival Silveira, Glauco Arbix, Daniel Arbix, Andre Pereira, Jorge Bermudez, Gabriela Chaves, among others. I have also benefitted from productive exchanges with Ken Shadlen, Nitsan Chorev, Nuria Homedes, Judit Ruiz, Analia Porras, James Fitzgerald, Donald Light, and Jesus Maria Garcia Calleja.

This book would not have been possible without the financial support of a Fellowship in Latin American Sociology from the Andrew W. Mellon Foundation. Additionally, as a Post-Doctoral Fellow in Health and Human Rights at the Bernard and Audre Rapoport Center for Human Rights and

xx *Acknowledgements*

Justice, University of Texas at Austin, I benefitted from insights from the Health and Human Rights Workshop which I co-directed with Neville Hoad. Georgia Southern University's Writing and Research Workshop, led by Larry Griffin, also provided additional opportunities to refine my work. Work experience with the University of Texas at Austin HIV/STD Research Support Team to the Texas Department of State Health Services HIV/STD Prevention and Intervention Unit allowed me to contextualize Brazil's experience and compare it to programs in the United States. Lastly, Taylor and Francis' anonymous reviewers provided important critiques and feedback, and their editors and project managers, including Natalja Mortensen and Lillian Rand, played an essential role in the publication process.

Lastly, I want to thank my many friends in Brazil for offering me their hospitality and assistance while I was in the field. Kirtan Smith provided vital assistance in translating and transcribing several interviews, and Danielle Brown assisted with proofreading earlier drafts. I also want to thank my wife, Ana Palacios, for her loving support and encouragement as well as her willingness to read previous drafts.

Introduction
Access to AIDS Medicines, Public Health, and the Brazilian Solution

Toni never thought that she would have to leave her native home in Florida in 2010 and return to Brazil in order to obtain access to life-saving medicines. She recalled the time several years ago when she surprisingly became seriously ill in Rio de Janeiro and required hospitalization for several days. While looking at Rio's iconic statue of Christ the Redeemer from her hospital room at the time, the physician informed her that she was infected with the human immunodeficiency virus (HIV), which causes the acquired immune deficiency syndrome (AIDS). Just as difficult as the stigma, loathing, and blame connected to the disease was her decision to return to her native Florida to receive comfort and support from family. She would have to leave her job as a business consultant, the band in which she played samba rhythms, and the land she adopted as her home.

After suffering bouts of depression back home in the United States, Toni jumped at the opportunity to return to Brazil when a friend offered her a place to stay and business contacts drummed up a steady stream of freelance work. Another factor that weighed heavily on her decision was determining how she was going to obtain access to treatment. Her disease had been in remission until a few months earlier when tests showed that the number of CD4 T lymphocyte cells, a type of white blood cell that fights infection, in her blood stream had begun to fall. Now she would have to start taking the "AIDS cocktail" and would have to continue taking these medicines for the rest of her life or risk contracting deadly opportunistic infections as her immune system weakens. Today, the treatment protocol recommends that those newly infected with HIV begin treatment immediately, but when Toni tested positive, prevailing guidelines recommended that drug therapy begin only when white blood cell counts fall below a certain level.

Known as the "Lazarus Drug" due to its ability to transform near-death patients with compromised immune systems into healthy individuals in a short period of treatment, the AIDS cocktail, a powerful combination of antiretroviral medicines (ARVs),[1] allows HIV-positive people to live active and productive lives. Daily compliance with treatment is important not only for achieving individual health improvements but also for addressing public health objectives. Since ARVs reduce viral loads, or the number of HIV

2 Introduction

particles in a person's system, people receiving treatment are 96% less likely to infect someone who has not been infected (Cohen et al. 2011).

A natural experiment comparing Brazil and South Africa demonstrated the importance of these medicines. Both countries had similar HIV prevalence rates in the early 1990s. But whereas Brazil aggressively rolled out the AIDS cocktail in 1997, South Africa resisted efforts to scale up government-sponsored treatment programs until 2008. By 2009, South Africa's HIV population reached an estimated 5.6 million compared to Brazil's 635,000 (UNAIDS 2010). While treatment is not the only factor affecting the spread of HIV, especially in two countries as different as Brazil and South Africa, a steady supply of medicines nonetheless is fundamental to any health program to address the disease.

In Florida, Toni faced paying $15,000 out of pocket annually for the medicines. Private insurance companies turned down her application for health coverage due to her HIV-positive status, so she had to rely on government programs.[2] However, due to local and state austerity measures in response to the Great Recession of 2007, these programs were cut back. State governments slashed publicly funded AIDS Drug Assistance Programs (ADAPs), which are designed to provide access to ARVs to those without insurance and below certain income thresholds. In September 2011, there were 8,785 people in ten states placed on waiting lists to access ARVs. Toni's native Florida led the country with 4,098 people waitlisted (AIDS Healthcare Foundation 2011). Such a high number of people without access to the life-saving medicines in the United States is ironic since the US government is the largest provider of AIDS treatments to the developing world. In 2003, George W. Bush announced the Presidential Emergency Plan for AIDS Relief (PEPFAR), committing billions of dollars to fight the disease worldwide. Successive US governments have renewed commitments to provide funds for treatment, prevention, and care to nations around the world.

Back in Rio de Janeiro, the only obstacle Toni faced when obtaining her medication was waiting several hours in line at the clinic. Armed just with a doctor's prescription, she obtained enough medicines to last a month. Although she was on a legal visa in Brazil, she was not asked about her citizenship status or insurance coverage in order to obtain the life-saving drugs. She looked at the back of the box of efavirenz, a widely used ARV in Brazil, and was surprised to notice that it was actually manufactured by a pharmaceutical company controlled by the Brazilian government's Ministry of Health. Upon leaving the clinic, Toni wondered how it was possible for a country like Brazil to provide essential medicines to its population for free, whereas many people with HIV in the US must forgo treatment or face penury.

Toni's experiences[3] draw attention to the stark differences in how countries approach health care throughout the world. In Brazil, access to health care is considered a human right enshrined in the country's Constitution and guaranteed by the state. By contrast in the US, access to adequate

Introduction 3

health remains a significant economic burden for families and the economy, especially with continual rise in healthcare costs. Although Brazil's health system lacks sufficient funds to deliver comparable levels of care seen in high-income countries, its HIV/AIDS program has demonstrated to the world that resource-strapped countries can also provide technologically advanced care and treatment to their populations. In fact, the "Brazilian Model" has galvanized global responses to fighting the pandemic that currently infects an estimated 33 million people throughout the world, 95% of whom live in the developing world.[4]

Brazil's AIDS Program is a remarkable success story. The first cases of HIV appeared in São Paulo in 1980 but were only confirmed as HIV in 1982. The first programmatic efforts to address the disease began in the southwestern state of São Paulo by a group of progressive-minded health workers. In partnership with civil society organizations, like the AIDS Prevention Support Group (*Grupo de Apoio à Prevenção à Aids*—GAPA), started in 1985, these health professionals transformed AIDS from just a medical problem into a human rights issue. As of 2014, Brazil's National AIDS Program[5] estimated a total of 797,000 people with HIV, of which 123,000 do not know their status. The incidence rate stood at 20 cases per 100,000 inhabitants with some 39,000 new cases in recent years. Without the struggles by AIDS activists to fight discrimination, clean up the blood supply, and promote harm reduction, the number of infections and human suffering would be much higher.

One of the most important successes achieved by Brazilian AIDS activists was access to treatment. In 1996, the Brazilian government mandated the distribution, free of charge, of life-saving ARVs. By 2013, the AIDS Program was distributing 21 different antiretroviral medicines that make up the AIDS cocktail to over 352,000 people (see Appendix One). Access to drugs translated into lives saved. AIDS-related deaths fell from 9.7 per 100,000 in 1995 to 6.4 per 100,000 by 1999 after the introduction of treatment. And median survival times from the date of diagnosis also increased from five months in 1989 to five years in 2002 (Galvão et al. 2009).

Until recently in the rest of the developing world, access to treatment was unthinkable. Given the high price of the medicines, the policy consensus in the 1990s favored prevention over treatment.[6] Providing AIDS medicines was not "cost-effective" for treating the global poor. Only after tremendous pressures from social movements, the availability of cheaper generic medicines, and promising successes of countries like Brazil has the situation dramatically changed (Kapstein and Busby 2013). In what is dubbed as the first ever "global entitlement" scheme, access to treatment has expanded significantly (Over 2008). PEPFAR and the Global Fund for AIDS, Tuberculosis and Malaria, run by the United Nations (UN), are the key funding sources for addressing the market failure in HIV medicines. These efforts have resulted in major improvements to expand access. By the end of 2009, the UN estimated 5,254,000 people in low- and middle-income

4   *Introduction*

countries were on treatment, a remarkable increase from the mere 400,000 people in 2004. Despite efforts to scale up treatment and the millions of deaths averted, just over one-third of those requiring treatment had access to life-saving ARVs by the end of the decade, leaving some 10 million people to fall through the cracks of a weak global safety net (UNAIDS 2010; WHO 2010). Sadly, an estimated 914,000 children under 15 years and 658,000 pregnant women requiring services for preventing mother-to-child transmission do not receive life-saving medicines (WHO 2010). In addition, those who began treatment with inexpensive, first-line treatments will need to migrate to more expensive second-line therapies.

Recent economic difficulties have put worldwide treatment expansion in check. Donors only disbursed US$6.9 billion in 2010 for HIV prevention, treatment, and care, a reduction of US$740 million compared to the year before. In order to achieve universal access goals, UNAIDS estimates that at least US$22 billion will be needed by 2015 (Kaiser Family Foundation 2010). Why are not the basic prescription needs of the world's population being met? In the view of Pedro Chequer, a physician who directed Brazil's AIDS Program, the problem of providing essential medicines is rooted in an economic system that is incompatible with providing for human needs. "If the world decided today to provide ARVs to the nine million people who needed them, besides the current three million currently with access, there would not be any medicines, because you cannot guarantee human rights based on a business proposition," he claimed.[7] The former director's assertion stems from a view that profit-based economic systems have inherent limitations. Firms do not invest millions in R&D in order to market their products to the billions who live off of a few dollars a day.

The current "business proposition" of the global pharmaceutical industry is to research and develop blockbuster drugs that can be sold at inflated prices to a limited number of buyers who can afford to pay those prices. Central to high-margin, low-volume markets are patents. By providing temporary monopolies to producers, patents reduce competition that would lower prices. Generic makers of the same medicine are not allowed to market their version of the drug until the patent period expires, a period that lasts for 20 years. Industry justifies the policy due to the high costs of researching and developing new medicines compared to the fraction of expense required to make copies. However, access to high-priced medicines remains limited to those consumers with private insurance schemes offering coverage for high-priced drugs or to citizens in government-sponsored programs with sufficient financial resources.

The patent-based business model, once restricted to the most advanced countries, now encompasses nearly the entire globe with the establishment of the World Trade Organization (WTO) in 1995. Before the creation of this international government organization, many countries did not award patents for pharmaceuticals due to the impact they would have on their health systems and to their limited technological abilities to produce innovative

Introduction 5

products. With practically all countries as members of the WTO, there is now a minimum baseline, including a 20-year patent on new drugs, established worldwide with serious implications for public health.

The WTO's patent rules include humanitarian safeguards, such as the use of compulsory licenses that allow for more generic competition, but few countries such as Brazil have dared to use them. In 2007, the Brazilian health officials issued a compulsory license for the ARV efavirenz, effectively rescinding the patent monopoly Merck Sharpe & Dohme (MSD) had on the drug's sale in Brazil. If the Brazilian government had not taken such a measure, Toni would not be holding the box of the medicines manufactured by its Ministry of Health's public lab Farmanguinhos. Instead, MSD would be the sole supplier and the price of the medicine would be much higher.

Brazil's experience demonstrates the challenges and possibilities regarding the dissemination of life-saving medical advances in the brave new world of patents. In providing a full spectrum of AIDS medicines, the country had to defy international health experts who said that providing treatment was not cost-effective for developing countries, defend itself against WTO panels concerned about enforcing new patent laws, confront the United States government which sought to protect the interests of its pharmaceutical companies, and allay fears of its citizens concerned about the country's economic growth and the quality of generic medicines. Despite political uncertainties and economic pressures, the country prevailed against what Ellen 't Hoen (2009), the former director of the Doctors without Borders' campaign for access to essential medicines, calls the "monopoly power of the global pharmaceutical industry."[8] This book provides a nuanced picture into the roles state, society, and industry played to secure the prescription drug needs of the Brazilian population, or what I call pharmaceutical autonomy.

NOTES

1. In the medical literature, the AIDS cocktail is also referred to as Highly Active Antiretroviral Therapy (or HAART).
2. Starting January 1, 2014, the Affordable Care Act forbids private insurance companies from rejecting health insurance applications based on prior conditions like HIV.
3. Toni is a fictional character developed from several nonfictional experiences.
4. Without a doubt, the AIDS pandemic is one of the most devastating epidemics of modern times. According to the *2010 Global Report* from the Joint United Nations Programme on HIV/AIDS (UNAIDS), more than 60 million people have been infected by the disease and 30 million people have died from HIV-related causes since the epidemic began more than three decades ago (UNAIDS 2010). The UN body estimates that nearly 33.3 million were infected as of 2009. This number includes the estimated 1.8 million deaths and 2.6 million estimated new infections in that year.
5. Brazil's National AIDS Program later became the Department of STDs, AIDS and Viral Hepatitis.

6   *Introduction*

6. When zidovudine (AZT), the first drug to demonstrate antiretroviral activity, first arrived on the market in 1987, Burroughs-Wellcome (now GlaxoSmith-Kline) priced the medicine at US$10,000 per person per year. Citizens in developed countries could count on government-funded health programs to finance purchases.
7. Pedro Chequer. Interview with author. Brasilia, DF. July 12, 2008.
8. Nobel Prize-recipient Doctors without Borders is also known by its name in French *Médecins sans Frontières* and acronym MSF.

REFERENCES

AIDS Healthcare Foundation. 2011. "Proposed AIDS Funding Amount Is 'Inadequate.'" Retrieved September 29, 2011 (www.aidshealth.org/news/press-releases/ahf-to-senate-proposed-aids.html).

Cohen, Myron S. et al. 2011. "Prevention of HIV-1 Infection with Early Antiretroviral Therapy." *The New England Journal of Medicine* 365(6): 493–505.

Galvão, Jane, Paulo Roberto Teixeira, Marco Vitória, and Mauro Schechter. 2009. "How the Pandemic Shapes the Public Health Response—the Case of HIV/AIDS in Brazil." Pp. 135–50 in *Public Health Aspects of HIV/AIDS in Low and Middle Income Countries*, edited by David D. Celentano and Chris Beyrer. New York: Springer.

't Hoen, Ellen F. M. 2009. *The Global Politics of Pharmaceutical Monopoly Power*. Diemen: AMB.

Kaiser Family Foundation. 2010. "Financing the Response to AIDS in Low- and Middle-Income Countries: International Assistance from the G8, European Commission and Other Donor Governments in 2010." Retrieved September 28, 2011 (www.kff.org/hivaids/7347.cfm).

Kapstein, Ethan B., and Josh Busby. 2013. *AIDS Drugs For All*. Cambridge: Cambridge University Press.

Over, Mead. 2008. "Prevention Failure: The Ballooning Entitlement Burden of U.S. Global AIDS Treatment Spending and What to Do About It—Working Paper 144." Retrieved September 27, 2011 (www.cgdev.org/content/publications/detail/15973/).

UNAIDS. 2010. "Global Report: UNAIDS Report on the Global AIDS Epidemic 2010." Geneva: Joint United Nations Programme on HIV/AIDS 2010. Retrieved January 2, 2011 (www.unaids.org/globalreport/Global_report.htm).

WHO. 2010. "Towards Universal Access: Scaling up Priority HIV/AIDS Interventions in the Health Sector—Progress Report 2010." World Health Organization. Geneva: Switzerland. Retrieved September 27, 2011 (www.who.int/hiv/pub/2010progressreport/report/en/index.html).

1 Pharmaceutical Autonomy
Technology, Alliances, and Norms

"Forget everything I have said and wrote. The world has changed." Brazil's President Fernando Henrique Cardoso allegedly made this statement after he entered politics. He had supposedly disavowed his former work after adopting several policies that his critics characterized as an embrace of neoliberal economic philosophy. Accusations that Cardoso was pushing policies that he had once critiqued in his previous career as an academic seemed like direct attacks on his character. Before entering politics, Cardoso had achieved international recognition as a sociologist for his work on socio-economic development. In his academic work, he argued that Latin America's colonial past and continued ties to advanced capitalist economies presented formidable obstacles towards achieving widespread improvements to Latin Americans' well-being. His writings informed what is known as dependency theory, which was a popular way of explaining the failures and prospects of development in the 1970s.

During his presidency from 1994–2001, Cardoso's opponents on the left argued that his economic policies would reinforce Brazil's subordinate position in the world economy and stifle efforts to achieve sustained growth and a more equal society. These critics argued that Cardoso's support for privatizing state-owned firms and monetary policies based on large capital inflows would increase the country's dependency. With these policies, Brazil's economic development would continue to be stunted and historic socio-economic disparities would never be addressed. In his defense, Cardoso reiterated that he never told anyone to forget his former academic work and that his writings on dependency were completely valid for the specific "situations" he sought to illuminate decades ago. In other words, specific conjunctures in the world historic economy provide different opportunities for economic growth and space for governments to enact policies to ensure equitable distribution of the fruits of development. Specifically, he argued that today's multipolar world whereby no one country dominates the international economy allows for more space for governments to pursue social democratic objectives (Cardoso 2009). The counterargument is that the rules of the global economy favor the powerful at the expense of social justice.

8 *Pharmaceutical Autonomy*

As we shall see in subsequent chapters, Cardoso's policies had contradictory effects on Brazil's efforts to achieve what I call pharmaceutical autonomy. Importantly, his administration initiated reforms to improve state managerial capacity and implemented social policies based on broad social democratic criteria, including HIV programs. However, in other aspects, his economic policies increased the structural power of foreign capital over Brazil's economy, which was evident in the pharmaceutical industry. For example, his administration passed new legislation providing patents on new drugs in 1996—several years in advance of the 2005 deadlines set by the World Trade Organization (WTO). After adhering to the new trade agreements, Cardoso and his successors had to negotiate the complicated terrain of drug patents, on the one hand, and the upsurge in citizens' demands for essential medicines, on the other, that are detailed throughout this book.

This chapter reviews the theories and writings of Cardoso and other scholars in order to develop an analytical framework for understanding the origins, challenges, and contests surrounding Brazil's policy of providing high-cost AIDS medicines. I argue that the structural-historical lens developed by dependency theories offers an insightful viewpoint for understanding strategies to increase policy space related to a country's AIDS treatment program. Specifically, the analytic framework sheds a critical light on contemporary institutions and social inequality, the indeterminacy of political actions, and alternative possibilities (Heller, Rueschemeyer, and Snyder 2009). However, applying the dependency perspective requires a number of caveats regarding the theory's shortcomings, such as conceptual clarity and lack of attention to social movement actors.

AN ANALYTICAL FRAMEWORK FOR UNDERSTANDING PHARMACEUTICAL AUTONOMY

The concept of pharmaceutical autonomy I use throughout this book refers to a country's ability to fulfill the prescription drug needs of its populations, especially in the face of structural constraints. As an ideal type, the concept also encompasses all the stages in the research, production, and distribution of essential medicines. At the research stage, pharmaceutical autonomy involves the application of resources into discovering and developing treatments for diseases that most burden a society. Next, autonomous capability at the production stage, including the combination of various raw materials at various steps in the manufacturing process, ensures the availability of medicines at suitable prices. Given the limitations imposed by scale economies, not every country can develop an integrated pharmaceutical base. But having firms that can enter a product line and increase competition can lead to lower prices and reduced monopoly power.

In terms of distribution, pharmaceutical autonomy refers to effective health systems that can ensure that essential drugs reach consumers and can guarantee their rational use. Health systems should include qualified doctors, nurses, and pharmacists to diagnosis ailments and administer treatments; regulatory oversight to police substandard drugs; and logistics systems to ensure safe, timely, and effective delivery of medicines. Needless to say, pharmaceutical autonomy implies access to essential medicines regardless of one's social class, sexual orientation, race, gender, or type of disease. Fulfilling a population's medical needs thus requires an inclusive institutional framework—such as laws, national Constitutions, and international treaties—that outline the roles and responsibilities of various actors in society to ensure universal access.

Pharmaceutical autonomy is the opposite of pharmaceutical dependency. In previous studies of the pharmaceutical industry, Gereffi (1983) recognized dependency as inequitable distribution of benefits and reduced policy options available to government. Countries that are dependent on the research prerogatives of foreign scientists and firms, have no production capabilities, lack developed health systems, and have weak institutional settings experience higher disparities in access to essential medicines and reduced policy space to pursue public health objectives. More importantly, strong political coalitions necessary for formulating, implementing, and sustaining universalistic pharmaceutical policies are not likely to develop.

The objective of this book is to examine the factors affecting the movement between the two ideal types of pharmaceutical dependency and autonomy. What accounts for Brazil's broadening of its policy space and its overcoming pressures from the transnational drug industry? And conversely, what factors constrained policymakers from taking more aggressive actions affecting distributional gains and losses? Focusing on just one sector—pharmaceuticals—allows for the exploration of the linkages and distributional consequences between production and access, including the role of both industrial and social policies to discern the evolution of Brazil's socio-economic development. In more general terms, what does the Brazilian case tell us about the structure of the international political economy and the nature of domestic politics for achieving social democratic goals in the developing world through time? An idiographic case study of Brazil's AIDS treatment program will allow us to compare current and past social structures (Stake 1995; Yin 1989).

To interrogate Brazil's pharmaceutical autonomy, my account draws from Haydu's approach to analyzing history and policy outcomes (Haydu 1998, 2010; Howlett and Rayner 2006). In applying this framework, my narrative of historical events focuses on the "the connections between events in different time periods as reiterated problem solving" (Haydu 1998: 341). The methodology seeks to uncover casual sequences not only by comparing discrete periods of time to discern important variations but also by placing these time periods into broader temporal trajectories. As such, "reiterated problem solving" differs from path dependency models in their understanding of public policies. While both models emphasize the importance of

10   *Pharmaceutical Autonomy*

previous historical events as shaping subsequent actions, Haydu's method views important turning points in history, known as "crucial junctures" in the path dependency literature, not as historical accidents but as developments rooted in previous historical trajectories (Howlett and Rayner 2006).

Explanation in path dependency begins with the "critical juncture" in which prior historical experiences cannot explain the contingent nature of an event. A critical juncture often cannot be predicted or foreseen based on prior events. In these moments, uncertainty and agency often determine the subsequent flow of events and historical processes. After a critical juncture, powerful lock-in mechanisms are set in motion that rule out the possibility of moving on to a new historical pathway. For example, a critical juncture marks the introduction of the QWERTY keyboard, which, despite its inefficiencies in typing, remains to this day due to lock-in mechanisms such as feedback loops and social entrenchment through the keyboard's widespread adoption in society (Mahoney and Rueschemeyer 2003).

Despite its merits in demonstrating how history constrains subsequent options, path dependency models have two methodological problems. First, the approach has difficulty in addressing broader historical processes that transcend time periods encompassing various discrete critical junctures and lock-in mechanisms. Second, and perhaps more importantly, path dependency provides little conceptual space for historical reversals (Haydu 2010). For example, lock-in mechanisms should prevent a country that transitions from an authoritarian regime to a democracy to switch back into a dictatorship. The path dependent model employed by Nunn (2008) to understand Brazil's AIDS treatment policies faces difficulty in understanding the various policy reversals regarding the introduction of neoliberal reforms. For example, in the 1990s the Brazilian government dismantled industrial policies and introduced patents for the pharmaceutical sector only later to re-introduce state initiatives for the sector and re-work patent laws from the turn of the century onward.

Haydu's "reiterated problem solving" does not analyze time periods as discrete units of analysis separated by crucial junctures and lock-in mechanisms. Instead, the methodological approach focuses on how actors face recurring problems over time (Haydu 1998, 2010). In the case of Brazil, the question was how to maintain the sustainability of its AIDS treatment program with increasing number of enrollments each year and high prices charged by the introduction of patented medicines. The "sequence of problem solving" traces how the various "multiple causal trajectories—such as fleeting political opportunities, slower-moving changes in economic resources or strategic allies, and long-standing cultural repertoires—are brought together in episodes" (Haydu 2010: 32). A close case study of the Brazilian AIDS treatment program thus considers the evolution of the country's technological capabilities, entrenchment of political alliances, and intersection of cultural frames with political opportunities.

My account focuses on the recurrent episodes from 1991 to 2011 in which Brazil faced the problem of procuring high-cost antiretrovirals (ARVs). My detailed analysis of these two decades reveals swings between pharmaceutical autonomy and dependency, and in doing so, reveals the current nature of the contemporary global economy and available policy space for achieving broad-based development. But in order to do so, these recurrent episodes are situated within a broader account of the trajectories of the international pharmaceutical industry and Brazil's domestic institutions in recent decades. In contrast to Nunn's approach focused on critical junctures, I analyze the multiple technological, political, and normative trajectories through different "situations" of dependency over a 40-year period. The advent of new global trade regimes, new communication technologies, and the rise in democratic politics present new constraints and opportunities with what Wade (2003) calls a country's "development space" compared to previous situations of dependent development.

Figure 1.1 provides a broad outline of my argument. The decades from approximately the 1950s to the 1980s represent a distinct timeframe of "national" development. During this conjuncture, Brazil grew its pharmaceutical industry using policies based on import-substituting industrialization (ISI) development strategies. Military rule from 1963 to 1985 dominated the political scene, and social policies favored those with formal employment. The country experienced significant changes during re-democratization in the 1980s. From the 1990s onward, the government introduced new social policies based on broad social democratic criteria and, concomitantly, implemented various neoliberal economic reforms that removed various protective measures against foreign competition, thereby integrating the country into the global economy.

During the subsequent period from the 1990s onward, the "global turn," I trace three key processes affecting Brazil's pharmaceutical autonomy: the

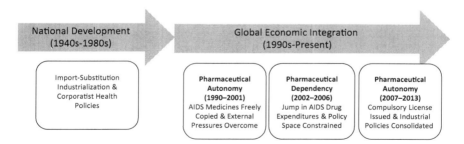

Figure 1.1 Broad Historical Conjunctures (1940s–1980s and 1990s–Present) and Short-Term Episodes (1990–2013) in Brazil's Pharmaceutical Autonomy

12   *Pharmaceutical Autonomy*

development and decline of technological capabilities; creation and maintenance of political alliances; and strategic use of normative framing. This conceptual framework draws from traditional sociological concerns that relate to the economic, political, and symbolic dimensions of social power. Importantly, these processes can be traced back to the earlier period that predates Brazil's change in its political economy. In the three subsequent periods, I demonstrate Brazil's achievements and challenges in achieving pharmaceutical autonomy when it first rolled out AIDS medications. In the first period (1990–2001), the country developed Brazilian copies of ARVs and overcame external challenges to its patent policies. In the subsequent period (2002–2006), Brazil experienced more dependency due to the inclusion of high-cost medicines and reduced capabilities to produce local medicines, demonstrating the limits of previous political strategies. In response to these constraints, activists inside and outside of the government initiated new forms of coalition building premised on the roll out of new industrial policies for the pharmaceutical sector in the final period (2007–2013).

Technological Capabilities

A key component for achieving pharmaceutical autonomy involves local control over technology necessary to provide essential medicines required by society. Scholars of dependency theory recognized that technology, markets, and trade are intertwined, not as apolitical arenas for exchange, but as fields of power where actors dispute the control of society's economic resources. In the 1970s, Cardoso and others coined the term *dependent development* to understand the new structure of the political economies in Latin America and their external economic relations that continued to condition a country's growth potential (Cardoso and Faletto 1979; Evans 1979; Gereffi 1983).[1] In their view, industrial deepening required the manufacturing operations of foreign-based multinational corporations whose control over capital, technology, and market distribution reproduced situations of dependency.

In the past, the dependency approach has been useful in explaining the impact of external economic constraints on pharmaceutical industries and policies in the Third World (Bermudez 1995; Bertero 1972; Evans 1979; Gereffi 1983). In the case of Mexico, Gereffi (1983) demonstrates the increasing control that foreign capital assumed over the nation's steroid hormone industry from 1944 to 1982. Despite a comparative advantage in terms of resource endowments for producing strategic inputs, Mexico lost control of the production technologies as foreign companies acquired the most lucrative segments of the production chain and moved these productive activities outside of the country. Gereffi (1983: 240–43) also demonstrates how drug prices, marketing, end products, and local production of raw materials have failed to meet the development needs of host countries. In past studies like

Gereffi's, technological dependency rested on the physical control over the assets of production and resulted in inequitable distribution of benefits and constrained government action.

Towards the end of the 1980s, dependency theory fell out of favor amongst scholars as new ideas about globalization gained popularity.[2] One group of scholars developed the theory of global capitalism to understand the qualitatively different changes occurring in economies, polities, and societies (McMichael 2004; Robinson 2004; Sklair 1995, 2001). Like dependency theorists, they emphasized the role of transnational corporations (TNCs) in directing contemporary world capitalism but argued that the world economy had entered a new age of accumulation. Since TNCs run their operations on a global basis, the relationship between capital and labor has moved beyond the confines of the nation state and has become transnational. Global subcontracting and flexible production has diffused across the globe while the command over capital, investment decisions, and resources has become increasingly centralized in corporate organizations no longer domiciled in any one country. Ensuring TNC control over technological capabilities in a globalizing economy requires the construction of a "transnational state" including formal organizations such as the World Trade Organization (WTO), the International Monetary Fund, and the World Bank, as well as political bodies such as the G-7/8 and expanded G-22, and informal groupings like the Trilateral Commission, the International Chamber of Commerce, and the World Economic Forum (Robinson 2004).

The class-domination perspectives of dependency theory and global capitalism reveal the powerful actors and their ability to achieve their objectives in relation to trade liberalization, de-regulation, and adherence to international trade accords. Despite their differences,[3] both perspectives emphasize the unequal political and economic relationships inherent in the global economy. Also, the objective of both schools of thought concerns growing social inequality and structural barriers to government action. In today's global economy, new trade agreements have "kicked away the ladder" and reduced the "development space" for governments to enact catch-up strategies once employed by other countries to climb the technological ladder (Chang 2002; Wade 2003). The new rules make copying existing technologies from abroad or using industrial policies to privilege local firms increasingly difficult for developing countries to employ.

The type of technology under consideration is also qualitatively different between the previous studies of dependency and current analysis of global capitalism. In the past, economic power rested upon control over tangible physical assets, such as iron ore mines, steel making, and car manufacturing. Nowadays, technological control involves new networks of production based on intangible assets that are central to the knowledge-based economy and which, in turn, require robust legal frameworks and juridical bodies

14 *Pharmaceutical Autonomy*

(Castells 2010; Richards 2004). Securing surplus value increasingly relies on the commodification of such intangibles as science and mental labor that are the focus of new intellectual property claims. A case study can evaluate the assertions made by theories of dependency and global capitalism. How has the adoption of WTO agreements affected the control over technology? What are the connections between technology capability and the policy space available to achieving developmental goals, including public health programs?

In analyzing the development and control of technology in the pharmaceutical sectors, I consider two distinct but related forms of power—market power and patent power. Market power refers to the various ways in which actors, including industrial firms and their partners, exercise control over one or more steps in a production process. Pharmaceutical markets involve various actors, including CEOs, scientists, and consumers, who engage in research and development, production, marketing, distribution, and consumption activities divided among various organizations, both private and public, in distinct locations. These various stakeholders seek to appropriate relative surplus gains at the various nodes of the production chain. The idea of market power attempts to capture the implications that production technologies have disseminated to newly industrialized countries like Brazil, India, China, amongst others. That these countries have become important producers of generic medicines, as well as important players in international trade, adds credence to Cardoso's optimistic view of a more multipolar world.

Patent power, in contrast, refers to the structural power that TNCs and their contenders have in establishing the "rules of the game" or the legal codes and normative expectations undergirding market operations. Specifically, patents involve state intervention into pharmaceutical markets by granting 20-year monopolies to grantees. Both market power and patent power, described in more detail in Chapter Two, directly affect the availability of medicines and, in turn, prices and accessibility. Indeed, more scholars are examining the impact that intellectual property regimes have on pharmaceutical markets in developing countries and the challenges they pose to public health goals (Coriat 2008; Deere 2009; Löfgren and Williams 2013; Shadlen, Guennif, and Chavez 2011). A focused case study on Brazil's ability to produce AIDS medicines contributes towards this growing literature.

Brazil's pharmaceutical capabilities put the country in a contradictory position. On the one hand, the country is home to a number of competent scientists, technicians, and firms capable of producing a variety of medicines and formulations. On the other hand, its pharmaceutical sector has never sustained the type of coherent government support necessary to become a global player like firms in advanced industrialized countries or in other emerging markets like India. This situation has important implications for sustaining access to high-priced AIDS medicines. Previous studies have emphasized the important role of Brazil's pharmaceutical industry in the

Pharmaceutical Autonomy   15

production of AIDS medicines and treatment program (Cohen and Lybecker 2005; Nunn 2008; Orsi et al. 2003; Shadlen 2009). But few trace the subsequent weakening in generic production of ARVs to new patent legislation of 1996 (Flynn 2013b; Possas 2008). As I demonstrate in this book, the decline in pharmaceutical capabilities places constraints on the country's policy space, but also leads to new forms of state intervention and political alliances.

Political Alliances

While historical-structural analysis of dependency theory and global capitalism sheds light on the development of technological capabilities and the resulting impact of new forms of structural power based on international trade accords, political alliances offer what Albert Hirschman (1971) calls the "bias for hope" for overcoming situations of dependency. Building coalitions and pursuing political avenues thus play a crucial role in asserting pharmaceutical autonomy. More importantly, they are important when confronting powerful actors such as transnational drug companies or pressures from foreign governments. But in contrast with dependency theorists or contemporary scholars of global capitalism, the changing nature of state bureaucratic capacity, the rise of democratic politics, and the influence of social movements lead to new opportunities to achieve social democratic goals and expand space for government action.

In the past, focusing on the relationships across elite groups appeared sufficient to the dependency framework's analysis. In the 1970s, Cardoso (1972: 89) called the close connections between private capital, the state, and transnational capital the "joint venture enterprise" and Evans (1979) "the triple alliance." In these formulations, TNCs have an interest in maintaining social inequality since a cheap workforce keeps costs low and a wealthy upper class provides a profitable market. Local industrialists develop subsidiaries in alliance with TNCs, while the state's techno-bureaucracy bargains with TNCs to attract investment. The state employs nationalism as a means of social control, justifying coercive incorporation of the masses, legitimating the role of the local bourgeoisie, and negotiating favorable terms with the TNCs.

By positing a transnational capitalist class based on the fundamental interest of the continued accumulation of private wealth, theoreticians of global capitalism also focus on elite ties (Robinson 2004; Sklair 2002). Global capitalism differs from previous forms of dependency by positing that these elite political alliances are increasingly disconnected from national interests. Nonetheless, both perspectives employ a top-down or power elite perspective. Given their social position, especially in command of large-scale economic organizations and control over the policy-making process, elites have the resources and capabilities to achieve their class interests and impose their policies on the rest of society (Domhoff 2006; Mills

16   *Pharmaceutical Autonomy*

1957). The crux of the argument is that the power elite, at both the global and national levels, achieve higher levels of coherency and collective agency than their fragmented opponents.

In contrast to power elite perspectives, another view emphasizes the relative autonomy of the state to pursue its interests (Evans, Rueschemeyer, and Skocpol 1985; Evans 1995). The concept of embedded autonomy, developed by Evans (1995), argues that successful states are both *autonomous* from particularistic interests yet *embedded* in society through various informal social networks. Autonomy is achieved through meritocratic recruitment and clear career paths within the state bureaucracy. Public examinations, salaries comparable to the private sector, and common educational backgrounds not only attract highly trained and skilled personnel to serve in civil service, but also reduce various forms of nepotism and clientelism. Autonomy, Evans argues, also rests on state actors who develop a collective sense of mission that motivates them beyond material gain and instills purpose into working towards the benefit of the nation. However, autonomy without embeddedness would result in inappropriate policies due to the lack of information from the rest of society (Evans 1995).

Evan's ideal types are useful for understanding state structures in Latin America. Countries throughout the region have made improvements in their state institutions to design and carry out social policies, respond to public demands, and provide needed services (Bresser-Pereira 1999; Portes 2009; Roberts 2005). In fact, Brazil has made gradual and progressive improvements in its bureaucratic capabilities in recent years (Souza 2013). No longer can state actors and structures be reduced to broad-based claims of clientelism and patrimonial politics. Consequently, compared to dependency and global capitalist theory, technically capable states are better equipped with negotiating more advantageous agreements with TNCs (Holton 2011). Thus, as I and others have argued (Biehl 2004; Flynn 2013b), a reformed and "activist state" plays a crucial role for understanding Brazil's AIDS policies through the development of political alliances and broadening the space for action.

Pharmaceutical autonomy rests not only on an increasingly competent state bureaucracy but also requires backing from a mobilized civil society. In previous studies of dependent development, the role of subordinate groups received little attention. Based on his studies in the 1970s, Evans states that "Brazil's population are absent from this analysis because they are absent from the decision making that is being described," (Evans 1979: 13). The view is that pressures from below, including the actions of social movements, workers, and other non-elite groups, play no role in determining policy outcomes or acting as agents of history. This statement appears ironic given the crucial role that labor unions and other subordinate actors played in the country's transition to democracy from the late 1970s onward.

Democratic politics transforms the nature of state-society relations and allows for more claim making. Indeed, Cardoso argues that democracy

Pharmaceutical Autonomy   17

is a precondition for achieving a socially just society and reducing social inequality (Cardoso and Magalhaes 2001; Cardoso 2009). Other scholars concur that political institutions based on democratic principles provide more openings and possibilities for rights claims to be translated into reality (Dagnino 2004; Foweraker 2005; Huber and Stephens 2012; Jelin 1996). For example, Huber and Stephens (2012) contest that democratic elections, and especially rule by left-of-center political parties, leads to more social policies premised on "basic universalism" due in part to party competition seeking votes. Additionally, improvements in state bureaucratic capacities can facilitate the construction of state-society political alliances. Scholars of social movements argue that underprofessionalized state bureaucracies will discourage challengers, while "coherent state bureaucracies with social policy missions will encourage challengers targeting those issues" (Amenta and Young 1999: 161).

In sum, bureaucratically capable states and democratic regimes facilitate the political coalitions necessary for pharmaceutical autonomy. These political alliances stretch across the state-society divide. In comparison to elite ties in the public and private spheres, Evans' (1996) concept of "synergy" describes the "mutually reinforcing relations between government and groups of engaged citizens" (Evans 1996: 1119). This involves the channeling of information and productive collaboration to achieve development objectives such as universalistic drug policies. But synergy does not adequately capture the highly politicized nature of the political economy of development (see Hickey and Mohan 2005) or access to medicines. Conflicts over drug prices and threats of using compulsory licenses create political opportunities for the creation and re-creation of political alliances between state and civil society.

Another key change in today's current "conjuncture" concerns the internationalization of social movements. While not even imagined by past versions of dependency theory, theorists of global capitalism emphasize that social movements must transnationalize in order to achieve progressive change (Richards 2004; Sklair 2002; Tilly 1995). And social movement scholars have undertaken in-depth studies of the composition, motivation, and outcome of these movements that constitute a central element to a contentious global civil society (Pleyers 2010; della Porta 2006; Tarrow 2005). In relation to AIDS treatments, others have noted that social movement pressures from below have made important impacts internationally to increase access to medicines ('t Hoen 2009; Kapstein and Busby 2013; Matthews 2011).

Epistemic communities also play an important role in understanding the construction of Brazil's political coalitions. These include professionals and experts who research, practice, and disseminate highly rationalized forms of knowledge in the sciences, administration, law, among others. Contrary to most writing on the sociology of professions that depict epistemic communities as self-serving corporate entities that seek to develop occupational

18 *Pharmaceutical Autonomy*

cartels, these professionals can also embrace social movement ideals. When occupying a place in the state, they become "social movement insiders" (Santoro and McGuire 1997), that is, professional managers in the state who are activists themselves and are interested in achieving social movement goals.

Still, political leadership does matter. Synergistic relations for addressing HIV have varied, in part due to what Huber and Stephens (2012) call "veto points" inherent in most political structures. For example, civil society has been present in both South Africa and Brazil. But in South Africa, President Thabo Mbeki and his top ministers, having adopted the view that HIV does not cause AIDS, blocked efforts to address the disease and roll out treatment. In contrast, Brazil's President Cardoso and his ministers were more open to the science behind the disease, although they were not enthusiastic about funding costly HIV programs.

Prior work on Brazil's AIDS policies have illustrated the important role of social movements in constructing political alliances and funneling information and resources to social movement organizations across state agencies and with citizens on the outside (Biehl 2004; Cohen and Lybecker 2005; Galvão 2002; de Mello e Souza 2007; Nunn 2008). This book coincides with much of this previous work and develops my previous writings on the topic (see Flynn 2011, 2013b) that considers the proactive role of the state and the construction of political alliances between state and society. I also emphasize international coalition building in which activists, in both the state and civil society, seek out support from the global civil society and establish South-South connections. More importantly, I demonstrate the limits of civil society pressure due to patent power, and how facing new obstacles led to the development of a triple alliance composed not only of state and civil society but also Brazil's private pharmaceutical industry.

Normative Framing

Another important feature of pharmaceutical autonomy concerns the value systems undergirding markets, including the struggles over the definitions of right and wrong and legitimacy of state policies. These are crucial when considering not only moral issues such as access to medicines and property rights but also the construction of social movements and political alliances essential for expanding the scope of government action. For scholars of dependency theory and global capitalism, such cultural considerations play a less important role in policy outcomes. For instance, Cardoso and Faletto (1979: 173) focus on the "networks of interests and coercions that bind some social groups to others, some classes to others." Ideology plays a role, but mainly reflects the material interests of capitalist classes or represents a counter-ideology to capitalist consumerism, as is the case in global capitalism accounts (see Sklair 1995).

Pharmaceutical Autonomy   19

Most political economists fail to acknowledge the reflective nature of social actors as they devise competing ethical codes in their struggles over technology and politics. My account thus seeks to delve into the symbolic dimension of the "dismal science" of economics and move beyond game-theoretic political realism to evaluate the communicative and symbolic processes that tap into and express concrete interests. This is not to assert that culture determines in the last instance but rather to recognize the crucial role of opposing moral orders.

Fourcade and Healy (2007: 299–300) remind us that "markets are explicitly moral projects, saturated with normativity." In other words, economic actors actively legitimate or criticize market products, the rules of the game, and the institutional pillars undergirding economic systems based on different political positions. When considering the role of commodities in social life, anthropologist Norman Long suggests analyzing not only the rational calculations of agents but also the discursive strategies that legitimate or delegitimize economic actions. "Methodologically this means examining the contestation of value in different domains and arenas of social action . . . [and] the deployment of specific language strategies and discourses that represent the 'political' positioning of the different actors in the networks and arenas concerned," explains Long (2001: 229). In sum, markets are not reducible to marginalist claims of utilitarian preference or the crude Marxist notion of labor power incorporated into commodities. In this book, the normative foundations of essential drug markets are readily apparent during price negotiations in which the Brazilian government threatens to rescind a company's patent monopoly. During these political opportunities, a common frame Brazilian activists employ is that "health is not for sale."

Frame analysis reveals the discursive efforts varied social actors deploy in order to define and make moral claims about social issues (Goffman 1986). For social movements, various mobilizing frames play an important role in understanding grievances and ideational sources of protest and mobilization (Snow et al. 1988). In this sense, frames can be used strategically to focus attention on a particular issue or problem, influence public opinion, legitimate claims, and assign blame. More specifically, activists employ naming and shaming tactics when targeting more powerful opponents. Such "public stigmatization" affects corporate behavior (Winston 2002). Social movement organizations, moreover, can develop a "master frame" for organizing diverse protest groups interested in a variety of loosely connected issues (Snow and Benford 1992). Activists employ normative frameworks to marshal increased support from other groups and actors in society. In previous writing on the topic of Brazil's battles over access to medicines, I emphasize the naming and shaming tactics used by social movement activists (Flynn 2013b).

In addition to legitimating markets and mobilizing social movements, normative frameworks also influence policymakers. Weyland (2006) argues that the "cognitive heuristics," or the shortcuts policymakers take when

20   *Pharmaceutical Autonomy*

making quick decisions in less than an optimal timeframe, explain policy outcomes better than the rational-actor model assumed by economists. The concept of "bounded rationality" recognizes the uncertainty regarding policy effectiveness. For example, Jose Serra (2004), Brazil's Minister of Health when the high cost of AIDS medicines became apparent in the late 1990s, acknowledged significant amount of uncertainty and unforeseen risks when choosing different policy options in the face of foreign pressures. Amidst uncertainty and possible options, why choose a specific policy?

Facing the crucible of drug patents, prices, and access, politicians like Serra are influenced by various normative frameworks, including natural rights claiming the sacredness of property, utilitarian concerns dealing with economic progress, human rights based on notions of the social dignity of persons, and even more radical critiques about the socio-economic system (explained in more detail in Chapter Two). Various actors, including diplomats, economists, industry associations, and activists, push these frameworks. In the literature, they are described as "policy entrepreneurs" (Kingdon 2011) or "institutional entrepreneurs" (Campbell 2004), but in essence they are "moral entrepreneurs" (Fourcade and Healy 2007). The key "moral entrepreneurs" in this case were members of Brazil's health reform movement and their allies in civil society organizations.

As previous authors have noted (Berkman et al. 2005; Galvão 2002; Nunn 2008), the overarching framework of human rights is the key normative framework and mobilizing tool in Brazil's AIDS program. These authors focus on the use of the human rights banner at the national level in the order to obtain treatment. This strategy later expanded to the international arena when Brazil had to contest international pressures. Compared to other scholars that depict Brazil's actions as a form of soft power related to traditional geopolitical concerns (Lee and Gomez 2011), Brazil's actions, as I have argued elsewhere (Flynn 2013a), stem from its normative commitment to health as a human rights issue and efforts to defend a domestic social program (see also Nunn et al. 2012). Changing normative frameworks demonstrates the important differences between the period of dependent development and today's more globalized world.

BOOK OUTLINE

In this chapter, I argued that the methodological approach of dependency analysis provides a useful framework for understanding efforts to sustain access to high-priced medicines. Its approach, similar to that of scholars of global capitalism, seeks to delineate how structures of the global economy affect prospects for achieving broad-based development. Increasing social inequities and decreased policy space demonstrate situations of dependency. The opposite is also true: expanding the scope of state action to achieve social justice objectives exemplifies autonomy. Additionally, the framework

Pharmaceutical Autonomy 21

is not overly deterministic when analyzing political outcomes yet provides critical insights into alternative pathways.

Applying Haydu's approach of "recurring problem solving" complements the dependency approach by emphasizing how slow-moving structural conditions pose challenges to reflective social actors. The key dimensions underpinning dependency versus autonomy include the control and development of technological capabilities, the establishment of political alliances, and use of normative frameworks. Process tracing of these dimensions across the different time periods informs the theoretical discussion. I argue that Brazil prevailed against the interests of corporate power when it demonstrated control over pharmaceutical technology; developed political alliances between state, society, and industry; and employed the use of a human rights framework. These factors also help to explain why Brazil did not pursue even more aggressive measures against patent owners.

The following chapters apply this framework and develop this argument by detailing Brazil's ability to confront threats to its AIDS treatment program. Chapter Two outlines recent changes in the global political economy and demonstrates the growing power of global pharmaceutical companies, predicated upon the establishment of the WTO. The chapter provides an overview of the pharmaceutical production process and the roles *market power* and *patent power* play in the pendulum between autonomy and dependency. Along with explaining the origins and implications of intellectual property rights, especially those related to Trade-Related Aspects of Intellectual Property (TRIPS), I discuss country-level compliance to the new international regime of intellectual property rights (IPRs). The chapter concludes with a review of the normative frameworks related to contests over intellectual property rights and access to medicines derived from natural rights perspectives, utilitarian accounts, human rights claims, and critical views.

Chapter Three provides background about Brazil's pharmaceutical capabilities, medicines policies, and AIDS treatment program. Due to its macro-economic situation, changing political system, and large-scale changes to its health system during the 1980s and 1990s, Brazil had few of the conditions necessary to implement an HIV treatment program comparable to First World standards. Neoliberal economic reforms weakened the country's pharmaceutical sector and increased Brazil's dependency on imports. Despite an underfunded public health system and continued health inequalities, reformers implemented an effective treatment program premised on the extension of formal social rights secured during the country's democratization. The irony in the case of Brazil is the passage of new patent protections on pharmaceuticals the same year that it passed a law mandating free and universal treatment for those with HIV/AIDS.

Chapters Four through Six, which trace the recurring episodes of Brazilian capabilities to produce AIDS medicines locally and increasing conflicts with the global pharmaceutical industry, are divided chronologically to

22 *Pharmaceutical Autonomy*

demonstrate the impact of patents on the treatment program. Chapter Four describes the evolution of Brazil's technological capabilities to produce the first generation of ARVs. Brazilian firms, in both private and public sectors, reverse engineered these medicines, thereby breaking the monopoly power of transnational drug firms. After the passage of a federal law guaranteeing universal and free access to these medicines, policymakers decided to mobilize state resources to produce ARVs for Brazil's national treatment program in public labs that had not been privatized during neoliberal reforms of the 1990s. Since patent laws were not in place, policy space existed for a quick response to the AIDS crisis and for achieving pharmaceutical autonomy. Political tensions increased when Brazil sought to produce patent-protected ARVs. The WTO panel the United States brought against Brazil concerning its intellectual property laws created a political opportunity that not only crystallized alliances between the Brazilian state and national activists, but also created the necessary conditions to scale up the pro-access coalition to the global level. The country's successful treatment program based on local production of ARVs provided a rallying point for activists and policymakers. The naming and shaming tactics premised on human rights notions trumped the material interests of transnational drug corporations.

Chapter Five, covering the period from 2002 to 2006, shows increasing foreign dependency of Brazil's pharmaceutical sector due to the impact of patents. Over the next few years, domestic drug-making capabilities declined while the total number of clients enrolled increased. The rising number of people in treatment and the inclusion of more expensive second-generation, patent-protected treatments doubled annual ARV expenditures to R$1 billion (about US$500 million).[4] The patent power of originator companies and the market power of low-cost producers in Asia squeezed Brazil's local ARV manufacturing abilities resulted in pharmaceutical dependency. But confrontations between the government and TNCs created another political opportunity concerning the use of compulsory licenses, which resulted in increased societal mobilization and the need to include another domestic ally—local private sector pharmaceutical industrialists—into the AIDS alliance that had consisted of progressive health professionals and AIDS activists.

Chapter Six traces the development of industrial policies for Brazil's pharmaceutical sector. Essential drugs and medicines used in the country's public health system are increasingly defined as "strategic" goods. Through public labs, the Ministry of Health established public-private partnerships with local pharmaceutical companies in order to nationalize the production of strategic medicines. These initiatives solidified the support of national drug makers for the country's aggressive AIDS policies. Industrial policies, at the same time, increased the distance between the state and transnational drug companies. The institutionalization of these domestic political coalitions organized by the Ministry of Health formed the backdrop for using TRIPS humanitarian safeguards. After several episodes of contentious price

Pharmaceutical Autonomy 23

negotiations and threats over the use of compulsory licenses, Brazil finally issued a compulsory license in 2007 for Merck's efavirenz. By this time, members of the domestic alliance assumed concrete roles to support the decision that a global community of experts and activists readily endorsed.

The final chapter reviews the current situation of Brazil's health system and pharmaceutical access. I contrast the problem of Brazil's health system and pharmaceutical policies with the successes of its AIDS program. In addition, I summarize my findings and highlight the lessons for other countries looking to emulate the Brazilian model and achieve pharmaceutical autonomy. I conclude with a review of the problems of accessing medicines at the global level.

NOTES

1. Dependency theory focuses on the economic ties between countries of the "periphery" that trade low value-added goods for high value-added goods from "core" countries. In *Dependency and Development in Latin America*, first published in 1969, Fernando Cardoso and co-author Enzo Falleto (1979) argued that external processes such as the worldwide expansion of capitalism and international division of labor determines the prospects of economic growth and political institutions in the Third World. Their ideas echoed the thoughts of Andre Gunder Frank (1967), who argued that colonialism, international economic integration, and exploitative enclave economies led to underdevelopment. But Cardoso and Falleto countered that, instead of increasing deprivation, dependent economic growth still occurred in Latin America due to industrialization. Nevertheless, external economic relations continued to condition a country's growth potential. Industrial deepening required the manufacturing operations of foreign-based multinational corporations whose control over capital, technology, and market distribution reproduced situations of dependency.
2. While dependency theory is no longer in vogue, it continues to inspire studies of dependent development and influences debates and research about the possibilities of broad social improvements outside the advanced developed world; see *Studies in Comparative International Development*, vol. 44, issue 4, 2009. Its macro-sociological framework based on historical-structural analysis informs political economy perspectives and debates of health (Morgan 1987; Muntaner et al. 2011; Whiteford and Manderson 2000).
3. Scholars of global capitalism dismiss country classifications of core and periphery traditionally used by dependency theorists.
4. Unless otherwise indicated, all figures in Brazilian currency units can be converted into US dollars at a rate of 2:1, R\$2 equals US\$1.

REFERENCES

Amenta, Edwin, and Michael P. Young. 1999. "Democratic States and Social Movements: Theoretical Arguments and Hypotheses." *Social Problems* 46(2): 153–68.
Berkman, Alan, Jonathan Garcia, Miguel Muñoz-Laboy, Vera Paiva, and Richard Parker. 2005. "A Critical Analysis of the Brazilian Response to HIV/AIDS:

24 *Pharmaceutical Autonomy*

Lessons Learned for Controlling and Mitigating the Epidemic in Developing Countries." *American Journal of Public Health* 95(7): 1162–72.

Bermudez, Jorge. 1995. *Industria Farmaceutica, Estado E Sociedade: Critica Da Politica de Medicamentos No Brasil.* São Paulo: Hucitec/Sobrevime.

Bertero, Carlos Osmar. 1972. "Drugs and Dependency in Brazil—An Empirical Study of Dependency Theory: The Case of the Pharmaceutical Industry." (Dissertation). Ithaca: Cornell University.

Biehl, João. 2004. "The Activist State: Global Pharmaceuticals, AIDS, and Citizenship in Brazil." *Social Text* 22(3): 105–32.

Bresser-Pereira, Luis. 1999. "Managerial Public Administration: Strategy and Structure for a New State." Pp. 1–14 in *Reforming the State: Managerial Public Administration in Latin America*, edited by Luiz Carlos Bresser Pereira and Peter Spink. Boulder: Lynne Rienne.

Campbell, John L. 2004. *Institutional Change and Globalization.* Princeton: Princeton University Press.

Cardoso, Fernando Henrique. 1972. "Dependency and Development in Latin America." *New Left Review* 74: 83–95.

Cardoso, Fernando Henrique. 2009. "New Paths: Globalization in Historical Perspective." *Studies in Comparative International Development* 44(4): 296–317.

Cardoso, Fernando Henrique, and Enzo Faletto. 1979. *Dependency and Development in Latin America.* Berkeley: University of California Press.

Cardoso, Fernando Henrique, and Mariana Magalhaes. 2001. "Democracy as a Starting Point." *Journal of Democracy* 12(1): 5–14.

Castells, Manuel. 2010. *The Rise of the Network Society.* 2nd ed., with a new pref. Chichester: Wiley-Blackwell.

Chang, Ha-Joon. 2002. *Kicking Away the Ladder—Development Strategy in Historical Perspective.* London: Anthem Press.

Cohen, Jillian Clare, and Kristian M. Lybecker. 2005. "AIDS Policy and Pharmaceutical Patents: Brazil's Strategy to Safeguard Public Health." *The World Economy* 28(2): 211–30.

Coriat, Benjamin. 2008. *The Political Economy of HIV/AIDS in Developing Countries: TRIPS, Public Health Systems and Free Access.* Cheltenham: Edward Elgar Publishing.

Dagnino, Evalina. 2004. "Sociedade Civil, Participação E Cidadania: De Que Estamos Falando?" Pp. 95–110 in *Políticas de ciudadanía y sociedad civil en tiempos de globalización*, edited by Daniel Mato. Caracas: FACES, Universidad Central de Venezuela.

Deere, Carolyn. 2009. *The Implementation Game: The TRIPS Agreement and the Global Politics of Intellectual Property Reform in Developing Countries.* London: Oxford University Press.

Domhoff, G. William. 2006. *Who Rules America? Power and Politics, and Social Change.* Boston: McGraw-Hill.

Evans, Peter. 1979. *Dependent Development: The Alliance of Multinational, State, and Local Capital in Brazil.* Princeton: Princeton University Press.

Evans, Peter. 1995. *Embedded Autonomy: States and Industrial Transformation.* Princeton: Princeton University Press.

Evans, Peter. 1996. "Government Action, Social Capital and Development: Reviewing the Evidence on Synergy." *World Development* 24(6): 1119–32.

Evans, Peter, Dietrich Rueschemeyer, and Theda Skocpol. 1985. *Bringing the State Back In.* New York: Cambridge University Press.

Flynn, Matthew. 2011. "Corporate Power and State Resistance: Brazil's Use of TRIPS Flexibilities for Its National AIDS Program." Pp. 149–77 in *Intellectual Property, Pharmaceuticals, and Public Health: Access to Drugs in Developing*

Countries, edited by Kenneth Shadlen, Samira Guennif, and Georgina Alenka Guzman Chavez. Cheltenham: Edward Elgar Publishing.

Flynn, Matthew. 2013a. "Brazilian Pharmaceutical Diplomacy: Social Democratic Principles Versus Soft Power Interests." *International Journal of Health Services* 43(1): 67–89.

Flynn, Matthew. 2013b. "Origins and Limitations of State-Based Advocacy: Brazil's AIDS Treatment Program and Global Power Dynamics." *Politics & Society* 41(1): 3–28.

Fourcade, Marion, and Kieran Healy. 2007. "Moral Views of Market Society." *Annual Review of Sociology* 33(1): 285–311.

Foweraker, Joe. 2005. "Towards a Political Sociology of Social Mobilization in Latin America." Pp. 115–36 in *Rethinking Development in Latin America*, edited by Charles H. Wood and Bryan R. Roberts. University Park: Penn State University Press.

Frank, Andre Gunder. 1967. *Capitalism and Underdevelopment in Latin America*. New York: Monthly Review Press.

Galvão, Jane. 2002. "A política brasileira de distribuição e produção de medicamentos anti-retrovirais: privilégio ou um direito?" *Cadernos de Saúde Pública* 18(1): 213–19.

Gereffi, Gary. 1983. *The Pharmaceutical Industry and Dependency in the Third Word*. Princeton: Princeton University Press.

Goffman, Erving. 1986. *Frame Analysis: An Essay on the Organization of Experience*. Boston: Northeastern University Press.

Haydu, Jeffrey. 1998. "Making Use of the Past: Time Periods as Cases to Compare and as Sequences of Problem Solving." *American Journal of Sociology* 104(2): 339–71.

Haydu, Jeffrey. 2010. "Reversals of Fortune: Path Dependency, Problem Solving, and Temporal Cases." *Theory and Society* 39(1): 25–48.

Heller, Patrick, Dietrich Rueschemeyer, and Richard Snyder. 2009. "Dependency and Development in a Globalized World: Looking Back and Forward." *Studies in Comparative International Development* 44(4): 287–95.

Hickey, Sam, and Giles Mohan. 2005. "Relocating Participation within a Radical Politics of Development." *Development and Change* 36(2): 237–62.

Hirschman, Albert O. 1971. *Bias for Hope: Essays on Development and Latin America*. 1st ed. New Haven: Yale University Press.

't Hoen, Ellen F. M. 2009. *The Global Politics of Pharmaceutical Monopoly Power*. Diemen: AMB.

Holton, Robert J. 2011. *Globalization and the Nation State: Second Edition*. Newbury Park: Palgrave Macmillan.

Howlett, Michael, and Jeremy Rayner. 2006. "Understanding the Historical Turn in the Policy Sciences: A Critique of Stochastic, Narrative, Path Dependency and Process-Sequencing Models of Policy-Making over Time." *Policy Sciences* 39(1): 1–18.

Huber, Evelyne, and John Stephens. 2012. *Democracy and the Left Social Policy and Inequality in Latin America*. Chicago: University of Chicago Press.

Jelin, Elizabeth. 1996. "Citizenship Revisited: Solidarity, Responsibility, and Rights." Pp. 101–19 in *Constructing Democracy: Human Rights, Citizenship, and Society in Latin America*, edited by Elizabeth Jelin and Eric Hershberg. Boulder: Westview Press.

Kapstein, Ethan B., and Josh Busby. 2013. *AIDS Drugs for All*. Cambridge: Cambridge University Press.

Kingdon, John W. 2011. *Agendas, Alternatives, and Public Policies*. Updated 2nd ed. Boston: Longman.

26 *Pharmaceutical Autonomy*

Lee, Kelley, and Eduardo Gomez. 2011. "Brazil's Ascendance: The Soft Power Role of Global Health Diplomacy." *The European Business Review*. Retrieved February 4, 2011 (www.europeanbusinessreview.com/?p=3400).

Löfgren, Hans, and Owain David Williams. 2013. *The New Political Economy of Pharmaceuticals: Production, Innovation and TRIPS in the Global South*. Basingstoke: Palgrave Macmillan.

Long, Norman. 2001. *Development Sociology: Actor Perspectives*. London: Routledge.

Mahoney, James, and Dietrich Rueschemeyer. 2003. *Comparative Historical Analysis*. Cambridge: Cambridge University Press.

Matthews, Duncan. 2011. *Intellectual Property, Human Rights and Development: The Role of NGOs and Social Movements*. Cheltenham: Edward Elgar Publishing.

McMichael, Phillip. 2004. *Development and Social Change*. London: Sage.

De Mello e Souza, Andre. 2007. "Defying Globalization: Effective Self-Reliance in Brazil." Pp. 37–63 in *The Global Politics of AIDS*, edited by Paul G. Harris and Patricia D. Siplon. Boulder: Lynne Rienner Publishers.

Mills, C. Wright. 1957. *The Power Elite*. New York: Oxford.

Morgan, Lynn M. 1987. "Dependency Theory in the Political Economy of Health: An Anthropological Critique." *Medical Anthropology Quarterly* 1(2): 131–54.

Muntaner, Carles, Carme Borrell, Edwin Ng, Haejoo Chung, Albert Espelt, Maica Rodriguez-Sanz, Joan Benach, and Patricia O'Campo. 2011. "Politics, Welfare Regimes, and Population Health: Controversies and Evidence." *Sociology of Health & Illness* 33(6): 946–64.

Nunn, Amy. 2008. *The Politics and History of AIDS Treatment in Brazil*. New York: Springer.

Nunn, Amy, Samuel Dickman, Nicoli Nattrass, Alexandra Cornwall, and Sofia Gruskin. 2012. "The Impacts of AIDS Movements on the Policy Responses to HIV/AIDS in Brazil and South Africa: A Comparative Analysis." *Global Public Health* 7(10): 1031–44.

Orsi, Fabienne, Lia Hasenclever, Beatriz Fialho, Paulo Tigre, and Benjamin Coriat. 2003. "Intellectual Property Rights, Anti-AIDS Policy and Generic Drugs." Pp. 109–35 in *Economics of AIDS and Access to HIV/AIDS Care in Developing Countries. Issues and Challenges*. Paris: Agence Nationale pour Recherche sur le Sida.

Pleyers, Geoffrey. 2010. *Alter-Globalization: Becoming Actors in the Global Age*. Cambridge and Malden: Polity.

Della Porta, Donatella. 2006. *Globalization from Below: Transnational Activists and Protest Networks*. Minneapolis: University of Minnesota Press.

Portes, Alejandro, ed. 2009. *Las Instituciones En El Desarrollo Latinoamericano: Un Estudio Comparado*. 1st ed. México, D.F.: Siglo Veintiuno Editores.

Possas, Cristina de Albuquerque. 2008. "Compulsory Licensing in the Real World: The Case of ARV Drugs in Brazil." Pp. 150–66 in *The Political Economy of HIV/AIDS in Developing Countries*, edited by Benjamin Coriat. Cheltenham: Edward Elgar Publishing.

Richards, Donald. 2004. *Intellectual Property Rights and Global Capitalism*. Armonk: M. E. Sharpe.

Roberts, Bryan. 2005. "Citizenship, Rights, and Social Policy." Pp. 137–58 in *Rethinking Development in Latin America*, edited by Charles H. Wood and Bryan R. Roberts University Park: Penn State University Press.

Robinson, William I. 2004. *A Theory of Global Capitalism*. Baltimore and London: Johns Hopkins University Press.

Santoro, Wayne A., and Gail M. McGuire. 1997. "Social Movement Insiders: The Impact of Institutional Activists on Affirmative Action and Comparable Worth Policies." *Social Problems* 44(4): 503–19.

Serra, José. 2004. "The Political Economy of the Brazilian Struggle against AIDS." *An Institute for Advanced Study Friends Forum*. Brown University. Retrieved October 25, 2008 (www.sss.ias.edu/files/papers/paper17.pdf)

Shadlen, Kenneth. 2009. "The Politics of Patents and Drugs in Brazil and Mexico: The Industrial Bases of Health Policies." *Comparative Politics* 41: 178–201.

Shadlen, Kenneth, Samira Guennif, and Georgina Alenka Guzman Chavez, eds. 2011. *Intellectual Property, Pharmaceuticals and Public Health Access to Drugs in Developing Countries.* Cheltenham: Edward Elgar Publishing.

Sklair, Leslie. 1995. *Sociology of the Global System.* Baltimore: Johns Hopkins University Press.

Sklair, Leslie. 2001. *The Transnational Capitalist Class.* Oxford: Basil Blackwell.

Sklair, Leslie. 2002. "The Transnational Capitalist Class and Global Politics: Deconstructing the Corporate: State Connection." *International Political Science Review/Revue internationale de science politique* 23(2): 159–74.

Snow, David A., and Robert D. Benford. 1992. "Master Frames and Cycles of Protest." Pp. 133–55 in *Frontiers in Social Movement Research*, edited by Aldon D. Morris and Carol McClurg Mueller. New Haven: Yale University Press.

Snow, David A., E. Burke Rochford, Jr., Steven K. Worden, and Robert D. Benford. 1988. "Frame Alignment Processes, Micromobilization and Movement Participation." *American Sociological Review* 51: 464–81.

Souza, Celina. 2013. "Modernisation of the State and Bureaucratic Capacity-Building in Brazilian Federal Government." Pp. 39–52 in *Policy Analysis in Brazil*, edited by Jeni Vaitsman, Lenaura Lobato, and Jose M. Ribeiro. Bristol: Policy Press.

Stake, Robert E. 1995. *The Art of Case Study Research.* Thousand Oaks: Sage.

Tarrow, Sidney. 2005. "The Dualities of Transnational Contention: 'Two Activist Solitudes' or a New World Altogether?" *Mobilizations* 10(1): 53–72.

Tilly, Charles. 1995. "Globalization Threatens Rights." *International Labor and Working-Class History* 47: 1–23.

Wade, Robert Hunter. 2003. "What Strategies Are Viable for Developing Countries Today? The World Trade Organization and the Shrinking of 'Developmental Space.'" *Review of International Political Economy* 10(4): 621–44.

Weyland, Kurt Gerhard. 2006. *Bounded Rationality and Policy Diffusion Social Sector Reform in Latin America.* Princeton: Princeton University Press.

Whiteford, Linda M., and Lenore Manderson. 2000. *Global Health Policy, Local Realities: The Fallacy of the Level Playing Field.* Boulder: Lynne Rienner Publishers.

Winston, Morton. 2002. "NGO Strategies for Promoting Corporate Social Responsibility." *Ethics & International Affairs* 16(1): 71–87.

Yin, Robert. 1989. *Case Study Research: Design and Methods.* Newbury Park: Sage.

2 Elements of Global Pharmaceutical Power

In 2007 Christopher Singer, a mild-mannered former executive for Glaxo-SmithKline's operations in Latin America, was the director of international affairs at the Pharmaceutical Research and Manufacturers of America (PhRMA), one of the world's most powerful lobbying organizations. From his Washington, DC, office lying between the White House and the Capital Building, Singer is responsible for working towards the global harmonization of intellectual property systems and regulatory affairs in the interests of the pharmaceutical industry. PhRMA's members include some of the biggest companies in the industry, including Pfizer, Merck, GlaxoSmithKline (GSK), and Abbott.[1] Created in 1958 to advocate for public policies, PhRMA promotes the view that the privately owned and operated pharmaceutical industry drives technological innovation and improves health and well-being.

As an executive of GSK in Latin America in the 1990s, Singer witnessed the conflicts between transnational drug companies and governments over the price of medicines. Now at PhRMA, he lobbies to ensure that the intellectual property rights of companies are enforced worldwide and included in international trade accords. Because finding cures for diseases is a global concern, and given that the drug industry operates internationally, PhRMA's chief objective is promoting a patent-based business model worldwide. Singer argues that even middle-income countries that have resources should help support research and development. "Granted there is a huge divide between the rich and poor like in Brazil, but they still have means," he said in an interview.[2] According to the industry, every country, except perhaps the most destitute, should contribute to funding research and the development of new medicines.

PhRMA is also concerned about prices and the ability of its members to recoup its investments and generate profits. For the trade group, intellectual property does not represent an obstacle to access medicines. "In fact, we had a study done by the Boston Consulting Group that showed that even . . . Brazil's government policy to purchase and provide more generic products actually didn't serve to expand access. So our belief is this alleged tension between intellectual property and access in the developing world is a real tenuous one," Singer asserted. In his view, countries should promote a free market, and governments should only target social policies to those individuals in society that are the worst off.

Setting aside the equity issues with respect to financing R&D and the validity of corporate sponsored studies, the transnational pharmaceutical industry resembles the ideal type of corporate power. The concept of power here is understood in the classic Weberian sense as the ability to obtain one's objectives even in the face of adversity. Corporate power rests on the means to continuously generate profits and depends on institutions that enable the expansion of profitable activities. Since social institutions remain fragile and subject to various human interests, they must constantly be defended and upheld. The basis of corporate hegemony rests on the creation and control of economic resources, the ability to affect public policy through influential policy-making networks, and constant public persuasion that private markets are the best means to achieve social objectives.

This chapter delves into the dimensions of corporate power of the global pharmaceutical industry. My objective here is not to critique or add to the growing literature on the pharmaceutical industry.[3] Rather it is to outline the changes in the international pharmaceutical industry in recent decades that are relevant to the Brazilian case study. Without this prior knowledge, it will be difficult to understand the various challenges and constraints related to Brazil's efforts to obtain pharmaceutical autonomy. I begin with a review of the pharmaceutical production process broken into to the discovery of new medicine, bulk manufacturing of inputs, and formulation into finished products. The chapter develops the concepts of *patent power* and *market power* to draw attention to the role that patents play in the current business model of pharmaceutical innovation as well as to understand the rise of market power from low-cost generic producers of medicines. Next, I describe how the industry's political power translated into the Agreement on Trade-Related Aspects of Intellectual Property Rights (TRIPS), which mandates that all member countries of the World Trade Organization (WTO) adhere to a patent-based business model. I detail TRIPS flexibilities and humanitarian safeguards including the use of compulsory licenses and parallel importing, and review TRIPS compliance in various countries. Lastly, I outline competing normative frameworks regarding intellectual property rights, especially as they relate to innovation, development, and access of new medicines.

THE PHARMACEUTICAL INDUSTRY

The Pharmaceutical Production Cycle

To understand the prospects for controlling technology in Brazil's attempts to achieve pharmaceutical autonomy, it is important to understand the many steps involved in the pharmaceutical production cycle. Monopolizing any step in the process impacts negotiating power between different market participants. The tendency towards monopolization is offset by generic producers who reverse engineer new medicines and thus lower the price towards the marginal cost of production. Developing and producing pharmaceuticals involves numerous actors, including academic scientists, firms, and regulatory bodies that, networked together, contribute to the creation of a new drug, ensure safe manufacturing practices and products, and police reliable distribution systems.

The pharmaceutical production cycle can be broken into three distinct steps (see Figure 2.1): 1) discovery research, 2) manufacturing of raw materials, such as the active pharmaceutical ingredients (APIs), and 3) pharmaceutical formulation.[4] Discovery research begins with basic research into discovering new pharmaceutical interventions and ends with clinical testing of new chemical entities. Basic research seeks to unveil the progression and causal mechanisms of disease and ill health. By identifying therapeutic targets, researchers look for new chemical and biological entities capable of arresting infection, providing relief from suffering, and even curing disease. Basic research involves tracing disease pathogenesis and the discovery of new therapeutic agents. Due to the uncertainty of how specific diseases work and the risks inherent in finding effective therapeutic agents, few private companies invest in basic research. Consequently, much of the initial funding comes from public resources and is carried out in government-sponsored

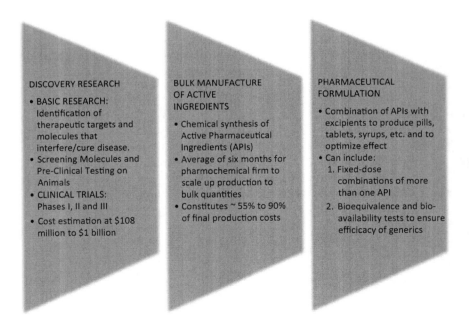

Figure 2.1 The Pharmaceutical Production Cycle

research centers such as the National Institute of Health, public-private partnerships, and university laboratories (Angell 2004; Goozner 2004). At later stages in the research process, venture-capital firms, equity stakes, and partnerships with established pharmaceutical firms provide resources and guide the development process (Pisano 2006).

The time it takes basic research to discover a new drug can last from three months to 30 years. Insights about the spread and development of disease are followed by the synthesis, screening, and testing of new compounds. Scientists employ advance technology at relatively inexpensive costs to carry-out initial screenings of 5,000–10,000 possible candidates. Next, laboratory tests and animal studies gauge effectiveness and toxicity before proceeding with research on human subjects (Boston Consulting Group 2001).

In order to conduct clinical trials in human hosts, a company or researcher must submit an Investigational New Drug Application with regulatory authorities, such as the Food and Drug Administration (FDA). At this point, the chance of failure for a new compound completing the trials and reaching the market is roughly 1:10 or 2:10 (Goozner 2004). The most expensive step in bringing a new drug to market is conducting clinical trials, which include three distinct phases with progressively larger numbers of volunteers. Phase I trials, involving between 200 to 400 healthy volunteers, seek to determine maximum doses before the chemical becomes toxic and to learn how the drug is absorbed and metabolized by the body. Phase II trials focus on drug efficacy in groups of 400–600 patients and often include comparisons to a placebo.

Clinical trials culminate with Phase III trials, which are large-scale, randomized trials, often using double-blind studies so that neither patients nor administrators know who are in the treatment and control groups. The goal of the trial, ranging upward from 3,000-plus patients and sometimes numbering in the tens of thousands, is to confirm the effectiveness of the drug versus a placebo or current standard medication. Phase III trials account for around 75% of total R&D costs. At this point, the odds that a drug successfully completes the trial and reaches market decreases to around 1:2 or 1:3 (Goozner 2004). A cost study on new rotavirus vaccines revealed that Phase III trials involving 63,000–68,000 volunteers cost between US$126 million and US$204 million (Light, Andrus, and Warburton 2009). It is important to note that vaccine trials tend to be some of the largest, compared to trials of new cancer or antiretroviral medicines used against HIV/AIDS. After completing all the clinical trials, companies submit a new drug application to regulatory authorities who assess clinical data and determine whether or not to grant marketing approval. Additional post-market trials, which are rarely completed, should identify adverse reactions by monitoring their use on a large-scale setting by a diversified population (Light 2009).

Bringing a new drug to market can be a time-consuming process, but recent years have witnessed a speeding-up in the process. According to one

32 Elements of Global Pharmaceutical Power

study, the total time expended from regulatory approval for human trials to the completion of Phase III tests has fallen, on average, from eight years in 1992 to five in 2002 (Keyhani, Diener-West, and Powe 2005). While an expedited review process results in medicines reaching consumers quicker, which is justifiable in limited life-threatening cases, such as Ebola, they also result in additional risks to patients (Abraham and Lewis 2014; Goldacre 2013). Needless to say, private industry continues to lobby for quicker regulatory approval in order to take advantage of the time a drug is under patent.

Researchers and companies typically apply for a product patent at the pre-clinical stage when a new chemical entity appears promising. Subsequent drug development, testing, and regulatory review may take an additional five years before a drug reaches the market, providing the patent holder with an effective monopoly of 15 years. In the case of the antiretroviral ritonavir, which received expedited FDA approval, Abbott Pharmaceuticals filed its first patent for the drug in December 1993 and received marketing approval in March 1996. The company's market exclusivity for the product extended for close to 18 years, not including additional tactics to extend the period of market exclusivity.

The second stage in the production cycle involves the mass production of raw materials, including the combination and transformation of chemical intermediates, to obtain active pharmaceutical ingredients (APIs). "The synthesis of an API usually requires several chemical processing steps in which new chemical bonds are formed and molecular complexity increases," explain Pinheiro, Antunes, and Fortunak (2008: 2). Producers begin with large quantities of chemicals. At each step of the production process, which may include fermentation, distillation, crystallization, among other techniques, drug makers synthesize chemicals and produce ever smaller amounts of output until obtaining the desired active pharmaceutical agent. Typically, API producers can choose from various processes or different routes in order to arrive at the final product. In the case of AZT, the first known effective agent against HIV and known by its generic name as zidovudine, producing the API was, at first, extremely expensive since it was developed from herring and salmon sperm extract.[5] Not until scientists developed synthetic chemical processes did manufacturing costs fall.

Countries must have significant industrial and technological capacity to engage in the mass production of APIs. Given the global market in medicines and technological possibilities, pharmaceutical companies can achieve significant economies of scale at this stage of the production cycle. In a review of some the most widely used and expensive ARVs, the API accounts for 55% to 90% of the direct manufacturing costs (i.e. not including R&D costs) of the finished end product (Pinheiro et al. 2005). Mass production of the API requires stringent quality controls to avoid contamination of the drug at each stage of the refining process. To reduce costs and rationalize production, pharmochemical producers who make APIs prefer to know, as much as possible, demand horizons. Switching between product lines and starting new products can be a time-consuming and expensive process. During field visits in Brazil that I conducted, API makers said they needed about six months in order to scale up production from the laboratory setting to industrial scale for producing the API of a reverse-engineered drug. Such timeframes are crucial when government officials negotiate prices and seek out alternative suppliers.

The third step in the production process involves manufacturing the finished dosage form, or pharmaceutical formulation. At this stage, drug makers combine the API with inactive ingredients known as excipients in the form of capsules, tablets, syrups, serums, creams, and aerosols. Drug formulation evolves during clinical trials in order to optimize treatment, but the dosage of the API may also vary to make a drug more or less potent depending on the population taking the drug. For example, children, due to their distinct metabolism and size, may require smaller or higher dosages compared to adults and often require easier-to-use formulations such as syrups or chewable tablets. Additionally, a drug's stability and solubility affects the number of pills a patient requires to take per day. Drug formulators, for example, made improvements to the antiretroviral drug efavirenz by increasing the dosage from 200mg to 600mg so that, instead of three pills per day, patients need only take one.

Other examples of innovations in drug formulas are enteric versions and fixed-dose combinations. Digested through the intestine instead of the stomach, enteric formulas include delayed-release mechanisms that result in longer-lasting tablets and optimized treatment schedules. The fewer pills required, the better the adherence to treatment protocols. Additionally, formulations with more than one API, called fixed-dose combinations (FDCs), reduce the number of pills required and improve treatment compliance. Compared to the early days of ARV treatment when individuals had to consume twelve or more tablets during the day and night, current treatment protocols emphasize a three-in-one combination pill taken once a day. For example, the brand name drug Atripla combines 600mg of efavirenz with 300mg tenofovir and 200mg emtricitabine.[6] The drawback with FDCs is that they can increase the risk of adverse reactions and limit the range of dosage adjustments.

There are many different classifications of medicines. A new medicine that arrives on the market is called a reference drug, or initial innovator drug. Generic medicines, in contrast, are dosage forms comparable to reference drugs based on bioavailability and bioequivalence tests. Bioavailability refers to the duration the body metabolizes and removes the API from its system; bioequivalency means that the drug has the same therapeutic effect on a patient as the reference drug. These tests ensure that generic drugs have the same levels of quality, safety, and efficacy as initial innovator drugs.[7] While regulatory authorities uphold the compatibility between generic and reference drugs, originator companies employ media campaigns to question

34 Elements of Global Pharmaceutical Power

the quality of generic competitors. Companies also invest resources in marketing and advertisements in their "branded generics" in order to differentiate their products from other generic competitors.

Pharmaceutical production occurs in tightly controlled environments to ensure purity and potency, and regulatory authorities regularly inspect manufacturing sites to certify the use of current Good Manufacturing Practice (cGMP). In today's global trading system, regulatory authorities have begun to expand their activities abroad. The United States' Food and Drug Administration (FDA) inspects sites in India, and Brazil's comparable authority, the National Health Surveillance Agency (ANVISA—*Agência Nacional de Vigilância Sanitária*) inspects upstream API facilities.

Global procurement agencies have established worldwide certification standards for drugs used in international health programs. The Global Fund for AIDS, Tuberculosis and Malaria, which procures medicines for distribution around the developing world, uses the World Health Organization's prequalification program to guarantee quality, safety, and efficacy of its bulk purchases (see Kapstein and Busby 2013). There is debate within the drug industry concerning the level of certifications and standards on generic medicines. The FDA, for example, is known to be more stringent than the WHO prequalification program. While tighter standards may appear as more desirable, especially where the therapeutic window between efficacy and toxicity remains narrow, excessively tight standards could disproportionately benefit originator companies that produce the reference drugs and thus discourage generic competition that results in lower prices.

A Globalizing Industry

Understanding the pharmaceutical production process sheds light on the resources involved and steps required for bringing a drug to market. A "drug company" may be involved in all the steps of the pharmaceutical production chain described in Figure 2.1. In this case, they are called a vertically integrated firm. Firms that concentrate in chemical synthesis to produce APIs and/or their chemical intermediates are called pharmochemical companies or API makers. Drug formulators do not partake in discovery research or API production and focus on producing finished dosage forms.

In today's global economy, the operations of vertically integrated firms, such as the transnational drug industry, often are dispersed throughout the world. Having operations in several countries allows transnational corporations (TNCs) to take advantage of economies of scale and global sourcing strategies. In fact, drug companies were one of the first industries to internationalize their operations in the first half of the 1900s in order to secure their *market power* in various countries by obtaining economies of scale.

Market power refers to firms' abilities to produce at any node in the pharmaceutical production chain at a lower cost than their competition. A number of factors affect the expansion of TNCs: uneven development of capitalism (i.e. cheaper wages in different countries), government support (i.e. tax breaks and subsidies), and improvements in productivity or organization of work. Consumers can also exert *market power* through a monopsony or buyers' cartel. The more concentrated the demand side, such as a government representing thousands of individuals, the stronger their bargaining position. Conversely, the greater degree to which production and distribution is centralized through mergers and acquisitions, as well as by licensing agreements, the greater the market power on the supply side.

Exercising economic power in the global marketplace is a high stakes game. IMS Health (2012a) estimated that the global pharmaceutical market reached US$956 billion in 2011. Despite its enormous size, distribution remains highly skewed. About 18% of the world's population consumes 88% of the world's pharmaceuticals, with 82% of that population accessing the remaining 12% (Tempest 2010). Growth, however, is slowing in traditional markets, hovering between 3.5–3.9% from 2007 to 2011 in North America and Europe, compared to emerging markets which experienced a 12.3–15.5% increase for the same period (IMS Health 2012b). These trends are likely to continue in the near future. For the 2012 and 2016 period, IMS Health forecasted market growth in the developed countries between 1–4% compared to 10–13% elsewhere. IMS Health analysts coined the term "pharmerging" to describe the countries of Brazil, Russia, India, China, Mexico, South Korea, and Turkey, which accounted for 51% of the total market growth in 2009, compared to 16% of growth in the recession-plagued traditional markets (Campbell and Chui 2009). Despite market saturation in developed economies, the United States still accounts for the largest amount of sales revenue, roughly one-third, in the world, and US consumers also spend the most per capita, $992 per year, followed by Canada's $736, in 2009 (OECD n.d.). While market growth is shifting towards the "pharmerging" markets, the top pharmaceutical firms remain based in the developed world. Table 2.1 lists the top ten largest drug companies in the world according to total sales in 2006. The sales of the top companies often outstrip the entire budget of health ministries.

The world's largest pharmaceutical companies operate on a global scale, and executives plan their strategies at this level. However, local distribution and marketing continues to segment markets into national domains due to differing national regulations and health care systems. Compared to other industries, wide-scale competition in pharmaceuticals practically does not exist between producers, except when a patent expires and generic manufacturers enter the market. Instead, the global pharmaceutical industry remains heavily oligopolistic with companies specializing in certain product lines within specific therapeutic classes (Bermudez 1995). This is observed even in the field of HIV medicines when, for instance, Roche decided to exit the ARV market while other companies such as Merck and GlaxoSmithKline (GSK) expanded their portfolios of antiretrovirals (Reuters 2008). In

36   *Elements of Global Pharmaceutical Power*

Table 2.1   Global Company Sales Summary (Billions US$) in 2006

Rank	Company	Sales US$ billions	Market Share (%)	Sales Growth (%)
1	Pfizer (US)	45.1	8.6	1.8
2	GlaxoSmithKline (UK)	36.9	7.1	8.9
3	Sanofi-Aventis (French)	35.6	6.8	4.9
4	Novartis (Swiss)	28.9	5.5	17.9
5	Roche (German)	26.6	5.1	21.4
6	AstraZeneca (UK)	25.7	4.9	10.5
7	Johnson & Johnson (US)	23.2	4.4	4.2
8	Merck & Co (US)	22.6	4.3	2.8
9	Wyeth (US)	15.7	3.0	9.8
10	Eli Lilly (US)	14.8	2.8	7.5

Source: Gray (2007)

total, Bermudez (1995) estimated that the planet's ten largest pharmaceutical firms controlled 40% of the world market during the 1990s.

A number of industry strategies mark the growth and evolution of the pharmaceutical industry in recent decades. First is increasing centralization and consolidation. As part of their development strategies in the 1960s thru the 1980s, many newly industrialized countries in Asia, Latin America, and elsewhere promoted the development of nationally owned firms, either as privately owned companies or state enterprises. Governments promoted the purchase of technology and machinery from the developed world; provided a policy environment with weak intellectual property protection; incentivized local firms to reverse engineer existing products; protected against import competition; and attracted foreign investors to establish local manufacturing facilities. With several countries implementing these policies at the same time, such as Brazil and South Korea, the market experienced a production glut. Large, internationally experienced drug producers responded to widespread overcapacity and capacity underutilization by initiating mergers and acquisitions and by increasing market consolidation through strategic alliances. For example, GSK and Pfizer announced a strategic alliance in their antiretroviral divisions in 2009 (Reuters 2010).

Second, global drug companies are increasingly outsourcing and/or subcontracting elements of the production process. During the 1980s and 1990s, the tendency was to centralize production of active pharmaceutical ingredients and decentralize end-production and marketing (Zeller 2000). Nowadays, large firms increasingly concentrate on marketing and distribution of final products while outsourcing R&D activities to small biotech companies and clinical testing to contract research organizations (Homedes and Ugalde 2006; Tarabusi and Vickery 1998). Furthermore, centralization

Elements of Global Pharmaceutical Power 37

has led to increased intra-firm trade between separate branches of the same company. When conducted internationally, intra-firm trade allows companies to engage in transfer pricing strategies. This accounting procedure occurs when a TNC charges itself higher prices for an input in low-tax regions, sometimes by a factor of 10, than for the same input priced in the high-tax countries (Sikka and Willmott 2010).[8]

Third, transnational drug companies have changed their research strategies in order to respond to a decline in new molecular entities (Homedes and Ugalde 2006). In 2002, the FDA approved only 17 new drugs for sale in the US, the lowest number of approvals since 1983 and a drop from the 56 that entered the market in 1996, a significant decrease despite the industry's rising R&D expenditures (Cockburn 2004). The situation may be even worse than these figures reveal. According to in-depth reviews, the percentage of truly innovative drugs that represent important therapeutic breakthroughs over existing treatments account for only 2–3% of new drug candidates in recent decades (Light 2009). Increasingly, the industry's strategy has focused more on the discovery and launching of "blockbuster" drugs that amount to over US$1 billion in sales, with competitors attempting to produce comparable treatments called "me-too" drugs, which use the same action mechanism and result in similar effects (Homedes and Ugalde 2006). However, companies have experienced difficulties in producing new "blockbuster" drugs to replace existing product lines. The productivity crisis in the global pharmaceutical industry amounts to a "patent cliff" in which future sales and profits in key markets will likely decline due to patent expirations (Tempest 2010).

Fourth, the pricing of patented medicines is carried out secretly by top executives and hired specialist consultants. Light (2008: 67) explains the pricing system: "The value of a new drug is made up of the *reference value*, the price of the best alternative, and the added or *differential value* of the new drug [italics in original]." The added or differential value includes all the advertising and marketing techniques employed to convince doctors and patients that a specific drug is better and has fewer side effects than competitor drugs. At the global level, prices of the same drug vary considerably. In the US, for instance, insurance companies negotiate with drug companies, whereas in Canada and the United Kingdom, a pricing board negotiates with the drug firms. In the developing world, prices also vary considerably according to market competition, patent regimes, and public health systems (Silverman, Lydecker, and Lee 1992).

Lastly, the rise of India and China as important producers of medicines and raw materials has shifted *market power* away from incumbent Western firms. In recent decades, India has become a powerhouse in producing generic medicines with firms like Cipla, Ranbaxy, and Aurobindo becoming lead suppliers of inexpensive global medicines to treat AIDS and other diseases. The growing market power of Indian and Chinese firms has undercut not only incumbent pharmaceutical firms from high-income countries but

38 *Elements of Global Pharmaceutical Power*

has also squeezed generic firms based in other middle-income countries such as Brazil. Large Western firms have responded by acquiring firms in newly industrialized countries. For example, Japan's Daiichi Sankyo paid US$4.6 billion in 2008 for a controlling stake in Ranbaxy, based in India (Gibbs and Tripathy 2008). These firms are also entering the branded generics market, seeking more revenue growth in the developing world and outsourcing more activities to other countries (Tempest 2010).

The growing division of labor in the global pharmaceutical industry continues apace as low-cost Asian producers advance in global markets, but R&D remains concentrated in developed countries, especially in the biotech offshoots from university labs. Clinical trials of new therapies, meanwhile, are undertaken throughout the world. Understanding the shifting counters of *market power* provides insight into the strategies originator companies employ to maintain market share and obtain surplus rents. The increasing salience of *patent power* can be viewed as a response to uneven development of pharmaceutical production across the world. In response to the rise of cheap, generic producers from the developing world that are able to exploit their *market power* based on quick reverse engineering of new medicines and exploiting less expensive production costs, incumbent pharmaceutical corporations from wealthy, industrialized companies have pushed a global patent agenda.

POLITICAL POWER OF THE GLOBAL PHARMACEUTICAL INDUSTRY

PhRMA's lobbyists have been extremely effective in achieving the industry's objectives that include a market with few price controls, a strong intellectual property system, and quick regulatory approvals of its medicines. PhRMA, together with its sister organization, the International Federation of Pharmaceutical Manufacturers & Associations (IFPMA), which is based in Geneva and represents national and regional industry associations across five continents, promote corporate pharmaceutical power throughout the world. One strategy is lobbying. In the US, the pharmaceutical industry is one of the biggest political spenders. According to the Center for Responsive Politics (2011), between 1998 and 2009 the pharmaceutical industry spent US$1.23 billion in political donations and, in one year, employed up to 800 lobbyists.

Corporate pharmaceutical power is not only based on money alone, but also on the revolving door between government and industry. Billy Tauzin, who played an instrumental role in the US's Medicare Prescription Act of 2003 as a member of the House of Representatives, later became the president of PhRMA. Harvey Bale served for 12 years in the Office of the United States Trade Representative (USTR) before becoming the director-general of the IFPMA. PhRMA maintains direct relations with the USTR through advisory committees that provide input into trade accords. IFPMA has formal consultative status with specialist bodies of the United Nations such as the World Health Organizations and formal relations with the World Trade Organization (WTO). These industry associations tend to have privileged access to trade accords and negotiations that are conducted outside the public's view (Sell 2003).[9]

Industry lobbies, the use of the revolving door, and privileged access to international governance organizations allows transnational drug firms to protect its most lucrative market—the United States—and to win a powerful backer to enforce *patent power* across the world. *Patent power* refers to the state's codification of intellectual property into laws specifying the rights accorded to the patent holder. As sole providers of the drug, the patent holder or licensee can charge monopoly rents for a certain length of time before the invention falls into the public domain, that is, when other producers can enter the market. During the period of market exclusivity, the inventor or producer can charge prices far higher than the marginal cost of production. With generic competition, prices fall and profit margins decline (see Appendix Two).

Patent power illustrates the political power of certain groups in the value chain to formulate and obtain policies in their interests. Without a doubt, the most important accord expanding the industry's patent power in recent years has been the Agreement on Trade-Related Aspects of Intellectual Property (TRIPS).

Patents and the Lead-Up to TRIPS

Intellectual property refers to various "creations of the mind" that include a number of enforceable rights over patents, trademarks, industrial designs, and copyrights. The "rights" over intellectual property grant their owners with a number of exclusive entitlements concerning their use and transferability, with a limited number of exceptions. Various forms of intellectual property date back to antiquity, but the modern patent system originated in Venice in 1474 and later became formalized into a statutory system of standardized applicability in the US with the Patent Act of 1836 (Bracha 2004; May and Sell 2006). May and Sell (2006) contend that the evolution of the intellectual property laws resulted from changes in technology, political systems, and conceptualization of individuals as knowledge producers. "The rise and expansion of the patent system . . . had little to do with inventiveness and much more to do with the rise, expansion, and growing institutionalization of the capitalist mode of market organization," they claim (May and Sell 2006: 86–87).

What conditions must be fulfilled in order to achieve a patent? Typically, a patent is awarded when the applicant demonstrates three criteria in an application: novelty, inventiveness, and industrial applicability. Novelty refers to whether or not the invention already exists. If the invention is already available or described in printed documents, then the claim fails the

40 Elements of Global Pharmaceutical Power

novelty test. Patent claims must also detail an inventive step, which means that the invention is not obvious. The invention must go beyond current practices in a specialized field of knowledge, that is, advances on what an average skilled technician or engineer in the field already knows. Industrial applicability means that the alleged invention has a practical utility or usefulness, conforms to the natural laws of the universe, and does not involve aesthetic or expressive content. Accordingly, only when these three conditions are fulfilled should patent offices award patents.

Depending on the scope of national legislation, applicants can obtain numerous patents on the same drug. Companies can obtain patents on the molecule comprising the API and on the various formulations of that molecule with inert ingredients or with other fixed dosages of other ingredients. The processes to create a drug as well as the chemical processes and the chemical intermediates involved in the production process can also be patented. Lastly, there are patent claims on a drug's second medical uses, polymorphs, and analogues.

According to the Commission on Property Rights Innovation and Public Health Patents (2006), set up by the World Health Organization, patents play a number of roles in the innovation process. First is the incentive function. Without the guaranteed absence of rents, inventors would not expend the necessary efforts and resources to make new discoveries, and society would achieve less than optimal rates of innovation. A second function is transactional. Patents contribute to the creation of new markets in technological goods and inter-firm R&D collaboration. Third, patents perform a signaling function. A patent, for example, informs potential venture capital funds which firms look promising while indicating to other firms not to replicate potentially laborious scientific and R&D studies. Lastly, patents play a disclosure function. By providing the details of their invention to the public, inventors are given legal protection. A skilled person in the art should be able to understand the details and schematics in the patent filling.

The role of patents in the economy and society touches upon various normative frameworks that are described in more detail latter in this chapter. Needless to say, the general assumption is that patents encourage more innovation in society. The timeframes regarding different forms of intellectual property protection reflect this concern. While copyrights can last for at least 50 years after the death of an author, patents last for a much shorter time. Longer patent durations would dissuade others from developing more downstream innovations as well as inhibit optimal levels of diffusion.

Patents operate as negative rights. The state provides patent owners with legal protections to prevent others from commercializing their inventions. In the US, disagreements over patent approvals, infringements, and claims are decided in the courts, whereas the ultimate usefulness of a patented invention is determined by market demand. Where economic demand for a patented product remains strong, patents allow companies to control markets. Typically, those firms with a technological advantage push for stronger forms of intellectual property (IP) protection in order to secure a monopolistic position, especially if other forms of protecting proprietary knowledge, i.e. trade secrets, are not available. In comparative terms, the degree of patent protection historically has been associated with a country's level of development. Those countries that dominate the leading sectors of the world economy seek out stronger forms of IP protection, while other countries engaging in catch-up adopt weaker forms of protection. In the early 1900s, for example, the US pharmaceutical industry, trailing foreign competitors in technological progress, argued that German drug firms enjoyed excessively strong patent protection and were not completely disclosing information on their patent applications (Dutfield 2003).

Increases in international trade often accompany new demands for patent rights across countries with distinct economic, technological, and innovative capabilities. The last half of the 1800s witnessed a rise in foreign trade and concerns that patents would not be respected in other countries. Due to the lobbies representing commercial interests, countries established new international agreements. The 1883 Paris Convention for the Protection of Industrial Property represents one of the first international agreements addressing patents. The agreement enshrined the concept of national treatment: a foreigner applying for a patent in any member state would be accorded the same treatment as if they were a national making the same application. Member states, however, could still determine the level of patent protection that best fit their development needs—mainly a question of whether they were technological leaders or followers.

Economic nationalism, cartel formations, and two World Wars halted new international efforts related to patents until the 1970s when commercial interests began to lobby again for substantive changes. The General Agreement on Tariffs and Trade (GATT) that governed international commerce at the start of the post-War era, for example, did not include provisions regarding intellectual property. But in the final decades of the 20th century, Correa (2000) argues that a number of factors converged to explain the renewed push for patent power at the international level, especially by the US. First, US firms increasingly faced international competition in the high-tech field at the same time that many private companies started to invest more resources into research and development, especially in science-intensive areas. Second, reaping the results of large R&D expenditures in new fields such as computer software, biotechnology, and semi-conductors required the extension of intellectual property rights to these leading sectors. Meanwhile, US court cases and legislation provided domestic intellectual property protection for these fields. Third, the elimination of trade barriers to the developing world improved the bargaining power of TNCs, which no longer had to transfer technology in exchange for market access. Fourth, US economic and political leaders characterized the erosion of US manufacturing supremacy as caused by unfair competition from Japan and newly industrializing countries that had weak intellectual property protections and that had engaged

42 *Elements of Global Pharmaceutical Power*

in "piracy" and the "counterfeiting" of US innovations. In sum, growing concerns about US technological competitiveness, coupled with a growing trade deficit, led US policymakers to adapt a more assertive role towards intellectual property rights internationally.

Since the 1970s, the US initiated a number of unilateral efforts to protect the intellectual property interests of its transnational corporations. In 1974, lawmakers amended Section 337 of the Tariff and Trade Act of 1930 allowing the International Trade Commission the power to act on requests from domestic right holders by seizing goods being imported into the US. To address concerns about IP infringements in foreign countries, the US Congress included in Section 301 of Trade Act of 1984 provisions that granted the United States Trade Representative (USTR) the power to investigate the intellectual property regimes in foreign countries and, where necessary, initiate trade sanctions. Specifically under Section 301, the USTR could withhold preferential access to the US market for developing countries' exports under the Generalized System of Preferences.

Section 1303 of the Omnibus Trade and Competitiveness Act of 1998 strengthened the USTR's power to pressure other countries on their IP enforcement. According to the legislation, mandatory actions must be taken by the USTR according to a non-compliant country's classification. A "Priority Foreign Country" indication means that a country's policies or practices have the most adverse impact on US products; a "Priority Watch List" designation implies that a country has some but not all of the criteria for a "Priority Foreign Country"; and a "Watch List" classification means that a country has some problematic IP-related issues (Sell 2003). "The amended Section 301 was a mandate to the USTR to defend US intellectual property rights in the global economy," claims Matthews (2002: 15).

Different classifications resulted in different levels of responses from the US government. Section 301 provided unprecedented power to US business interests through their ability to pressure other countries on their IP regimes. The USTR, due to limited staff and resources, largely relies on US firms' information, figures, and surveillance. Every year, when the agency calls for submissions from trade associations, this "business-government partnership is formalized" (Matthews 2002: 26). And every year, industry groups like PhRMA provide their assessments of other country's efforts to protect the interests of its members. Brazil was one of the first countries to experience the US's new approach. In 1988, acting on complaints by PhRMA about inadequate domestic patent protection on pharmaceuticals, the US imposed tariffs of 100% on $39 million of Brazilian products coming into the US.

US multilateral initiatives to raise the level of IP protections complimented bilateral pressures. Including IP into trade talks that led to the creation of the World Trade Organization (WTO) represents one of the clearest examples of corporate interests writing the rules of global government. Indeed, Sell (2003: 96) details how "twelve corporations made public law for the world." Lobbying efforts began through the US President's

Advisory Committee on Trade Policy and Negotiations (ACTPN), which, since the 1974 Trade Act, institutionalized business input into trade negotiations. ACTPN set up the Task Force on Intellectual Property whose members included Ed Pratt, CEO of Pfizer, and Abraham Cohen, president of Merck's international division, along with executives from the software and entertainment industries. Focusing on the single issue of intellectual property allowed top US executives to develop a coherent and effective plan for US negotiators (Matthews 2002; Sell 2003). But not all credit goes to US corporate interests. While the US government played an important role in applying bilateral pressure on behalf of US corporations, Matthews (2002) argues that equally important were contributions from the corporate sectors in Europe and Japan. "In practice the interests and concerns of multinational companies, which by their nature transcend national boundaries, also ensured that global business had a vested interest in achieving a TRIPS agreement regardless of the country in which their head office was located," he writes (Matthews 2002:27).

Developing countries resisted efforts by developed countries to tie intellectual property to trade agreements. Brazil and India, concerned about their ability to achieve development objectives, preferred to keep the topic at the World Intellectual Property Organization (WIPO), a United Nations' agency created in 1967 that, until the creation of the WTO, held primary authority for the administration of intellectual property agreements. During the Uruguay Round of trade talks leading up to the creation of the WTO, policymakers from developed countries and their corporate advisors considered the WIPO too weak a forum to achieve the level of protection they desired. The WTO, on the contrary, would include a powerful enforcement mechanism to ensure member states complied with treaty obligations.

Apart from a few advanced developing countries such as Brazil and India, most other trade delegations from the Global South lacked the skills to successfully negotiate the technical intricacies of IP, especially compared to the input wealthy country negotiators received from corporate lobbyists. In fact, only ten developing countries sent IP experts to the TRIPS negotiations. Importantly, the views of the generic drug industry and civil society groups were marginalized during the initial Uruguay round of negotiations, and important UN-based organizations such as the World Health Organization (WHO) or the United Nations Conference on Trade and Development (UNCTAD) were sidelined. Lastly, US bilateral trade pressure through the Special 301 forced recalcitrant developing countries to concede to the inclusion of new IP rules in the WTO (see Matthews 2002).

The World Trade Organization and Agreement on Trade-Related Aspects of Intellectual Property (TRIPS)

With the creation of the World Trade Organization (WTO) in 1995, TRIPS extended the pharmaceutical industry's *patent power* to the rest of the world

44 Elements of Global Pharmaceutical Power

by establishing an overarching international legal code governing patents, copyrights, and trademarks. The Agreement goes beyond previous international treaties, including the Paris Convention for the Protection Intellectual Property signed in 1883, and incorporates most of the demands of executives from the transnational drug industry based in the US, Europe, and Japan. Details of the agreement reveal a new form of structural power that reduces the policy space available to developing countries to pursue development strategies available up to that time.

TRIPS establishes a minimum baseline of intellectual property protection that all WTO members must include in their national legislation. The agreement stipulates that a patent holder is guaranteed exclusive rights for the exploitation of product, process, and use over a specified period of time. Article 27.1 specifies that "patents shall be available for any inventions, whether products or processes, in all fields of technology, provided they are new, involve an inventive step and are capable of industrial application." Minimum obligations include a patent period of 20 years for pharmaceuticals—the timeframe in the US—and national treatment, that is, no discrimination between the patent rights of foreigners and nationals. Members, however, may exclude from patentability diagnostic, therapeutic, and biological processes for the production of plants and animals.

The accord was cast as mutually benefiting to both producers and consumers of intellectual property. Article 7 states the objective of TRIPS: "The protection and enforcement of intellectual property rights should contribute to the promotion of technological innovation and to the transfer and dissemination of technology, to the mutual advantage of producers and users of technological knowledge and in a manner conducive to social and economic welfare, and to a balance of rights and obligations." Consequently, TRIPS provides a number of flexibilities, exceptions, and humanitarian safeguards for members when formulating national legislation. In terms of transition periods, high-income countries had until 1996 to change their laws; middle-income countries, 2005; and least developed, 2016. With more time to adjust their patent legislation in accordance to TRIPS, developing countries with a pharmaceutical base would have more time to develop their generic pharmaceutical industry and could legally reverse engineer drugs patented elsewhere. India and China waited until 2005 to change their intellectual property laws, while Brazil anticipated the deadline by nine years by becoming TRIPS compliant in 1997. Once a country adopts its national legislation to become TRIPS compliant, it cannot go back on its commitments. IP laws can be tweaked to include TRIPS flexibilities.

The most important flexibilities affecting medicines are humanitarian safeguards. Article 8 states that countries may adopt "measures necessary to protect public health and nutrition, and to promote the public interest in sectors of vital importance to their socio-economic and technological development" as well as take additional action "to prevent the abuse of intellectual property rights by right holders." An important legal instrument for

Elements of Global Pharmaceutical Power   45

correcting abuses by patent holders is the compulsory license (CL), which allows for the exploitation of a patent by third parties without the consent of the patent holder. TRIPS allows for the use of a CL in three main instances: national emergency, cases of anti-trust, and for public, non-commercial use. Before issuing a CL, a government must first attempt to reach a negotiated settlement with the patent holder, who, in the case of the CL, still has the right to receive royalties. Only in cases of national emergency and public, non-commercial use can governments dispense with prior negotiations.

Due to the increasing number of disputes between countries and pharmaceutical companies, several WTO members from the developing world successfully lobbied for stronger legal protection to use humanitarian safeguards outlined in TRIPS. Along these lines, the *Doha Declaration* of 2001 reaffirmed the rights of WTO member states to circumvent patents in order to uphold public health obligations. Instead of placing decision-making power in an international body like the WTO, the *Declaration* upholds the sovereignty of member nations to determine the criteria to issue CLs ('t Hoen 2009). The resolution represented a major defeat for the transnational drug industry, which sought to restrict the use of CLs.

Following the *Doha Declaration*, there has been increased use of CLs by developing countries as a means to lower the cost of medicines, especially in the case of HIV medicines. Table 2.2 lists those countries that have resorted

Table 2.2   Recent Uses of Compulsory Licenses for Antiretrovirals, 2003–2012

Year	Country	Royalty Rate	Antiretrovirals
2003	Malaysia	4%	didanosine; zidovudine; zidovudine/lamivudine
2003	Zimbabwe	NA	HIV-related medicines
2004	Mozambique	2%	lamivudine/stavudine/nevirapine
2004	Zambia	2.50%	lamivudine/stavudine/nevirapine
2004	Indonesia	0.55%	lamivudine; nevirapine
2005	Ghana	NA	HIV-related medicines
2006	Thailand	0.50%	efavirenz
2007	Thailand	0.50%	lopinavir/ritonavir
2007	Indonesia	0.50%	efavirenz
2007	Brazil	1.50%	efavirenz
2010	Ecuador	0.42% of US price	ritanovir
2012	Indonesia	0.50%	abacavir; didanosine; efavirenz; lopinavir/ritonavir; tenofovir; tenofovir/emitricitabine; tenofovir/emitricitabine/efavirenz
2012	Ecuador	5% of US price	abacavir/lamivudine

Source: WHO (2014)

46 *Elements of Global Pharmaceutical Power*

to this humanitarian safeguard and the specific antiretroviral medicine for which a CL was issued. It is important to note that a compulsory license does not abolish a patent. It just removes a company's market exclusivity to sell the drug based on a patent. The most common CL is for government, non-commercial use, so a patent remains in place for private market sales.

What is surprising is not the number of countries that have resorted to the use of CLs; instead, it is the limited use of this legal measure to reduce prices given the extent of the AIDS epidemic and the impact of high-priced medicines.

The *Doha Declaration* left open a crucial issue that has only been partially resolved. What will countries do if they decide to use CLs for public health reasons but do not have the manufacturing capabilities to produce those medicines locally? Even if a country issued a CL for a humanitarian reason, it would have to import medicines from another country. But the drug-producing country would not be able to export it without also issuing a CL. Paragraph 6 of the *Declaration* instructed the TRIPS council to resolve the issue. After years of discussion, WTO members agreed to allow drug-making countries to export pharmaceuticals to countries with no or insufficient manufacturing capabilities. To date, Rwanda is the only country that has taken advantage of the Paragraph 6 exception, leading critics to charge that the requirements are too onerous.

While TRIPS establishes a minimum baseline of patent protection of 20 years, member states still retain a degree of maneuverability in terms of compliance and criteria used for adjudicating patentability. Besides the use of CLs, member states can also incorporate provisions that allow for parallel importation.[10] Countries also determine which government organizations grant patents and whether other public or private organizations may participate in the analysis of patent applications. Member states also have some leeway in determining the scope of patentability. For example, patent examiners may take a narrow versus broad definition of what constitutes novelty, inventiveness, and industrial application for approving or rejecting patent applications. Lastly, patent offices may take into account public health concerns when issuing patents on medicines and diagnostic equipment. Since drug companies often engage in patent strategies involving numerous claims over different aspects of a drug, they can extend the effective timeframe in which they enjoy market exclusivity. The process, known as "ever-greening," constrains generic competition that would reduce the prices of medicines. A public health approach towards patenting attempts to reduce awarding patents based on frivolous claims, minor adaptations, and secondary uses of existing treatments.[11]

National IP laws sometime go beyond TRIPS minimum requirement. Indeed, many countries have embraced numerous TRIPS-plus measures; that is, they fail to incorporate all the proscribed safeguards, either due to domestic political considerations or as a result of bilateral or regional trade agreements that demand more restrictive intellectual property laws (Smith, Correa, and Oh 2009). One TRIPS-plus measure relates to the use of CLs—trade agreements may limit the use of this humanitarian safeguard to cases of emergency and urgency, and not as an anti-trust measure or for government, non-commercial uses.[12] Another TRIPS-plus requirement is patent linkage. This rule restricts generic companies from registering their product until patent(s) on a drug expires. Additionally, various forms of data exclusivity provisions restrict generic companies from using the clinical test data that originator companies submit to regulatory officials for approving a new medicine. Besides increasing costs of replicating clinical tests to ensure safety and efficacy, the provision raises bioethical concerns about unnecessary experimentation on human subjects. TRIPS-plus measures, while increasingly commonplace in trade agreements, restrict drug generic competition that could reduce prices and limits policy space available to governments to achieve development or public health objectives.

TRIPS Implementation and Consequences

TRIPS represents a qualitative change in the governance in all member countries of the WTO regardless of their level of development or regional economic activity. What has been the impact of TRIPS on developing countries and what accounts for the diverse country experiences in implementing the accord? In one view, the agreement institutionalizes power differentials between wealthy and poor countries, whereby the former with developed intellectual property infrastructures and cultures has a clear advantage over the latter (Carolan 2009). Before TRIPS, countries decided the level of intellectual property protection they deemed compatible with their level of development. Most countries, even while respecting patents in other industries, did not provide patents for pharmaceuticals since they were considered a strategic input for the health system. In effect, the accord reduces the policy space available for developing country governments so that they cannot replicate the successes of developed countries (Chang 2002; Wade 2003). Other scholars remain sanguine about the potential that intellectual property has on growth, trade, and market development which, presumably, would translate into overall welfare gains (Maskus 2008).

Patents have mixed impact on national pharmaceutical sectors. One large, cross-country study concluded that there is no association between pharmaceutical patent protection and domestic innovation or foreign direct investment, and positive spillover effects only occur in countries with high levels of education, development, and economic freedom (Quian 2009). However, a study by Odagiri (2010: 26), focusing on intellectual property regimes in developing countries, concludes that intellectual property does not affect catch-up strategies of late developers since the effects are too varied and

48   *Elements of Global Pharmaceutical Power*

difficult to assess across the various dimensions of economic development. The one exception is in pharmaceuticals in which patents clearly matter.

In some cases, domestic pharmaceutical firms from developing countries are interested in patent protection due to their desire to enter the US market, irrespective of TRIPS (Chaudhuri 2009; Shadlen 2009). Nonetheless, reviews of patent applications and approvals before and after TRIPS show that foreign firms tend to outstrip domestic patent applicants up to a factor of five (Laforgia, Montobbio, and Orsenigo 2009). Indeed, the six most developed countries of the world accounted for up to 84% of all patent applications (Shadlen 2011). Consequently, it is not difficult to see how *patent power* is one of the many strategies originator companies employ to maintain market share and high rents. Incumbent pharmaceutical corporations from wealthy, industrialized companies have pushed a global patent agenda in order to arrest the rise of cheap, generic producers from the developing world that are able to exploit their *market power* based on less expensive production costs and quick reverse engineering of new medicines on the market.

One important factor affecting the consequences of TRIPS involves domestic implementation of the accord. There has been a significant degree of variation across countries regarding the timing and extensiveness of the reforms they carried out in their domestic IP laws. Oddly, many sub-Saharan African countries that would have few foreseeable benefits from awarding patents revised their patent laws in accordance with TRIPS several years in advance of the 2015 deadline. Deere (2009) highlights international pressures on developing countries in the form of direct trade, diplomatic, and industry pressures but also emphasizes the role of competing knowledge communities, framing and counter-framing, and ideology. Susceptibility to these external pressures varies according to government capacity and degree of coordination across state agencies, both domestically between different ministries and internationally with foreign diplomats and representatives. Accordingly, global experts appear to play an important role in disseminating pro-business views towards patents (Deere 2009).

Developing countries are also experimenting with humanitarian safeguards to shore up their health commitments (see Shadlen, Guennif, and Chavez 2011). One of the more powerful instruments at their disposable, the use of compulsory licenses to protect the public interest, has been rare due to the politics and powerful forces involved. Nonetheless, despite new global norms justifying their use (Chorev 2012), recourse to this policy will be limited if there are no supplies of cheap, generic alternatives. After India and China adjusted their legislation in 2005 to make them TRIPS-compliant, experts forecast that firms from China and India will continue to supply cheap, finished drugs and bulk raw materials, but newer medicines will no longer be available at inexpensive prices, or perhaps at all (Grace 2004). The case of Brazil thus illustrates the possibilities for governments to expand policy space despite the new structural constraints imposed by TRIPS.

NORMATIVE FRAMEWORKS CONCERNING INTELLECTUAL PROPERTY RIGHTS AND MEDICINES

So far, I have argued that large incumbent transnational drug companies, in political alliance with trade ministers from developed countries, pushed for the TRIPS accord in order to maintain control over lucrative segments of the pharmaceutical industry. A new, international property regime governing "creations of the mind" also includes discursive strategies to justify the creation and maintenance of the new institutional framework. Consequently, transnational drug companies and their allies employ normative frameworks to justify why such strong intellectual property projects are good, just, and right for society. They must also contest counter-frames from those opposed to the strong patent regimes. These various normative frameworks can be categorized along the natural rights, utilitarian, human rights, and critical perspectives.

Natural Rights Perspective

In the natural rights perspective, intellectual property represents a natural extension of inalienable right to property. The roots of modern notions concerning property rights date back to John Locke's philosophy and political theory positing natural rights as absolute and transcendent over governmental authority. Compared to previous notions of private property rooted in religious ideas of Earth as God's domain for mankind to nurture, Locke argues in the fundamental sovereignty of the individual. Individuals retain ownership over themselves and their labor. As they invest their labor in the land, individuals establish a natural claim to what they produce. Property rights thus represent a natural right over the fruit of one's labor. Casting property rights along these essentialist lines, Locke argues that the purpose of government is to protect individual's property from encroachment by others.

While Locke bases his notion of labor's fruit in ideas about the natural world such as land and its output, contemporary scholars extend the principle to "creations of the mind." Just as individuals expend their sovereign labor to create tangible products and thus lay rightful claim to its output, they also invest considerable time in the production of intangible, knowledge-based goods and therefore may claim ownership over their production and distribution. Resnik (2003: 322) argues that Locke's "libertarian perspective" seems to apply best to "original works and inventions where people have invested time and effort in their products, such as books, paintings, airplanes, and new drugs." Not surprisingly, the pharmaceutical industry and its allies invoke Lockean arguments when justifying a strong patent regime and frame unauthorized copying of their formulas as forms of "piracy" and "theft."

Purveyors of the natural rights view of intellectual property often conflate the individualistic notions of property with a collectivistic approach

50 Elements of Global Pharmaceutical Power

towards property represented by nation-states. For example, countries that use compulsory licenses "amount to 'constructive takings' of exclusive US private property, and thus, violate US companies' constitutional rights. The President and the Congress have sworn to protect these rights no matter where such property is located," argues Kogan (2006). Furthermore, countries' illegal use of US intellectual property affects the US's international competitiveness, technological leadership, and economic growth, as well as the US's advantages in international trade and innovation, thus the country's living standards (Kogan 2006). Attacks on the fundamental and inalienable right of private intellectual property thus represent encroachments on nation-states and its citizens.

The Lockean framework of natural property rights couples with the pharmaceutical companies' emphasis on the large, up-front expenditures necessary to bring a product to market. The cost to produce and bring a new drug to market remains highly contested. Estimates at the high end, such as those produced by DiMasi and his colleagues at the industry-financed Tufts Center for Drug Development, concluded that it costs US$802 million dollars to research, develop, and bring to market a new chemical entity (DiMasi, Hansen, and Grabowski 2005). The figure includes attrition rates and cost of capital. Other estimates claim that the costs of new drug development reach as high as US$1.7 billion (Gilbert, Henske, and Singh 2007).

High estimates concerning R&D costs have not escaped scrutiny. Researchers at the public interest group Public Citizen (2003) calculate R&D costs of US$108 million per new drug. Adjusting for tax deductions on R&D expenses, they calculate the actual cost per new drug comes to US$71 million. Cost studies of specific innovator drugs estimate prices at US$115 million to US$240 million for new anti-tuberculosis drugs (Goozner 2004) and US$208 million to US$878 million for new rotavirus vaccines (Light, Andrus, and Warburton 2009). The debate concerning the costs of drug discovery and development is complex and goes beyond the scope of this study.[13] Needless to say, a strong intellectual property regime is particularly important for the pharmaceutical and chemical industries, since their products may be easily copied. The cost of reverse engineering a product is far less expensive than the time-consuming process of discovery, research, and development of new therapeutic agents. Compared to the estimated US$108 million to US$2 billion cost to develop a new drug, Brazilian informants said that the estimated costs for generic drug producers to reverse engineer a medicine and bring it to market hover around US$2.5 million (R$5 million).

The natural rights perspective is not the sole province of corporate defenders of intellectual property. Accusations of "piracy" and "theft" are also applied to situations when outsiders appropriate knowledge from traditional communities. Biopiracy refers to the commercial use of traditional knowledge without providing compensation, acknowledgement, or informed consent to those that hold or practice this knowledge. For example, the serpent tree in India has been used to treat mental illness and now is the active ingredient in reserpine used to treat epilepsy and high-blood pressure

(Robinson 2010). In these cases, the Lockean justification of labor's fruit applies to an entire community. Applying the piracy frame is both a rhetorical tool to name and shame appropriators of traditional knowledge and also as a legal device to sue for redress in the court system. One challenge facing the piracy frame when referring to theft of intellectual property of traditional communities revolves around different cultural notions of what constitutes ownership of knowledge (Nagan et al. 2010). Contrasting ideas about ownership and property suggest that the Lockean argument about intellectual property is not as natural or transcendent as many from the natural rights perspective purport.

Utilitarian Arguments

Utilitarian perspectives influence most economistic views on intellectual property, which tend to eschew arguments about the transcendental nature of property rights. Rather, providing rules of ownership are embedded in incentive mechanisms. For economists, intellectual property goods are both non-rival and intangible, which distinguishes their market characteristics compared to other goods and services. Creations of the mind are qualitatively different from transforming materials into something else as in the natural rights account. In classical economic thinking, property rights are necessary to address the problem of scarcity that results from the fact that physical goods rival one another; that is, my acquisition of an automobile prevents you from acquiring it.

In the neoclassical universe of unlimited wants and limited goods (also known as scarcity), market mechanisms are used for allocating goods based on what people are willing to spend on a product compared to the alternative. Prices operate as signals for gauging consumer preferences and indicating profitable ventures to producers. The same logic does not apply to intangible goods for which the costs of replication are non-existent or marginal. Intellectual property goods, like music, can be consumed by more than one individual at the same time, resulting in no zero-sum loss. For example, two listeners of recorded music can hear the same song at the same time in different places without one waiting for the other to complete their consumption. In this sense, intellectual property goods are non-rival.

The alleged problem concerning non-rivalrous goods, according to the utilitarian perspective, is the lack of incentive mechanisms for the creation of the intangible knowledge- and information-based goods. To resolve this market failure of optimal rates of innovation, intellectual property law creates a temporary monopoly, or artificial scarcity. According to May and Sell (2006: 19), "One of the central functions of the institution of the property in knowledge is to construct scarcity where none necessarily exists. . . . In a capitalist economy the construction of rivalrousness is the central role of intellectual property." Intellectual property rights are legal creations, not based on absolutist notions of property employed by the natural rights frame, but predicated on a functionalist logic, i.e. a means to an end—allegedly more

52   Elements of Global Pharmaceutical Power

innovation. The primary function of a patent is to stimulate the production of new products, processes, and technologies. The legal framework assumes that people and firms will not innovate unless granted additional material incentives through monopoly pricing. Accordingly, stronger patents translate into more incentives that produce more innovation.

But the problem is that monopolies, while addressing one market failure due to underinvestment in innovative activities, create others. Monopolies distort equilibrium prices necessary for achieving socially optimum outcomes. Indeed, none other than the great proponent of free markets and strong property rights Friedrich von Hayek (1963: 114) wrote, "In the field of industrial patents in particular, we shall have seriously to examine whether the award of a monopoly privilege is really the most appropriate and effective form of reward for the kind of risk bearing which investment in scientific research involves." Since patent holders can charge higher than average prices, fewer consumers are able to obtain the product.

Besides inducing market scarcity for knowledge- and information-based goods, utilitarian notions also undergird the principles of temporality and disclosure. Patents involve specific time restrictions in order to allow developers to use the patented product and process. Extending the patent period for too long or providing excessive patenting, critics argue (see Heller 2008), inhibit the innovative process since those who would like to add on to a previous invention confront legal restrictions or must pay exorbitant fees for licensing the patented technology. After the patent period expires, the patented knowledge enters the public domain where anyone can access the invention, and produce more add-on innovation. With respect to disclosure, utilitarian views assume that inventors would not disclose their inventions unless granted legal based protections for controlling its production and distribution. In exchange for a temporary monopoly, the inventor agrees, in theory, to disclose all the specifics about it. Lastly, disclosure provides signals to other inventors not to replicate the same efforts in discovering a new product or process. Resources for research and development can thus flow into other productive areas.

The utilitarian frame undergirds the claim that a strong intellectual property system helps developing countries advance economically (Maskus 2008; US National Law Center for Inter-American Free Trade 2008). One version argues that Europe, the United States, and Japan developed economically vis-à-vis the rest of the world because they provided stronger patent systems than in other countries which had weaker laws and enforcement mechanisms. In today's contemporary world, intellectual property advocates claim that strong intellectual property laws encourage development by attracting foreign direct investment, encouraging technological transfer and learning, promoting domestic entrepreneurship and inventive activity, and stimulating overall economic growth. In this "optimistic view," intellectual property rights can "play an important and positive role in economic advancement with the role becoming larger as economies grow richer," even for the least developed countries (Maskus 2008: 170). Such a frame often resonates with policy experts, politicians, and policymakers in both developed and developing countries. Indeed, this is the main argument of US trade officials when negotiating new treaties and agreements.

Utilitarian logic plays an important role for the research-based pharmaceutical industry. Pisano (2006) argues that the "monetization of intellectual property," i.e. the trading, valuing, and appropriation of know-how as an asset, is an essential mechanism for addressing uncertainty as well as managing and rewarding risk for a science-based industry such as pharmaceuticals. Allowing firms holding patents to charge prices hundreds of times the cost of production, patents permit industry to secure monopoly rents. Since the costs of developing new medicines remain high (although the exact cost is debatable), patents are viewed as a necessary economic incentive for attracting investment and dissuading competitors from simply copying new innovations. "Biopharmaceutical intellectual property (IP) protections, such as patents and data protection, provide the incentives that spur research and development. They help ensure that the innovative biopharmaceutical companies that have invested in life-saving medicines have an opportunity to justify their investments," claims PhRMA (n.d.) on their website.

Critics of patents from the utilitarian perspective, such as economists Boldrin and Levine (2012: 20), contend that the legal instrument involves more problems than social benefits because they encourage "failing monopolists to inhibit competition by blocking innovation." Since patents provide for the chance to achieve windfall profits, pharmaceutical firms prefer investing in a few blockbuster drugs that can achieve high sales volumes. A study of the expansion of patent protection of quinolones used to treat bacterial infections estimated the gains to a foreign firm at US$53 million per year compared to the US$713 million in annual welfare losses to the Indian economy, mainly Indian consumers (Chaudhuri, Goldberg, and Jia 2006). Besides encouraging firms to maximize the benefits of market exclusivity of new drugs, critics contend that the patent system encourages the pharmaceutical industry to extend the life of their monopolies through practices that provide few social benefits. Patent holders make minor modifications on their existing medicines, tweaking formulas, in order to obtain an additional patent. This process, known as ever-greening, combined with other patent strategies employed to block a competitor from producing a similar product (i.e. "patent thickets"), has led to a veritable explosion of patents (Correa 2000).

Additional patents for the antiretroviral ritonavir provide a clear example of ever-greening. Figure 2.2 illustrates a patent map, developed by the World Intellectual Property Organization (WIPO), showing all the patents and patent applications gathered from patent databases across the world. The map is organized around 805 patent families, with each patent family representing a collection of interrelated individual patents. These families are linked to downstream innovations to the compound, including variants and derivatives, polymorphs, combinations with other drugs, production processes, and methods of use. Each branch in the map represents a new and additional downstream innovation. According to the authors of the

54 *Elements of Global Pharmaceutical Power*

Figure 2.2 Patent Map for Ritonavir

study, "Innovation tracks illustrate important protection related to Ritonavir as subsequent generations continue to narrow the scope of protection in a wide area of technologies while still maintaining protection from the first Ritonavir Patent" (WIPO 2011: 4). The first filings of each patent family were done in the United States, and Abbott Pharmaceuticals was the most common filer. Figure 2.2 reveals the complexity related to different patent strategies and the lengths companies go in order to extend patent monopolies and fend off generic competition.

Elements of Global Pharmaceutical Power   55

One of the biggest public health problems with the current patent-based system of pharmaceuticals is the failure to address the health needs of the poor. The WHO's Commission on Intellectual Property Rights Innovation and Public Health (2006: 32) states, "Where the market has very limited purchasing power, as is the case for diseases affecting millions of poor people in developing countries, patents are not a relevant factor or effective in stimulating R&D and bringing new products to market." Patents operate as incentive mechanisms so that companies can develop products for wealthy consumers, while diseases affecting the global poor receive less attention. The end result is that only 10% of total R&D expenditures are invested in diseases affecting some 90% of the world's population, located mainly in developing countries (Global Forum on Health Research 2004). This "10/90 gap" in investments into the disease burdens that affect much of the developing world has spurned global debate and several initiatives to address the health needs of the global poor in relation to neglected tropical diseases, malaria, and tuberculosis, among others.

Human Rights Claims

International human rights norms, practices, and institutions have grown steadily since the end of World War II. The core document concerning human rights perspectives is the *Universal Declaration on Human Rights*. Human rights claims in the *Declaration* include both rights to health and rights to intellectual property. Article 25 states that "Everyone has the right to a standard of living adequate for health and wellbeing, including food, clothing, housing, medical care and necessary social services." Soon thereafter, Article 27 outlines the rights to intellectual property: "Everyone has the right to the protection of the moral and material interests resulting from any scientific, literary or artistic production of which he is the author."

Subsequent international human rights accords reproduce these two cultural ideals, which can lead to confusing mandates and contradictory obligations for states. For example, Article 12 in the *International Covenant on Economic, Social and Cultural Rights* (United Nations 1966) declares that "States Parties to the present Covenant recognize the right of everyone to the enjoyment of the highest attainable standard of physical and mental health," which is followed by Article 15 (c) which recognizes the right of everyone "to benefit from the protection of the moral and material interests resulting from any scientific, literary or artistic production of which he is the author." These apparently separate claims come into sharp contradiction when high-priced, patented medicines have life or death consequences. Only at the turn of the 21st century did the Committee on Economic, Social and Cultural Rights (CESCR) specify a hierarchy of rights: "The Committee wishes to emphasize that any intellectual property regime that makes it more difficult for a State party to comply with its core obligations in relation to health, food, education, especially, or any other right set out in the

56 Elements of Global Pharmaceutical Power

Covenant, is inconsistent with the legally binding obligations of the State party," states CESCR (2001: 5).

The contradictory orientation of rights-based norms stems from their origin in Lockean natural philosophy and the evolution of citizenship rights embedded in welfare states during the 1900s. Regarded as inherently inalienable and inviolable for all human beings, contemporary rights claims retain the essentialist version of human nature propounded by John Locke. Initially, these were negative rights, protections against state encroachments on the sovereign individual and her beliefs, property, and expression. Only later with the construction of the welfare states did positive rights oblige states to ensure economic welfare, security, and social heritage, according to the prevailing standards of society. The right to health, outlined in international accords and embedded in state Constitutions, falls within the category of positive rights that have diffused throughout the world. Nowadays, roughly two-thirds of countries have Constitutional guarantees to the right to health (Kinney and Clark 2004).

At the international level, debates concerning the right to health revolve around what falls within its scope and who is responsible for upholding it. With regard to scope, the CESCR's (2000) general comment No. 14 links access to medicines to various elements of the right to health. But the first resolution that specifically outlines access to essential medicines as a right to health is *Access to Medication in the Context of Pandemics Such as HIV/AIDS*, passed by the United Nations Commission on Human Rights in April 2001 (United Nations High Commissioner on Human Rights 2001). Additional motions passed at the World Health Organization, United Nations' General Assembly Special Session, and United Nations Sub-commission on Human Rights later that year. The UN Special Rapporteur on Human Rights stated that international trade agreements with IP provisions "have had an adverse impact on prices and availability of medicines, making it difficult for countries to comply with their obligations to respect, protect, and fulfill the right to health" (Grover 2009: 28). While not addressing whether intellectual property rights are also human rights, this statement calls on countries to incorporate all the flexibilities outlined in TRIPS to ensure that obligations to the right to health can be upheld.

As developed in international treaties and resolutions, the right to health frame provides powerful justification for trumping intellectual property. But the right to health approach provides less direction in how the right should be implemented. From a pro-business perspective, Goodman (2005) argues that legal mandates to health individualize access, represent claims on other people's resources, and amount to increasing government control over health care. "Access to health care cannot be a human right, since there is no shared understanding of what constitutes good health care," he concludes (Goodman 2005: 655). Accordingly, the right to health sidesteps the political process by imposing claims on the state through the court system and disrupts public health objectives. Goodman raises important issues regarding new forms of health stratification that may result from individuals using the court system; however, his view does not take into consideration how the right to health also represents a collective right. Important principles in the human rights approach include non-discrimination and progressive realization, which oblige states to ensure equal access to baseline standards of care across their entire population. Limited resources do not excuse states from their responsibilities, only that they must universalize health goods from the bottom-up as more resources become available.

Freeman (2009) also recognizes that the right to health provides little guidance for priority setting. Instead of questioning the appropriateness of legal frameworks, he emphasizes its inherent limitations. The right to health involves not only access to health care but also the underlying social determinants of health, including employment, education, poverty, water, sanitation, among others. According to Freeman, however, the right to health does not address deeper socio-structural conditions. For example, life expectancy and other health indicators are strongly correlated with socio-economic status, which is bound up in the economic system. Economic inequalities translate into health inequalities. Consequently, the right to health is not the same as health justice—the equitable distribution of health within and across countries: "Equal rights do not produce equal outcomes, and the legalization of rights does not necessarily 'empower' the poor," he says (Freeman 2009: 52). While human rights may not address the underlying power differentials between groups in society, alleging that legal rights do not lead to increased mobilization may also represent misplaced causality; for the converse may be true—the institutionalizing of rights may result from social movement pressures.

The work of Gideon Sjoberg on human rights bridges debates about the appropriateness and limitations of the right to health. According to him and his colleagues, human rights are social claims upon social power arrangements (Sjoberg, Gill, and Williams 2001). Along these lines, the most significant human rights abuses stem from large-scale organizations, the most powerful actors in society. Human rights thus represent claims made upon powerful organizations to "respect, protect, and fulfill." Therefore, the normative framework of human rights shapes the relationships between states and their citizens concerning both property rights and welfare. But governments are not the only powerful, large-scale organizations in society; so too are corporate actors. Accordingly, powerful business entities also become subject to social claims regarding human rights objectives (Sjoberg 2009). In fact, the UN Special Rapporteur issued guidelines for drug companies regarding transparency, pricing, ethical marketing, lobbying for more protection in intellectual property laws, and patenting strategies (Hunt 2008).

The human rights framework might not address deeper socio-structural causes of health injustice, but as a master frame offers an umbrella for various constituencies, including health advocates, scientists, and activist bureaucrats, to make social claims against both governments and corporations.

58 *Elements of Global Pharmaceutical Power*

The case of Brazil, explained throughout this book, demonstrates how the naming and shaming of more powerful organizations using a human rights frame contributed to the country's pharmaceutical autonomy.

Critical Views

Critical perspectives on intellectual property rights and their relationship to medicines fall into two lines of inquiry—a Marxian critique of the capitalist system and a cultural account concerning medicalization. The Marxian-inspired frame highlights the social dimension of labor, processes of commodification, and class-based social inequalities that are a consequence of capitalism (Richards 2004). Marx's labor theory of value resembles Lockean perspectives concerning "labor's fruit," but with an important distinction. While Locke emphasized the individual as sovereign over her or his works, Marx underscores the collective and social dimension of labor that allows societies to reproduce and develop as a whole. Capitalist property relations, according to Marx, mystify the cooperative element in social labor though exploitation. Instead of paying just compensation to laborers, capitalists acquire surplus value—the additional labor time and product—from their workers. When applied to creations of the mind, property rights mystify the cooperative element involved in knowledge and technological development. By individualizing patent awards and copyright criteria, intellectual property rights discount the many contributions made by previous generations and the intellectual labor contributions made by various individuals. Within capitalist firms, for example, workers witness their creative labor appropriated by capitalists to whom they are contractually bound to sign over rights.

Fundamental to Marxian notions of exploitation is the enclosure of the commons through the process of commodification. In other words, property once held in common has become parceled out to individual, private interests (May 2000). The tragedy of the intellectual commons does not result from its overuse, as in utilitarian accounts of physical property, but from its underuse in the form of privatized knowledge (Kapczynski 2010: 30–34). The counter-hegemonic movement against capitalist forms of privatized intellectual property thus emphasizes sharing, cooperation, and public goods. The scientific community in contradistinction to the business community often espouses this view. When asked who owned the patent to the Polio vaccine he invented, Jonas Salk replied: "There is no patent. Could you patent the sun?" Indeed, balancing the divergent value orientations of scientists who espouse openness, recognition, and sharing versus investors interested in efficiency, competition, and revenue represents one of the biggest challenges of a science-based industry like pharmaceuticals (Pisano 2006). Central to this conflict is the question of whether mental creativity should even be considered a form of property as asserted in the term "intellectual property."

Critical views of capitalism also highlight how private sectors obtain public resources in order to sell goods back to the public at inflated prices. In the US, public dollars fund 84.2% of basic research into new drugs through tax-funded research at the National Institute of Health (NIH) and universities, while pharmaceutical companies only spend 1.3% of their sales revenue on basic research after discounting tax credits and deductions (Light 2009). Despite US laws requiring that inventions developed with public resources be priced accessibly to the public and that the government retains "march-in" rights under the Bayh-Dole Act of 1980—permitting third-party commercialization of products that resulted from government-funded research—the US government has never approved requests by public interest groups attempting to force companies to make price concessions.

The intellectual property system has also resulted in an incentive structure that skews priorities towards short-term gains for shareholders and executives. According to Homedes and Ugalde (2006), patents and the profit motive have transformed the pharmaceutical industry "from scientists to merchants," from researching and developing new and useful medicines to pill pushers attuned only to their profit margins. "Our hypothesis is that capitalism has forced the pharmaceutical industry to spend a sizeable amount of R&D funds to produce drugs that do not add new therapeutic value to the market. The purpose of these drugs is to compete with innovative blockbuster drugs, those that generate more than US$1 billion of yearly sale," state Homedes and Ugalde (2006: 29). During the 1990s, the drug industry became five times more profitable than the average Fortune 500 companies with returns to shareholders at 18%, double the median for Fortune 500 shareholders. High profits are not ploughed back into R&D, as the industry asserts, but provide large dividends and lucrative compensation packages. Indeed, the ten largest drug firms paid their CEOs, on average, US$23 million in 2001, not including stock options (Homedes and Ugalde 2006). In 2011, John C. Martin, the chief executive officer of Gilead Sciences, a leading producer of antiretrovirals, received total compensation of US$43.2 million.

Critical perspectives also highlight how industry medicalizes common problems associated with everyday life. Industry promotes pharmaceutical solutions to health problems for which lifestyle changes would respond better. Light (2009b) argues that patents are partially to blame for the "Risk Proliferation Syndrome,"[14] whereby the benefits of new drugs are exaggerated but the risks downplayed if they are mentioned at all. As a consequence, adverse drug reactions now account for the fourth leading cause of death in the US; an estimated 111,000 to 256,000 deaths related to adverse drug reactions occur each year. Apart from the loss of life, the heavy mass marketing, hospitalizations, and lawsuits associated with prescription drugs also drive up social costs (Light 2009). The political power of industry also affects government agencies responsible for protecting public health due to

60 Elements of Global Pharmaceutical Power

their vulnerability to capture, lack of accountability, and inability to restrict extensive conflicts of interest (Abraham and Lewis 2014).

In the case of HIV/AIDS, prescription drugs play a necessary role in which the benefits outweigh risks. While Light illustrates both the benefits and risks of prescription drugs, extremist views concerning medicalization only emphasize drug risks. South Africa's President Thabo Mbeki, who denied the link between HIV and AIDS, notoriously said that antiretroviral medicines were poisonous. His government's reluctance to roll out ARV therapies in the public health sector had severe consequences for the South African population who suffered from the disease.

In summary, this chapter asserted that there are number of components that contribute to the power of the global pharmaceutical industry. First, large, incumbent firms dominate the latest technological processes from the research and development stages to end-state manufacturing. While many of these activities may be outsourced to smaller firms, established firms from advanced industrialized countries continue to control the most lucrative segments. Nonetheless, the generic firms from newly industrialized countries continue to challenge the market position of established companies. Western firms have contested the growing market power of new arrivals through their established political alliances with leading policymakers and trade agencies in the United States and Europe. These efforts resulted in a new form of structural power based on patents that they have institutionalized internationally. A powerful discourse connecting property to intellectual creations undergirds the establishment of a corporate-based patent system, which argues that intellectual property represents a natural right and/or provides the basis for an incentive structure that is necessary to spurn innovation and development. Counter-frames contest the normative frameworks employed by industry. A human rights approach argues for a hierarchy of rights in which the right to health trumps rights to intellectual property, while critical perspectives illustrate how drug patents increase social inequalities and health risks. These counter-frames assert that "health is not for sale."

NOTES

1. In 2011, Abbott spun off its pharmaceutical division and named it AbbVie. Since the company was known as Abbott for the timeframe under study, I will continue to use this name.
2. Christopher Singer. Interview with author. Washington, DC. August 5, 2007.
3. Recent books on the pharmaceutical industry include those by Angell (2004), Goozner (2004), Goldacre (2013), Pisano (2006), Huber (2013), Abraham and Lewis (2014), Werth (2014), Healy (2012), Light (2009b), and Abramson (2008).
4. Other authors stipulate marketing as a fourth step in the production process; see Bermudez (1995). Since TNCs' sales forces and commercialization

processes play less of a role in understanding Brazil's AIDS treatment program, the topic is not developed here.

5. Former Marketing Manager of Burroughs Wellcome. Confidential interview with author. October 21, 2009.
6. Throughout this book, I will use generic names of drugs instead of brand names. In cases of fixed-dose combinations, I often resort to brand names.
7. There is another classification of drugs called similars. They have the same active ingredients as reference drugs, but do not go through the bioavailability tests as generics. See Homedes and Ugalde (2005) for more details.
8. Some examples Sikka and Willmot cite include estimates that pharmaceutical TNCs make internal sales to their Latin American subsidiaries at prices between 33% to 314% above world market levels, and the case of GlaxoSmithKline, who, after years of litigation with the Internal Revenue Service concerning $5.2 billion in skirted taxes, agreed to pay a US$3.4-billion settlement in 2006.
9. Many consumer watchdogs, such as KEI (Knowledge Ecology International) and Health Gap, spend much of their time attempting to obtain access to negotiation documents.
10. Parallel importation allows countries to perform price arbitrage for the same patented product placed in both foreign and domestic markets. When this TRIPS flexibility is incorporated in national legislation, the domestic country can import a patented product that may be cheaper on a foreign market. The patent holder, once placing the patent on the foreign product, has exhausted her/his marketing rights to resale on the domestic market.
11. For a public health perspective on patentability outlined by an Argentine economist and lawyer, see Correa (2006).
12. Non-commercial use involves rescinding market exclusivity for government purchases to supply public health systems.
13. To follow the debate see Angell (2004); Commission on Intellectual Property Rights Innovation and Public Health (2006); DiMasi, Hansen, and Grabowski (2005); Goozner (2004); Homedes and Ugalde (2006); Light and Warburton (2005); Riggs (2004).
14. The various elements of Light's "Risk Proliferation Syndrome" include 1) conflict-of-interest testing of drugs; 2) approval speed-up of new medicines; 3) mass marketing of risky drugs; 4) an increase in unapproved uses; and 5) expanding the domain of health problems.

REFERENCES

Abraham, John, and Graham Lewis. 2014. *Regulating Medicines in Europe: Competition, Expertise and Public Health*. New York and London: Routledge.

Abramson, John. 2008. *Overdosed America: The Broken Promise of American Medicine*. 3rd ed. New York: Harper Perennial.

Angell, Marcia. 2004. *The Truth about the Drug Companies*. New York: Random House.

Bermudez, Jorge. 1995. *Industria Farmaceutica, Estado E Sociedade: Critica Da Politica de Medicamentos No Brasil*. São Paulo: Hucitec/Sobrevime.

Boldrin, Michele, and David Levine. 2012. *The Case against Patents*. St. Louis: Federal Reserve Bank—Research Division. Retrieved May 24, 2013 (http://research.stlouisfed.org/wp/2012/2012–035.pdf).

Boston Consulting Group. 2001. *A Revolution in R&D*. Boston: Boston Consulting Group.

62 Elements of Global Pharmaceutical Power

Bracha, Oren. 2004. "Commodification of Patents 1600–1836: How Patents Became Rights and Why We Should Care." *Loyola of Los Angeles Law Review* 38(1): 177–244.

Campbell, David, and Mandy Chui. 2009. "Pharmerging Shake-up: New Imperatives in a Redefined World." *Pharmaceutical Executive*, July, 1–8. Retrieved July 20, 2012 (www.imshealth.com/imshealth/Global/Content/IMS%20Institute/Documents/Pharmerging_Shakeup.pdf).

Carolan, Michael S. 2009. "The Problems with Patents: A Less Than Optimistic Reading of the Future." *Development and Change* 40(2): 361–88.

Center for Responsive Politics. 2011. "Pharmaceutical Manufacturing." Retrieved October 19, 2011 (www.opensecrets.org/industries/indus.php?ind=H04).

Chang, Ha-Joon. 2002. *Kicking Away the Ladder—Development Strategy in Historical Perspective*. London: Anthem Press.

Chaudhuri, Shubham, Pinelopi K. Goldberg, and Panle Jia. 2006. "Estimating the Effects of Global Patent Protection in Pharmaceuticals: A Case Study of Quinolones in India." *American Economic Review* 96(5): 1477–1514.

Chaudhuri, Sudip, ed. 2009. "Is Product Patent Protection Necessary to Spur Innovation in Developing Countries?" Pp. 265–91 in *The Development Agenda: Global Intellectual Property and Developing Countries*. Oxford: Oxford University Press.

Chorev, Nitsan. 2012. "Changing Global Norms through Reactive Diffusion: The Case of Intellectual Property Protection of AIDS Drugs." *American Sociological Review* 77(5): 831–53.

Cockburn, Iain M. 2004. "The Changing Structure of the Pharmaceutical Industry." *Health Affairs* 23(1): 10–22.

Commission on Intellectual Property Rights Innovation and Public Health. 2006. *Public Health, Innovation and Intellectual Property Rights*. Geneva: World Health Organization.

Committee on Economic, Social and Cultural Rights (CESCR). 2000. "General Comment 14: The Right to the Highest Attainable Standard of Health." Retrieved August 6, 2011 (http://cesr.org/generalcomment14).

Committee on Economic, Social and Cultural Rights (CESCR). 2001. "Human Rights and Intellectual Property. Statement Adopted by the CESCR, 14 December 2001." Retrieved August 6, 2011 (www1.umn.edu.humanrts/esc/escstatements2001.html).

Correa, Carlos. 2000. *Intellectual Property Rights, the WTO and Developing Countries*. London: Zed Books.

Correa, Carlos. 2006. *Guidelines for the Examination of Pharmaceutical Patents: Developing a Public Health Perspective*. Geneva: WHO/ICTSD/UNCTAD.

Deere, Carolyn. 2009. *The Implementation Game: The TRIPS Agreement and the Global Politics of Intellectual Property Reform in Developing Countries*. London: Oxford University Press.

DiMasi, Joseph A., Ronald W. Hansen, and Henry G. Grabowski. 2005. "Extraordinary Claims Require Extraordinary Evidence." *Journal of Health Economics* 24(5): 1034–44.

Dutfield, Graham. 2003. *Intellectual Property Rights and the Life Science Industries: A Twentieth Century History*. Aldershot and Burlington: Ashgate.

Freeman, Michael. 2009. "Right to Health." Pp. 44–67 in *Interpreting Human Rights—Social Science Perspective*, edited by Rhiannon Morgan and Bryan Turner. Hoboken: Routledge.

Gibbs, Edwina, and Devidutta Tripathy. 2008. "Daiichi to Pay up to $4.6 Billion for Control of Ranbaxy." *Reuters*, June 11. Retrieved July 21, 2014 (www.reuters.com/article/2008/06/11/us-ranbaxy-idINT34755720080611).

Elements of Global Pharmaceutical Power 63

Gilbert, Jim, Preston Henske, and Ashish Singh. 2007. "Rebuilding Big Pharma's Business Model." *In Vivo: The Business & Medicine Report* 12(10): 1–10.

Global Forum on Health Research. 2004. *The 10/90 Report on Health Research 2003–2004*. Geneva: Global Forum on Health Research. Retrieved February 4, 2014 (www.isn.ethz.ch/Digital-Library/Publications/Detail/?id=17141).

Goldacre, Ben. 2013. *Bad Pharma: How Drug Companies Mislead Doctors and Harm Patients*. Reprint ed. New York: Faber & Faber.

Goodman, T. 2005. "Is There a Right to Health?" *J Med Philos* 30(6): 643–62.

Goozner, Merrill. 2004. *The $800 Million Pill*. Berkeley: University of California Press.

Grace, Cheri. 2004. *The Effect of Changing Intellectual Property on Pharmaceutical Industry Prospects in India and China*. London: DFID: Health Systems Resource Centre.

Gray, Nicole. 2007. "Changing Landscapes: A Special Report on the World's Top 50 Pharma Companies." Retrieved October 10, 2014 (www.pharmexec.com/pharmexec/data/articlestandard/pharmexec/272006/354138/article.pdf).

Grover, Anand. 2009. *Report of the Special Rapporteur on the Right of Everyone to the Enjoyment of the Highest Attainable Standard of Physical and Mental Health*. Geneva: Human Rights Council.

Hayek, Friedrich A. von. 1948. *Individualism and Economic Order*. Chicago: University of Chicago Press.

Healy, David. 2012. *Pharmageddon*. 1st ed. Berkeley: University of California Press.

Heller, Michael. 2008. *The Gridlock Economy*. New York: Basic Books.

't Hoen, Ellen F. M. 2009. *The Global Politics of Pharmaceutical Monopoly Power*. Diemen: AMB.

Homedes, Nuria, and Antonio Ugalde. 2005. "Multisource Drug Policies in Latin America: Survey of 10 Countries." *Bulletin of the World Health Organization* 83: 64–70.

Homedes, Nuria, and Antonio Ugalde. 2006. "From Scientists to Merchants: The Transformation of the Pharmaceutical Industry and Its Impact on Health." *Societies without Borders* 1(1): 21–40.

Huber, Peter W. 2013. *The Cure in the Code: How 20th Century Law Is Undermining 21st Century Medicine*. 1st ed. New York: Basic Books.

Hunt, Paul. 2008. *Human Rights Guidelines for Pharmaceutical Companies in Relation to Access to Medicines*. Geneva: United Nations.

IMS Health. 2012a. *Total Unaudited and Audited Global Pharmaceutical Market, 2003–2011*. Retrieved July 20, 2012 (www.imshealth.com/deployedfiles/ims/Global/Content/Corporate/Press%20Room/Top-Line%20Market%20Data%20&%20Trends/2011%20Top-line%20Market%20Data/Global_Pharma_Market_by_Spending_2003-2011.pdf).

IMS Health. 2012b. *Total Unaudited and Audited Global Pharmaceutical Market by Region*. Retrieved July 20, 2012 (www.imshealth.com/deployedfiles/ims/Global/Content/Corporate/Press%20Room/Top-Line%20Market%20Data%20&%20Trends/2011%20Top-line%20Market%20Data/Regional_Pharma_Market_by_Spending_2011-2016.pdf).

Kapczynski, Amy. 2010. "Access to Knowledge: A Conceptual History." Pp. 17–56 in *Access to Knowledge in the Age of Intellectual Property*, edited by Gaëlle Krikorian and Amy Kapczynski. New York: Zone Books.

Kapstein, Ethan B., and Josh Busby. 2013. *AIDS Drugs for All*. Cambridge: Cambridge University Press.

Keyhani, Salomeh, Marie Diener-West, and Neil Powe. 2005. "Do Drug Prices Reflect Development Time and Government Investment?" *Medical Care* 43(8): 753–62.

64　Elements of Global Pharmaceutical Power

Kinney, Eleanor D., and Brian Alexander Clark. 2004. "Provisions for Health and Health Care in the Constitutions of the Countries of the World." *Cornell International Law Journal* 37: 285–355.

Kogan, Lawrence A. 2006. "Brazil's IP Opportunism Threatens U.S. Private Property Rights." *Inter-American Law Review* 38(1): 1–139.

Laforgia, Francesco, Fabio Montobbio, and Luigi Orsenigo. 2009. "IPRs and Technological Development in Pharmaceuticals: Who Is Patenting What in Brazil after the TRIPS." Pp. 293–313 in *The Development Agenda: Global Intellectual Property and Developing Countries*, edited by Neil Weinstock Netanel. Oxford: Oxford University Press.

Light, Donald W. 2008. "Pricing Pharmaceuticals in the USA." Pp. 63–79 in *Excessive Medical Spending*, edited by Norman J. Temple and Andrew Thompson. Oxford: Radcliffe.

Light, Donald W. 2009. "Bearing the Risks of Prescription Drugs." Pp. 1–39 in *The Risks of Prescription Drugs*, edited by Donald W. Light. New York: Columbia University Press.

Light, Donald W., Jon Kim Andrus, and Rebecca N. Warburton. 2009. "Estimated Research and Development Costs of Rotavirus Vaccines." *Vaccine* 27(47): 6627–33.

Light, Donald W., and Rebecca N. Warburton. 2005. "Extraordinary Claims Require Extraordinary Evidence." *Journal of Health Economics* 24(5): 1030–33.

Maskus, Keith E., ed. 2008. *Intellectual Property, Growth and Trade*. 1st ed. Amsterdam: Elsevier.

Matthews, Duncan. 2002. *Globalizing Intellectual Property Rights: The TRIPS Agreement*. London: Routledge.

May, Christopher. 2000. *A Global Political Economy of Intellectual Property Rights: The New Enclosures?* London: Routledge.

May, Christopher, and Susan K. Sell. 2006. *Intellectual Property Rights: A Critical History*. Lynne Rienners Publishers.

Nagan, Winston P., Eduardo J. Mordujovich, Judit K. Otvos, and Jason Taylor. 2010. "Misappropriation of Shuar Traditional Knowledge (TK) and Trade Secrets: A Case Study on Biopiracy in the Amazon." *Journal of Technology Law & Policy* 15(2): 143–59.

Odagiri, Hiroyuki, ed. 2010. *Intellectual Property Rights, Development, and Catch Up: An International Comparative Study*. Oxford: Oxford University Press.

OECD. n.d. "OECD Health Statistics 2014." *Health Policies and Data*. Retrieved July 20, 2014 (www.oecd.org/els/health-systems/oecd-health-statistics-2014-fre quently-requested-data.htm).

PhRMA. n.d. "Intellectual Property." *Intellectual Property Protections Are Vital to Continuing Innovation in the Biopharmaceutical Industry*. Retrieved November 5, 2013 (www.phrma.org/innovation/intellectual-property).

Pinheiro, Eloan dos Santos, Benjamin Gilbert, Maria Fernanda Macedo, Antonio Carlos Siani, Roberto Sacramento, and Leandro Safatle. 2005. *Identificação de Oportunidades de Investimentos No Setor de Fármacos: Lista Tentativa de Farmoquímicos E Introdução À Eleição de Uma Política Para Fitoterápicos E Fitofármacos*. LC/BRS/R.153. Rio de Janeiro: CEPAL. Retrieved October 25, 2008. (www.cepal.org/publicaciones/xml/6/22306/lcbrsr153farmacoseloangilbert.pdf)

Pinheiro, Eloan dos Santos, Octavio Augusto Ceva Antunes, and Joseph M.D. Fortunak. 2008. "A Survey of the Syntheses of Active Pharmaceutical Ingredients for Antiretroviral Drug Combinations Critical to Access in Emerging Nations." *Antiviral Research* 79(3): 143–65.

Pisano, Gary P. 2006. *Science Business: The Promise, the Reality, and the Future of Biotech*. 1st ed. Boston: Harvard Business School Press.

Elements of Global Pharmaceutical Power 65

Public Citizen. 2003. "America's Other Drug Problem." Retrieved January 16, 2010 (www.citizen.org/congress/reform/rxfacts/).

Quian, Yi. 2009. "Are National Patent Laws the Blossoming Rains?" Pp. 191–213 in *The Development Agenda: Global Intellectual Property and Developing Countries*, edited by Neil Weinstock Netanel. Oxford: Oxford University Press.

Resnik, David. B. 2003. "A Pluralistic Account of Intellectual Property." *Journal of Business Ethics* 46(4): 319–35.

Reuters. 2008. "Roche to Suspend H.I.V. Research." *The New York Times*, July 12. Retrieved July 21, 2014 (www.nytimes.com/2008/07/12/busines s/12bizbriefs-ROCHETOSUSPE_BRF.html).

Reuters. 2010. "Gilead Dominates HIV/AIDS Drugs Market." *Reuters*, July 19. Retrieved July 21, 2014 (www.reuters.com/article/2010/07/19/aids-drugs-id USLDE66C0FR20100719).

Richards, Donald. 2004. *Intellectual Property Rights and Global Capitalism*. Armonk: M. E. Sharpe.

Riggs, T. 2004. "Research and Development Costs for Drugs." *The Lancet* 363(9404): 184.

Robinson, Daniel F. 2010. *Confronting Biopiracy: Challenges, Cases and International Debates*. Washington, DC: Earthscan.

Sell, Susan K. 2003. *Private Power, Public Law: The Globalization of Intellectual Property Rights*. Cambridge: Cambridge University Press.

Shadlen, Kenneth. 2009. "The Politics of Patents and Drugs in Brazil and Mexico: The Industrial Bases of Health Policies." *Comparative Politics* 41(1): 178–201.

Shadlen, Kenneth. 2011. "The Political Contradictions of Incremental Innovation: Lessons from Pharmaceutical Patent Examination in Brazil." *Politics & Society* 39(2): 143–74.

Shadlen, Kenneth, Samira Guennif, and Georgina Alenka Guzman Chavez, eds. 2011. *Intellectual Property, Pharmaceuticals and Public Health Access to Drugs in Developing Countries*. Cheltenham: Edward Elgar Publishing.

Sikka, Prem, and Hugh Willmott. 2010. "The Dark Side of Transfer Pricing: Its Role in Tax Avoidance and Wealth Retentiveness." *Critical Perspectives on Accounting* 21(4): 342–56.

Silverman, Milton, Mia Lydecker, and Philip Randolph Lee. 1992. *Bad Medicine*. Redwood City: Stanford University Press.

Sjoberg, Gideon. 2009. "Corporations and Human Rights." Pp. 157–76 in *Interpreting Human Rights—Social Science Perspective*, edited by Rhiannon Morgan and Bryan Turner. Hoboken: Routledge.

Sjoberg, Gideon, Elizabeth A. Gill, and Norma Williams. 2001. "A Sociology of Human Rights." *Social Problems* 48(1): 11–47.

Smith, Richard D., Carlos Correa, and Cecilia Oh. 2009. "Trade, TRIPS, and Pharmaceuticals." *Lancet* 373(9664): 684–91.

Tarabusi, Claudio Casadio, and Graham Vickery. 1998. "Globalization of the Pharmaceutical Industry." *Journal of Health Care Industry* 28(1): 67–105.

Tempest, Brian. 2010. "A Structural Change in the Global Pharmaceutical Marketplace." *Journal of Generic Medicines: The Business Journal for the Generic Medicines Sector* 7(2): 113–17.

United Nations. 1966. *International Covenant on Economic Social and Cultural Rights*. Geneva: Office of the United Nations High Commissioner for Human Rights.

United Nations High Commissioner on Human Rights. 2001. *Access to Medication in the Context of Pandemics such as HIV/AIDS: Report of the Secretary-General*. UNHCR Resolution 2001/33 (April). Geneva: Office of the United Nations High Commissioner for Human Rights.

66 *Elements of Global Pharmaceutical Power*

US National Law Center for Inter-American Free Trade. 2008. "Strong Intellectual Property Protection Benefits the Developing Countries." Retrieved October 25, 2008 (http://natlaw.com/interam/ar/ip/sp/sparip11.htm).

Wade, Robert Hunter. 2003. "What Strategies Are Viable for Developing Countries Today? The World Trade Organization and the Shrinking of 'Developmental Space.'" *Review of International Political Economy* 10(4): 621–44.

Werth, Barry. 2014. *The Antidote: Inside the World of New Pharma.* New York: Simon & Schuster.

WHO. 2014. *Increasing Access to HIV Treatment in Middle-Income Countries.* Geneva: World Health Organization.

WIPO. 2011. "Patent Landscape Report on Ritonavir." Retrieved April 29, 2012 (www.wipo.int/patentscope/en/programs/patent_landscapes/reports/ritonavir. html).

Zeller, Christian. 2000. "Rescaling Power Relations between Trade Unions and Corporate Management in a Globalising Pharmaceutical Industry: The Case of the Acquisition of Boehringer Mannheim by Hoffman—La Roche." *Environment and Planning A* 32:1545–67.

3 The Brazilian Context
Contradictions between Democracy and Neoliberalism

Paulo Teixiera, despite his small stature and size, exhibits boundless energy when discussing the evolution of Brazil's HIV policies. He played an important role designing and implementing these policies ever since the disease first appeared in São Paulo city in the early 1980s. At the time, he was working in the leprosy division of the state health department. For Teixeira, HIV and leprosy shared many characteristics in terms of the stigma surrounding the disease. Confronting the new epidemic, in his view, required a human rights-based approach and a willingness to work directly with affected communities. Teixiera was part of a larger social movement occurring in Brazil—the health reform movement, *Movimento Sanitário*—composed of activist doctors, nurses, health care workers, and students that argued in favor of government provision of health care based on participatory decision making. These *sanitaristas* considered access to health care as a means to address broader issues of social exclusion in Brazil's highly unequal society. They believed the state should not only lead in the provision and delivery of care but should also address deprivations in housing, sanitation, education, and employment.

Teixeira embodies the activist professional that is central to understanding Brazil's HIV policies and to grasping how the country succeeded in confronting several challenges to the roll-out and sustainability of treatment. By infiltrating the state, these activists occupied formal positions within the government and used bureaucratic channels to achieve social movement objectives. When developing Brazil's domestic HIV treatment policies, *sanitaristas* allied with grassroots activists, employed rights-based rhetoric towards health, and disseminated expert knowledge about the disease, treatments, and patent monopolies.

At the time Teixeira saw his first HIV patient in the early 1980s, Brazil demonstrated few signs that the country would develop a model treatment program. The South American country was entering a period of hyperinflation and low economic growth that would last some 20 years. Economic elites were more concerned about macro-economic stability, foreign investment, and trade than expensive social programs. Only in recent years has the Brazilian economy boomed and incomes steadily risen. Developing a first-class treatment

68   *The Brazilian Context*

program faced multiple obstacles related to the production of medicines and access to the health system. Despite several efforts to build an industrial pharmaceutical base, the country remained dependent on foreign technologies and raw materials. And Brazil's health system mainly benefitted mobilized urban classes, until the 1990s when new policies were enacted.

This chapter details the recent history of Brazil's pharmaceutical and health policies over the past 50 years. Major transformations occurred in the country's political economy and social institutions between the country's authoritarian past (1964–1985) to the restoration of democratic governance. When considering new development models during the 1980s and 1990s, Brazilian policymakers could choose from three different options: neoliberal, state interventionist, and social democratic. I focus on the neoliberal recommendations and their relevance to pharmaceutical policies. In broad terms, these reforms are associated with the global pharmaceutical power described in the previous chapter, especially new forms of intellectual property protection. Implementing these policies, including trade liberalization, price deregulation, and new patent protection, increased the transnational drug industry's control over Brazil's drug market.

New democratic forms of governance, meanwhile, opened space for a surge in citizenship claims. The new Constitution of 1988 outlined an expansive set of social rights and duties of the state, and new groups came to power who enacted progressive social policies to reduce poverty, provide employment, raise the minimum wage, and expand educational opportunities (see Cohn 2012; Huber and Stephens 2012; Tendler 1997). The *sanitaristas* pushed a social democratic model and provided expertise for revamping the country's health system. While they failed to achieve the more comprehensive reforms they had envisioned, these health reformers succeeded in implementing their ideals with the establishment of the National AIDS Program.[1] The strategies *sanitaristas* employed at the domestic level—coalition building with activists groups and naming and shaming opponents—would inform their future efforts when foreign challenges threatened the sustainability of their treatment program. Understanding the Brazilian context helps to explain the shifts in pharmaceutical autonomy and dependency in AIDS medicines detailed in subsequent chapters.

NEOLIBERALISM AND ITS ALTERNATIVES

Neoliberal economic policies gained popularity in the 1980s and 1990s in response to several macro-economic challenges, including hyperinflation, balance-of-payments problems, and unsustainable government debts. Economists, especially those from the University of Chicago, presented a coherent set of arguments and policy responses to sluggish economic growth, high unemployment, and volatile currencies. In general, they favored a minimal role for government intervention in the economy and emphasized international economic integration. Their policy toolkit became known as the Washington Consensus and later the "Augmented" Washington Consensus (Rodrik 2006). Many of the policy instruments focus on public finance and monetary issues, but several have a direct impact on the health systems. The abridged list below highlights key neoliberal policies and their impact on industrial and social policies affecting pharmaceutical markets:

- **Fiscal discipline:** Strict limitations on budgets directly affect expenditures on publicly funded health systems and programs, including funds to purchase medicines.
- **Public expenditure priorities:** Prioritization of public expenditures often leads to the cessation of industrial policies that support infant industries.
- **Trade liberalization:** Reducing tariffs on imports and stimulation of exports expose local drug makers to foreign competition, directly affecting supply and demand for medicines and consequently prices.
- **Privatization:** Privatization of state-run enterprises transfers control over to private-sector owners. Those developing countries operating public, or state-run, labs that produce medicines and vaccines would no longer have these assets for public health objectives and would have to rely on private market suppliers.
- **Deregulation:** Removing government regulations allegedly facilitate the entry and exit of firms in a market. But deregulation also involves the removal of price controls, which could lead to price hikes of medicines.
- **World Trade Organization (WTO) agreements:** Joining the WTO obliges countries to adopt standard rules for the organization of global markets. WTO agreements including the General Agreement on Trade in Services (GATS) and the Agreement on Trade-Related Aspects of Intellectual Property Rights or TRIPS (explained in more detail in Chapter 2) have a direct impact on the governments' ability to address public health concerns. By stipulating that all developing countries provide a 20-year patent on pharmaceuticals, TRIPS directly impacts drug prices.
- **Targeted social policies:** State involvement in the provision of social welfare should be means-tested, targeting only those that cannot obtain services through private market mechanisms.

The adoption of policies represented a major transformation in the political economies of developing countries. Between World War II and the Debt Crises of the 1980s, the prevailing economic model emphasized industrial transformation using a set of policies premised on import substitution. Governments employed high tariff barriers to protect local industry, provided subsidies and public credit to producers, and created state enterprises in capital-intensive industries and strategic sectors of the economy. Many developing countries, including Brazil, created state-run or public labs to produce needed medicines for their health systems and to encourage the growth of a local pharmaceutical industry. Based on broad Keynesian ideas,

70 The Brazilian Context

the prevailing economic consensus of the day emphasized an active state role in the economy in order to transform the economy and create a growing consumer market. In contrast, neoliberal prescriptions sought to reign in the state so that market forces could "get prices right" and "free up" private sector actors to drive growth.

Neoliberal ideas also inspired changes in social policy paradigms. Most social welfare systems in Latin American were based on corporatist models in which states distributed public benefits to mobilized groups who were formally incorporated into state structures. Governments provided trade unions resources in exchange for loyalty and political support. Instead of reliance on state monopoly of provision and centralized decision making, neoliberal policy recommendations privileged greater use of non-state actors (including private business and nongovernment organizations), allocation models that would target those most in need, and decentralization of decision making and program administration to local authorities (Franco 1996; Homedes and Ugalde 2005a). Many of the new social policies sought to increase government efficiency and reduce overall expenditures, with the assumption that private and nongovernmental health insurers and providers would be more cost-effective in delivering care.

Neoliberal policies were not the only options available to politicians and policymakers. Two alternative models include the developmental state model and the social democratic model. Scholars who studied the rise of East Asian economies coined the term *developmental state* to describe a coherent set of government organizations capable of designing policies leading to high rates of economic growth combined with the capability to climb the technological ladder (Amsden 2001; Grabowski 1994; Johnson 1982; Wade 1990). The work of these scholars demonstrated that the state was not the problem but, rather, the solution. Strong meritocratic regimes that have institutionalized channels for sharing information with private sector actors provide the basis for strong economic growth (Evans 1995). Contrary to prevailing neoliberal philosophies, heterodox economists argue in favor of dynamic comparative advantages that actively encourage industrial upgrading (Lin and Chang 2009). In terms of pharmaceutical policies, this model would emphasize increased state support, protectionist measures, and industrial policies targeting national firms in order to develop the industry.

Whereas the concept of the developmental state model emphasizes the use of industrial policies, the *social democratic model* stresses democratic politics and expansive social provisions. Social democratic welfare systems combine full democratic participation with the extensive provision of public goods regardless of class, gender or racial/ethnic distinctions in order to reduce overall social inequalities (Marshall 1964). Social policies based on social citizenship reduce individuals' reliance on markets for their livelihood. Scandinavian countries best represent the social democratic ideal in that their social policies promote equality and solidarity irrespective of class or market position (Esping-Anderson 1990). Some scholars remain

The Brazilian Context 71

sanguine about the possibilities of a social democratic route in the developing world. Sandbrook et al. (2007) argue that Kerala (a state in India), Costa Rica, Mauritius, and Chile, albeit markedly different from social democratic regimes in the European tradition, demonstrate a model that is democratically thick, socially proactive, and economically inclusive. In these cases, access to health care and essential medicines is based not on income level or private insurance coverage but on citizenship rights, i.e. membership in a political community.

When formulating and implementing pharmaceutical policies, Brazilian policymakers therefore could select from various neoliberal, developmental, or social democratic models. The evolution of Brazil's pharmaceutical capabilities amidst new trade regimes, the construction of democratic politics leading to new coalition building, and the institutionalization of Constitutionally guaranteed rights would influence the subsequent policy choices.

SISYPHEAN ATTEMPTS TO CONTROL PHARMACEUTICAL TECHNOLOGY

The current situation of dependency in the Brazilian pharmaceutical sector stems from the penetration of foreign capital and from several unsuccessful attempts by the state to develop the pharmaceutical industry. In the early 1900s, Brazilian research institutes made significant advancements in vaccine research and tropical diseases, such as yellow fever and Chagas diseases. In fact, Brazilian pharmaceutical firms in 1930 largely resembled their counterparts in the United States and Europe. But with advancements in synthetic chemistry concentrated elsewhere and the absence of a strong chemical industry, local firms soon trailed behind foreign companies (Bermudez 1995; Bertero 1972).

From the 1940s to the 1980s, Brazil followed a set of policies, known as import substitution industrialization (ISI), encouraging the local production of imported goods and products. High tariffs, favorable credit lines, and state enterprises sought to induce local industrial development. These policies resulted in a considerable buildup of the pharmaceutical sector in Brazil. However, with no controls on the activities of transnational firms to operate in Brazil, acquisition of private national drug companies became the main strategy for foreign firms to enter the market. Between 1958 and 1972, the control of 43 private Brazilian labs was transferred to multinational drug companies who increased their share of Brazil's domestic market from 14% in 1930 to 73% by 1960 (Bermudez 1995). Meanwhile, imports of medicines fell from 70% of total consumption in 1953 to near zero by the end of the decade, but TNCs still imported raw materials used for production (Palmeira and Pan 2003).

Mazzolleni and Costa Póvoa (2010) attribute three factors to Brazil's denationalization during the ISI period. First, the strategy of transnational

72 The Brazilian Context

national corporations (TNCs) centered on establishing a presence in large developing country markets. Second, inflation and a deflated currency made acquisitions of Brazilian companies attractive. And third, industrial policies favored foreign direct investors. For example, essential goods that could not be sourced locally did not receive protective tariffs, which favored the local production of formulations at the expense of active pharmaceutical ingredients (APIs), the crucial ingredient in drug making, which could be imported cheaply. Additionally, Brazilian companies were at a disadvantage compared to local TNC affiliates who had access to cheaper sources of credit to import machinery. Most foreign-owned drug companies, consequently, focused on end-stage production and marketing. Apart from a few isolated cases, TNCs did not invest in API production or R&D activities, so there were few spillovers into the rest of the pharmaceutical industry (Mazzoleni and Costa Póvoa 2010). In cases when local firms achieved scale and technological prowess, TNCs would acquire their control and incorporate them into their global production processes.

The exception to denationalization from the 1950s onwards is public, or government-affiliated, labs. State governments, universities, and branches of the armed forces opened 20 public labs to produce medicines for the public health sector and to respond to outbreaks of tropical diseases (Flynn 2008). The Institute in Technology of Medicines (*Instituto de Tecnologia em Fármacos*—Farmanguinhos) operates under the direct control of the federal Ministry of Health and comprises part of the Oswaldo Cruz Foundation (*Fundação Oswaldo Cruz*—FioCruz) medical and health complex, similar to the United States' National Institute of Health (NIH). These public labs produce finished dosage forms and not crucial active principal ingredients (APIs). And most of their production supplements the needs of the health system.

By the late 1960s, Brazil's military government decided that developing the pharmaceutical industry was a strategic objective of the state. In 1969, lawmakers abolished patents on pharmaceutical processes as well as products, which had already been eliminated since 1945. This policy remained in vigor until the Industrial Property Act passed in 1996 that, once again, provided patent protection for products and processes in line with the country's new trade commitments. While Brazil continued to award patents in other industries through the National Institute for Patent Protection (*Instituto Nacional de Propriedade Intellectual*—INPI), the country's local pharmaceutical industry would be allowed to lawfully copy existing drugs until the new legislation passed in 1996 came into force.

To coordinate the sector's development, expand access to essential medicines, and centralize public procurement of medicines from both public and private labs with the aim of developing the country's pharmaceutical base, the federal government created in 1971 the Central Medicines Agency (*Central de Medicamentos*—CEME). At the time, it was estimated that 104 million people, roughly 80% of the Brazilian population, did not have sufficient means to afford essential medicines. The agency was also responsible for collecting regional epidemiological information, promoting research and technological development, and controlling and assuring quality (Bermudez 1995). CEME set out to streamline procurement of medicines, especially from public labs, for distribution to the country's social security system that served the poorest segments of the population. Up to this point, foreign firms, despite some complaints about the lack of patent protection, did not feel threatened by government initiatives. They still accounted for approximately 80% of the total market and even made sales to CEME whose market to the low-income groups did not compete against their traditional markets.

By the 1970s, ISI policies had led to the creation of a base chemical and petrochemical industry as well as the production of finished dosage forms, but the intermediate stages in the pharmaceutical production cycle remained weak or altogether missing. Consequently, the government enacted policies to attract investments for developing the fine chemical industry that would produce APIs and other chemical intermediates. Industrial policies in the 1970s incentivized upstream investments, and CEME also sponsored universities and research institutes to develop processes for the chemical synthesis of pharmochemicals. Nonetheless, expansion of the pharmaceutical base remained incipient.

Only in the following decade did government efforts to build upstream manufacturing plants gain traction. In 1984, the Ministries of Health and of Industry and Trade issued Interministerial Decree No. 4 *(Portaria Interministral No. 4)* to stimulate the local production of drugs and raw materials. Measures included investment incentives and increased tariffs on imports of raw materials, even prohibiting the importation of some items (Bermudez 1995; Palmeira and Pan 2003). State officials even threatened to purchase raw material inputs on the international market and distribute them on the national market if TNCs did not produce them locally (Mazzoleni and Costa Póvoa 2010). Other efforts focused on developing human resources by providing scholarships in chemical engineering and related fields. These policies led to the start of a number of industrial projects for the production of drugs, including APIs. A few notable examples of new Brazilian firms, often including collaborations between the state and private sector, were Codotec, Microbiologica, and Nortec. Viewed from the perspective of TNCs, these policies contributed to the global over-capacity mentioned in the previous chapter, disrupted global production chains, and impeded transfer pricing strategies employed to shift profits out of the country.

The investment surge of the 1980s in the fine chemicals ground to a halt by the end of the decade. Fernando Collor (1990–1992), Brazil's first democratically elected president since the end of military rule, pursued the Washington Consensus set of neoliberal economic policies. Trade liberalization, price deregulation, and privatization of state enterprises marked the end of the ISI period. Policymakers, pressured by international financial

74 *The Brazilian Context*

institutions, believed that curtailing the government's role in the economy could address sluggish economic growth, hyperinflation, and growing indebtedness. Even the public supported the drastic measures designed to stabilize the economy, which was suffering from hyperinflation and heavy foreign debts (Weyland 1998b).

Neoliberal policies had a dramatic impact on Brazil's pharmaceutical sector as the government slashed tariffs on imports, removed price controls on medicines, and abandoned industrial policies. One of Collor's first policies was rescinding Interministerial Decree No. 4. As tariffs fell from 60% to 20% and state petrochemical firms were privatized, several manufacturers producing APIs and chemical intermediates for the pharmaceutical industry went bankrupt. In the first half of the 1990s, 1,700 production lines of synthetic intermediates and inputs ended their operations (Orsi, Hasenclever, Fialho, Tigre, and Coriat 2003). The consequence was evident in the sector's trade balance: Imports of drugs and APIs climbed from $512 million in 1990 to $2.363 billion in 2002, while exports remained at just over $400 million during the same period (Palmeira and Pan 2003).

Neoliberal policies culminated in the approval of the Industrial Property Law No. 9.279 of 1996, which reinstated patents for pharmaceutical processes and products. When drawing up legislation regarding intellectual property, policymakers did not wait until the 2005 deadline set for middle-income countries to adhere to TRIPS. Brazilian officials began discussing a new patent law in 1991, but its passage did not occur until May 15, 1996, due to corruption scandals in the presidency and resistance from business interests, professional organizations, and organized civil society. The Ministry of Health and *sanitaristas* opposed and called into the question the characterization of medicines as just another commodity (Bermudez 1995).[2] One important group, however, remained unaware of the implications of the new patent legislation. Up to this point, AIDS activists focused their attention elsewhere on education, prevention, and treatment rollout.

Fernando Henrique Cardoso, Brazil's president at the time of passage and chief sponsor of the legislation,[3] refused to comment on his motivations for pushing intellectual property legislation, when interviewed by Nunn (2008), but two factors stand out. First, Cardoso and his economic team believed that embracing IPRs would be a positive step for Brazil's economic liberalization, reduce Brazil's dependence on technology imports, and attract foreign investment. "Cardoso's support for the Industrial Property Law was one of his many endorsements of globalization," asserts Nunn (2008: 82).

Second, policymakers alleged that IPRs would improve trade with the US. Since many lawmakers were tied to the export industry in Brazil, deputies and senators were susceptible to US trade threats. In fact, the proposed legislation had divided business interests (Tarchinardi 1993). Concerns over intellectual property protection had marred US-Brazil trade relations since the 1980s. In 1988, US President Ronald Reagan used Section 301 of the Trade Act of 1974 to impose a 100% tariff on imports of Brazilian paper

The Brazilian Context   75

products, consumer electronics, and Brazilian medicines. In the view of Brazil's Ambassador to General Agreement on Tariffs and Trade (GATT), Rubens Ricupero, the US could never prove that its companies were losing profits due to the lack of patent protection on pharmaceuticals. Furthermore, Ricupero maintained the unilateral trade sanctions were illegal under international trade law. "We lost out because of power politics," he said.[4] The Ambassador believed that the US's strategy was to pressure Brazil on intellectual property in order to obtain concessions from other countries like India and China who waited until the 2005 deadline.

Nelson Brasil, executive vice-president of the Fine Chemical and Pharmochemical Trade Association (*Associaçao Brasileira das Indústrias de Química Fina e suas Especialidades*—ABIFINA) also pointed to US pressure behind a bill that incorporates few of the flexibilities outlined in the TRIPS accord.

> The initial bill was approved by consensus in the House of Deputies in 1993–1994 and was very good—ABIFINA had taken part in the negotiations with [then President] Itamar Franco and [then Minister of Foreign Relations] Cardoso. But when it went to the Senate, which at the time Cardoso had become president and had other commitments, the bill changed form. Because of pressure from the US, such as in 1995–96, [Luiz Felipe] Lampreia, the Minister of Foreign Relations, warned that if Brazil did not pass the TRIPS-plus legislation, there would be trade sanctions on steel, orange juice, and other Brazilian products.[5]

The TRIPS-plus legislation refers to several provisions that went beyond the mandatory minimum. For example, issuing compulsory licenses could only be used for purchases of medicines produced locally (until later changes were made). In addition, the legislation included pipeline protection, which provided patent protection for drugs that had had their patents approved in other countries without an examination by Brazilian agencies. Appendix Three details TRIPS flexibilities and Brazilian legislation.

Contrary to policymakers' belief that increased protection of intellectual property (IP) would encourage more foreign investment, foreign companies scaled back domestic activities (except in clinical testing, marketing, and end-stage production). The impact on local product innovation had also been lackluster. Six years after the Industry Property Act was passed, Brazilian firms accounted for only 3.1% of the industry's total 6,934 patent claims. The vast majority came from countries home to the world's leading pharmaceutical companies (Bermudez and Oliveira 2004). With strong patent protections on medicines, transnational drug companies consolidated their position in the most lucrative segments of the economy, while the nationally owned pharmaceutical industry focused on commodity and branded generics, conventional dosage forms, and value-added formulations. The domestic pharmochemical sector continued as a weak link in the

76 The Brazilian Context

Brazilian domestic industry, an issue that became more apparent in subsequent chapters examining the production of AIDS medicines. In addition, despite highly trained engineers and competent scientists in Brazil, discovering new chemical entities and treatments remained limited.

Consistent with their economic beliefs, Brazilian economic policymakers during the 1990s no longer devised industrial policies. Pedro Malan, Brazil's finance minister from 1995 to 2002, is famously quoted as saying, "The best industrial policy is no industrial policy." The government's decision to close CEME in 1997 symbolized the end of government efforts to support local production efforts. Previous attempts to use CEME and public labs to develop the country's pharmaceutical industry fell short of their objectives. Instead of organizing and streamlining the country's network of public labs, CEME's activities revealed the conflicts between the public and private sectors, especially with regard to centralized purchases of medicines. Acquisitions, which declined to 20% of average levels in 1991 and 1992, increasingly came from private national and foreign companies at the expense of public labs due to the hegemonic position of foreign firms in the domestic market and allegations of corruption at CEME (Bermudez 1995; Ministry of Health 2002b). Even state governments looked to privatize public labs under their control (Oliveira 2007).

There is a lot of debate concerning the failure of Brazil to develop a strong pharmaceutical industry. While Brazilian companies acquired significant reverse-engineering capabilities and proceeded in the production of generic formulations, they never achieved the global position of Indian, Israeli, or Canadian generics industries. One argument is that the presence and strength of foreign capital in the Brazilian market continually placed Brazilian firms at a disadvantage or vulnerable to acquisition by foreign firms (Bermudez 1995). Defenders of strong property protection take the opposite position and claim that Brazil's underdeveloped pharmaceutical industry stems from a weak commitment to patent incentives necessary to attract investment and encourage innovation.[6] However, Mazzoleni and Costa Póvoa (2010) conclude that the low levels of education attainment and misguided policies account for the reduced absorptive capacity of indigenous drug companies more than pull mechanisms like temporary patent monopolies.

Another perspective highlights Brazil's weak institutions and incoherent pharmaceutical policies. Unlike strong bureaucracies of East Asian countries, Brazil's "semi-developmental state" remains susceptible to clientelist politics and political favoritism (Evans 1995; Weyland 1998a). In the early 1970s, the president's office was responsible for policies to develop the pharmaceutical industry, but in subsequent years government priorities shifted and various federal ministries assumed control of pharmaceutical policies and programs (Bermudez 1995). Without the focused attention of the presidency, industrial policies towards the pharmaceutical sector remained susceptible to clientelist politics and "bureaucratic rings," or informal channels

The Brazilian Context 77

between private sector interests and civil servants. According to Salama and Benoliel (2010: 682), these problems persist to this day: "Political framework in Brazil undermines long-term policies and favors shortsighted ones vis-à-vis R&D investments in the pharmaceutical industry . . . regardless of the strictness of Brazil's patent regime."

Lastly, Brazil's global economic integration was more pronounced than those observed in India and China. Besides the dismantling of several projects for producing raw materials for pharmaceutical production, Brazil's trade liberalization proceeded quicker than in other countries that continued to implement neo-mercantilist policies to penetrate foreign markets. A definitive assessment of the varied reasons for the relative backwardness of Brazil's pharmaceutical sector is beyond the scope of this work. But in subsequent chapters, a more focused view on Brazil's production of antiretroviral medicines (ARVs) used to treat HIV provides nuance into these different claims.

In 2007, the Brazilian pharmaceutical market ranked ninth largest in the world with sales of $12.2 billion or 2.91% of world total (2008). The country was home to 550 pharmaceutical companies that employed 69,000 people (Grupemef/Febrafarma 2007). Market concentration remains skewed towards foreign companies. Studies of Brazil's market at the start of the millennium reveal that 48 companies are foreign-based but are responsible for between 70–80% of the entire Brazilian market in terms of revenue; 18 public labs (or state sector labs) account for less than 5% (selling to the public health sector); and the rest are in the hands of local, privately owned firms, which vary in terms of size and markets (Hasenclever 2002; Palmeira and Pan 2003). The Brazilian company Aché is the largest drug firm with 6.94% of the market, ahead of France's Sanofi-Aventis, with 6.81% (Gadelha 2008).

While the Brazilian market remains dominated by foreign firms, the country is home to a variety of Brazilian-owned companies that produce at varied levels of technological sophistication. Few companies have research and development divisions capable of discovering innovative drugs, so most focus on the growing market of generic medicines. In 2009, Brazil's generic market represented 20% of the total unit sales, with Brazilian generic companies accounting for 88% of this market segment (Pro-Genericos n.d.). While indigenous firms are highly sophisticated in the ability to produce end products in a variety of formulations, few have vertically integrated operations that include research and development divisions or factories to produce APIs. Foreign firms, whose local operations focus on end-stage production and marketing of their products, invest few resources in local R&D, apart from clinical trials. Despite recent industrial policies to encourage both local and foreign firms to invest more R&D, local innovation remains embryonic.

The Brazilian pharmaceutical industry is heavily dependent in the production of APIs and other chemical intermediates required for the production

78   *The Brazilian Context*

of finished dosage forms. After neoliberal reforms of the 1990s, only 23 Brazilian firms remained that could produce active principals, and they accounted for only 17% of the domestic market. Brazilian firms and TNCs imported the remaining 83%. In 2006, medicines imports of $2.6 billion surpassed exports of $622 million; and pharmochemical imports amounted to $1.1 billion compared to US$286 million in exports (Gadelha 2008). The trade deficit in the pharmaceutical sector, which reached $2.8 billion in 2007, continues to stimulate efforts to reduce external dependency.

In Brazil's pharmaceutical market, TNCs retained control over product innovation, raw materials, and market sales. The state made various attempts to promote local industry and encourage upstream investments, but these initiatives never achieved the coherence and long-term planning necessary to develop a strong pharmaceutical base. Instead of the local pharmaceutical industry in a state-mediated alliance with the transnational capital, as described by Evans (1979), dependent development relied on the local health system focused on curative and individualized forms of care to dispense its products. Mendes (1993) described the triple alliance between state, private sector, and foreign capital, which gained hegemony in the 1970s in the following terms:

1) The state is the main financier through the social welfare system;
2) The national private sector is the largest provider of services and medical attention; and
3) The private international sector is the largest producer of inputs, especially biomedical equipment and medicines.

Neoliberal reforms including trade liberalization, price deregulation, and, most importantly, new intellectual property protections only increased the power of foreign capital. While the transnational drug industry complained about local industry copying their products, national firms never posed much of a threat and only accounted for 20% of total market sales. Meanwhile, the *sanitaristas* attempted to break the alliances between the state, the private sector health sector, and the foreign dominated medical-industrial complex.

SOCIAL DEMOCRATIC HEALTH CARE REFORMS AND MEDICINES POLICIES

In contrast to the neoliberal policies adopted in the pharmaceutical sector, policymakers pursued reforms in the health system and medicines inspired by social democratic criteria. As several past studies have demonstrated, a strong professional movement made up of middle-class public health workers criticized the country's health system and led efforts to make changes (Costa 2013; Escorel 1999; Falleti 2009; McGuire 2010; Weyland 1995).

This *Movimento Sanitário* (health reform movement) both criticized the health system under the military regime and later cooperated with it during the early days of the democratization process in order to enact their reforms. Initially tied to the Brazilian Communist party *(Partido Communista Brasileira)*, these progressive public health workers made the following criticisms about the prevailing model of care at the time: the outsourcing of health services to private sector providers, an incentive structure geared towards providing excessive and unnecessary services, an emphasis on curative versus preventative care, and the unequal distribution of public resources to the benefit of the middle and upper classes.

The first initiatives to provide social insurance began in the 1930s and throughout the decades various government initiatives had increased formal coverage to the majority of the population. Most significantly, Brazil's military created the Assistance Fund for Rural Workers *(Fundo de Assistência ao Trabalhador Rural*—FUNRURAL), which increased insurance coverage from 9% of the population to 90% in the early 1970s. Such coverage, however, did not translate into access. Urban workers and government employees continued to receive the bulk of resources slated for the health system. State agencies like the National Social Security Medical Assistance Institute *(Instituto Nacional de Assistência Médica da Previdência Social*—INAMPS), responsible for contracting out services that privileged private medical facilities, incentivized the construction of medical facilities in wealthy, urban areas as opposed to those under the control of the state (Falleti 2009; McGuire 2010). In addition to widespread fraud and waste in disbursements, funding remained volatile due to tax evasion, poor investments, and economic downturns. Claimants often relied on personal connections to an administrative official in order to obtain needed care. In fact, the military government gave the administration of FUNRURAL to rural workers' organizations in order to co-opt labor organizing in the countryside (Falleti 2009)

Costa (2013) reviews the *sanitarista* critiques of the health system during the 1970s and 1980s and their proposals for reform. Through their teaching positions in medical schools, new professional associations, and academic journals, the initial work of leading figures like Hesio Cordeiro and Sergio Arouca, amongst others, espoused the critical normative framework outlined in the previous chapter that linked the country's dependent development to skewed distribution of health outcomes and health resources. Their writings showed how state measures overlooked preventative and collective health needs of the vast majority of the population. To address the system's multiple problems, *sanitaristas* defended a comprehensive set of benefits funded through mandatory disbursements from government budgets through the decentralization of care and resources to state and municipal levels of government. Moreover, they sought to create a more powerful public sector that would displace commercial health interests and ensure universal access.

80   The Brazilian Context

The *sanitarista* movement had two strategies to revamp the country's health system: engage in grassroots mobilization and occupy formal positions in the country's bureaucracy (Escorel 1999; Falleti 2009; Weyland 1995). *Sanitaristas* worked with marginalized communities and encouraged them that the only way to achieve quality and regular access to care was through a major restructuring of the health system. However, poverty and persistent clientelism stymied these efforts. Due to the failure to obtain a strong grassroots base, these health activists looked to the state to achieve their goals. Although critical of the military regime in power, *sanitaristas* infiltrated government health agencies, starting at the municipal and state levels and later the federal government, to implement their ideas. In 1976, they created the Interiorization of Health and Sanitation Program (*Programa de Interiorização das Ações de Saúde e Saneamento*—PIASS), which combined preventative health measures with projects to improve water distribution. With the support of state health secretariats, they started Integrated Health Actions (*Ações Integradas de Saúde*—AIS) to decentralize more resources from INAMPS (Falleti 2009).

By the time Brazil began its democratic transition (1985–1990), *sanitaristas* had already articulated health as a human right, carried out several successful pilot programs throughout the country, and outlined a coherent plan of action for restructuring the health system based on universal access. Additionally, they demanded state-mandated minimums of public resources slated for the health system as well as the prominent role of the state in service delivery. During the writing of Brazil's new Constitution in 1988, these activist health professionals presented a coherent proposal for outlining the role and duty of the state in relation to the health system. Through their ties to reform-minded politicians in charge of writing the document, they were able to influence various articles related to health (196–200). Article 196 of the Constitution of 1988 states that health is a fundamental right:

> Health is a right of all and a duty of the State and shall be guaranteed by means of social and economic policies aimed at reducing the risk of illness and other hazards and at the universal and equal access to actions and services for its promotion, protection and recovery.[7]

Article 200 justifies continued state intervention in the production of strategic inputs: "The single health system shall . . . participate in the production of drugs, equipment, immunobiological products, hemoproducts, and other inputs." Health became a universal right no longer associated with affiliations to a social insurance coverage, and the state assumed responsibility for leading the provision of preventative and curative care (Ferraz 2011; Weyland 1995).

The 1990 Federal Health Law *(Lei 8.080)* codified how the constitutional right to health should be implemented and specified the organization, guiding principles, and operations into a new Unified Health System (*Sistema*

Única da Saúde—SUS). These include constitutional directives regarding decentralization of management to the federal, state, and municipal spheres; integrality of service provision so that health problems of individuals and communities are treated in their entirety; and social participation. To this effect, the public health system has been decentralized to 26 states and 5,508 municipalities, and health councils have been established at the municipal, state, and federal levels to make decisions, provide directives, and monitor actions. The 1990 Federal Law on Health reinforced the principles of universality (health is everyone's right) and equity (everyone has the equal opportunity to use the public health system irrespective of social class).

Contrary to the wishes of *sanitaristas*, the law also enshrined the role of the private sector and did not achieve more expansive reforms desired by the *sanitaristas*. Article 199 in the Constitution specifies that private enterprise may participate in the provision of health assistance in a supplementary manner yet regulated by the state. "Medical business, established bureaucrats, and clientelist politicians had blocked the effort at profound health reform. These conservative forces had survived the attack from the sanitary movement and succeeded in preserving many parameters of the existing system," argues Weyland (1995: 1709).

While SUS offers care for the entire population, roughly 25% of the population, mainly 40 million middle- and upper-class Brazilians, purchase tax-deductible private insurance plans. In effect, a two-tiered health system came into existence. First is a system of universal public provision geared towards the general population and known as the SUS. Through this system, health reforms have expanded access to primary and preventative care, resulting in drastic reductions in infant mortality and other public health problems (McGuire 2010). The second is the entrenched system of private hospitals and insurance policies that cater to the middle and upper classes that *sanitaristas* had failed to transform.

Medicines policies and programs trailed the evolution and reforms in the rest of the health sector. In the 1970s, CEME distributed a list of essential medicines to those earning the official minimum wage or less, while the rest of the sector faced price controls. Access remained a problem. In the 1980s, CEME estimated that only 47% of the population had regular access to essential medicines (Bermudez 1995). In the view of the *sanitaristas*, the middle and upper classes obtained better access to medicines through social insurance schemes administered through government programs that favored urban and wealthy classes. Oliveira and Teixeira (1986: 209) critique the system in the following terms:

> . . . state intervention in the area of health, opting for curative and individual medical practice through the Social Security system, led to the creation of a medico-industrial-complex, responsible for high rates of capital accumulation of the great international monopolies in the production of medicines and medical equipment.

82 The Brazilian Context

In their view, public resources favored urban middle and upper classes' access to medicines and profiteering by transnational drug companies.

Federal efforts to provide basic medicines continued to run up against institutional barriers and problems. The Ministry of Health started the Basic Pharmacy *(Farmacia Basica)* in 1987 with the provision of 60 medicines to municipalities throughout Brazil. However, in the evaluation of Bermudez (1995), political clientelism that negatively impacted the operations of CEME undermined the program. Successive governments initiated neoliberal policies in the early 1990s that removed price regulations, and policymakers finally closed CEME in 1997 amidst allegations of corruption. With the closure of CEME, the Ministry of Health's lab, Farmanguinhos, assumed responsibility for producing and procuring a kit of basic medicines used by the federal Family Health Program (see Ministry of Health 2002a). The federal government later initiated a Basic Pharmacy Program in 1998, which subsequently was decentralized to state governments, who, in turn, began to craft their own programs (Cosendey et al. 2000).

With the federal government reorganizing the health system and providing minimal forms of pharmaceutical coverage, the public remained dependent on accessing medicines at local pharmacies. Purchasing medicines at pharmacies increased consumer dependence on market fluctuations. As trade liberalization and market deregulation of the pharmaceutical sector progressed, the prices of prescription drugs increased. Between 1989 and 1999, drug prices rose 54% above inflation while per capita consumption fell (Ministry of Health 2000). In a country with widespread inequality, consumption varies greatly according to income strata. One sector analysis estimated that by the end of the 1990s, 40% of the Brazilian population from lower income brackets did not have sufficient resources to purchase medicines at retail pharmacies (Callegari 2000).

The promotion of neoliberal pharmaceutical policies came to a halt at the end of the 1990s as demands for sector re-regulation increased. A veritable crisis in the pharmaceutical market due to price hikes and falsification of products gained the media's spotlight, resulting in congressional investigations in November of 1999. Media attention led to renewed state market intervention and policies aimed at increasing access. In addition, a new health minister, Jose Serra, who had the backing of the presidency, pushed for expansive pharmaceutical reforms.

In October 1998, the Ministry of Health issued the New Medicines Policy *(Portaria n° 3.916)* for supplying medicines through SUS. Initiatives included an updated list of essential medicines, minimum levels of care, and decentralization of basic pharmaceutical services. In principle, the federal government finances 50% of the budget for medicines purchases, and state and municipal governments each provide 25% of the funding. The policy led to increased transfers of federal resources to state and municipal governments. Additional measures focused on rational use of pharmaceuticals, improved logistics and operations, incentives to improve drug production,

The Brazilian Context   83

and price transparency. Lastly, the Ministry revamped centralized purchases for the procurement of high-cost medicines. The new law precipitated two additional reforms affecting access to medicines—ANVISA and rules governing generics.

The National Health Surveillance Agency (*Agência Nacional de Vigilância Sanitária*—ANVISA), modeled after the United States' Food and Drug Administration (FDA), was created in January 1999. The agency represented the start of a new regulatory framework for medicines, as well as for food and other areas of health surveillance. Since the mid-1980s, health professionals had been demanding the creation of an agency that would have administrative independence and financial autonomy. Drug companies interested in protecting their brand names also lobbied for a strong enforcement agency to investigate fraud. Besides approving registrations for the commercialization of pharmaceutical products and inspecting factories at home and abroad, ANVISA has additional responsibilities, such as monitoring and controlling prices of certain drugs and medical inputs.

One of the most polemical federal rules was a Presidential Directive *(Medida Provisória)* in 1999 that requires the National Institute of Industrial Property *(Instituto Nacional de Propriedad Intellectual*—INPI), responsible for ruling on patentability, to consult with ANVISA before conferring a drug patent (Basso 2006). Health officials at the time believed that the patent office did not have the expertise to analyze patent claims for drugs, especially to ensure that the novelty requirement is truly satisfied. The Presidential Directive later became law in 2001, specifying that a pharmaceutical product cannot receive a patent until ANVISA gives "prior consent." The change has resulted in a turf wars between the two government agencies and has resulted in a large backlog in patent approvals. PhRMA and the US government continue to pressure their Brazilian counterparts to remove what is known as the "prior consent" mechanism (Shadlen 2011).[8]

The last major policy initiative of the 1990s was the Generics Act of 1999. The law established the conditions for licensing, as well as technical standards and norms for reference, innovative, generic, and similar drugs. While both generics and similars are copies of off-patent medications, only generics have passed tests of bioavailability and bioequivalence. In other words, both generics and similars contain the same active pharmaceutical ingredient, but only generics are proven to be interchangeable to the reference or innovator product in terms of safety, efficacy, and quality.[9] INTERFARMA, the industry association representing transnational drug companies, lobbied against the legislation and launched campaigns aimed at consumers and physicians questioning the quality of generic medicines (Bermudez and Oliveira 2004). After the bill's passage, the government launched successive media campaigns to educate the public about the safety and effectiveness of generics, as well as their cheaper price. Ten years after the ruling, local drug makers control most of this growing market segment (Pro-Genericos n.d.).

84   The Brazilian Context

Since the turn of the century, the Ministry of Health has increased expenditures on medicines and investments in public labs, as well as initiated industrial policies for the sector (see Chapter 6). Federal expenditures on medicines increased from R$1.9 billion in 2003 to a proposed R$4.7 billion in 2007, and spending has increased in all categories. For "high cost medicines" outlays have increased by R$1 billion, and expenditures on AIDS medicines have nearly doubled in the five-year period. Between 2002 and 2006, federal spending on medicines jumped 124% versus a 9.6% increase on total health outlays (Ministry of Health/Secretaria Executiva 2007). Part of the reason for the difference in growth rates is due to the low level of public drug purchases in the 1990s and renewed efforts to increase pharmaceutical coverage. The other factor is the high costs of medicines now protected by patent, and/or have few suppliers. A more focused examination of antiretrovirals (ARVs) in subsequent chapters provides insight into the costs of pharmaceutical autonomy.

Pharmaceutical acquisitions by the Ministry of Health occur on a yearly basis (unless emergency purchases need to be made) and follow strict procurement guidelines. Public procurement made by all sectors of the Brazilian government, including the Ministry of Health and public labs, is governed by Public Procurement Law 8.666. Approved after a corruption scandal involving Brazil's first elected president after the military dictatorship, Fernando Collor, the law was passed by Congress in 1993 to reestablish credibility in government purchases. The guidelines set forth in the law have led to an increase in bureaucratic procedures while establishing as a reference the lowest price for purchases without consideration of national production or other criteria. While important for addressing corruption in the public sphere, the law has become an obstacle when attempting to use the purchasing power of the state to develop the domestic pharmaceutical industry, especially with regard to the local production of ARVs (Marques and Hasenclever 2008).[10]

Contrary to other accounts that emphasize changes to Brazil's health reforms occurring as a result of a "critical juncture" of Brazil's return to democracy, my assessment concurs with the work of Falletti (2009) that the *sanitarista* movement began laying the foundations for a federally integrated and universally accessible health system since the early 1970s. Brazil's democratic transition presented new opportunities for their goal to achieve universal care through state provision. Despite the increase in funding and consolidation of countrywide health programs, Brazil's public health system continues to suffer from lack of funding, long lines, and shortages to such a degree that the principles of SUS—universality, integrality, and equity—remain a challenge (a topic that is taken up again in the conclusion). *Sanitaristas* laid the normative foundations based on broad social democratic criteria but failed to achieve their ideals due to the lack of a grassroots base.

Nonetheless, the health sector represents a dramatic change in state-society relations from military rule to more inclusive government. Public participation in health policies and oversight has been institutionalized in the form of health councils at the municipal, state, and federal levels.[11] High prices and substandard medicines galvanized congressional investigations that led to the creation of new agencies and programs to address the country's pharmaceutical needs. The concept of citizenship rights, which achieved its most fervent expression when dealing with the HIV/AIDS epidemic, provides the institutional backdrop for understanding Brazil's treatment activism.

THE ORIGINS OF AIDS TREATMENT ACTIVISM

Compared to efforts in revamping the country's health system, the *sanitaristas* achieved the greatest success in achieving their ideals when implementing Brazil's AIDS program. In the case of SUS, these public health reformers faced conservative politicians, entrenched government bureaucrats, and private sector interests. AIDS policies were different. Besides gaining the support of Brazil's leading politicians, the program led to the creation of a new agency, the National AIDS Program, with new funding that sidestepped the traditional bureaucracy.[12] Private sector challenges only came later when the government adopted the strategy of local production of medicines and aggressive price negotiations with the transnational drug industry. Most importantly, the *sanitaristas* had the support of a mobilized, grassroots base. When attempting to mobilize a grassroots base in order to enact expansive health reforms, *sanitaristas* never had much of a popular following due to widespread poverty and persistent clientelism of communities they attempted to organize. In contrast, those affected by AIDS came from a different socio-economic profile. The epidemic was first diagnosed in São Paulo in the 1980s amongst urban, middle-class professionals. "One of the major risk factors was having traveled to the United States," recounts Marco Antonio Vitoria, a physician who helped establish Brazil's AIDS Program, of the early days of the epidemic.[13]

Apart from the socio-demographic characteristics of those infected, the political context also affected the shape of AIDS policies (Bastos 1999; Galvão 2005; Nunn 2008; Parker 1997, 2003). Brazil's democratic transition during the 1980s was a time rich with discussions of citizenship and the development of civic associations interested in redefining state-society relationships. The democratic opening provided a gateway for a new group of actors to make demands against the state. Vitória summed up the importance of socio-political context:

> There was a political decision on the part of the government to call out partners to sit and develop a participatory policy with the involvement of civil society in this whole process. Without the initiative of the government, it would have been difficult for the thing to have happened, and without the participation of civil society I think the process of a

86   The Brazilian Context

true synergism in that very favorable political moment would not have happened. AIDS was the first experiment of the new SUS model. That is why I say that if AIDS would have happened before or after SUS it would not have turned out the way that it did.[14]

Framing AIDS as a human rights issue provided the glue that undergirded state-society alliances.[15] Galvão (2000: 167–73) details the discourse of human rights was appropriated by people with HIV, national programs, religious organizations, international financial organizations, health professionals, and NGOs. Perspectives on human rights and AIDS varied. The World Bank took a narrow view in that human rights offer protections to those infected and the rest of the society.[16] AIDS activists in Brazil, on the contrary, equated the human rights dimension of the disease with expansive notions of citizenship rights that developed in their struggle against Brazil's military dictatorship—the "right to have rights." In Brazil's new democracy, theses activists viewed AIDS as part of a larger struggle for social justice, poverty alleviation, and social equality (Galvão 2000). "The rich social movement responding to AIDS in Brazil from 1985 to 1995 cannot be understood without reference to the international movement and to the historical moment lived then by Brazilian society, which was overcoming two decades of military rule," adds Bastos (1999: 149).

The characterization of AIDS as rooted in broader social issues resonated with international health activists and local *sanitaristas*. Jonathan Mann, who established the World Health Organization's first programmatic efforts to fight the disease, consistently argued that human rights violations increased the spread of HIV.[17] In Brazil, AIDS activists and health professionals published the *Declaration of Fundamental Rights of People with HIV (Declaração dos Direitos Fundamentais da Pessoa Portadora do Vírus da Aids)* in 1989. The document outlined that people with HIV have the right to participate fully in society, not to be subject to discrimination, and not have tests performed against their will, or be quarantined. Item three in the *Declaration* states that "Every carrier of the AIDS virus has the right to assistance and to treatment, given without any restriction, guaranteeing improved quality of life."[18]

Rights-based discourse influenced the constitution and strategies of AIDS NGOs (Galvão et al. 2009; Parker 1997). In the 1980s, the main routes of transmission were homosexual sex and intravenous drug use, and news articles and the Brazilian media characterized the disease in discriminatory and prejudiced terms. Civil society organizations combatted these images through media campaigns that provided information and unbiased messages about the new disease. Rio de Janeiro-based ABIA initiated a campaign to clean up the country's poorly regulated blood supply. AIDS NGOs also reached out to religious groups and opened care and information centers throughout the country, and provided support to lower socio-economic groups who increasingly comprised new HIV cases by the end of the decade.

When antiretroviral drugs (ARVs) for HIV became available by the end of the 1990s, AIDS NGOs already developed advocacy experience and strong ties to activist health professionals. These experiences informed treatment activism. Due to civil society pressure, SUS began to distribute medicines for opportunistic infections in 1988 (de Mello e Souza 2007). For their part, *sanitaristas* played a key role in stimulating public pressure and ensuring access to medicines on a collective and not individual basis. The city health department in São Paulo distributed zidovudine treatments as early as 1989 and combination therapy in 1995—a year before it became the worldwide standard in 1996. At the federal level, the National AIDS Program began to distribute zidovudine in the early 1990s.

Since the early days of treatment, AIDS bureaucrats emphasized that medicines should be provided free of charge in order to ensure compliance and avoid the development of gray markets.[19]Although initial supplies were limited and covered minimal amount of need, Teixeira asserts that providing treatment "was a deliberate initiative as part of a strategy to create a need, to generate demands, and to spark involvement by society on the issue" (Teixeira 2003: 185). The strategy worked as AIDS NGOs pressured local governments to address shortages. GAPA-São Paulo, which began mobilizing around access to medicines in 1992, brought the first court case requesting access to AIDS medicines on behalf of schoolteacher Nair Soares Brito. In July 1996, the Brazilian judge, basing his decision on the Constitution's mandate concerning health as a human right, ordered the state of São Paulo to supply her with zidovudine for free.

At the federal level, synergies between the state and the government increased with outside funding. In the early 1990s, the World Bank estimated that Brazil's epidemic would result in 1.2 million infections by the turn of the century. Notwithstanding modeling errors in these initial forecasts, the Bank's resources allowed for increased participation of NGOs in programmatic efforts (Mattos, Júnior, and Parker 2003). The National AIDS Program signed a $250 million loan agreement ($160 million from the World Bank and $90 million from the Brazilian government) in 1993 to establish prevention and control activities. In the case of HIV, technical personnel from the Bank involved in the loan agreement did not push a neoliberal stance but instead shared many of the views of their Brazilian counterparts (Biehl 2007).

World Bank loans led to the development of a relatively autonomous bureaucracy (Gomez 2011; Nunn 2008; Rich 2013). While AIDS directors determined overall policy direction, the loan agreement gave UNESCO (The United Nations Educational, Scientific, and Cultural Organization) control over the management of the AIDS budget. This arrangement allowed AIDS officials to sidestep cumbersome government rules on spending, staffing, and salaries in order to hire experienced professionals, some of whom came from civil society. Increasingly, leaders of the NGO community began working as consultants for the National AIDS Program, as was the case of

88 *The Brazilian Context*

Stalin Pedrosa, a director from Pela VIDDA, who was chosen to interface with civil society organizations bidding on projects (Bastos 1999; see also Nunn 2008).

Brazil's approach to AIDS resembles the ideal approaches praised by experts in the field. "Many of the best government programs are the ones that have co-opted the NGOs, sucked up their experience, their know-how, sometimes their staff," claims epidemiologist Elisabeth Pisani (2009: 179). Contrary to the trend of outsourcing services and competing with NGOs (Roberts 2005), the Brazilian state centralized AIDS policy making and established clear lines of action between the state and civil society organizations. The National AIDS Program focused on treatment and national prevention strategies, while NGOs worked at the community level and outreach programs with high-risk groups.

While some civil society campaigners raised concerns about possible co-optation and changing efforts from "protest to proposal" when receiving government grants, the merging of state and society proved crucial in terms of treatment activism. First, international experts, the World Bank included, argued that it would be more cost effective for developing countries to invest their limited resources in prevention instead of costly treatments. But the AIDS officials and civil society partners resisted these pressures and maintained that treatment was a right that could not be denied to their citizens (Galvão 2005; Mattos, Júnior, and Parker 2003). Second, although the state had begun to distribute AIDS medicines for free by the mid-1990s, coverage remained incomplete, stock-outs frequent, and funding limited. AIDS activists staged nationwide protests in 1995 to demand access to the expensive medicines and used the court system to press their demands. As if by design, the World Bank loan that provided monies to NGOs to carryout prevention and education activities also provided the means to increase treatment activism.

In November 1996, the efforts of treatment activists culminated in the passage of Law 9.313, known as Sarney's Law, or *Lei Sarney,* which mandated that the state provide *free* AIDS treatments through the public health system to everyone in need. It is named after conservative politician Jose Sarney, a former president and senator, who was able to use his political position to obtain rapid approval of the law by overcoming objections from then President Cardoso and other lawmakers (Nunn 2008).

The law goes beyond Brazil's Constitution of 1988, which mandates that the state will guarantee access to health, yet does not obligate the government to provide all treatments for free. The passage of the legislation came on the heels of announcements by the scientific community that triple-therapy is successful combating the disease. Monotherapy failed in treating HIV, but the use of up to three different ARV drugs attacking various points of viral replication changed AIDS from a death sentence to a chronic disease. While medicines policies throughout SUS remained underfunded and increasingly decentralized to states, Sarney's Law resulted in a vertical and centralized

The Brazilian Context 89

program for the provision of free AIDS treatments throughout the country. The National AIDS Program assumed responsibility for procuring expensive ARVs, while decentralizing the procurement of medicines used to treat opportunistic infections to state and local governments. The legislation also instructed the Ministry of Health to standardize treatment protocols, that is, establish guidelines for when people should begin taking medicines and determine which medicines should be used as first-, second-, and third-line treatments. Consequently, an advisory group to the National AIDS Program meets regularly to review scientific findings concerning ARVs. Their conclusions constitute the therapeutic consensus which physicians are encouraged to follow when prescribing medications.[20]

Sarney's Law gave the state a powerful mandate to distribute AIDS treatments above and beyond current initiatives, but there were no guarantees that Congress would budget enough funding, especially during Brazil's turbulent economy of the 1990s. Politicians and even some health officials worried about the cost. Nunn (2008) provides rich details about the social movement tactics employed during the early history of treatment rollout. When Health Minister Carlos Albuquerque opined in 1997 that too much of the ministry's budget was being spent on AIDS and Congress considered spending cuts, AIDS officials and civil society partners went on the offensive. Pedro Chequer, the AIDS Director at the time, publicly denounced his boss, warned about stock-outs, and emphasized the state's legal obligations, while NGOs staged protests and threatened to flood the courts with lawsuits. In the end, politicians balked. Albuquerque's subsequent exit from the Ministry of Health demonstrated the political costs of challenging AIDS treatment activists. Treatment activists convinced politicians like Sarney, Cardoso, and Albuquerque's replacement, Jose Serra, about the potential losses and political gains in relation to essential medicines (Nunn 2008).

Another World Bank loan disbursed in 1998 provided AIDS bureaucrats with the resources to establish the necessary treatment infrastructure throughout the country and further institutionalized treatment activism through grants to NGOs. The World Bank loan, used in combination with federal funding, helped to establish treatment infrastructure. Besides hospitals operated by SUS and outpatient services, the National AIDS Program set up the National Network of 66 laboratories for testing HIV viral load, 78 laboratories for measuring CD4+ cell count, and a national ARV logistic control system of 480 dispensary units (Serra 2004). Even the country's 1999 monetary crisis and ensuing fiscal austerity did not affect AIDS budgets.

Recent history of citizenship struggles and successful AIDS programs laid the domestic foundation for battles that would later occur at the international level. The social context, institutional framework, and most importantly, the strength of social ties across the state-society proved fundamental for achieving universal access to AIDS treatment. In fact, President Fernando Henrique Cardoso claims that the "state and the social movement

90   *The Brazilian Context*

practically fused" (quoted in Biehl 2004: 114). Brazil's AIDS policies, compared to the rest of the health care system, demonstrate the important role of institutional activists and shared notions of health as a social justice issue.

In combatting the AIDS epidemic, the *sanitaristas* appear to have achieved their ideals. These included a rights-based approach to health, emphasis on both treatment and prevention, social participation by society, and a strong role of the state in system delivery. AIDS policies differed from the rest of the system because the *sanitaristas* developed strong links with a grassroots base and could construct a new health agency as opposed to revamping a large, complex system. Their political strength swayed politicians skeptical of the high costs of medicines. The next chapter highlights Brazil's efforts to produce the first generation of HIV medicines and foreign challenges from the US government and foreign-based drug companies against Brazil's efforts. Control over technology, new international alliances, and the extension of the human rights framework would play critical roles in Brazil's ability to achieve pharmaceutical autonomy in the brave new world of patents.

NOTES

1. Previous scholars have written about the connections between the *sanitaristas* and Brazil's HIV policies (Bastos 1999; see Berkman et al. 2005; Nunn 2008; Teixeira, Vitória, and Barcarolo 2003).
2. Eloan Pinheiro. Interview with author. Rio de Janeiro. June 8, 2008.
3. Cardoso was in charge of pushing the legislation dating from the time he was Minister of Foreign Affairs, October 1992 to May 1993.
4. Rubens Ricupero. Interview with author. São Paulo, SP. October 15, 2007.
5. Nelson Brasil. Interview with author. Rio de Janeiro, RJ. June 30, 2008.
6. Jorge Raimundo. Interview with author. Rio de Janeiro, RJ. June 20, 2008.
7. English translation from Brazil's Federal Supreme Court: www.stf.jus.br/repositorio/cms/portalStfInternacional/portalStfSobreCorte_en_us/anexo/constituicao_ingles_3ed2010.pdf.
8. The prior consent mechanism is permitted by TRIPS, since the accord says that member countries can determine the procedures and government agencies responsible for evaluating claims.
9. See Homedes and Ugalde (2005b) concerning the differences of multi-source drugs in Latin America.
10. Chapter Four addresses the challenges posed by Law 8.666 to the development of local ARV capacity, and Chapter Five changes to the law.
11. There continue to remain problems with particularistic interests prevailing over the common welfare by those who participate in health councils (see Pereira Neto 2012).
12. The National AIDS Program later achieved the status of a department in the Ministry of Health, Department of STDs/AIDS and Viral Hepatitis. The Department's location in a recently constructed, modern building contrasts with the Ministry of Health's structure that was built in the 1960s.
13. Marco Antônio Vitória. Interview with author. Geneva, Switzerland. August 15, 2006.
14. Ibid.

15. Several other scholars have highlighted the synergistic role between state and society (see Bastos 1999; Biehl 2004; Galvão 2000; Gomez 2009; Nunn 2008; Passarelli and Júnior 2003; Rich 2013; Teixeira, Vitória, and Barcarolo 2003).
16. "Because people can be infected with HIV and transmit it to others for years before they become ill, the disease defines and creates a new minority group in society. Government responses to the difficult task of balancing the interests of the infected against the interests of others have varied widely." World Bank (1997) *Confronting AIDS: Public Priorities in a Global Epidemic* (quoted in Galvão 2000: 168 ft. 5).
17. See also Farmer (1999).
18. Ministry of Brazil. National AIDS Program. *Direitos Fundamentais.* www. aids.gov.br/pagina/direitos-fundamentais. In 1996, the National AIDS Program also created the National Network of Human Rights of HIV *(Rede de Direitos Humanos em HIV/AIDS),* but the network appears to have little impact on policy since many civil society participants questioned the necessity of another organization.
19. Paulo Teixeira. Interview with author. São Paulo, SP. May 7, 2008.
20. Appendices Three and Four list ARVs according to their drug classification and provides the date they were included in the therapeutic consensus and producers registered to distribute the drug.

REFERENCES

Amsden, Alice. 2001. *The Rise of "The Rest."* Oxford: Oxford University Press.
Basso, Maristela. 2006. "Intervention of Health Authorities in Patent Examination: The Brazilian Practice of the Prior Consent." *International Journal of Intellectual Property Management* 1(1/2): 54–74.
Bastos, Cristiana. 1999. *Global Responses to AIDS.* Bloomington and Indianapolis: Indiana University Press.
Berkman, Alan, Jonathan Garcia, Miguel Muñoz-Laboy, Vera Paiva, and Richard Parker. 2005. "A Critical Analysis of the Brazilian Response to HIV/AIDS: Lessons Learned for Controlling and Mitigating the Epidemic in Developing Countries." *American Journal of Public Health* 95(7): 1162–72.
Bermudez, Jorge. 1995. *Industria Farmaceutica, Estado E Sociedade: Critica Da Politica de Medicamentos No Brasil.* São Paulo: Hucitec/Sobrevime.
Bermudez, Jorge, and Maria Auxiliardora Oliveira. 2004. *Intellectual Property in the Context of the WTO Trips Agreement: Challenges to Public Health.* Rio de Janeiro: ENSP.
Bertero, Carlos Osmar. 1972. "Drugs and Dependency in Brazil—An Empirical Study of Dependency Theory: The Case of the Pharmaceutical Industry." (Dissertation). Ithaca: Cornell University.
Biehl, João. 2004. "The Activist State: Global Pharmaceuticals, AIDS, and Citizenship in Brazil." *Social Text* 22(3): 105–32.
Biehl, João. 2007. *Will To Live.* Princeton: Princeton University Press.
Callegari, L. 2000. *Análise Setorial—A Indústria Farmacêutica—Panarama Setorial.* São Paulo: Gazeta Mercantil.
Cohn, Samuel. 2012. *Employment and Development under Globalization: State and Economy in Brazil.* Hampshire and New York: Palgrave Macmillan.
Cosendey, Marly Aparecida, Jorge Bermudez, André Luis de Almeida dos Reis, Hayne Felipe da Silva, Maria Auxiliadora Oliveira, and Vera Lúcia Luiza. 2000. "Assistência Farmacêutica Na Atenção Básica de Saúde: A Experiência de Três Estados Brasileiros." *Cadernos da Saúde Pública* 16: 171–82.

92 The Brazilian Context

Costa, Nilson do Rosário. 2013. "Expert Community and Sectoral Policy: The Brazilian Sanitary Reform." Pp. 219–32 in *Policy Analysis in Brazil*, edited by Jeni Vaitsman, Lenaura Lobato, and Jose M. Ribeiro. Bristol: Policy Press.

Escorel, Sarah. 1999. *Reviravolta Na Saúde: Origem E Articulação Do Movimento Sanitário*. Rio de Janeiro: Editora Fiocruz.

Esping-Anderson, Gøsta. 1990. *The Three Worlds of Welfare Capitalism*. Cambridge: Polity Press.

Evans, Peter. 1979. *Dependent Development: The Alliance of Multinational, State, and Local Capital in Brazil*. Princeton: Princeton University Press.

Evans, Peter. 1995. *Embedded Autonomy: States and Industrial Transformation*. Princeton: Princeton University Press.

Falleti, Tulia. 2009. "Infiltrating the State. The Evolution of Health Care Reforms in Brazil, 1964–1988." Pp. 38–62 in *Explaining Institutional Change: Ambiguity, Agency, and Power*, edited by James Mahoney and Kathleen Thelen. Leiden: Cambridge University Press.

Farmer, P. 1999. "Pathologies of Power: Rethinking Health and Human Rights." *American Journal of Public Health* 89(10): 1486–96.

Ferraz, Octavio Luiz Mo. 2011. "Health Inequalities, Rights, and Courts: The Social Impact of the Judicialization of Health." Pp. 76–100 in *Litigating Health Rights: Can Courts Bring More Justice to Health?* edited by Alicia Ely Yamin. Boston: Harvard University Press.

Franco, Rolando. 1996. "Social Policy Paradigms in Latin America." *CEPAL Review* 58: 9–23.

Flynn, Matthew. 2008. "Public Production of Anti-Retroviral Medicines in Brazil, 1990–2007." *Development and Change* 39(4): 513–36.

Gadelha, Carlos. 2008. *Estudo Setorial Sobre a Indústria Farmacêutica*. São Paulo: Fundação Instituto de Pesquisas Econômicas (FIPE).

Galvão, Jane. 2000. *AIDS No Brasil: A Agenda De Construção De Uma Epidemia*. 1st ed. Rio de Janeiro and São Paulo: Associação Brasileira Interdisciplinar de AIDS-Editora 34.

Galvão, Jane. 2005. "Brazil and Access to HIV/AIDS Drugs: A Question of Human Rights and Public Health." *American Journal of Public Health* 95(7): 1110–16.

Galvão, Jane, Paulo Roberto Teixeira, Marco Vitória, and Mauro Schechter. 2009. "How the Pandemic Shapes the Public Health Response—The Case of HIV/AIDS in Brazil." Pp. 135–50 in *Public Health Aspects of HIV/AIDS in Low and Middle Income Countries*, edited by David D. Celentano and Chris Beyrer. New York: Springer.

Gomez, Eduardo J. 2009. "The Politics of Receptivity and Resistance: How Brazil, India, China, and Russia Strategically Use the International Health Community in Response to HIV/AIDS: A Theory." *Global Health Governance* 3(1): 1–29.

Gomez, Eduardo J. 2011. "How Brazil Outpaced the United States When It Came to AIDS: The Politics of Civic Infiltration, Reputation, and Strategic Internationalization." *Journal of Health Politics, Policy and Law* 36(2): 317–52.

Grabowski, Richard. 1994. "The Successful Developmental State: Where Does It Come From?" *World Development* 22(3): 413–22.

Grupemef/Febrafarma. 2007. "Mercado Farmacêutico—Brasil." Retrieved October 25, 2008 (www.febrafarma.org.br).

Hasenclever, Lia. 2002. *Diagnóstico Da Indústria Farmacêutica Brasileira*. Brasília/Rio de Janeiro: UNESCO/Fundação Universitária Joaquim Nabuco—Instituto de Economia—Universidade Federal do Rio de Janeiro (UFRJ).

Homedes, Nuria, and Antonio Ugalde. 2005a. "Why Neoliberal Health Reforms Have Failed in Latin America." *Health Policy* 71(1): 83–96.

Homedes, Nuria, and Antonio Ugalde. 2005b. "Multisource Drug Policies in Latin America: Survey of 10 Countries." *Bulletin of the World Health Organization* 83: 64–70.

The Brazilian Context 93

Huber, Evelyne, and John Stephens. 2012. *Democracy and the Left Social Policy and Inequality in Latin America.* Chicago: The University of Chicago Press.

Johnson, Chalmers. 1982. *MITI and the Japanese Miracle: The Growth of Industrial Policy, 1925–1975.* Stanford: Stanford University Press.

Lin, Justin, and Ha-Joon Chang. 2009. "Should Industrial Policy in Developing Countries Conform to Comparative Advantage or Defy It? A Debate between Justin Lin and Ha-Joon Chang." *Development Policy Review* 27(5): 483–502.

Marques, Felipe, and Lia Hasenclever. 2006. "Política de Compra Governamentais: O Caso Das Compras de Anti-Retrovirais E Seus Efeitos Nocivos À Indústria Nacional." Rio de Janeiro: UFRJ-Instituto de Economia.

Marshall, Thomas H. 1977. *Class, Citizenship, and Social Development: Essays by T. H. Marshall.* Chicago: University of Chicago Press.

Mattos, Ruben Araújo de, Veriano Terto Júnior, and Richard Parker. 2003. "World Bank Strategies and the Response to AIDS in Brazil." *Divulgação em Saúde para Debate* 27: 215–27.

Mazzoleni, Roberto, and Luciano Martins Costa Póvoa. 2010. "Accumulation of Technological Capabilities and Economic Development." Pp. 280–314 in *Intellectual Property Rights, Development, and Catch Up: An International Comparative Study,* edited by Hiroyuki Odagiri. Oxford: Oxford University Press.

McGuire, James W. 2010. "From Laggard to Leader in Basic Health Services." Pp. 149–80 in *Wealth, Health, and Democracy in East Asia and Latin America,* edited by James McGuire. New York: Cambridge University Press.

De Mello e Souza, Andre. 2007. "Defying Globalization: Effective Self-Reliance in Brazil." Pp. 37–63 in *The Global Politics of AIDS,* edited by Paul G. Harris and Patricia D. Siplon. Boulder: Lynne Rienner Publishers.

Mendes, Eugênio Vilaça. 1993. "As politicas de saude no brasil e a construção da hegemonia do projeto neoliberal." Pp. 19–91 in *Distrito sanitário: o processo social de mudança das práticas sanitárias do Sistema Unico de Saúde,* edited by Eugênio Vilaça Mendes and Carmen Fontes Teixeira. São Paulo-Rio de Janeiro: Hucitec-Abrasco.

Ministry of Health. 2000. *A Dor Dos Remédios.* Brasília: Ministry of Health.

Ministry of Health. 2002a. *Far-Manguinhos: Remédio Para O Brasil.* Rio de Janeiro: Ministry of Health/FioCruz.

Ministry of Health. 2002b. *Política Federal de Assistência Farmaceutica 1990 a 2002.* Brasilia: Ministry of Health.

Ministry of Health/Secretaria Executiva. 2007. "Evolução Dos Gastos Do Ministério Da Saúde Com Medicamentos." Brasília: Ministry of Health.

Nunn, Amy. 2008. *The Politics and History of AIDS Treatment in Brazil.* New York: Springer.

Oliveira, Egléubia. 2007. "Política de Produção Pública de Medicamentos No Brasil: O Caso Do Laboratório Farmacêutico Do Estado de Pernambuco (LAFEPE)." (Doctoral Thesis). Rio de Janeiro: Escola Nacional de Saúde Pública Sergio Arouca, Fundação Oswaldo Cruz.

Oliveira, Jaime Antônio de Araújo, and Sonia Maria Fleury Teixeira. 1986. *(Im)previdência social: 60 anos de história da previdência no Brasil.* Petropolis: Vozes.

Orsi, Fabienne, Lia Hasenclever, Beatriz Fialho, Paulo Tigre, and Benjamin Coriat. 2003. "Intellectual Property Rights, Anti-AIDS Policy and Generic Drugs." Pp. 109–35 in *Economics of AIDS and Access to HIV/AIDS Care in Developing Countries. Issues and Challenges,* edited by Benjamin Coriat. Paris: Agence Nationale pour Recherche sur le Sida.

Palmeira, Pedro, and Simon Shi Koo Pan. 2003. "Cadeia Farmacêutica No Brasil: Avaliação Preliminar E Perspectivas." *BNDES Setorial* 18: 3–22.

Parker, Richard. 1997. *Políticas, Instituicões E AIDS: Enfrentando a Epidemia No Brasil.* Rio de Janeiro: Jorge Zahar/ABIA.

94 The Brazilian Context

Parker, Richard. 2003. "Building the Foundations for the Response to HIV/AIDS in Brazil: The Development of HIV/AIDS Policy, 1982–1996." *Divulgação em Saúde para Debate* 27: 143–83.

Passarelli, Carlos André, and Veriano Terto Júnior. 2003. "Non-Governmental Organizations and Access to Anti-Retroviral Treatments in Brazil." *Divulgação em Saúde pare Debate* 27: 252–64.

Pereira Neto, Andres. 2012. *Conselho de Favores: Controle Social Na Saúde.* Rio de Janeiro: Garamond.

Pisani, Elizabeth. 2009. *The Wisdom of Whores: Bureaucrats, Brothels and the Business of AIDS.* New York: W.W. Norton & Company.

Pro-Genericos. n.d. "Mercado." *Mercado.* Retrieved January 23, 2012 (www.proge nericos.org.br/index.php/mercado).

Rich, Jessica. 2013. "Grassroots Bureaucracy: Intergovernmental Relations and Popular Mobilization in Brazil's AIDS Policy Sector." *Latin American Politics and Society* 55(2): 1–25.

Roberts, Bryan. 2005. "Citizenship, Rights, and Social Policy." Pp. 137–58 in *Rethinking Development in Latin America,* edited by Charles H. Wood and Bryan R. Roberts. University Park: Penn State University Press.

Rodrik, Dani. 2006. "Goodbye Washington Consensus, Hello Washington Confusion? A Review of the World Bank's Economic Growth in the 1990s: Learning from a Decade of Reform." *Journal of Economic Literature* 44(4): 973–87.

Salama, Bruno M., and Daniel Benoliel. 2010. "Pharmaceutical Patent Bargains: The Brazilian Experience." *Cardozo Journal of International and Comparative Law* 18(3): 633–85.

Sandbrook, Richard, Marc Edelman, Patrick Heller, and Judith Teichman. 2007. *Social Democracy in the Global Periphery.* Cambridge: Cambridge University Press.

Serra, José. 2004. "The Political Economy of the Brazilian Struggle against AIDS." *An Institute for Advanced Study Friends Forum.* Retrieved October 25, 2008 (www.sss.ias.edu/files/papers/paper17.pdf)

Shadlen, Kenneth. 2011. "The Political Contradictions of Incremental Innovation: Lessons from Pharmaceutical Patent Examination in Brazil." *Politics & Society* 39(2):143–74.

Tarchinardi, Maria. H. 1993. *A Guerra Das Patentes.* Rio de Janeiro: Editora Paz e Terra.

Teixeira, Paulo. 2003. "Universal Access to AIDS Medicines: The Brazilian Experience." *Divulgação em Saúde pare Debate* 27: 184–91.

Teixeira, Paulo, Marco Antônio Vitória, and Jhoney Barcarolo. 2003. "The Brazilian Experience in Providing Universal Access to Antiretroviral Therapy." Pp. 69–86 in *Economics of AIDS and Access to HIV/AIDS Care in Developing Countries. Issues and Challenges.* Paris: Agence Nationale pour Recherche sur le Sida.

Tendler, Judith. 1997. *Good Government in the Tropics.* Baltimore: John Hopkins University Press.

Wade, Robert Hunter. 1990. *Governing the Market.* Princeton: Princeton University Press.

Weyland, Kurt. 1995. "Social Movements and the State: The Politics of Health Reform in Brazil." *World Development* 23(10): 1699–1712.

Weyland, Kurt. 1998a. "From Leviathan to Gulliver? The Decline of the Developmental State in Brazil." *Governance: An International Journal of Policy and Administration* 11(1): 51–74.

Weyland, Kurt. 1998b. "Swallowing the Bitter Pill: Sources of Popular Support for Neoliberal Reform in Latin America." *Comparative Political Studies* 31(5): 539–68.

4 Asserting Antiretroviral Autonomy (1990–2001)

Eloan Pinheiro exemplifies the activist professional who combines the brains, guts, and heart that made the Brazilian AIDS treatment a reality. As the director of Farmanguinhos, the pharmaceutical manufacturer owned and operated by the federal government, she played a central role in the production of antiretroviral (ARVs) medications used by Brazilians with HIV throughout the country. In her position, Pinheiro had to balance demands from politicians, pressures from private industry, and collaborations with civil society. Despite the various challenges she faced, Pinheiro had always remained committed to *sanitarista* ideology. "Health is a social justice issue, especially in developing countries," she contends. "If you have only seven rich countries—what about the rest of us? Countries that depend on economic relations with the rich countries must have hope for a better future."[1] This normative framework informed her work and undergirded her support for social movement organizations.

In the fight for access to medicines, Pinheiro was not afraid of taking risks and bending the rules. In 2001, she sold medicines to activists from the humanitarian group Doctors without Borders and knew that these drugs may be illegally transported to South Africa. A typical government bureaucrat in her position would have conferred with government lawyers to seek approval since the transaction may contravene intellectual property laws governing Brazil and South Africa. Regardless of the implications, she shared in the same goals and values of the activists—providing access to life-saving medicines. At the time of the sale, 39 transnational drug companies, wanting to maintain their market position based on high-priced, patented medicines, had sued the South African government over a law that would allow for the importation of cheaper medicines.

In Brazil, Pinheiro also faced the growing problem of patents on medicines and was concerned about the impact that they might have on the public health system. She was confounded by the fact that private patent rights provided to industry could take precedence over the collective rights to health guaranteed by Brazil's Constitution. "How is it that a public law remains subordinate to a private law? . . . Who is being exploited here? It is society; it is our money that is in play," she contends. As director of

96 Asserting Antiretroviral Autonomy (1990–2001)

Farmanguinhos, she saved Brazilian taxpayers millions of dollars in purchases of medicines by reverse engineering and producing the first generation of ARVs at prices significantly cheaper than originator firms. The know-how she brought from working as a chemist for transnational drug companies made her a formidable opponent in the fight to control pharmaceutical technology.

Before her tenure as director of Farmanguinhos, Pinheiro already had gained 20 years of experience working for transnational drug companies, including Beecham from the United Kingdom, before it was acquired by Glaxo, now GlaxoSmithKline. Her specialty was product *tropicalization*, that is, the adoption of pharmaceutical formulas developed elsewhere to local Brazilian conditions using locally sourced excipients. Despite the attractive salary, she left the company due to her involvement in Brazilian politics and re-democratization efforts. Pinheiro says that she had been a political activist since she was a student in the 1960s. Later, she became the president of the chemical workers union and contributed to the formation in 1979 of the left-leaning Workers Party. While contributing to *sanitarista* efforts to reform the health system in the late 1980s and early 1990s, she began to work as a consultant to Brazil's public labs and completed a specialist training in hot-melt extrusion drug-making techniques at the University of London. In 1994, Pinheiro was elected director of Farmanguinhos, which is housed at the Oswald Cruz Foundation (FioCruz), Brazil's federal research and training facility. FioCruz' tradition of holding internal elections to select administration appealed to her democratic values, and the institute's mission serving the country's public health needs inspired her *sanitarista* ideals. "FioCruz is the NIH of the poor," she proudly proclaimed with a laugh. While the National Institutes of Health researched health issues common to the middle class in the US, FioCruz focused its efforts on neglected tropical diseases common amongst the poor majority in Brazil.

The rest of this chapter traces the efforts of Pinheiro and other Brazilians who contributed towards the successes in controlling technology, developing political alliances, and using normative framing to achieve pharmaceutical autonomy in the production of ARVs. Despite the end of state intervention in support of industrial deepening detailed in the previous chapter that resulted in the closure of several upstream firms involved in the pharmaceutical chain, a few companies involved in chemical synthesis and pharmaceutical formulations such as public labs remained. Previous studies have noted the public-private collaboration behind Brazil's ability to produce the first generation of ARVs (Biehl 2007; Nunn 2008). My version bolsters these accounts about Brazilian firms, both private and public, reverse engineering these medicines[2] and breaking the monopoly power of transnational drug firms, not by focusing on crucial junctures, but in terms of recurrent problem solving on the one hand and the evolving institutional terrain on the other. Specifically, I consider how a few API makers survived the neoliberal reforms that led to the closure of several firms involved in chemical synthesis and detail their commercial decisions in the face of declining state support of industrial policies as well as policy makers' rationale to produce drugs in public labs as opposed to private industry.

While controlling technology in pharmaceutical production encountered few obstacles when producing non-patented medicines, new patent protections on medicines entering the market from 1997 onward reduced the "development space" to freely copy existing technologies. The World Trade Organization (WTO) panel that the United States brought against Brazil concerning aspects in its intellectual property laws added additional pressure on the government. In the face of these obstacles, new political alliances and strategic framing expanded the scope of government action. *Sanitaristas* like Pinheiro worked to improve state administrative capacity to operate complex health programs, but they were not afraid to collaborate with the civil society in the use of naming and shaming tactics against powerful opponents. Tactics such as the strategic use of legal systems, protests, and media exposure that had played such an important role at the domestic level to roll out treatment would be used at the international level. Brazilian health officials mobilized their base and reached out to transnational advocacy groups under a common frame: "Access to life-saving medicines is a human right." And human rights groups supported Brazil's threat to use a compulsory license when negotiating prices with patent holders.

"BRAZILIAN AZT": THE STORY OF MICROBIOLOGICA

The first medication found to have an effect on HIV/AIDS was the antiretroviral medication zidovudine (AZT). Although the compound had been synthesized in the 1960s, it was only when the virus that causes AIDS was discovered in 1984 that companies could begin to screen for potential drugs to treat the disease. Burroughs Wellcome (now GlaxoSmithKline—GSK) working in collaboration with the National Cancer Institute, a branch of the United States' National Institute of Health and Duke University, discovered AZT's antiretroviral activity and began conducting clinical trials. By January 1987, the Food and Drug Administration gave accelerated approval of the drug. But the hopes of people with HIV/AIDS were dashed when Burroughs Wellcome set a price tag at around $10,000 for a year's supply. Corporate executives justified the high price on the high costs and risks of development as well as an expensive manufacturing process. AIDS activists did not remain idle. Within a few months, the US-based direct-action group AIDS Coalition to Unleash Power (ACT UP) had formed and launched protests for lower prices and more research efforts (Siplon 2002).

Despite the costs, the side effects, and the subsequent failure of monotherapy (i.e. the use of one ARV drug to treat the disease), a few Brazilian organizations risked distributing the drug. In the face of the growing AIDS epidemic, the Secretary of Health of São Paulo State became the first

98 Asserting Antiretroviral Autonomy (1990–2001)

government body to initiate free distribution of AZT in 1989. The federal government's National AIDS Program as well as a number of large Brazilian firms followed São Paulo's lead and began limited distributions of AZT in the early 1990s. The sole supplier at the time was Burroughs Wellcome, which won all the contracts until a new Brazilian start-up company, Microbiologica (MB), began producing its version, known as "Brazilian AZT." The new start-up threatened the transnational drug company's market control, not only in Brazil but worldwide.

Microbiologica was a product of Brazil's industrial policies of the 1970s and 1980s. The company began as an offshoot of the Federal University of Rio de Janeiro in 1981. Contrary to Brazilian academic culture, chemistry professors decided to enter the world of business. Microbiologica first produced cultures and reagents for the diagnosis of tropical diseases. In response to a government initiative for the national production of strategic medicines and active pharmaceutical ingredients (APIs), the company decided to enter the line of chemical synthesis. With funding from the federal Central Medicines Agency (CEME), Microbiologica established a chemical division and brought in Jaime Rabi, a Chilean-born chemist trained in the United States and professor at the university, as a consultant. By the end of the 1990s, the lab had established its credibility and competence in the production of nucleoside-based compounds, such as mercaptopurine and azathioprine (Rabi 2007).

Due to its small scale and specialization in niche markets, Microbiologica survived the market liberalization of the early 1990s while many other manufacturers of fine chemicals went bankrupt. Lelio Maçaira, a chemical engineer and former student of Rabi, who joined Microbiologica to assist his former supervisor, said that "Microbiologica never risked much, to do large investments, and never had loans. Thus when the neoliberal wave hit, we were not a risk because we were not in debt."[3] The new key niche market that Microbiologica entered was the production of AZT. The highly emotional aspect of the disease, the unmet needs by the community, and the opportunity to enter a class of medicines that were at its infancy were factors that contributed to MB's decision to invest in the drug. The company already had experience with nucleosides and industrial chemistry. Plus Rabi, who later became the firm's director, explained that there were no competitors in Brazil, only the transnational company Burroughs Wellcome. "Of political interest is the fact that for the first time a Brazilian company was taking advantage of the possibility to make in Brazil a new medicine which was protected by patents outside Brazil," highlighted Rabi.[4] In 1992, Microbiologica officially launched "Brazilian AZT" and won its first public bid to sell 16,600 cases (equal to 100kg of AZT). The firm's price was $100 per 100 tablets versus Burroughs Wellcome's price of $140 (Abrahams 1992).

In the early 1990s, Brazil's federal treatment program was in its nascence. The Ministry of Health had placed some AZT orders for federal medicines programs, but Microbiologica's most important clients were a few large

Brazilian companies that provided medicines directly to their employees. Maçaira explains that the firm's commercial strategy remained "very conservative" and never aimed to attend the whole market, the remainder of which was supplied by Burroughs Wellcome and later on by the public lab Lafepe, when it began to produce the ARV.[5] Microbiologica, lacking a marketing department, sold all that it could produce, which amounted to about half of the public sector market. "We opened up an office just to sell to individuals too. Patients used to go directly to the factory to buy medicines since the product was not sold in pharmacies," explained Maçaira. Because it owned few of its installations, the API maker subcontracted most of the production to other companies, including the production of finished dosage forms. In hindsight, Maçaira regrets not making a larger investment. "We had something very important in our hands; only we knew how to do it. We should have done the investment that was necessary, to do a world-scale plant, so that the whole world could become a consumer of our products."[6]

Risk averse, the owners of Microbiologica missed an opportunity to increase the scale of its activities in the early 1990s. But the company also operated in an environment with declining government support and in a market dominated by large pharmaceutical firms. As Rabi (2007) details in an industry journal, Microbiologica obtained resources from two government programs that supported the move into AZT. First, the Scientific and Technological Development Support Program (*Programa de Apoio ao Desenvolvimento Científico e Tecnológico*—PADCT), using World Bank funds to support science and technology initiatives, allowed Microbiologica to invest in quality control and in synthetic processes at the laboratorial scale. Second, the Financing Agency for Studies and Projects (*Financiadora de Estudos e Projetos*—FINEP) provided financing to purchase the necessary machinery and equipment for industrial production. Despite this support, protectionist policies such as high tariffs on imports to protect infant industries or guaranteed public procurement contracts were no longer available. The reigning philosophy of the time is best summed up by Pedro Malan, Brazil's Finance Minister from 1995 to 2002: "The best industrial policy is no industrial policy."

Burroughs Wellcome quickly responded to Microbiologica's entrance into the market. The transnational lowered its price in order to drive Microbiologica out of business. "The extreme dumping consisted of donations," Rabi said.[7] This occurred not only in Brazil but also in export markets such as Chile. "The size of Wellcome compared to us at the time made us look insignificant," he said. Microbiologica took the originator company to court on charges of systemic dumping, but withdrew its case because of an inability to achieve a ruling in Brazil's notoriously slow judicial system.[8] Another front against Microbiologica opened in the press where articles appeared that questioned the quality and safety of its products.[9] Despite the absence of an independent regulatory agency (ANVISA was not established

100 *Asserting Antiretroviral Autonomy (1990–2001)*

until 1999), Microbiologica had already established itself as a producer of quality medicines during the 1980s.

Microbiologica was not the only Brazilian pharmochemical firm to enter the ARV market in the early 1990s. The year after the company launched "Brazilian AZT," another small start-up, Labogen, based in the city of Campinas, São Paulo State, produced its first batch of the drug in 1993 after three years of development. After failing in the field of biotechnology related to agriculture, the company's owners decided to enter the fine chemicals industry using its existing factory financed by the Brazilian National Development Bank (*Banco Nacional do Desenvolvimento Econômico e Social*—BNDES). "We knew that AIDS was a big problem and that there will be constant demand for products. [Former President] Collor opened up the market to imports in 1990, and we knew that AIDS products were value-added items," explained the company's former director, José Machado de Campos Neto.[10] Similar to Microbiologica, the firm had strong links to a local university. Labogen began as an incubator renting out an area from the Multidisciplinary Center on Chemical, Biological and Agricultural Research at the University of Campinas. It also had the support of FINEP, which provided R$1 million (about $1 million at the time) in funds required to reverse engineer AZT. Labogen only produced the API and established a partnership with Brazilian drug company Medley to produce the finished dosage form.

While most of the Brazilian pharmochemical sector was shrinking in the 1990s as a result of drastic trade liberalization, a few firms survived and demonstrated the technical ability to produce advanced molecules used in cutting-edge medicines. The institutional environment that did not provide patent protection for new drugs allowed these firms to undercut Burroughs Wellcome's monopoly prices.[11] In fact, due to their success, US diplomats and originator companies increased the pressure on Brazil to change its patent laws. The process of "learning by doing" that began with AZT carried over into the production of other antiretroviral medicines. Microbiologica began production of estavudine and lamivudine, and Labogen developed estavudine, didanosine, and nevirapine as well as the API for ganciclovir, a drug used for treating AIDS-related opportunistic infections.

The forays of Brazilian private labs into the ARV segment remained modest due, in large part, to the state's failure to engage in the necessary "midwifery" and "husbandry" that Evans (1995) says are necessary for new industries to thrive. Apart from modest support as a "midwife" through credits and grants for these companies to enter the new markets, government policies failed to engage in the "husbandry" that would allow them to address global pressures through limited forms of protection and additional funding to support more research and development. Instead, the state assumed the role of "demiurge," direct producer of goods that competed with private capital. The entrance of Brazil's public labs into the ARV

Asserting Antiretroviral Autonomy (1990–2001)

market would affect the success of the private companies Microbiologica and Labogen.

STATE MONOPOLIZATION OF ARV PRODUCTION

First Initiatives by Public Labs

Brazil is one of the few countries that have public (or state-run) pharmaceutical companies that produce medicines for the public health system. Brazil's public labs entered into the antiretroviral business, initially as a market opportunity to sell to the government and later as a result of government mandate. During the 1990s, most of Brazil's public labs operated below capacity, lacked resources to invest and modernize production, and were slated for privatization. Despite their difficult financial and management problems, many labs continued to play a vital role in public health programs (cf. Cosendey et al. 2000; Flynn 2008; Oliveira 2007). Public-private collaborations jump-started their entrance into the field of antiretrovirals. In fact, technicians from Microbiologica assisted public labs by providing analytical methodology and standards for the production of finished dosage forms of AZT (Nunn 2008).[12] Since public labs did not have capabilities with synthetic chemical processes to produce APIs, they focused on pharmaceutical formulations and end-stage production. When developing pharmaceutical technology for the fabrication of pills, capsules, and syrups, they also faced significant challenges in terms of human capital and equipment.

The biggest challenge of Brazil's public labs is the lack of in-house research and development divisions, especially before the federal government decided to pour funds into them for the production of AIDS medicines. Instead, most state sector labs relied (and continue to rely) on API suppliers to provide the pharmaceutical technology required to make the finished dosage forms.[13] In-house pharmaceutical technology in formulations allows producers to better specify the inputs and raw materials they require; otherwise, they become hostage to just one API supplier. In 1994, Lafepe was the first public lab to begin production of AZT, but was dependent on outside suppliers for the technology.[14] In contrast, Microbiologica and Labogen produced the API and contracted out the production of the final dosage form. In subsequent years, Lafepe established an internal R&D division under the leadership of Pedro Rolim, who had previously worked for Sanofi-Adventis in France. Under his direction, Lafepe developed formulations for a pediatric version of AZT, lamivudine, estavudine, and didanosine.

By the time Sarney's Law mandating free and universal distribution of AIDS medicines was passed in 1996, several public labs controlled by state governments were in a position to contribute to the program. According to data from the Ministry of Health (2008), in the first two years after Sarney's

102 *Asserting Antiretroviral Autonomy (1990–2001)*

Law passed (1997 and 1998), Lafepe sold up to R$72 million worth of zidovudine (both capsules and oral solutions) and stavudine, but foreign firms continued to dominate ARV sales to the government with sales of R$200 million. Meanwhile, sales from national firms such as Microbiologica and Labogen reached a mere R$5 million.

Public labs were also competitive in terms of pricing. Lafepe sold a 100-capsule box of AZT for R$54–56 compared to the private sector's price of R$97–120 (Junior 1997; Lins and de Paula 1996). In the case of zalcitabine, the Ministry made two purchases in 1997—one from the foreign lab at R$1.70/pill and one from the national lab at R$1.17/pill, and both acquisitions were for comparable volumes of 3.2 million pills. Comparisons between local private and local public production reveal similar prices: Public labs provided AZT oral solutions at R$9.89 per dose in 1997 compared to the national private sector's price of R$10.29 per dose in 1996.[15] Without access to the bids made to supply the medicines, generalizations cannot be drawn, but direct comparisons show that local producers, both private and public labs, often undercut the prices of imports.

Federal Government Begins ARV Production

While Lafepe and a few other public labs had already begun to produce some ARVs, the Ministry of Health turned to its in-house facility, the Farmanguinhos Institute in Medicines Technology (*Farmanguinhos Instituto de Tecnologia em Fármacos*—FM), to be the main supplier for its federal treatment program after the passage of Sarney's Law in 1996. Like other public labs during the 1990s, FM was under-financed and produced few medicines. But under the leadership of Eloan Pinheiro, the lab increased its product line from three products to 64. AIDS medicines became an important part of the lab's product portfolio.

The state's dependence on public labs for the supply of ARVs developed gradually, but the initiative began relatively early in the institutionalization of Brazil's program of universal access. From the perspective of the managers of public labs, a consensus emerged about how these state enterprises came to play an important role.[16] First, the AIDS program was directed by the federal government, and past public health initiatives depended on inputs supplied by public labs. At the time, several public labs were operating below productive capacity, so they had room to expand output and attend to the government's needs. Second, despite production from Microbiologica and Labogen, Brazil remained dependent on imported ARVs to supply its treatment program, so there was an interest in nationalizing the production of these vital medicines in order to reduce costs. Without a national private sector having developed the entire spectrum of medicines, the government turned to public labs and provided them with the necessary resources to improve their operations. Third, an additional role of the public labs is to train people in pharmaceutical production. In the advent of the

AIDS crisis, Brazilian society called upon the country's leading scientists and professionals to support the fight against the disease. Since most public labs had ties to public universities, they could draw on additional human capital and contribute to graduate level educational programs.

Another reason why the government relied on public labs is a certain level of distrust of the private sector. *Sanitaristas*, now responsible for pharmaceutical policies at the Ministry of Health, had criticized profit-making drug companies as detrimental to public health objectives and responsible for the country's health disparities. Pedro Chequer, former director of National AIDS Program (1996–2000; 2004–2005), best articulates the view that the state should be involved in the direct production of strategic goods for society and distrust the profit orientation of the private sector. "The state is not subject to variations in the market. . . . We cannot be subject to a factory being sold or the closing down of a line of production or simply believing that the price should be different," he emphasized.[17] For Chequer and other top policymakers, an AIDS treatment program represented an important entitlement program that requires the state's full participation. In fact, Article 200 (I) of the Brazilian Constitution states that the unified health system, also known as SUS, should "participate in the production of drugs, equipment, immunobiological products, blood products and other inputs."

The political climate at the end of the 1990s also contributed to policymakers' distrust in the private sector. Despite neoliberal economic reforms during the course of the decade, there were numerous scandals involving falsified products and exorbitant price hikes affecting access to medicines. The business strategies of Microbiologica and Labogen also should not be discounted in the government's decision to enter the ARV market. Brazil's pharmaceutical sector had and continues to have more companies that focus on the last stage of production—formulation and marketing—but only a few API manufacturers that, given the right conditions, could position themselves to control the market. Machado de Campos Neto, the former director of Labogen, explained that they sought to control the market in APIs by selling to public labs. "We established an informal agreement to divide the market between the two of us. Labogen would do estavudine and Microbiologica would do lamivudine, for example, in which each could develop economies of scale," he said.[18] Labogen and Microbiologica's ambitions to control the market had unforeseen consequences when public labs decided to import raw materials, not to mention that their strategy likely contributed to public officials' distrust in the private sector providers (see also Flynn 2008).

The last major element in Brazil's public production of ARVs concerns the role of José Serra.[19] Exiled from Brazil during the military dictatorship, Serra returned to Brazil and helped found the Brazilian Social Democratic Party (*Partido Social Democratico Brasiliero*—PSDB) together with Fernando Henrique Cardoso. Serra, before assuming command at the Ministry of Health in March 1998, served as Minister of Planning in the

104 *Asserting Antiretroviral Autonomy (1990–2001)*

administration. Serra was chosen to succeed Cardoso's two-term presidency (1994–2002). Known as one of Brazil's most powerful and capable Ministers of Health in recent history, with personal backing from the president and a strong following in Congress, Serra capitalized on the country's problems related to pharmaceuticals and pushed through significant legislation affecting the sector, including the New Medicines Policy, the Generics Law, and creation of ANVISA.

When Serra assumed control of the Ministry of Health, Brazil had already passed legislation mandating free and universal distribution of AIDS medicines and a new bill protecting patents on pharmaceuticals. While Lafepe had accounted for most of the production from public labs, FM had begun talks with the National AIDS Program and Ministry to supply ARVs by the time Serra assumed office. Pinheiro and Chequer convinced Serra that the lab directly under the control of the Ministry of Health had the technological capacity to produce the medicines and should take the lead role in organizing ARV production and developing new medicines. They developed a strategic plan to centralize production and procurement of non-patented ARVs before moving on to patented formulas (Nunn 2008).

According to Eloan Pinheiro,[20] the original plan foresaw the following market division of ARVs: 40% from FM, 30% from other public labs, and 30% from private labs. Since FM pertains directly to the Ministry of Health and also operates as a regulatory body for the Ministry of Health, it would provide transparent cost information to the Ministry, which, in turn, it would use to negotiate contacts with other public labs. For those products that FM developed itself, it could transfer the technology to other labs. The federal lab collaborated most with the São Paulo state lab (*Fundação para o Remédio Popular*—FURP) due the latter's capacity and adoption of Good Manufacturing Practices for drug production.[21] To organize the public production of medicines, the Ministry of Health selected those public labs that were in the best position to develop ARVs and had sufficient productive capacity from the 18 public labs located throughout the country.[22] Appendix Five lists the public labs registered to produce ARVs. FM provided reference prices for ARVs, but the Brazilian Association of Public Labs (*Associação dos Laboratórios Farmacêuticos Oficiais do Brasil*—Alfob) negotiated allocations and prices for the other public labs with the Ministry's Department of Pharmaceutical Assistance.

Farmanguinhos and other public labs were able to scale up production because Serra provided additional resources for investments to expand capacity. FINEP provided FM with resources to purchase machinery for controlling quality. And more importantly, the Ministry of Health's *Guarda Chuva* Project (Umbrella Project) provided R$41.3 million to the country's public labs between 2000 and 2002.[23] The federal initiative, designed not only for ARVs but for an entire spectrum of medicines produced by the public labs, increased drug production 368%, or from 1.89 billion to 8.87 billion units.

Asserting Antiretroviral Autonomy (1990–2001) 105

With the Ministry of Health providing resources and contracts to public labs, private, locally owned drugs became increasingly marginalized. Acquisitions from national private companies remained marginal except in 2000 when the Ministry purchased R$106 million worth of ARVs from this sector. By the end of 2002, there were 19 national drug makers registered with ANVISA to sell ARVs, but the only private companies to secure large contracts with the Ministry of Health were Laob, Eurofarma, Neo-Quimica, and Cristalia (Orsi et al. 2003).

Since the start of Brazil's universal treatment program, the government was interested in maintaining control of production in the public sector. The irony in Brazil's case is that the country had been implementing several neoliberal reforms during the 1990s, and now they began to change course. Elected officials in Pernambuco State had slated Lafepe for privatization but changed course with increased demand for AIDS medicines and the influx of federal funds for investments (see Oliveira 2007).

Developing ARVs and Sourcing Raw Materials

Not only were private Brazilian firms sidelined as public labs scaled up production of ARVs, so too were the few pharmochemical companies that produced the raw materials. As explained in Chapter Three, Brazil's public labs are not vertically integrated factories that produce the active ingredients. FM, the most technologically advanced of the public labs, has an in-house research and development unit that can produce raw materials at the laboratory scale but not at the industrial level necessary for production. Instead, it relies on inputs elsewhere.

Microbiologica followed by Labogen spearheaded initial domestic efforts to make ARV drugs, and they shared accumulated knowledge of drug development with Brazil's public labs. Despite these initial contacts across the public-private divide, public labs turned towards foreign suppliers for sourcing their raw materials. Why did this occur? The consequence of favoring foreign suppliers would later prove to be the Achilles' heel of Brazil's attempt to consolidate its pharmaceutical autonomy in the production of essential AIDS medicines used in its universal treatment program. To answer this question, it is necessary to look at how public labs organized their research and development of pharmaceutical formulas.

Cassier and Correa (2003, 2007) describe how Farmanguinhos established procedures to reverse engineer the composition of the finished dosage medicines as well as the synthetic process for obtaining the active pharmaceutical ingredient (API). First, the federal lab set up an analytic chemistry department for analyzing the quality of inputs. The department tested raw materials to determine whether it was the same as that purported by the supplier and compared generic APIs to proprietary drugs. Developing in-house quality control standards and methods allowed the federal lab to determine criteria for purity and the type of raw material necessary for production.

106   *Asserting Antiretroviral Autonomy (1990–2001)*

Second, Farmanguinhos created a team of chemists who reverse engineered formulations in order to identify which excipients were used. Understanding which formulation works best based on bioequivalence tests allowed the lab's chemists to determine the raw material they would want to use and the best synthetic process for the production of an in-house version of the drug. Lastly, technicians developed purity standards and molecule references that could be added to the Brazilian pharmacopoeia.[24] Since not all the information necessary for producing the ARVs was available in patents and pharmacopoeias, the lab's scientists had to rediscover the qualitative and quantitative composition of ARVs, a learning process, which in turn could be shared with other public labs and private-sector suppliers.

The story of the development of the protease inhibitor indinavir, marketed by Merck under the brand name Crixivan, is emblematic of the partnerships established and challenges faced when Brazil reverse engineered patented medicines. The US Food and Drug Administration approved indinavir in 1996, and it quickly became the standard for ARV therapy. Brazil's AIDS Program initiated distribution in 1997, and by the end of 2000, when FM began production, over 19,000 patients were using the drug. The federal lab responded to the Ministry of Health's request to produce indinavir and established a partnership with Indian companies Hetero and Aurobindo, who were gradually moving into the ARV market. At the time, only Merck produced the API and filed patents for the product in Brazil but not in those countries that had yet become TRIPS compliant.[25] Hetero provided the first batches of the raw material, which FM formulated into medicines. According to Nubia Boechat, the federal lab's director of research and development at the time,[26] Merck knew that all the details of making indinavir were not available in the public domain. In fact, there was an element of contamination undetectable by traditional methods of quality control and not described in the patents on the product. Merck obtained a batch of FM's product, completed its analysis, and published its findings in the media. "It caused quite an uproar, especially with all the AIDS NGOs. Merck knew that the product would be contaminated. They just wanted to discredit our production," Nubia Boechat, a research chemist with FM, recounts. The federal lab called in Rio de Janeiro-based API maker Nortec Química[27] and Hetero to correct the problem. After several tests, the research team discovered that the reaction to produce the compound had to be achieved by re-cooling at a very low temperature. After solving the technical difficulty, the FM scaled up production and cut the Ministry of the Health's expenses from $1.89 in 1999 to $0.47 per pill in 2001.

The episode illustrates the close working relationships with Indian raw material suppliers and the strategy by originator companies to question the quality of medicines produced by public labs when their products are copied. Domestic API producers, such as Nortec, were not entirely marginalized but were only contracted to work on specific programs. Besides Nortec,

Farmanguinhos sought out another domestic API maker, São Paulo-based Cristalia, to assist in the development and to supply the ritonavir. However, there were no strong institutionalized relationships between the state and the national private companies to produce the APIs used by public labs, nor was there an extensive fine chemical sector that could produce all the APIs necessary for the growing portfolio of drugs used to treat the disease. Indeed, the first raw material FM acquired to produce didanosine came from Germany.[28] In the case of new medicines like ARVs, there were few suppliers worldwide producing the raw materials used to make these drugs.

Another reason why public labs overlooked domestic suppliers of raw materials is due to the specifications of the type of raw material required to fabricate certain medicines. Since Farmanguinhos had developed in-house pharmaceutical technology, its chemists had specific criteria for inputs used in its production (Cassier and Correa 2003). The federal lab used rigid specifications when procuring raw material in order to ensure quality. Up until the establishment of ANVISA, Brazil had a weak regulatory structure to guarantee the quality of medicines since there were no regulations governing bioequivalence tests for the production of generic medicines. At times, the technical criteria specified in tenders seemed to favor foreign suppliers over domestic ones. But Pinheiro said that she was not going to redo all bioequivalence and solubility tests to satisfy a local API maker.[29] In effect, public labs like Farmanguinhos and Lafepe with R&D divisions capable of developing in-house formulations could decide which type of raw material they desired and not become dependent on just one API maker.

Another factor that favored foreign raw material suppliers was Brazil's Public Procurement Act (Law 8.666). The law, passed in the early 1990s to curb government corruption by establishing rigid criteria all public sector entities must follow when purchasing inputs, had a significant impact on upstream ARV production (Marques and Hasenclever 2006). When FM held international tenders to procure raw material from abroad, FM had to award contracts to the lowest priced supplier and local firms could no longer compete. "When they knew they could enter the Brazilian market, they increased the price of intermediates that they sold to us and began to sell AZT and other products much cheaper," explained Campos de Machado Neto from Labogen.[30] Brazilian API producers had neither the economies of scale nor the government support required to compete against Asian producers.

Compared to the developmental states in East Asia, Brazil no longer had coherent industrial policies to develop the pharmaceutical sector nor the time to plan a long-term strategy. Pinheiro sums up the situation:

> There was not a policy of public labs working with the private sector. There were not a lot of options available on the domestic market. It was an emergency situation. You had to produce in the fastest way possible.[31]

108 *Asserting Antiretroviral Autonomy (1990–2001)*

Although most people involved in ARV production in Brazil, including directors, scientists, and engineers all know each other, the government failed to establish trust across the public-private divide. The culture of developing public-private partnerships had not taken root, and there was no industrial policy to institutionalize collaborations across the state and industrial divide. In fact, while Jose Serra used the Ministry of Health to promote local production of medicines, economic policy making remained in the hands of Pedro Malan at Brazil's Finance Ministry. Brazil's economic team remained tied to a neoliberal view and worked towards dismantling the developmental state that had been in place for decades. This lack of a coordinated industrial policy became most apparent when Microbiologica opened up a factory in 1997 to produce 25t of zidovudine a year—enough to supply 10% of the world demand at the time. Although the company received support from the government financing arm FINEP to set up the facility, the lack of coordinated public sector initiatives and Serra's decision to obtain raw material from abroad forced Microbiologica to close the plant and subsequently exit the AZT market entirely in 2000.[32]

Despite attempts by originator companies to push Brazilian firms out of the market, to maintain industrial secrets in the production process, and to discredit the quality of Brazilian production, Brazilian scientists and pharmaceutical companies demonstrated the capability to reverse engineer and produce quality ARVs. They had the technical know-how and the ability to produce any ARVs and even began producing fixed-dose combinations, such as lamivudine with zidovudine. But in the face of significant budget constraints, the government focused on the lowest possible price.[33] Immediacy trumped long-term planning to develop a global competitive industry observed in the state-industry relationships in East Asia (Evans 1995). Lacking a coherent industrial policy to compete against the rising market powers of Indian and Chinese firms, the country was slowly becoming more dependent on the importation of key components of ARVs. Still, by the turn of the century, Brazilian labs had achieved technological control over major steps in the production process—a success that was only achievable due to the absence of patents.

FIRST PRICE CONFLICTS OVER PATENTED ARVS

Brazil's public and private labs reduced the prices of medicines by producing the first generation of medicines not protected by patents. Had the country not changed domestic patent laws until 2005 like India and China, it could have continued with this strategy for several more years. Instead patent owners occupied a monopoly position for medicines they introduced after 1997 when patent legislation took effect. The introduction of second-generation ARVs like protease inhibitors now contributed to the largest costs to the

Asserting Antiretroviral Autonomy (1990–2001)   109

growing program. Local generic firms could legally only produce these medicines if the government issued a compulsory license.

At the end of 1999, Serra began to publicly discuss the use of compulsory licenses for two ARVs. The first was Merck's efavirenz, which cost $2,540 for a year's supply per individual, and the second, Swiss-based Roche's nelfinavir, $5,585. During the 1999–2001 period when negotiations were taking place, the number of people using efavirenz rose from 2,460 to 23,313 and those on nelfinavir, from 11,761 to 21,717. The total number of people receiving ARVs increased from 73,000 to 105,000 over the three-year period. While the substitution of locally produced ARVs in public labs reduced overall expenditures from R$559 million in 1999 to R$501 million in 2001, amidst the rising number of people enrolled in the program, patented medicines increasingly accounted for larger share of overall expenditures. In fact, spending on nelfinavir and efavirenz rose from 22% to 49% of the total spent on acquiring ARVs over the same three-year period.

Meanwhile, Brazil faced increasing financial constraints. Jose Serra (2004: 9) states that, since policymakers were "aware that the *real*-dollar rate of exchange was strongly overvalued and that this situation could not continue, it was obvious that the AIDS program would soon become unfeasible if only as a consequence of the rising costs in national currency." In January 1999, the devaluation of the real confirmed his fears. The R$/US$ exchange rate that stood at R$1.21 before the crisis skyrocketed to R$2.16 before settling at R$1.79 by the end of the year. Imported ARVs priced in dollars jumped in price, while an International Monetary Fund agreement limited government spending.

On top of budget constraints, the US government became more aggressive in asserting the patent rights of transnational drug companies. A lawsuit from 39 drug companies against the South African government galvanized world attention on the link between intellectual property and drug prices and demonstrated to Brazilian policymakers and activists the challenges they faced. The South African government sought to revamp its inherited apartheid-based health system into a more inclusive and universalistic health system. Since the country had provided drug patents since 1978, the government looked to reduce the prices of medicines by making changes to its intellectual property laws. The South African 1998 Medicines Act allowed for parallel importation of drugs and expanded the scope of compulsory licensing. Transnational drug companies, alleging the Act contravenes World Trade Organization (WTO) commitments, sued South Africa and mobilized the US and European governments to apply political pressure (Bond 1999; Klug 2008).

Brazil also faced the combined pressures of foreign drug companies and a United States-sponsored World Trade Organization (WTO) panel questioning an article in Brazil's 1996 patent legislation. A major difference between Brazil and South Africa was that Brazil could trumpet the success of its

110 *Asserting Antiretroviral Autonomy (1990–2001)*

treatment program, while South African leaders resisted the inclusion of AIDS medicines in the public health system. South Africa's President Thabo Mbeki shocked the global AIDS community by questioning the link between HIV and AIDS at the Durban AIDS Conference in July 2000. Meanwhile at the same Conference, Brazilian officials presented data that attributed falling mortality rates and reduced hospitalizations of people with HIV/AIDS to access to treatment. Between 1997 and 2000, Brazil's health ministry estimated that 234,000 hospital admissions were avoided, representing savings of $677 million (Bermudez and Oliveira 2004). Brazil's success demonstrated that a developing country can provide First World levels of care and encouraged efforts to replicate its success. Concerns about inadequate health infrastructures, lack of treatment adherence, and the development of an uncontrollable strain of HIV melted away in the face of Brazil's experience.

In the face of new policy constraints resulting from patent protections and a WTO panel, Brazil turned to strategies and tactics developed at the national level for the role out of treatment, namely construction of new alliances and strategic normative framing.

New Changes to Patent Laws

The first step towards issuing a CL involved changes to the legal framework. Presidential Decree 3.201 of October 1999 defined and expanded the uses for issuing a CL by amending Article 71 of Brazil's Industrial Property Law (see Appendix Three). It specified "national emergency" and "public interest" as the criteria for issuing a CL. Besides the issue of compulsory licensing, another important change in legislation made while Serra was the Minister of Health was Law #10.196/2001 that modified articles of the Industrial Property Law No. 9.279/1996. This new law aimed to address public health concerns regarding Brazil's intellectual property laws by introducing the Bolar Exception and giving ANVISA—Brazil's version of the US's Food and Drug Administration—the power of "prior consent" before a patent is granted for pharmaceutical products. The Bolar Exception allows a company to carry out all the regulatory tests and obtain the approvals necessary to market a drug even before its patent expires. With this flexibility, a company can obtain a registration to sell a product from ANVISA, although it is still protected by patent. When the patent expires, generic competition can begin immediately, resulting in price declines. Additionally, when the government considers the use of a CL, a local producer would be in a position to market it to the government.

Due to the high price of patented AIDS medicines, policymakers began to correct a number of perceived problems associated with the Industrial Property Law No. 9.279 of 1996. The original law had few of the safeguards outlined in TRIPS, and those that were included required modifications. Outlining the grounds for issuing CLs had a direct relevance to the Ministry of Health's negotiations with companies selling patented medicines. The Bolar Exception, designed to increase competition with generic medicines and reduce prices for the final consumer, had important ramifications for the production and acquisition of ARVs. Foreign drug companies were unhappy with what they viewed as a weakening of IP laws, and the US pharmaceutical industry association PhRMA pressured the US government to take action. Indeed, US Secretary of Commerce William Daley, while travelling to Brazil in 2000 accompanied by Merck's president Raymond Gilmartin and Pfizer's vice-president for Latin America Ian Read, expressed his displeasure in the decree related to the use of compulsory licensing (Aith 2000), but the only issue in which the USTR took direct action concerned the "local working" clause in Brazil's Industrial Property Law No. 9.279 of 1996.

World Trade Organization Panel over "Local Working"

Since Brazil's threats of using a CL during negotiations with Merck and Roche coincided with a US panel against the country at the WTO, many observers refer to the conflict over "local working" between the two countries as the "Merck case" (Sell 2003; Serra 2004).[34] When Brazil passed its Industrial Property Law No. 9.279 of 1996, PhRMA praised the legislation but expressed concern over Article 68 concerning the "local working" for a patented product (PhRMA 1998). The provision states the government can issue a compulsory license if a patented good is not "worked" in Brazil either through domestic production or permission for its domestic use. According to transnational drug companies, Article 68 provides the government with the authority to issue compulsory licenses for items that are not manufactured in Brazilian territory, disrupting their strategies of achieving economies of scale through global supply chains.

A contrary view by some intellectual property experts interprets "local working" as a long-standing precedent related to making a patented item available on the domestic market for a country's development needs, however defined. Accordingly, patent owners cannot retain their rights if they do not supply the market with their patent-protected goods. Brazilian officials upheld the perspective that the local working clause can only be used in cases of abuse of economic power (Serra 2004: footnote 14). The vagueness surrounding the wording of "local working" in TRIPS—whether a firm must produce locally or merely make a patented item available commercially—appears to be more of a diplomatic compromise than an attempt to establish clear legal boundaries (Attaran and Champ 2002). Brazilian interviewees who worked closely on the trade dispute claim that it had been brewing since Brazil passed its new intellectual property legislation in 1996.[35] But it was not until the transition process outlined in TRIPS had expired, on June 8, 2000, that the United States Trade Representative (USTR) requested bilateral consultations. Coincidentally, the request for

112 *Asserting Antiretroviral Autonomy (1990–2001)*

bilateral talks occurred a month before the biannual International AIDS Conference took place in Durban, South Africa.

Up to this point, Brazil's AIDS activists had not been aware of the impact of intellectual property on medicines. "We were somewhat aware of patent laws when they were passed in 1996. But we really began to see the impact when the US set up the panel at the WTO," claimed one civil society activist.[36] Although activists began staging protests in front of US consulates, one challenge faced by civil society was motivating members to become involved in issues related to intellectual property, pharmaceutical formulations, and drug prices. "Negotiations and treatments have always been a very complex topic and not always very transparent for civil society. Within the priorities of the movement, it was not preferred or prioritized due to the technical level required, difficulty in acquiring information, and also lack of interest," claimed Mario Scheffer,[37] a coordinator from Grupo Pela VIDDA-São Paulo, who said volunteers preferred working directly with patients as opposed to studying abstract laws and regulations. *Sanitaristas* including Jorge Bermudez and Eloan Pinheiro, among others, however, had known about the implications of patents on medicines prices and fought against Brazil's patent reforms since the early 1990s. Their previous limited efforts would be boosted now that they had a mobilized grassroots base to coordinate actions. The National AIDS Program provided the organizational resources and institutional location within the state to interact with a variety of interests across society and with other state agencies. Health officials had to proceed strategically after witnessing South Africa's confrontation with foreign drug companies and trade threats from the US.

The International AIDS Conference in Durban, South Africa, in July 2000 provided the perfect venue for Brazil to use its AIDS program for its defense at the WTO. Paulo Teixeira, the director of Brazil's National AIDS Program during the trade dispute, explained that the Brazilian strategy of national production of medicines was becoming the reference for the world.[38]

> Brazilian national production started to be the reference for the world. The Brazilian Example! We got together with the Itamaraty [Ministry of Foreign Affairs] and came to a conclusion: The National AIDS Program could be Brazil's defense, which we would take to a variety of international venues. We did not have the support of all the ministries. The Ministries of Planning and Agriculture thought it inappropriate. . . .
>
> We began here in Brazil, in an organized way, international mobilization. We made an agreement with Brazilian NGOs, especially ABIA which was known internationally, as well as with GAPA and Pela VIDDA, to endorse the government's strategy against the panel and the price negotiations. We also reached out to the large international NGOs mainly CPTech, MSF, Oxfam, and ACT-UP, but many others also joined. We were the ones that sought them out. We telephoned them and said that there is a certain lack of trust in governments but

Asserting Antiretroviral Autonomy (1990–2001)

suggested they consult with Brazilian NGOs which they subsequently did. Along with a *New York Times* article about the program, we were able to sway international opinion in our favor.

Domestically, Brazilian AIDS officials encountered difficulty obtaining the support of ministries representing international business interests such as the agro-export industry. But Brazil's diplomatic corps institutionalized links with the health ministry to push the country's rights-based agenda regarding access to medicines. The WTO dispute brought the issue of patents and the price of medicines to the foreground, and Brazilian diplomats even began to visit and consult with activist groups like ABIA—a practice as of yet unknown to the insular foreign ministry.[39] AIDS bureaucrats also sought out support from international NGOs. Since 1999, leading international NGOs like Consumer Project on Technology (CPTech),[40] Health Action International (HAI), and Doctors without Borders (MSF) had been advocating the use of TRIPS humanitarian safeguards including the use of CLs ('t Hoen 2009).

Brazilian officials coordinated efforts with allied activist groups and like-minded countries to formalize human rights norms related to access to medicines in several international venues (Flynn 2013; Nunn, Fonseca, and Gruskin 2009). While international government organizations addressing human rights issues do not have the same enforcement mechanisms as other bodies, such as the WTO, they provide a venue for establishing societal ideals. The International Covenant on Economic, Social and Cultural Rights (United Nations 1966) asserts "the right of everyone to the enjoyment of the highest attainable standard of physical and mental health." Many states are signatories of this agreement and have incorporated its principles into their Constitutions. The treatment coalition thus sought to include access to biomedical innovations, such as medicines, into core obligations of the right to health. In doing so, Brazilian activists and officials replicated the strategies they employed at the domestic level. Along with invoking the Brazilian Constitution, they pointed towards the evolving framework on the right to health in international accords.

At the international level, Brazilian officials and civil society allies worked at various UN bodies. As mentioned by Teixeira above, these included the United Nations Commission on Human Rights (UNCHR), the World Health Assembly of the World Health Organization, and the UN General Assembly Special Session on HIV/AIDS (UNGASS). At the UNCHR, Brazil drafted and sponsored the resolution *Access to Medication in the Context of Pandemics such as HIV/AIDS*, which specifically outlines access to AIDS medicines as a fundamental human right. The resolution passed unanimously in April 2001, with only the United States abstaining. In June 2001, UNGASS's *Declaration of Commitment on HIV/AIDS* also declared that access to medicine is a fundamental human right and crucial to fighting the pandemic. Lastly, Brazilian health officials played a key role in the adoption

114 *Asserting Antiretroviral Autonomy (1990–2001)*

of the *WHO Medicines Strategy* and World Health Assembly resolution *Scaling Up the Response to HIV/AIDS* in 2001 (Flynn 2013; Nunn, Fonseca, and Gruskin 2009).

Despite Brazil's success in gathering world opinion behind its AIDS program and the inclusion of access to medicines as a human right, President Bill Clinton authorized the opening of the WTO dispute resolution panel on his last day in office on January 15, 2001. Remarkably, the USTR (2001b) specified that the WTO panel would not affect the country's "widely-praised [*sic*] anti-AIDS program" and did not affect the use of a compulsory license in cases of public interest or national emergency.[41] The view of US officials, while technically correct, circumvents the high level of politicization of the negotiating process. In either case, the strategy of Brazil's Ministry of Health—mobilizing international support from NGOs, public opinion, and the media, including paid advertisements in major US newspapers—turned the panel into a "public relations disaster for the United States," asserts de Mello e Souza (2007: 48).

Brazil's strategy of mobilizing support from local and foreign civil society succeeded. The US withdrew the WTO panel on June 25, 2001, alleging that Brazil had not actually used a compulsory license based on Article 68 of its patent law (USTR 2001a). Another factor that weighed in on the resolution of the conflict is Brazilian diplomats found "local working" provisions for patents developed with assistance from the federal government in the US Patent Code, so they began formal consultations in the ambit of the WTO for a possible panel against the US.[42] In the negotiated settlement, the two sides set up a Consultative Mechanism in which the Brazilian government agreed to give the US advanced notice were it to use a CL based on the "local working" clause.[43]

The WTO panel had three important consequences for Brazil's treatment coalition. First, the country both promulgated and invoked a human rights-based discourse when contesting drug company patent monopolies. In subsequent price talks for patented antiretrovirals, Brazilian negotiators used a human rights frame in order to obtain substantial price discounts. Brazil's discourse during negotiations referenced both national legislation that upholds social rights, such as its 1988 Constitution, and international treaties stipulating access to medicines as a fundamental human right. Second, Brazil's health and foreign relations ministries began to collaborate in global health diplomacy and partnered with like-minded civil society organizations. Rights-based discourse and ministerial cooperation shaped the country's subsequent health diplomacy, foreign assistance programs, and foreign technology partnerships (Flynn 2013). Third, Brazil's treatment coalition expanded to include international allies. Domestic battles to secure policies and financing for treatment involved only close collaboration between "social movement insiders" in formal positions in the state and civil society activists. Brazilians would increasingly develop ties to foreign activists in subsequent battles over drug prices and patents.

Brazil's Involvement in the *Doha Declaration*

One of the most strident achievements of the treatment coalition spearheaded by Brazilian officials and their civil society partners was the *Doha Declaration*. Because of the growing awareness of the AIDS crisis, the need to provide inexpensive medicines for treatment, and problems Brazil and South Africa had experienced with foreign drug companies, developing countries were able to place the issue on the next round of trade negotiations launched in Doha, Qatar, in November 2001, at the Fourth WTO Ministerial Conference.

Serra instructed Brazil's Ministry of Foreign Affairs to find a way for the country to never have to face pressure at the WTO concerning its patent legislation and use of CLs again (Nunn 2008; Serra 2004). The goal was to clarify the use of CLs outlined in TRIPs in terms of public emergency. The term "public emergency" remained vague and subject to broad interpretation. Brazilian negotiators insisted the goal was not to abrogate the TRIPS accord; instead, it was to rebalance the rights and privileges between private and public interests. Even though it initially resisted the *Declaration*, the US eventually capitulated after threatening to use a compulsory license during the anthrax attacks in Washington, DC, in the aftermath of the September 11th attacks. The US Secretary of Health and Human Services threated to use a CL to lower the prices of ciproflaxin, the only known medication to fight anthrax and whose patent was in the hands of German-based drug company Bayer. The threats exposed the US to accusations of hypocrisy. Activists charged that the US operated under a double standard by permitting itself to use compulsory licenses but not developing countries.

The *Doha Declaration on TRIPS and Public Health* was signed a month later, on November 14, 2001, and declared that each member of the WTO had the right to determine the grounds for using a compulsory license and to define what constitutes a national emergency (WTO 2001). The *Doha Declaration* did not have an immediate impact on Brazil's negotiations with Merck and Roche, nor did the *Declaration* fully resolve issues related to parallel importing and exports of medicines. Diplomat Francisco Cannabrava, Brazil's TRIPS negotiator, explained that his country's interest in the agreement was primarily to import raw materials necessary to make generics and not to export medicines (Nunn 2008). If there is no patent on the product in the country that will export the medicine, a CL is not required, but a decree would be necessary if there is a domestic patent on the product.

There is some debate about the significance of the *Doha Declaration*. Industry representatives, highlighting that it did not modify any articles of TRIPS, downplayed its significance (Sell 2003), but in legal circles, the opinion is different. Leo Palma, an attorney at the Advisory Centre on WTO Law involved in the negotiations, said that the *Declaration* has the force of law in international trade disputes and provides an extra layer of protection for countries to use the legal instrument.[44] More importantly, the *Declaration*

116 *Asserting Antiretroviral Autonomy (1990–2001)*

effectively sidelined the WTO as an arena for the US and transnational drug companies to pressure countries not to use compulsory licenses. In subsequent price negotiations, Brazilian health officials would always invoke the *Doha Declaration* when threatening to use a compulsory license. Nonetheless, the accord would not resolve the country's growing dependence on imported raw materials.

Negotiated Settlements with Merck and Roche

With the legal backdrop at the global and domestic levels in place for the use of a compulsory license, the Ministry of Health proceeded with its price negotiations with Merck and Roche. At the bequest of health officials, local pharmochemical labs such as Labogen and Microbiologica began to develop the synthetic chemical process of both efavirenz and nelfinavir.[45] Despite these initial efforts, public labs continued to rely on foreign producers for the active pharmaceutical ingredients. Farmanguinhos and Lafepe presented proposals to produce these patented medicines in their final dosage forms. In the case of efavirenz, the federal lab confronted problems to legal restrictions and poor raw material. Merck, alleging patent infringement, threatened a lawsuit after Farmanguinhos purchased a generic form of the active pharmaceutical ingredient used to make efavirenz from a producer in India (Darlington 2001). Merck never took Farmanguinhos to court, but the federal lab never completed the development of the drug since a negotiated settlement was achieved soon thereafter. The new price of $0.84 for a 200mg dose represented a 59% discount from $2.06. The National AIDS Program announced that the deal would save the program $39 million.

Negotiations with Roche dragged on further. Serra refused the company's initial price discount and pressed forward with the local development of nelfinavir. Farmanguinhos completed the bioequivalence tests and produced samples of the finished dosages. "We formulated nelfinavir and had a meeting with Roche and showed them the final product, although we still had to do the scale-up," explained Pinheiro,[46] upon which Serra threatened the compulsory license. The public lab still required another six months to begin industrial production, but there were no risks of stock-outs. With Farmanguinhos offering to produce nelfinavir at 40% less than the current price charged by Roche, Serra announced a compulsory on August 22, 2001, but added that he was still open to negotiations. A week later, Roche capitulated and cut the price from $1.07 a pill to $0.64—a 40% discount and comparable to Farmanguinhos' cost parameters. The Swiss drug company also agreed to move production of nelfinavir to Brazil since the agreed volume of purchases made it economically viable (Roche 2001).[47]

The reaction by foreign pharmaceutical companies to Brazil's aggressive approach to copy drugs in public labs and threatened use of compulsory licenses varied. On one extreme, executives were upset that their products were being "pirated" and demanded action from the US government to protect their interests, but Brazil's large pharmaceutical market remained attractive. Other critics highlighted that Serra used the occasion to be the in the media spotlight. Trumpeting a positive government program such as Brazil's AIDS program and threatening to break patents is not uncommon for any politician with future political ambitions. Indeed, Serra left the Ministry of Health in February 2002 to launch his campaign for Brazil's presidency.

Bringing price negotiations to the public spotlight would have lasting effects on corporate strategies.[48] Foreign drug companies that did not have dedicated offices and personnel for negotiating directly with the government later established local divisions. However, local autonomy to negotiate contracts would increasingly become more restricted as home offices set pricing criteria. Under the industry-backed Accelerating Access Initiative[49] and other firm-level efforts, originator firms began to establish global differential pricing schemes. Typically, the criteria depended on World Bank classification of a country as high-, medium-, or low-income as well as domestic HIV prevalence rates. Countries with the highest prevalence rates and lowest levels of income would receive ARVs at the cost of production.

UNDERSTANDING ANTIRETROVIRAL AUTONOMY

During the first period under study, Brazil asserted antiretroviral autonomy by demonstrating technological capabilities to produce ARVs, developing larger political coalitions, and pushing the norm of access to essential medicines as a human right. Expenditures on ARVs increased from R$191 million in 1997 to R$496 million in 2002, but PPPY costs for ARVs fell from R$6,223 in 1998 to R$4,158 in 2002 (Grangeiro et al. 2006). Autonomy understood as more equitable distribution of benefits and increased policy space characterized the period.

State actors led many of the policy outcomes. Why did "policy entrepreneurs" like Serra decide to address the issue of high-cost AIDS medicines? Nunn (2008) argues that such a decision represents a critical juncture in Brazil's AIDS treatment program with long-lasting consequence. While Serra could not have ignored mobilized AIDS constituencies, she notes that he could have deflected attention back on President Cardoso or Congress. In his position as Minister of Health, he could have even limited the number of drugs on treatment protocols and negotiated drug prices in private. Given the high level of politicization around AIDS in the media and international avenues, Nunn and several interviewees emphasized Serra's political ambitions in using the access to medicines to boost his political stature. According to his written account, Serra (2004: 15) denies any "political-electoral strategy" aimed at benefiting his presidency, and instead highlights the "bounded rationality" of policymakers:

> An orthodox examination of all the prior conditions required for an effective battle against AIDS would, without doubt, have greatly

118 *Asserting Antiretroviral Autonomy (1990–2001)*

discouraged the governmental and social energies that were eventually mobilized in a concerted effort to cope with the disease.

Apart from Serra's political motives, this statement resonates with the cognitive heuristics model advanced by Weyland (2006). In other words, not knowing all the relevant facts and lacking time to evaluate all courses of action ironically led policymakers' decision on taking an aggressive stance.

Focusing solely on the rational calculations of key political leaders must also be weighed against other factors. Viewed from the perspective of recurrent problem solving, *sanitaristas* convinced Serra and other reluctant ministries that the strategies based on political alliances and the human rights frame they developed in the national struggle for treatment would also prevail over pressures from transnational drug companies. The political coalition comprised of activist policymakers in the National AIDS Program and domestic civil society groups defined drug markets not in terms of a business proposition but as a human right, as a means to achieve a social end. This alliance grew to include transnational advocacy networks when the US applied trade pressure concerning Brazil's patent laws. Had the US not brought a WTO panel against the country, it is unlikely that Brazil's domestic AIDS coalition would have gone global. Treatment activism prevailed in the international arena by linking access to medicines as core obligation of the right to health and naming and shaming more powerful actors.

Brazil's experience in transnational activism contrasts with other theories concerning international relations and social movements. Growing discussion about the role of health diplomacy in international relations posit that Brazil's actions regarding access to medicines on the international stage represent a new form of "soft power" (Lee and Gomez 2011). The notion of "soft power" implies an instrumental rationality for achieving geopolitical objectives related to power politics and trade. In my account, Brazil's health diplomacy reflect less traditional foreign policy concerns but rather efforts to defend the values and programs that embody the right to health at the domestic level (see Flynn 2013). Brazil's strategy used the soft law of the international human rights regime to build flexibility into the hard law of trade agreements concerned with patents. Brazil's international actions also vary from the "boomerang" model of transnational activism developed by Keck and Sikkink (1998). Instead of grassroots activists seeking outside support to press claims against a domestic government in their model, state actors sought support from global civil society to contest powerful actors.

Still, pharmaceutical autonomy was not complete. Scaling up production in public labs in the face of fiscal austerity, a weak domestic pharmochemical sector, and the absence of coherent industrial policy led to growing foreign dependency on raw materials. At this time, AIDS NGOs were not interested in the industrial challenges faced in the production of life-saving medicines. The situation changed when patents began to impact Brazil's strategy to produce medicines locally. The next chapter details how Brazil's

Asserting Antiretroviral Autonomy (1990–2001) 119

control over pharmaceutical technology declined as a result of patent power and market power.

NOTES

1. This quote is taken from an interview that Eloan gave in a documentary film about the global HIV movement. See Anne-Christine d'Adesky, Shanti Avirgan, and Ann T. Rossetti (2003).
2. See Appendix Four and Five for a list of ARVs used in Brazil's program. First generation ARVs refer to those without patent protection: zidovudine, didanosine, zalcitabine, stavudine, lamivudine, nevirapine, delavirdine, saquinavir, ritonavir, indinavir and fixed-dose combination lamivudine + zidovudine.
3. Lelio Maçiara. Interview with author. Rio de Janeiro, RJ. November 28, 2007.
4. Jaime Rabi. Interview with author. Rio de Janeiro, RJ. April 16, 2008.
5. Maçiara interview.
6. Ibid.
7. Rabi interview.
8. Ibid.
9. Jorge Raimundo, who worked for Burroughs Wellcome before it merged with GlaxoSmithKline, said the company attempted to convince federal authorities to purchase only their product by arguing that their product's quality was superior, but the government was satisfied by MB's standards. Jorge Raimundo. Interview with author. Rio de Janeiro, RJ. June 20, 2008.
10. José Machado de Campos Neto. Interview with author. São Paulo, SP. July 7, 2008.
11. Drug firms in other developing countries also began to develop versions of AZT. India's Cipla in collaboration with the Council of Scientific and Industrial Research (CSIR) began making its version of AZT, also in 1991 but only launched capsules the following year. In Thailand, the Government Pharmaceutical Organization began producing its formula of AZT in 1996 at less than half the originator's price. Due to South Africa's Patents Act (1978), local generic companies were legally barred from producing the medicine.
12. Rabi interview; and Maçiara interview.
13. Typically, this would come in the form of a Drug Master File, which usually contains confidential details about the manufacture and production of APIs and finished dosage forms. The Drug Master File is often provided to regulatory officials in order to register a medicine for commercial distribution.
14. It is not entirely clear why Lafepe decided to start production of AZT. According to Nunn (2008), Lafepe entered the AZT product line to exploit a market niche selling to the state and federal health programs based on APIs and technology supplied by Microbiologica. Rabi (interview with author), while confirming the provision of some technical assistance, explained that there is some controversy regarding Lafepe but suspects that a local competitor unable to compete against its produces used imported raw material and technology to enter the market using Lafepe. Pedro Rolim, Industrial Director at Lafepe from 1996 to 2005, confirmed during an interview with the author (Recife, PE, July 28, 2008) that Lafepe had been dependent on API suppliers' technology but did not know the specifics, and Leduar Guedes, Lafepe's Director (interview with author, Recife, PE, July 23, 2008), did not elaborate.
15. A few caveats are necessary when comparing costs between public and private labs. Public labs do not have to pay taxes, import duties on raw materials, dividends to shareholders, or overhead on marketing and advertisement. In

120 *Asserting Antiretroviral Autonomy (1990–2001)*

addition, most employee salaries in public labs come from public sector budget outlays. However, since most labs operate under rules and regulations governing the public sector, they cannot raise their own capital nor have working capital in order to make purchases of inputs required for production. Typically, the state government would have to provide the resources required to purchase APIs and other raw materials. For the federal lab Farmanguinhos, the Ministry of Health would forward the money necessary to purchase medicines. Private labs are more efficient in terms of hiring and firing personnel as well as establishing supply contracts, but they must pay taxes that can account for up to one-third of their sales as well as generate profits for their owners and high payouts to executives.

16. Interviews with author: Ricardo Oliva, Director of FURP and ALFOB, São Paulo, SP, December 17, 2007; Carlos Alberto Pereira Gomes, Director of Funed, Belo Horizonte, MG, August 25, 2008; Eloan Pinheiro, Rio de Janeiro, RJ, June 4, 2008; Pedro Rolim interview.
17. Pedro Chequer. Interview with author. Brasilia, DF. July 12, 2008.
18. Machado de Campos Neto interview.
19. Research and conclusions in this section are limited by the fact that Jose Serra was unavailable for an interview, and Barjas Negri and Platão Fischer, second-tier level officials working at the Ministry of Health during Serra's term, refused interview requests. But third-tier officials Fernando Cardenas and Carlos Alberto Pereira Gomes were interviewed.
20. Pinheiro interview.
21. Pinheiro interview.
22. For more information on Brazil's public labs see Flynn (2008) and Oliveira, Labra, and Bermudez (2006).
23. Fernando Cardenas. Interview with author. Piracicaba, SP. July 10, 2008.
24. The references provided in pharmacopoeias contain the directions for the preparation of medicines and are accessible to any generic drug manufacturer interested in reproducing a drug.
25. Merck's patent was not applicable to countries like India and China that had not incorporated TRIPS legislation. Brazil's patent office would later deny Merck's indinavir patent request in 2003.
26. Nubia Boechat. Interview with author. Rio de Janeiro, RJ. April 22, 2008.
27. Nortec began as a partnership between Farmanguinhos/FioCruz and the private petrochemical holding company Norquisa in the early 1980s to produce APIs for the federal lab. The company, whose shareholders include the federal development bank BNDES, maintains an accord with Farmanguinhos to help develop and supply APIs. Nortec survived the sector's market liberalization since it was not accustomed to policies of import substitution and developed a competitive product profile that included exports, according to its Director of Business Development, Marcos Soalheiro. Marcos Soalheiro. Interview with author, Rio de Janeiro, RJ. June 17, 2008.
28. Pinheiro interview.
29. Ibid.
30. Campos de Machado Neto interview.
31. Pinheiro interview.
32. Rabi interview.
33. Ibid.
34. Although Roche is a Swiss company that marketed the drug, the US still had a direct economic interest in the negotiations since US-based Agouron Pharmaceuticals had licensed the product to Roche. Agouron later became a subsidiary of Pfizer.

Asserting Antiretroviral Autonomy (1990–2001)   121

35. Otavio Brandelli. Email Correspondence. February 14, 2008. And Paulo Teixeira. Interview with author. São Paulo, SP. May 7, 2008.
36. Coordinator of an AIDS NGO who preferred to remain anonymous. Interview with author. 2008.
37. Mario Scheffer. Interview with author. São Paulo, SP. April 4, 2008.
38. Teixeira, interview.
39. Veriano Terto. Interview with author, Rio de Janeiro, RJ. July 4, 2005. Often times, international NGOs tended to have closer relationships with Brazilian diplomats than domestic AIDS NGOs; see also Matthews (2011).
40. CPTech (Consumer Project on Technology) later changed its name to Knowledge Ecology International (KEI).
41. "On February 1, 2001, a WTO panel was established. Since the establishment of this panel, however, Brazil has asserted that the US case will threaten Brazil's widely-praised anti-AIDS program, and will prevent Brazil from addressing its national health crisis. Nothing could be further from the truth. For example, should Brazil choose to compulsory license antiretroviral AIDS drugs, it could do so under Article 71 of its patent law, which authorizes compulsory licensing to address a national health emergency, consistent with TRIPS, and which the United States is not challenging. In contrast, Article 68—the provision under dispute—may require the compulsory licensing of any patented product, from bicycles to automobile components to golf clubs. Article 68 is unrelated to health or access to drugs, but instead is discriminating against all imported products in favor of locally produced products. In short, Article 68 is a protectionist measure intended to create jobs for Brazilian nationals," stated the USTR (2001b: 10).
42. US Code, Title 35, Patents, Chapter 18 [38]. See *Serra (2004*: footnote 14).
43. To date, this Consultative Mechanism has never been used but draws attention to how much sovereignty a country has when taking advantage of TRIPS flexibilities.
44. Leo Palma. Interview with author. Geneva, Switzerland. June 11, 2006.
45. Maçiara, interview; Campos de Machado Neto interview.
46. Pinheiro interview.
47. The company later closed the facility due to increasing costs and reduced sales volumes.
48. Marcos Levy, then Director of Public Affairs at Merck Brazil, said, "Merck had been conducting price negotiations with the Health Ministry since 1995, but it was done very quietly back then, and the government still got a good deal. It was José Serra who took this whole thing public when he was running for President" (quoted in Nunn 2008: 139).
49. In May 2000, several UN agencies entered into a partnership with five pharmaceutical companies (Boehringer Ingelheim; Bristol-Myers Squibb; GlaxoSmithKline; Merck & Co., Inc.; and Hoffmann-La Roche; later joined by Abbott Laboratories) to offer price discounts in 80 countries.

REFERENCES

Abrahams, Paul. 1992. "Wellcome Faces Further Generic Competition over AZT Drug." *Financial Times*, July 1, 27.
D'Adesky, Anne-Christine, Shanti Avirgan, and Ann T. Rossetti (producer-directors). 2005. *Pills, Profits, Protest Chronicle of the Global AIDS Movement*. (Video-recording). New York: Outcast Films.

122 *Asserting Antiretroviral Autonomy (1990–2001)*

Aith, Marco. 2000. "Patent Laws Can Generate Conflict with US." *Folha de São Paulo*, February 12. Retrieved November 22, 2008 (www.cptech.org/ip/health/c/brazil/).

Attaran, Amir, and Paul Champ. 2002. "Patent Rights and Local Working under the WTO TRIPS Agreement: An Analysis of the U.S.-Brazil Patent Dispute." *Yale Journal of International Law* 27: 365–93.

Bermudez, Jorge, and Maria Auxiliardora Oliveira. 2004. *Intellectual Property in the Context of the WTO Trips Agreement: Challenges to Public Health*. Rio de Janeiro: ENSP.

Biehl, João. 2007. *Will To Live*. Princeton: Princeton University Press.

Bond, Patrick. 1999. "Globalization, Pharmaceutical Pricing, and South African Health Policy: Managing Confrontation with U.S. Firms and Politicians." *International Journal of Health Services* 29(4): 765–92.

Cassier, Maurice, and Marilena Correa. 2003. "Patents, Innovation, and Public Health: Brazilian Public-Sector Laboratories' Experience in Copying AIDS Drugs." Pp. 89–103 in *Economics of AIDS and Access to HIV/AIDS Care in Developing Countries: Issues and Challenges*, edited by Jean-Paul Moatti. Paris: Agence Nationale de Recherches sur le SIDA.

Cassier, Maurice, and Marilena Correa. 2007. "Intellectual Property and Public Health: Copying of HIV/Aids Drugs by Brazilian Public and Private Laboratories." *Electronic Journal in Communication, Information and Innovation in Health* 1(1): 83–90.

Cosendey, Marly Aparecida, Jorge Bermudez, André Reis, Hayne Felipe Silva, Maria Auxiliadora Oliveira, and Vera Lucia Luiza. 2000. "Assistência Farmacêutica Na Atenção Básica de Saúde: A Experiência de Três Estados Brasileiros." *Cadernos Da Saúde Pública* 16: 171–82.

Darlington, Shasta. 2001. "Brazil AIDS Drug Dispute Courtbound." *Reuters*, March 27. Retrieved November 24, 2008 (http://lists.essential.org/pipermail/ip-health/2001-March/001138.html).

Evans, Peter. 1995. *Embedded Autonomy: States and Industrial Transformation*. Princeton: Princeton University Press.

Flynn, Matthew. 2008. "Public Production of Anti-Retroviral Medicines in Brazil, 1990–2007." *Development and Change* 39(4): 513–36.

Flynn, Matthew. 2013. "Brazilian Pharmaceutical Diplomacy: Social Democratic Principles Versus Soft Power Interests." *International Journal of Health Services* 43(1): 67–89.

Grangeiro, Alexandre, Luciana Teixeira, Francisco I. Bastos, and Paulo Teixeira. 2006. "Sustainability of Brazilian Policy for Access to Antiretroviral Drugs." *Revista Saúde Púbica* 40: (Suppl).

't Hoen, Ellen F. M. 2009. *The Global Politics of Pharmaceutical Monopoly Power*. Diemen: AMB.

Junior, Gonçalo. 1997. "Lafepe Fecha Contrato de R$ 42 Mi Con O Governo." *Gazeta Mercantil*, June 26, 6.

Keck, Margaret, and Kathryn Sikkink. 1998. *Activists beyond Borders: Advocacy Networks in International Politics*. Ithaca: Cornell University Press.

Klug, Heinz. 2008. "Law, Politics, and Access to Essential Medicines in Developing Countries." *Politics & Society* 36(2): 207–45.

Lee, Kelley, and Eduardo Gomez. 2011. "Brazil's Ascendance: The Soft Power Role of Global Health Diplomacy." *The European Business Review*. Retrieved February 4, 2011 (www.europeanbusinessreview.com/?p=3400).

Lins, Leticia, and Isabel de Paula. 1996. "Saúde Não Paga a Fabricante E Pode Ficar Sem AZT." *O Globo*, November 27, 12.

Marques, Felipe, and Lia Hasenclever. 2006. "Política de Compra Governamentais: O Caso Das Compras de Anti-Retrovirais E Seus Efeitos Nocivos À Indústria Nacional." Rio de Janeiro: UFRJ-Instituto de Economia.

Asserting Antiretroviral Autonomy (1990–2001) 123

Matthews, Duncan. 2011. *Intellectual Property, Human Rights and Development: The Role of NGOs and Social Movements.* Cheltenham: Edward Elgar Publishing.

De Mello e Souza, Andre. 2007. "Defying Globalization: Effective Self-Reliance in Brazil." Pp. 37–63 in *The Global Politics of AIDS*, edited by Paul G. Harris and Patricia D. Siplon. Boulder: Lynne Rienner Publishers.

Ministry of Health. 2008. *Custo Dos Medicamentos AIDS.* Brasilia: Ministry of Health.

Nunn, Amy. 2008. *The Politics and History of AIDS Treatment in Brazil.* New York: Springer.

Nunn, Amy, Elize Massard da Fonseca, and Sophia Gruskin. 2009. "Changing Global Essential Medicines Norms to Improve Access to AIDS—Treatment: Lessons from Brazil." *Global Public Health: An International Journal for Research, Policy and Practice* 4(2): 131.

Oliveira, Egléubia Andrade de. 2007. "Política de Produção Pública de Medicamentos No Brasil: O Caso Do Laboratório Farmacêutico Do Estado de Pernambuco (LAFEPE)." (Doctoral Thesis). Rio de Janeiro: Escola Nacional de Saúde Pública Sergio Arouca, Fundação Oswaldo Cruz.

Oliveira, Egléubia Andrade de, Maria Eliana Labra, and Jorge Bermudez. 2006. "A Produção Pública de Medicamentos No Brasil: Uma Visão Geral." *Cadernos da Saúde Pública* 22(11): 2379–89.

Orsi, Fabienne, Lia Hasenclever, Beatriz Fialho, Paulo Tigre, and Benjamin Coriat. 2003. "Intellectual Property Rights, Anti-AIDS Policy and Generic Drugs." Pp. 109–35 in *Economics of AIDS and Access to HIV/AIDS Care in Developing Countries. Issues and Challenges*, edited by Jean-Paul Moatti. Paris: Agence Nationale pour Recherche sur le Sida.

PhRMA. 1998. "1998 National Trade Estimate Submission to USTR." Retrieved November 23, 2008 (www.cptech.org/ip/health/phrma/nte-98/brazil.html).

Rabi, Jaime. 2007. "Politicas Publicas E Empreendedoreismo Em Quimica No Brasil: O Caso Da Microbiologica." *Quimica Nova* 30(6): 1420–28.

Roche. 2001. "Roche and the Brazilian Ministry of Health Reach Agreement for Supply of HIV Drug Viracept." *Roche*, August 31. Retrieved November 25, 2008 (www.roche.com/static/app/news/media-news-2001-08-31-e.pdf.).

Sell, Susan K. 2003. *Private Power, Public Law: The Globalization of Intellectual Property Rights.* Cambridge: Cambridge University Press.

Serra, José. 2004. "The Political Economy of the Brazilian Struggle against AIDS." *An Institute for Advanced Study Friends Forum.* Brown University. Retrieved October 25, 2008 (www.sss.ias.edu/files/papers/paper17.pdf).

Siplon, Patricia D. 2002. *AIDS and the Policy Struggle in the United States.* Washington, DC: Georgetown University Press.

United Nations. 1966. *International Covenant on Economic Social and Cultural Rights.* Geneva: Office of the United Nations High Commissioner for Human Rights.

USTR. 2001a. "United States and Brazil Agree to Use Newly Created Consultative Mechanism to Promote Cooperation on HIV/AIDS and Address WTO Patent Dispute." Retrieved November 27, 2008 (www.ustr.gov/Document_Library/ Press_Releases/2001/June/United_States_Brazil_agree_to_use_newly_created_ Consultative_Mechanism_to_promote_cooperation_on_HIV-AIDS_address_ WTO_p.html).

USTR. 2001b. *USTR Special 301 Report.* Washington, DC: USTR.

Weyland, Kurt Gerhard. 2006. *Bounded Rationality and Policy Diffusion Social Sector Reform in Latin America.* Princeton: Princeton University Press. Retrieved May 22, 2013 (www.UTXA.eblib.com/patron/FullRecord.aspx?p=445568).

WTO. 2001. *Doha Declaration on TRIPS and Public Health.* Geneva: WTO.

5 Patent Power and the Limits of Treatment Activism (2002–2006)

Since its formation in 1987, the Brazilian Interdisciplinary AIDS Association (*Associação Brasileira Interdisciplinar de AIDS*—ABIA) has played a leading role in gathering and disseminating information about the growing AIDS epidemic in Brazil. While most civil society organizations that developed in the 1980s engaged in direct assistance to those affected by the disease, ABIA's mission since its founding in 1987 has been "to promote education and information geared towards preventing and controlling the epidemic" and "oversee the formulation and implementation of public policies." The technical sophistication of its researchers and work made ABIA into a leading civil society organization capable of influencing policymakers and informing the public about the growing epidemic in Brazil. But it is not just the levels of competence that made ABIA such an important player in the country's response to the crisis. Equally significant is the organization's ideology. Its founding members viewed AIDS as a disease that required not just biomedical solutions—doctors, therapies, and condoms—but a broader response to the social exclusion that unjustly placed some people at greater risk than others. ABIA's values expressed on its website resemble those of the *sanitarista* movement: "Defending rights as an integral part of the preservation of health and the reconceptualization of health, including reproductive and sexual health and full citizenship, and as a question of social justice is the banner that directs ABIA's current projects."

ABIA's creation in the 1980s reflected the dramatic increase in civil society organizing around the notion of the "right to have rights" that influenced Brazilian citizenship during the country's democratic transition. No other person combines citizenship claims and the fight against AIDS than ABIA's founder Herbert José de Sousa, also known as Betinho. A sociologist by training, Betinho was active in the leftist Catholic circles in the early 1960s until the military coup in 1964 forced him into exile. Returning to Brazil after a general amnesty in 1979, Betinho established several civil society organizations to address Brazil's historic levels of poverty and endemic hunger, including the Brazilian Institute of Social and Economic Analysis (*Instituto Brasileiro de Analises Sociais e Economicas*—IBASE). He strongly

Patent Power and the Limits of Treatment Activism (2002–2006) 125

believed in an active civil society for addressing the country's historic social problems. In fact, one of his famous phrases is "Only citizen participation is capable of moving the country."

Betinho's interest in AIDS came from the condition of hemophilia that he shared with his brother, the famous cartoonist Henfil, and his exposure to HIV through a blood transfusion. With the physician Walter Almeida, Betinho began meeting with progressive leaders from other social movements and health officials to discuss ways to address the growing epidemic. Start-up funds from Brazilian government organizations and the Ford Foundation provided ABIA the resources to obtain the latest computer and information technology and begin work. Betinho, the president of the entity, did not involve himself in the day-to-day administration but focused on the political campaigns, including the *Declaration of the Fundamental Rights of People Living with HIV*. The *Declaration* served as a national reference of the growing network of Brazil's AIDS NGOs. When HIV treatments became available in the early 1990s, ABIA organized with other NGOs to pressure the government to pay for supplies. Unfortunately, Betinho succumbed to the disease in 1997.

Betinho's legacy continues to inspire the work of ABIA in mobilizing civil society responses to the disease, disseminating information through the media, and lobbying the government for policies based on citizenship and human rights. The United States-sponsored World Trade Organization (WTO) panel against Brazil in 2000 drew ABIA's attention to the connection between patents and high-priced AIDS medicines. Since the episode, the advocacy organization has defended the use of compulsory licenses in order to ensure the medium- and long-term sustainability of its treatment program.

Prior to 2000, Brazil had been able to legally copy most of the first-generation medicines used in the "AIDS cocktail" and contain costs. And in 2001 Brazil obtained price discounts on two patented medicines sold by Merck and Roche after the conclusion of the US-sponsored WTO panel. Despite these successes, Brazilian expenditures on medicines doubled from R$496 million to nearly R$1billion (about US$500 million) between 2002 and 2005. Two factors contributed to the huge outlays. First, the therapeutic consensus included more medicines in the program, raising the number from 13 to 18. These new ARVs, now under patent, significantly increased costs. Second, the number of patients in the program rose from 125,000 in 2002 to 165,000 in 2005. Government negotiators, asking for price discounts on imported medicines, returned to the bargaining table with a compulsory license in 2003 and 2005.

The price negotiations and threats of the compulsory created another political opportunity for social mobilization on patents and Brazil's treatment program. Activists continued to pressure for the issue of compulsory licenses for vital ARVs. Despite the political and legal pressures, the government once again backed off their threats after obtaining some price

126 *Patent Power and the Limits of Treatment Activism (2002–2006)*

discounts. The episode reveals the limits of social movement pressures. One of the main reasons for not using compulsory licenses, I argue, is the decline in local pharmaceutical capabilities as a result of patent power of originator companies and the rise of market power of low-cost producers in Asia. Nonetheless, the confrontation renewed the alliance between social movement insiders and human rights activists, and revealed the need to include another domestic ally—local pharmaceutical industrialists.

RESTRUCTURING THE LOCAL PRODUCTION OF AIDS MEDICINES

Jose Serra, despite attracting international attention in leading Brazil's struggle against AIDS and defending countries' rights to use TRIPS flexibilities, suffered a loss in Brazil's 2002 presidential elections. Left-of-center candidate Luiz Inacio "Lula" da Silva received 61% of the votes against Serra in a runoff election. After eight years of Fernando Henrique Cardoso, Brazilians opted for the candidate from the leftist Workers' Party (*Partido dos Trabalhadores*—PT) who promised to redistribute Brazil's wealth and expand social programs tackling chronic poverty. Lula, whose candidacy was backed by social movements interested in addressing Brazil's social inequalities and the local industrialists affected by neoliberal policies of the past decade, was Brazil's first president to come from the country's popular classes. The new administration, however, promised not to rescind Cardoso's reforms or past economic commitments. Instead, Lula streamlined and expanded existing social programs, halted additional privatization projects, and kicked off industrial policies to support strategic sectors of the economy.

AIDS activists did not expect any significant changes to Brazil's universal treatment program during the presidential transition, given the program's institutionalization and the fact that *sanitaristas* directing the program retained strong ties to social movements. In fact, many activists believed that Lula's administration would be more aggressive in its pursuit of compulsory licenses for AIDS medicines. The one concern was that, since Serra had used the AIDS banner during his political campaign, the new administration would undertake personal changes at the Ministry of Health that could affect the local production of ARVs.

Humberto Costa, a physician from the northeastern state of Pernambuco, was chosen to assume command of the Ministry of Health in Lula's new government. Although he did not command the same degree of political capital as Jose Serra, Costa led a new group of *sanitaristas* into the top positions of the health ministry. The *petistas* (name given to PT politicians) and their allies created the new Secretary of Science, Technology and Strategic Inputs within the ministry under which the Department of Pharmaceutical Assistance would be subordinated and given responsibility for implementing pharmaceutical policies. They consolidated the 23 different programs

Patent Power and the Limits of Treatment Activism (2002–2006)   127

related to pharmaceutical assistance left over from the Serra era. Internal debates about which medicines should receive priority revealed an interest in local production to ensure sustainability of strategic health programs.

The PT continued to invest in modernization of the country's network of 18 public labs. The Umbrella Project *(Projeto Guarda Chuva)*, the investment program undertaken during Serra's administration, only invested in new machinery and productive capacity, according to Norberto Rech, the Director of the Department of Pharmaceutical Assistance at time.[1] A new round of investments under the new administration focused on adapting new technologies, improving human capital, and bringing the labs up to date with the stringent regulations published by the recently created National Sanitary Surveillance Agency *(Agencia Nacional de Vigilância Sanitária*—ANVISA). Total investments in public labs increased significantly in subsequent years. Table 5.1 shows that during Serra's administration, annual investments did not top R$15 million. But the PT, committed to ending Cardoso's emphasis on privatizing state assets, kicked off the Modernization Program of Public Drug Production with investments of R$36 million in the first year and nearly double that amount in subsequent years. Total production of medicines increased, but surprisingly ARV production began to drop, nearly in half in 2004, until peaking again in 2005.

Why did ARV production in public labs decline? Despite the investments in capacity and technology, Brazilian labs began to lose their competitive

Table 5.1   Investments (R$) and Production (Pharmaceutical Units) in Public Labs, 1997–2007

Year	Investments (R$ million)	Production (billions of units*)	Production of ARVs (millions of units*)
1997	–	2.1	71.9
1998	–	2.3	86.2
1999	–	2.5	103.9
2000	–	3.5	136.8
2001	14.5	4.0	202.4
2002	11.4	5.3	194.2
2003	36.0	5.3	153.6
2004	77.9	5.6	118.5
2005	60.7	7.5	209.0
2006	67.9	7.8	163.2
2007	56.4	4.8	163.3

* The Ministry of Health defines a pharmaceutical unit based on its pharmaceutical form; that is, for solids—one pill, one capsule, one vial containing sterile powder; for liquids— one vial; for semi-solids—one collapsible tube; for intravenous—one blister, one vial. The unit is not necessarily comparable to private sector units.

Source: Ministry of Health (2008)

128 *Patent Power and the Limits of Treatment Activism (2002–2006)*

position versus other more aggressive generic producers of ARVs located in the developing world. Brazil's entrance into the generic ARV market in the late 1990s reduced annual patient costs to less than one-third of the $15,000 or more that individuals in the US had to pay, but Indian suppliers began offering prices in the hundreds of dollars for the same medication. According to one study, Brazil paid an excess amount of $110 million from 2001 to 2005 for locally produced generics compared to international reference prices paid by other developing countries (Nunn et al. 2007). Another study showed a difference of $57.6 million just in 2005 (Marques and Hasenclever 2006). Aggressive negotiations with patent holders, nonetheless, resulted in savings of $1.2 billion (Nunn et al. 2007). Why did health authorities continue to pay more for ARVs produced domestically in its public labs instead of economizing resources by sourcing ARVs from abroad?

Brazil's continued support for its public labs is associated with maintaining pharmaceutical autonomy and avoiding foreign dependency. Specifically, having local production of medicines allows for a tougher negotiating stance. The $1.2 billion in savings would not have been achieved without Brazil's ability to produce ARVs in public (or private) labs. According to health authorities, purchasing cheaper AIDS medicines from abroad, while temporarily cheaper, would in the long term lead to higher prices as Brazilian national production and technological capacity declines. "This would place us in a situation of being hostages to decisions made abroad," claims Norberto Rech,[2] one of the new policymakers who entered the Ministry of Health with the PT in power. While international reference prices for first-generation ARVs began to fall, Brazilian health authorities believed it was necessary to continue investing and purchasing medicines made by public labs in order to boost their bargaining position when negotiating prices for patented medicines.[3]

The main reason why Brazilian public labs became less competitive in producing generic ARVs stems from organizational challenges in achieving economies of scale.[4] The country's network of 18 public labs is controlled by distinct branches of government at the federal and state levels. Under Serra, the allocation of ARVs was centralized under Farmanguinhos and the Brazilian Official Pharmaceutical Lab Association (*Associação Brasileira de Laboratórios Oficiais do Brasil*—ALFOB), an industry association representing the public labs. Still, Farmanguinhos ended up accounting for the majority of the production. Under Lula, the Ministry of Health attempted to streamline the public labs' production of ARVs and other medicines used in federal health programs and redirect ARV production away from Farmanguinhos to other public labs.[5]

Efforts to better coordinate the network's production failed, although ARV purchases from other public labs increased at the expense of Farmanguinhos. In 2001, the federal lab produced 135 million pharmaceutical units of ARVs worth R$145 million, more than double the amount procured from other public labs combined. By 2005, the situation had reversed—other public

Patent Power and the Limits of Treatment Activism (2002–2006)   129

labs supplied triple the amount relative to Farmanguinhos. The changes had significant and unforeseen consequences that would increase the country's pharmaceutical dependency. Instead of working together, public labs began to compete against one another for federal contracts to supply ARVs, considered high-end products compared to other generic drugs. Lafepe's Pedro Rolim emphasized that the network of public labs never worked together. "It ended up being a little cannibalistic—each one seeking out their own development and pride since they have distinct juridical bases," he said.[6]

One area that revealed Brazil's dependency as a result of increasing globalization were problems sourcing raw materials—the active pharmaceutical ingredients (APIs) and chemical intermediates required to make final dosage forms. As detailed in Chapter Three, Brazil has a many companies to make finished products but few that produce APIs and other raw materials. Since most public labs produce low value-added medicines, they obtain about two-thirds of their inputs from Asian raw material suppliers, according to ALFOB president Carlos Alberto Pereira Gomes.[7] A few public labs have in-house laboratory scale operations to produce small batches of APIs for a limited range of orphan drugs, but industrial scale production of bulk active principals goes beyond their capabilities.

Sourcing of foreign APIs not only increased dependence as market power of Asian suppliers grew, but increasingly put the country's universal AIDS treatment program at risk. First, part of the administrative changes enacted by the new PT government that came into power in 2003 affected how public labs obtained their raw materials. During the scale-up of ARV production under Minister Serra, procurement of raw material was, to a large extent, centralized in Farmanguinhos under the supervision of Eloan Pinheiro. When the system moved towards decentralized purchases in the various public labs, economies of scale were lost. Possible benefits of spreading risk (i.e. faulty material or delivery delays) were not achieved since most labs ended up buying from the same suppliers, explained MSF's coordinator Michel Lowtroska.[8]

Second, global demand for ARVs skyrocketed as national and global efforts attempted to replicate the success of Brazil's treatment program in other parts of the developing world. Multilateral initiatives included the Global Fund to Fight AIDS, Tuberculosis and Malaria, begun in 2002; the US President's Emergency Plan for AIDS Relief (PEPFAR), launched in 2003; and the World Health Organization (WHO) and the Joint United Nations Programme on HIV/AIDS (UNAIDS)'s "3 by 5" strategy, jointly launched in December 2003 with the aim to have 3 million people on treatment by 2005. Marco Vitoria Antonio, who had helped establish Brazil's National AIDS program and later became a medical officer at the WHO, warned that there could be a "stock out, not because of a lack of political will, but because there are not enough producers of APIs."[9] Rising demand for APIs strained procurement by Brazilian public labs already burdened by highly restrictive rules governing public tenders.

130 *Patent Power and the Limits of Treatment Activism (2002–2006)*

Third, strict tender laws, designed to limit public corruption, favored awarding procurement contracts to suppliers that offered the lowest price. As described in the previous chapter, the Public Procurement Law 8.666 of 1993 established formal procedures that all public sector entities, whether a municipal government or state enterprise, must follow when issuing call-for-tenders and awarding contracts. The rigid legislation did not provide departments or agencies with the flexibility to establish internal rules specific to their objectives. Moreover, tenders could not distinguish between foreign versus local suppliers nor impose technical restrictions, such as quality, apart from price criteria. In sum, price auctions awarded contracts regardless of other criteria. When carrying out auctions for the procurement of raw materials, public labs were legally obliged to award contracts based solely on price and, only afterwards, could they analyze quality. "As a consequence [of Law 8.666], national suppliers have been losing space to Chinese and Indian producers that offer lower prices since they fulfill fewer phytosanitary demands," summed up an analysis by Marques and Hasenclever (2006: 13–14).

Cumbersome procurement laws and weak state support to develop the pharmaceutical industry adversely affected the ability of the local pharmaceutical industry to contribute to Brazil's AIDS treatment program. Campos de Machado Neto from the São Paulo-based API maker Labogen explained that importers connected to trade networks in Asia would always undercut bids during price auctions. "The Chinese representative would hear all the bids then get on his phone and place a lower bid than all those that were submitted," he claimed.[10] In addition, Brazilian firms were at a disadvantage compared to Asian competitors whose government provided various forms of industrial support. Drawback measures, for example, allow companies to assemble products in export processing zones without having to pay taxes on the value added. Brazilian pharmochemical producers argued they would be competitive against Asian imports if they could export their products to a tax-exempt destination like the Cayman Islands and then re-import the product for sale in Brazil. While Asian production chains could take advantage of these tax exemptions to sell to the Brazilian market, local producers would get in trouble with Brazil's tax authorities.

In extreme forms, fiscal benefits transform into export subsidies that result in dumping. "There were even some instances that I would export my product to China and then the Chinese would sell it back to Brazil. They said they could still make money because they receive a lot of fiscal benefits from their government," said Campos de Machado Neto.[11] Local pharmochemical producers lobbied Brazil's trade authorities to take anti-dumping measures against Chinese imports. But Brazilian trade officials would not risk the billions of dollars in Brazilian steel, iron ore, and soy exports in order to support a small pharmochemical industry. Between 2000 and 2010, Brazil exports to China jumped from $55 billion $202 billion.[12]

Patent Power and the Limits of Treatment Activism (2002–2006)

Evidence of the rising market power of Asia in the global pharmaceutical business stems from the fact that production chains linked workers from the Chinese hinterlands to Brazilian patients. Lelio Maçaira, the former Microbiologica director, explained the dynamic process: "The Indians obtained scale and acted in world markets as large suppliers and now obtain their raw materials from the Chinese. The Chinese that speak English buy the materials from the non-English speaking Chinese in the interior. It is a chain that starts in China and goes to the Indians."[13] Between January 2002 and February 2005, foreign suppliers won 82% of the 68 auctions held by Brazilian public labs to procure APIs for making stavudine, didanosine, indinavir, lamivudine, and zidovudine. The contracts totaled $26.3 million (Lages 2007). Maçaira claimed that Brazilian API suppliers would be as competitive as foreigners if they were to circumvent the commercial intermediaries and obtain basic raw materials from the interior of China.

The sourcing of foreign APIs by public labs was not without risks, especially in regard to quality control. Public labs operated by state governments suffered the most from their inability to prequalify suppliers and from burdensome procurement laws. "It is a prostitute market. They show one product that is good quality, and then when they send the whole batch, it is of horrible quality. It is not possible to identify a *picareta* [cheat] during the tender process. If we reject some raw material, it could take up to 15 days, at best, to get another batch," recounted Pedro Rolim from Lafepe.[14] In one instance, a South Korean supplier that had their product rejected by public lab Vital Brazil located in Niteroi, Rio de Janeiro, sent the same item to Lafepe in Pernambuco without even removing the rejection label off the top of the box. Purchasing raw material at the lowest price did not economize resources. Maçaira estimated that public labs paid an extra 30% on the cost of producing ARVs due to the need to re-process or purify poor quality APIs.[15]

In sum, Brazilian public labs became increasingly dependent on Asian suppliers of the key ingredient, the API, for the production of its AIDS medicines. Procurement decentralization based on each facility purchasing APIs individually fragmented a streamlined process that had previously been organized by Farmanguinhos and ALFOB. The shift in procurement occurred at a time when global demand for ARVs spiked. Previous stable supplies and quality controls worsened as foreign producers, rushing to fill the jump in demand, began to outsource their production to poorer quality subcontractors. Strict interpretation of Public Procurement Law 8.666 forced Brazilian purchasers to remain beholden to lowest priced foreign bidders even though quality dropped. In the market disruption, the Brazilian pharmochemical industry lost an opportunity to grow and instead became a service provider for purifying imported raw material. The Achilles' heel of Brazilian local production would threaten its universal access program, but also presented new problems for policymakers to solve.

132 *Patent Power and the Limits of Treatment Activism (2002–2006)*

Supply Problems of the National AIDS Program

At the start of 2005, supply problems with Brazil's model treatment program put 30,000 people at risk. Part of the problem resulted from the rationing of medicines due to the aforementioned problems related to imported APIs. Another issue was the federal government's delay in approving the 2005 budget. Since public labs rely on the government for working capital to purchase inputs, they had to postpone their production timeframes. According to Carlos Alberto Pereira Gomes, director of the public lab Funed and ALFOB's president, supply contracts with the Ministry of Health only occurred in December and not the usual October. "We buy by the Law 8.666, so it was delayed. Since the process of signing contracts got backed up, the purchase of raw material took place later," he was quoted as saying by a news service (Leite 2005).

Failing to manage the symbolic currency of the program weakened ministers of government as well as provided opportunities for image management by originator firms. Supply problems revealed administrative problems and political infighting at the highest levels of government. An editorial in the *Estado de São Paulo* newspaper, often critical of the left-leaning PT government, underscored the "screaming technical incompetence of the Minister Humberto Costa" and the "administrative disorder that delayed in almost three months purchasing orders and the release of funds for the public labs" (Editoria 2005). Asked about the reports of delays in the delivery of raw material, Minister Costa responded: "If we had been advised on the first day about the delays, we would have taken the measures we took now" (Constatino 2005). The Ministry ended up importing three tons of medicines from Argentina using contacts established by Pedro Chequer who helped set the neighboring country's AIDS efforts before returning as director of Brazil's National AIDS Program.[16]

The Health Ministry's budget and administrative problems were not restricted solely to public labs, but also affected direct purchases from foreign companies. In early 2005, health officials claimed stock-outs of patented ARVs were the consequence of companies not lowering their prices. The situation placed companies in a dilemma, but also presented a public relations opportunity. The difference in tactical responses can be seen at the company level. Gilead, the supplier of tenofovir to the program, ended up trading accusations with the Ministry of Health. Health officials said the company did not have its importation papers in order and could be fined, whereas company representatives claimed the ministry did not have US$6 million available for payment (FSP 2005).

Bristol Meyers Squibb (BMS) saw the ministry's budget problems as an opportunity to improve its relationship with the public and portrayed itself as a partner to Brazil's AIDS program. Antonio Salles, director of corporate relations for the company's local division, explained that the company kept warning the government about the stock of medicines. When local media

Patent Power and the Limits of Treatment Activism (2002–2006) 133

contacted the company, BMS's executives revealed all the letters it had sent to health officials. The government and the firm made an informal agreement to purchase ARVs without a contract. "If you look in the newspaper, Bristol made a statement saying there was no contract with the government. We even advised all the NGOs what was going on," recounted Salles.[17]

Despite cultivating some positive relations with a few civil society organizations, companies like BMS still could not win the ideological battle concerning patents. Asked about the rationing of medicines, Rubens Duda, President of São Paulo State AIDS/NGO Forum, was quoted as saying: "The movement does not want to know the motive behind the stock outs; it wants a medicines policy. We want the breaking of patents" (Leite 2005).

HEALTH MINISTERS BACK OFF COMPULSORY LICENSES

Brazil's problems with local production of ARVs compounded the country's ability to take advantage of the humanitarian safeguards provided in TRIPS. In 2003 and 2005, Brazil threatened to issue compulsory licenses (CLs) for the purchase of patented AIDS medicines. But on both occasions, the Minister of Health backed off the threats and reached a negotiated settlement. The two events reveal the problems associated with local production and increased dependency on foreign suppliers.

Besides the budget and administrative problems at the Ministry of Health, there are several other factors that contributed to the failure to take advantage of the TRIPS flexibilities. These included higher standards in pharmaceutical production, perceived US retaliation, and, most importantly, the inability to obtain access to patented inputs used for making drugs. Nonetheless, the ongoing problems with local production and the continued clashes with foreign companies over high-priced medicines increased civil society's mobilization around issues of patents and local production.

Changing Negotiating Strategy Based on Imports

When the left-of-center government of Luiz Inacio Lula da Silva assumed power on January 1, 2003, the treatment coalition expected an even more aggressive approach towards patented medicines. But activists ended up dismayed. Instead of ending patent monopolies, Brazil's clashes with Abbott, Gilead, and MSD revealed additional obstacles in the development and sourcing of generic alternatives, especially given the short time horizons of drug negotiations. AIDS officials developed a new strategy to negotiate with companies by providing two options: either lower prices or provide a voluntary license for the production of medicines in Brazil; otherwise, Brazil could resort to a compulsory license. To make Brazil's bargaining position effective, generic alternatives had to be readily available. But local firms would not invest in production until a market is available. "This is a vicious

134 *Patent Power and the Limits of Treatment Activism (2002–2006)*

cycle: without a market they did not have production ready, and in an emergency they wouldn't be ready. To produce these medicines in Brazil, it would take one to two years," explained Grangeiro, the director of Brazil's AIDS Program from 2002 to 2003.[18]

To keep their options open, the Brazilian policymakers issued Decree #4.830 in 2003, which allows for parallel importation of products when a compulsory license (CL) is issued. When Brazil had threatened CLs in previous years, the threat was backed by the capability to produce the medicine *locally*. Importation was not considered a possibility because it had not been legal under the intellectual property legislation in force at the time that specified national as opposed to international exhaustion of rights. In other words, a drug company could legally restrict importation but not local production. The new decree allowed Brazil to import drugs from countries in which the product was not protected by patent. Since India and China took advantage of the complete transition process to adopt the TRIPS accord, by waiting until 2005 to implement the agreement instead of 1997 like Brazil, they developed several second-generation ARVs that were protected by patent in Brazil but not in their countries.[19] Indian drug companies, for example, had produced generic versions of nelfinavir and efavirenz but had yet to register them with ANVISA in Brazil. The decree represents a continuous learning curve regarding the use of TRIPS flexibilities that resulted from price negotiations officials held with patent holders (Oliveira, Chaves, and Epsztejn 2004).[20]

Increasing the flexibility of intellectual property laws did not change the fact that producers of second-generation ARVs enjoyed market exclusivity based on patent power. Originator companies including Roche, Abbott, and Merck now enjoyed a legal monopoly when marketing their new medicines in Brazil. This situation contrasts with the 1990 to 2002 period when Brazil demonstrated its capability to quickly copy medicines and ramp up production. In the first confrontation over the price of patented medicines and threats to issue a CL, Brazil was able to make a credible threat of local production of Roche's nelfinavir. The initial face-off, despite ending in a negotiated settlement and price reduction, foreshadowed the challenges in subsequent years.

Despite increasing the policy space for issuing CLs, policymakers remained hesitant to use them. First, it was unlikely that President Lula would spend political capital on a CL during his first year in office and potentially scare off foreign investors. The leftist president's arrival to power had already alarmed investors who threatened an economic meltdown by speculating against the country's currency and demanding higher premiums on government debt. Second, some top health officials believed that the threat of compulsory licensing of ARVs is most effective as a deterrent and, if used, would only be effective once. Despite Lula's claims that Brazil would not be "held hostage" to foreign drug companies, some top officials in the Health Ministry described it as an "atomic bomb."[21]

Patent Power and the Limits of Treatment Activism (2002–2006) 135

Despite the hesitation to issue a CL, Brazil's threat remained an effective negotiation tool. Of the options presented to drug companies—either lower prices or voluntarily license local manufacturer of their medicines—they chose the former. Negotiated settlements with patent holders finalized in January 2004 allowed the Ministry of Health to save R$299 million, an economy of 37% of its ARV budget (Oliveira, Chaves, and Epsztejn 2004). The savings coincided with the enrollment of 20,000 new patients in the program and inclusion of two additional ARVs, tenofovir and atazanavir, in its treatment arsenal.

Patent Obstacles to Research and Develop Patented ARVs

After having successfully developed and produced most off-patent ARVs by 2001, AIDS officials looked to develop generic versions of patented medicines. But in subsequent years, Brazil's public labs achieved limited success making copies of second-generation ARVs under patent. Brazil even passed Law 10.196 in 2001 that allows a local drug company to carry out all the necessary tests and procedures required for the registration of generics before a patent expires. Despite the incorporation of this TRIPS flexibility known as the Bolar Exception (i.e. the legal right to obtain all the regulatory approvals before a patent expires), why did Brazilian firms not make greater use of this allowance?

One factor was new regulatory rules. Brazil's new drug regulatory agency, ANVISA was tightening product standards to improve consumer protection on the domestic market. The agency was looking to increase the quality of Brazilian pharmaceutical products on global markets. In 2001, some pharmaceutical companies and even a few NGOs, he added, challenged the quality of Brazil's generic drugs. But, during the reign of Eloan Pinheiro at Farmanguinhos (1994–2002), most quality tests were carried out in-house without ANVISA's external verification. Attempts to discredit the quality of Brazilian generic drugs never succeeded, but regulations governing the market later became more stringent. "So, in 2001 it was much more politically feasible to produce these drugs. In 2003, it was unthinkable," stated Grangeiro.[22]

Besides the ratcheting up of quality standards set forth by ANVISA for obtaining product registration, administrative changes disrupted R&D processes at Farmanguinhos. Eloan Pinheiro, who directed the facility since 1994, left at the end of 2002. The new PT administration felt that she was too closely tied to Lula's former presidential challenger. Indeed, Jose Serra requested Pinheiro to continue as Farmanguinhos' director until the presidential elections, contravening the organization's bylaws that mandated a vote for a new director every three years. An adjunct director assumed control for three months until Farmanguinhos' employees elected Nubia Boechat, an organic chemist and Farmanguinhos career employee, as the new head of the federal lab. She removed personnel associated with Pinheiro

136 *Patent Power and the Limits of Treatment Activism (2002–2006)*

and brought in a new team of researchers and scientists. It is not uncommon for a new administration to enact personnel changes, but interviewees acknowledged that she made substantial changes. Boechat defended that the company was in disarray even before she assumed control since the interim director did not sign any contracts to obtain raw material nor make any operational decisions.[23]

The administrative transition under Boechat came at an inopportune time. The Ministry of Health was redirecting purchases away from Farmanguinhos to other public labs. As a result, the substantial sums of money brought in from ARV purchases during Pinheiro's administration, which, in turn, she used to finance additional R&D projects, fell. "In 2003, the resources available for R&D disappeared," said Boechat. When Pinheiro left Farmanguinhos in 2002, she had eight projects related to ARVs in development. The federal lab continued to invest in ARV development, but there were no new ARV launchings under Boechat's watch.[24]

Other public labs operated by state-run governments did not undergo complicated transitions like Farmanguinhos and were in a better positioned to continue R&D efforts. However, there was no central authority to coordinate efforts. With the Ministry of Health allocating more production towards other public labs, they would have more resources for R&D. But lab managers did not want to risk investing scarce resources without purchase guarantees from the Ministry of Health.

The situation of São Paulo State lab FURP, a close partner of Farmanguinhos, demonstrated the importance of federal contracts and inherent investment risks without a strategic plan to develop medicines under patent. In 2005, FURP sold R$50 million in medicines (both ARVs and other generics) to the Ministry of Health and R$22 million the subsequent year. The revenue difference made significant impact on the laboratory's cash flow. In principle, FURP has the technological capabilities to reverse engineer ARVs and the ability to develop partnerships with the national pharmochemical industry, but the problem involved investment outlays and market guarantees. "I am going to invest some US$2.5 million in two years to do any ARV in advance, to do the reverse engineering and necessary investments . . . and afterwards [the Ministry of Health] turns to me and says it is going to work with Lafepe and Farmanguinhos instead?" posed Ricardo Oliva, FURP's director.[25] Although São Paulo state has the largest seropositive population, Oliva says that it would be a waste of the state government's resources if it were to develop and produce ARVs just for distribution within the state since the program had been federalized. "The Ministry of Health buys the medicines and distributes them," he said in an interview.

Another state lab, Lafepe based in Pernambuco, risked developing new ARV formulations, but the results could not keep pace with changing treatment protocols. In 2004, the company registered a 200mg formulation for efavirenz, but in the same year the therapeutic consensus began recommending a 600mg formulation recently launched by Merck. Instead of taking

Patent Power and the Limits of Treatment Activism (2002–2006)   137

three tablets a day, the new formula required patients take only one tablet, thereby improving treatment adherence. Changing protocols affected not only patented products, but also the development of fixed-dose combinations. Pedro Rolim said he had to cease the development of the three-in-one pill comprised of stavudine-lamivudine-nevirapine after the National AIDS Program stopped recommending the usage of stavudine.[26]

Coordinating R&D and staying abreast of changing treatment protocols are internal problems related to administering a complex social program. These administrative challenges were exacerbated by external constraints imposed by originator companies who were able to use their patent power to restrict the development of generic copies. Despite the Bolar Exception allowing for registration of generics before a patent expires, foreign drug companies filed several injunctions restricting access to patented APIs. Their legal argument is that market exclusivity provided by a patent allows for research and development of the patented product but not its commercialization. Consequently, if a company wanted to develop the pharmaceutical technology required to produce the 600mg formulation of efavirenz, they would still require a CL to *purchase* the API—the key ingredient for making the medicine, but also under patent.

Patent thickets also became a problem for Farmanguinhos. In 2005, the last year of her administration, Boechat said that she signed an agreement with the National AIDS Program to develop efavirenz, atazanavir, and lopinavir.[27] The agreement included R$8 million in funding through Fiotec (the funding arm of the FioCruz Foundation) for the purchase of raw material and development to the industrial scale. But the main obstacle was obtaining APIs in order to reverse engineer and develop the drug. Boechat explained that while she was the director of Farmanguinhos she attempted to purchase 200kg of efavirenz, 100kg of lopinavir, and other APIs from patent holders, but they refused and only wanted to sell the finished product. She then opened the bidding process to local and international competitors who provided bids. Seeing the potential loss of their market, the patent holders of these drugs filed court injunctions to stop the sale. She explained:

> The patent owners said that the law in Brazil permits purchases of raw materials, development of the product, and even registration but not *commercialization!* You need raw material in order to do the development and also to do the registration. The [patent owners] prohibited these companies to commercialize in Brazil.[28]

Although Law 10.196 in 2001 allows for the research and development of patented products without the consent of the patent holder, foreign drug companies used the Brazilian courts to limit access to the necessary raw materials that Farmanguinhos required to develop medicines.[29]

Other public labs faced similar obstacles when attempting to develop formulations of patented ARVs. Lafepe's development of new ARV formulations,

138 *Patent Power and the Limits of Treatment Activism (2002–2006)*

despite the registration of 200mg efavirenz, remained problematic due to restricted access to APIs. In 2003, the state lab was commemorating its insertion in international markets after obtaining approval from the Pan American Health Organization for its pediatric formula of AZT.[30] Pedro Rolim, the former director of production at Lafepe, explained that the public lab had an interest in developing efavirenz, tenofovir, and an FDC lopinavir-ritonavir but had difficulty accessing raw material due to the restrictions imposed by the patent owners of these medicines. As with other public labs, Lafepe did not have the means to produce the API in house, only the finished dosage forms. In the end, he succeeded only in doing limited development work of patented versions of nelfinavir and efavirenz thanks to donated raw materials from suppliers in India.

Managers from other public labs also confirmed that the main problem with developing next-generation, patented ARVs were restrictions imposed by intellectual property rights. They were able to circumvent this obstacle, on limited occasions, through donations provided by private sector companies. Since the product was *donated* and not *commercialized*, there was no legal impediment. But donations of APIs remained limited. Private domestic firms do not want to make a larger investment in donating raw material without having market guarantees or viable commercial opportunity. The effects of patent power would affect Brazilian price negotiations in 2005.

US and NGO Pressures during the Abbott Negotiations

The year 2005 proved a pivotal one in Brazil's AIDS treatment program. ARV costs had jumped to close to R$1 billion, and 165,000 Brazilians were in treatment. Health Minister Humberto Costa demanded discounts or voluntary licenses from Merck for efavirenz, from Abbott for Kaletra (ritonavir/lopinavir), and from Gilead for tenofovir. Abbott was the most intransigent during the negotiations, and on June 24, 2005, Costa declared the fixed-dose combination lopinavir/ritonavir (brand name Kaletra) to be in the public interest. The declaration is the first step for issuing a CL, and the patent holder would have ten business days to respond. From 2002 to 2005, the number of patients using the medicine had jumped sevenfold to 23,400 and annual expenditures reached $91.6 million, representing about a fifth of the budget spent on ARVs. Health officials forecast that the number of patients would increase to 60,000 over the next four years. Negotiations with Abbott began in March, and negotiators demanded a price reduction from $1.17/pill to $0.68/pill—the cost that Farmanguinhos could allegedly produce the medicine. The talks with Abbott were complicated by the fact that Costa left office after supposedly reaching an agreement and were resumed under the new Minister José Saraiva Felipe.

The price negotiations of 2005 illuminate the varied framing of interests, alliance construction, and lobbying pressures. Corporate defenders of strong intellectual property rights quickly began to lobby the USTR to apply

Patent Power and the Limits of Treatment Activism (2002–2006)   139

pressure on Brazil soon after Humberto Costa threatened a CL in March. They couched their arguments in terms of natural rights claims and US national interests. "This theft has gone on at the expense of the American people and the US economy," said Nancie Marzulla, president of Defenders of Property Rights (2005). This frame captured the attention of members of the US Congress who lobbied the US Trade Representative (USTR) to fight Brazilian "theft" and "piracy" of US intellectual property as well as questioned Brazil's national "emergency" since its successful AIDS program kept prevalence rates comparable to those in the US (Wilson 2005). In a letter to USTR, members of the US Congress demanded action against Brazil and expressed concerns of the US's competitiveness being threatened by another rising economic power: "Brazil, with an economic output comparable to Germany, appears to be seeking a way to develop its generic manufacturing capacity through confiscating our pharmaceutical technology," they said (Palmedo 2005). An additional concern was that Brazil would begin competing against US companies for export markets such as Africa. Indeed, Lafepe had just obtained quality approval from PAHO to export pediatric formulas of AZT to Ecuador.

In contrast to US political leaders, treatment activists framed the issue not along nationalist lines, i.e. US versus Brazil, but in terms of greedy corporations whose excessive prices keep access to drugs out of the hands of those who need them. Activists invoked Brazil's image and reputation as being the leader in the fight against AIDS that had been constructed in previous years. "Brazil has let itself be bullied by big drug companies long enough. It's time for Brazil to stand up to them and show the world the kind of global leadership this issue so desperately needs," wrote Dr. Paul Zeitz, Executive Director of Global AIDS Alliance (Health GAP 2005). Treatment activists worldwide led petition drives through the Internet, arguing that Brazilian officials were not assuming their leadership position at the WTO and other international bodies. By refusing to issue a CL, they argued, Brazil was behaving like a "tiger without teeth." Activist efforts were capable of gaining the support of influential media such as the *New York Times* (2005), which defended "Brazil's Right to Save Lives" in an editorial.

At the domestic level, civil society activists looked to improve their organizational and lobbying capacity regarding patents and drug prices in the light of the WTO confrontation. In 2003, they created the Working Group on Intellectual Property (*Grupo de Trabalho sobre Propriedade Intelectual*—GTPI) as part of the Brazilian Network for the Integration of the Peoples (*Rede Brasileira pela Integração dos Povos*—Rebrip), comprised by the following local NGO groups: ABIA, CONECTAS, FENAFAR, GAPA-SP, GAPA-RS, Gestos, GIV, GRAB, IDEC, MSF, and Grupo Pela VIDDA. These organizations hired professional lawyers and pharmacists to sift through the technicalities of patent law and pharmaceuticals. While some of their members have gone on to work for the National AIDS Program, the working group developed similar tactics developed at the

140 *Patent Power and the Limits of Treatment Activism (2002–2006)*

domestic level to achieve universal access. These included channeling information to government contacts concerning prices and the patent situation of specific medicines; gaining attention in the media to explain the connections between trade accords, patents and prices; and filing court cases to keep pressure on the government.

GTPI's objectives were to mitigate the impact that patents have on the health system and to ensure access to essential medicines. Locally, NGOs explained to the public the reasons why medicine prices remain high due to patents, the options at the government's disposal, and the right to health in domestic and international law. ABIA, for example, published fliers that explained the "conflict that exists between intellectual property rights (patent rights) and that of fundamental human rights (the right to health) since the establishment of the TRIPS accord at the WTO."[31] Besides monitoring price negotiations and lobbying for CLs for all those medicines that weigh heavily on the public health system, the group submitted opinions to the patent office questioning patent claims on important medicines and sponsored lawsuits against the legality of pipeline patents.[32]

US diplomats were another important lobbying group. When Brazil first threatened a CL in 2001, US pressure consisted of a Dispute Settlement Panel at the WTO. The US withdrew the panel after Brazil successfully framed the conflict as one of an attack on its successful AIDS program and a human rights issue (see Chapter Four). US authorities, however, retained other instruments of pressure. The USTR produces the annual "Special 301" Report that identifies countries that fail to improve the intellectual property protection (see Chapter Two). If a USTR investigation discovers that a country is at fault, then trading privileges under the General System of Preferences (GSP) could be withdrawn.[33] In 2001, the agency placed Brazil on its Watch List and then on the Priority Watch List in 2003 after Brazil decreed the use of parallel imports in cases of a CL. During the confrontation with Abbott in 2005, members of the US Congress urged the USTR to withdraw Brazil's trade privileges provided under the GSP. Estimates of Brazilian exports affected by the possible trade retaliation ranged from $48 million (Boletín Farmacos 2005) to $3.6 billion (Kogan 2006).

A request made under the Freedom of Information Act (FOIA) of US Department of State Cables between 2004 and 2006 provide insight into the interactions between US and Brazilian officials concerning the use of CLs. The cables reveal the depth of US involvement in monitoring price negotiations, the politics of patents, and the defense of US companies involved in the negotiations—Abbott, Merck, and Gilead. A cable dated June 3, 2005, from the US Embassy Brasilia (2005) with the subject heading "Ambassador Meets with US Pharmaceutical Firms Threatened with Licensing" makes the conclusion: "We continues [sic] to believe that to resonate with the [Government of Brazil], the arguments will need to provide a sound analysis as to why compulsory licensing would be damaging to Brazil's economic and public health interests." In subsequent cables, US diplomats warned

Patent Power and the Limits of Treatment Activism (2002–2006) 141

Brazilian officials that a CL could harm the country's interests in attracting foreign investment and dissuade foreign drug companies to introduce new medicines into the market. Interestingly, US diplomats did not frame the conflict in the terms of "piracy" or "theft" employed by other defenders of strong IP protection, but rather evoked utilitarian and developmentalist arguments. In addition, the diplomatic cables note that the Brazilian government invoked "public interest" and not "national emergency" when negotiating compulsory licenses. In this way, Brazilian authorities could avert criticism that they were suffering from an out-of-control AIDS epidemic, since in fact their model program had kept prevalence rates at levels comparable to those in the US. Defenders of strong intellectual property rights argued that compulsory licenses should only be used during times of national emergency and not for government, non-commercial use as provided by TRIPS.

The details provided under the FOIA request do not detail the full extent of US pressures since many sections in the cables were excised. Agenor Alvares, who was second in command at the Ministry of Health under Saraiva Felipe and present during the negotiations, described the extent of US pressures:

> What was strange during the negotiations was the interference on behalf of the US Embassy. Diplomats from the US Embassy requested a meeting with us, and explicitly threatened that if a compulsory license is used the US would review all the partnerships between the US and Brazil, including training partnerships of Brazilians in research centers in the US. This was explicit. We took into consideration all the bilateral agreements and the interest of the Brazilian government to send Brazilian scientists to the US for training, we reaffirmed our intention that it is important for Brazil's technology development to continue sending scientists there, but we would not accept the threat.[34]

Such explicit bilateral pressures demonstrated how far US diplomats would go to defend the interests of US drug firms.

Direct threats did not convince officials from Brazil's Ministry of Health but led to increased intervention by other ministries. Both Alvares and Saraiva Felipe said that the Minister of Development, Industry, and Trade, Luiz Fernando Furlan, convened a meeting concerning the use of a CL in order to pressure health officials to find an alternative—an action outside of Furlan's ministerial jurisdiction. The fear of trade retaliation hit a nerve at the economic centers of Brazil's agro-export economy. Previous US bilateral pressure during the 1980s and 1990s focused on Brazil's powerful agricultural industry.

The Brazilian government was feeling pressure not only from the US government, but also from Brazilian civil society. On August 11, the National Health Council (*Conselho Nacional da Saúde*—CNS) approved a resolution

142 *Patent Power and the Limits of Treatment Activism (2002–2006)*

recommending the immediate issue of a CL for lopinavir/ritonavir, efavirenz, and tenofovir, "as well as other patented anti-retrovirals that burden or come to burden the budget of the Unified Health System—SUS." The CNS, composed of representatives from civil society, is the highest instance of social participation in the country's health system. Although Health Minister and CNS president Saraiva Felipe stated at the August meeting that "the only inviolable patent is that of life itself" (Boletín Farmacos 2005), he never signed the resolution and thereby never sanctioned its legal power.

When Saraiva Felipe assumed command of the Ministry of Health on July 8, 2005, he attempted to depoliticize price negotiations. Alvares explained that the first change the new minister initiated was to remove the "emotional weight of the negotiations and place the talks on a professional level."[35] They assured US officials of this and to keep the negotiation process transparent. Pressures from the treatment coalition to "break patents" symbolized the "emotional weight" brought to bear on the administration.

The second change concerned the sources and uses of price parameters. When Costa led the negotiations, the target price was $0.68 per pill that Farmanguinhos could allegedly produce the medicine. That price dropped to $0.41 per pill after the *New York Times* (Prada 2005) quoted a Ministry Health official saying that an internal review of local producers demonstrated that they could provide the drug at the lower price. This price then became the new baseline that NGOs demanded and subsequently sanctioned in the CNS resolution. In hindsight, the new baseline appeared more of a negotiating tactic than concrete reality.[36]

Despite the allegedly cheaper prices, the problems of sourcing Kaletra if a compulsory license were issued continued to haunt top officials. Jarbas Barbosa, who was the Secretary of Health Surveillance at the time and involved in the negotiations, recounted that one of the biggest factors weighing in on the decision to use a CL or not was the lack of available generic alternatives that had been approved by regulatory authorities, either by Brazil's Anvisa or by the World Health Organization.[37] Additionally, generic producers did not have Kaletra in stock and would have to scale up production, a problem that also plagued the government's top lab. "Farmanguinhos still could have used an Indian supplier of the API, but it still would have taken two years to complete the development. We did not divulge this because it would have weakened our bargaining position," explained Barbosa. Since no producer had completed the quality tests, health officials worried that doctors would not prescribe the medication to their patients. Abbott eventually offered a price below that of Indian producers. The final agreement, signed on October 10, cut the price of Kaletra to $0.63 per pill (the lowest price Abbott offered outside of Africa).

AIDS bureaucrats and their NGO partners were outraged by the accord and kept up the pressure. One of their chief complaints was that the contract was valid until 2011 and did not foresee the possibility of future price reductions or technology transfer. On December 1, World AIDS Day, treatment

Patent Power and the Limits of Treatment Activism (2002–2006) 143

activists filed a civil lawsuit requesting an injunction against the contract signed with Abbott and an immediate compulsory license for the drug. Pedro Chequer, the AIDS director at the time, said that he provided all the necessary information to NGOs to carry out legal actions.[38] But the courts did not uphold the injunction, arguing that a CL would harm the country's economic interest due to possible US retaliation. More importantly, the court questioned whether there was technical proof of the country's local capacity to produce the medicine at $0.41 per pill.[39]

Representatives from Brazil's private sector drug companies said that Chequer actively sought companies that could provide the key inputs to Brazil's public labs. During the negotiations, the Brazilian Fine Chemical Industry Association (*Associação Brasileiro das Indústrias de Química Fina, Biotecnologia e suas Especialidades*—ABIFINA), the most vocal of the private sector lobbying groups representing domestic companies, did not make any declarations in favor or against the use of a CL for Kaletra. But the entity and its members did provide health officials with information about the sector's capabilities.[40]

A number of organizations outside of government also began to carry-out evaluations of Brazil's pharmaceutical capacities, including the Clinton Foundation (2006) and the United Nations Development Program (UNDP 2006). Besides these important studies, Doctors without Borders teamed up with ABIA to finance a study of Brazil's local production capabilities (Fortunak and Antunes 2006). At this point, activist groups concerned themselves with industrial policies and established closer ties to the domestic pharmaceutical sector. The timing could not have been more auspicious, since the Lula government had just initiated more state support to the domestic pharmaceutical sector.

PHARMACEUTICAL DEPENDENCY AND THE LIMITS OF TREATMENT ACTIVISM

The time period from 2002 to 2006 marks increasing pharmaceutical dependency. The Ministry of Health paid ever larger amounts to acquire patented ARVs. Had Brazil delayed the incorporation of patents on pharmaceuticals until the TRIPS deadline of 2005, like China and India, local generic companies could have continued to legally reverse engineer and supply the country's treatment program as it did the previous period from 1996 to 2002. Graph 5.1 details how generic production, mainly carried out in public labs and factories, substituted the unpatented medicines supplied by the transnational drug industry. By 2002, supplies of non-patented medicines from TNCs had all but disappeared. Consequently, expenditures on unpatented medicines declined from a high of R$400 million in 1999 to almost half that amount two years later. Overall expenditures remained roughly flat, hovering around R$500 million, from 1998 to 2003, while

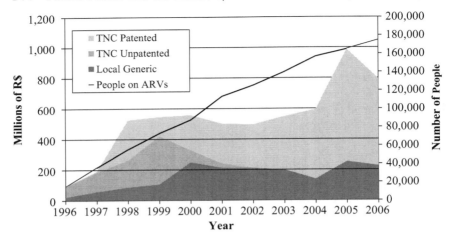

Graph 5.1 Brazilian Expenditures on ARVs (R$ millions*) and Number of People in the Treatment Program, 1996–2006.

Sources: Department of STDs, HIV, and Viral Hepatitis; Ministry of Health; and Banca de Preços.

*Nominal Reais.

the number of people in the program increased by 15,000 to 20,000 annually. Although expenditures remained steady, the Ministry of Health paid ever larger amounts of total spending on patented medicines from TNCs. These expenditures skyrocketed in 2005. In that year, imported ARVs accounted for 77% of total costs of R$1 billion (about $500 million). Three second-line drugs—efavirenz, tenofovir, and lopinavir/ritonavir (Kaletra)—accounted for the bulk of expenditures on these patented medicines. Further compounding the costs of the program is the migration of more patients from first-line medicines that cost US$667 PPPY compared to second-line medicines amounting to US$2,114 PPPY.

Increasing pharmaceutical dependency occurred not only due to ever larger expenditures on imported medicines, but also because of policy constraints. Legally, Brazil could use a compulsory license. National laws and international rules, such as the *Doha Declaration*, authorized compulsory licenses for government, non-commercial use, even without prior negotiations with patent holders. Politically, the treatment coalition including "social movement insiders" working at the National AIDS Program and activists from civil society provided support. Why did they not achieve their objectives for achieving a compulsory license in the case of Kaletra? Lacking the necessary material conditions, such as alternative sources of ARVs, constrained the treatment alliance's power. Brazil had the technical personnel, the material resources, and advanced firms to produce generic versions of all the ARVs on the market, but the country's pharmaceutical capabilities were weakened by a more restrictive patent

Patent Power and the Limits of Treatment Activism (2002–2006) 145

regime and by the inability to organize the various players, from scientists to manufacturers.[41]

According to Nunn (2008: 114), Serra had laid the foundations for labs to complete all the research and development of patented drugs. Articles 42 and 43 of the 1996 Industrial Property Law, combined with Law #10.196 passed in 2001, allow for this exception (see Appendix Three). These flexibilities, outlined in intellectual property legislation, permit researchers and scientists to legally obtain limited quantities of patented APIs to develop medicines and register them with ANVISA before the patent expires. But these provisions did not suffice. According to interviews with directors and researchers, public labs still faced court injunctions when attempting to obtain patented raw material. Patent holders were able to find sympathetic judges that interpreted their actions as forms of *commercialization* instead of merely scientific research. Compared to private industry, public labs must publicly announce their tenders for inputs, thereby notifying patent holders. Indeed, originator firms reportedly spend resources fighting other firms who have registered their products with ANVISA to ensure that they do not sell their product before the patent has expired.[42]

Meanwhile, activists across the state-civil society divide continued to engage in naming and shaming tactics rooted in a human rights-based discourse and pressured politicians through the court system. But in the case of ARVs, TNCs reaped the largest monetary rewards. Class interests rooted in neoliberal globalization prevailed over the efforts of civil society to change power structures. The price negotiations of the Abbott episode left many activists exhausted and demonstrated the limits of previous strategies to force politicians and powerful companies to their will. The experience, nonetheless, provided an opportunity to include another important ally into Brazil's efforts to overcome the patent power of the transnational drug industry—the domestic pharmochemical sector.

NOTES

1. Norberto Rech. Interview with author. Brasilia, DF. September 10, 2008.
2. Ibid.
3. Brazil, nonetheless, tapped into cheap international markets when it joined forces with other South American countries and engaged in collective negotiations in order to obtain better prices. For an evaluation of the first round of collective negotiations in 2003 and the difficulties encountered, see the study carried out by the Center for Pharmaceutical Policies (Cristante, Osorio-de-Castro, and Oliviera 2008: 8).
4. Other reasons include the lack of incentives for administrators in public labs to reduce costs, poor production planning, lack of administrative flexibility illustrated by Law 8.666 (explained in Chapter Four), and the Ministry of Health's willingness to pay more for ARVs to cover the fixed costs of public labs (Clinton Foundation 2006).
5. Hayne Felipe. Interview with author. Rio de Janeiro, RJ. September 22, 2008.

146 *Patent Power and the Limits of Treatment Activism (2002–2006)*

6. Pedro Rolim. Interview with author. Pernambuco, PE. July 28, 2008.
7. Carlos Alberto Pereira Gomes. Interview with author. Belo Horizonte, MG. August 25, 2008.
8. Michel Lowtroska. Interview with author. Rio de Janeiro, RJ. March 25, 2008.
9. Marco Vitoria Antonio. Interview with author. Geneva, Switzerland. August 15, 2006.
10. Campos de Machado Neto. Interview with author. São Paulo, SP. July 7, 2008.
11. Ibid.
12. Trade data obtained from Brazil's Ministry of Trade and Development. Secretary of Foreign Trade. 2013. "Brazilian Trade Balance." Available at www. mdic.gov.br/sitio/interna/interna.php?area=5&menu=3385&refr=576.
13. Lelio Maçiara. Interview with author. Rio de Janeiro, RJ. November 28, 2007.
14. Rolim interview.
15. Maçiara interview. This provided a new niche for some Brazilian pharmochemical firms, such as Labogen, which became a service provider re-processing poor quality imported APIs, claims Campos de Machado Neto, in interview with author.
16. Brazil later paid back the Argentine government with R$3.9 million worth of ARVs. Brazil and Argentina have increased collaborations across a number of issues affecting their health systems and pharmaceutical policies.
17. Antonio Salles. Interview with author. São Paulo, SP. May 8, 2008.
18. Alexander Grangeiro. Interview with author. São Paulo, SP. May 7, 2008.
19. Appendix Three includes a list of TRIPS flexibilities and related Brazilian legislation.
20. Shadlen (2009) notes that a lawyer from Brazil's fine chemical industry association ABIFINA drafted Decree #4.830 outlining the uses of a compulsory license. Incorporating TRIPS flexibilities were not always successful. In 2002, Brazil passed Law 10.603 which grants protection for undisclosed data drug firms provide to regulatory officials in order to obtain marketing approval. Extending the timeframe for protecting undisclosed data, a TRIPS-plus measure, restricts competition from generic drug makers that could lower prices. The law was passed after Jose Serra had left the Ministry of Health to campaign for the presidency and before new PT officials had assumed control of government. The law may have been more difficult to pass had it not been pushed through during this window of opportunity between administrations.
21. Grangeiro interview.
22. Ibid.
23. Nubia Boechat. Interview with author. Rio de Janeiro, RJ. April 22, 2008.
24. During this time, Farmanguinhos only registered one product. Boechat adds that ANVISA's stricter regulations were also a factor. "Eloan was able to approve eight medicines in one year. Afterwards, ANVISA began its operations and it became difficult even to renew registrations," she said.
25. Ricardo Oliva. Interview with author. São Paulo, SP. December 17, 2007.
26. Pedro Rolim interview.
27. Boechat interview.
28. Ibid.
29. Private generic drug companies do not face the same restrictions as public labs when taking advantage of the Bolar Exception. Since they are not required to publicize their tenders, patent holders do not have knowledge of their R&D strategies and therefore cannot lodge any injunctions restricting access to patented products.
30. "We did do some donations of AZT syrup to other countries in Latin America and Africa. We were the only public lab that did AZT syrup. It was also

Patent Power and the Limits of Treatment Activism (2002–2006)   147

important in confronting TNCs, which said that we did not have quality, at the moment when we started producing a lot of ARVs. They did not want us to start exporting to Asia and Africa at cheaper prices. All the TNCs with patents viewed Brazil as a competitor and wanted our product to just stay in Brazil. One impediment to exporting was the necessary registrations that we needed to have in that country. All these countries wanted to buy our product," said Pedro Rolim, in interview with author.

31. See www.abiaids.org.br/_img/media/cartilha_patentes_es.pdf (author's translation).
32. See GTPI's website "De Olha nas Patentes" (www.deolhanaspatentes.org.br) for a list of their actions.
33. Sell (2003) has detailed PhRMA's influence on the USTR's decision-making process. Based solely on information provided by the lobbying group, USTR withdrew trade preferences worth US$260 million from Argentina in 1997 (Sell 2003: 136). In the case of Brazil, PhRMA requested the USTR to include it on the Special 301 for lack of IP protection.
34. Agenor Alvares. Interview with author. Brasilia, DF. July 12, 2008.
35. Ibid.
36. US State Department cables, however, related that Brazil's Health officials said the Clinton Foundation could source efavirenz at the 41-cent price per pill.
37. Jarbas Barbosa. Phone interview with author. October 23, 2008.
38. Pedro Chequer. Interview with author. Brasilia, DF. July 12, 2008.
39. See GTPI's "De Olha nas Patentes," Caso Lopinavir/Ritonavir (Kaletra) www.deolhonaspatentes.org.br/caso_lopinavirritonavir_kaletra.html; and Benjamin Coriat, Fabienne Orsi, and Cristina d'Almeida (2006).
40. Alvares, in interview with author, said that Cristalia offered the API to Farmanguinhos at a price of R$0.47 per pill, about US$0.23. Farmanguinhos, in turn, said they could have the final product ready in two years' time, as long as there were no problems at any stage of development. Here again, policymakers remained trapped in a Catch-22—the time delay between having a readily available alternative in case a CL is issued and the time necessary to complete a drug's development and certification.
41. See also Possas (2008).
42. Jorge Raimundo, 2008. Interview with author. Rio de Janeiro, RJ. June 20.

REFERENCES

Boletín Farmacos. 2005. "Brasil, Abbott Y Sida: Continúan Las Negociaciones. El Consejo Nacional de Salud Recomienda Quebrar Patentes." *Boletín Farmacos*, September.

Clinton Foundation. 2006. "Analisis Da Situacao Da Producao Local de ARVs: Precos, Custos, Planejamento de Producao E Competitividade Internacional." Retrieved January 31, 2009 (www.aids.gov.br/data/documents/storedDocumen ts/%7BB8EF5DAF-23AE-4891-AD36–1903553A3174%7D/%7BD51846A2–744D-4D83-B324-A3E2E553EC1A%7D/RNP2.pdf).

Constatino, Luciana. 2005. "Governo Acompanhará Compras de Laboratórios." *Folha de São Paulo*, March 2.

Coriat, Benjamin, Fabienne Orsi, and Cristina d' Almeida. 2006. "TRIPS and the International Public Health Controversies: Issues and Challenges." *Industrial and Corporate Change* 15(6): 1033–62.

Cristante, Maruja, Claudia Garcia Serpa Osorio-de-Castro, and Maria Auxiliadora Oliviera. 2008. *Methodology for the Evaluation of Price Negotiations of Anti-Retrovirals in Latin American and Central American Countries*. Rio de

148   *Patent Power and the Limits of Treatment Activism (2002–2006)*

Janeiro: Center for Pharmaceutical Policies, Sergio Arouca National School of Public Health—ENSP.

Defenders of Property Rights. 2005. "Defenders of Property Rights Applauds USTR Comments on Brazil's Theft of US Drug Patents." Retrieved February 12, 2009 (http://goliath.ecnext.com/coms2/gi_0199–4243740/Defenders-of-Property-Rights-Applauds.html).

Editoria. 2005. "Novo Escândalo Na Saúde." *Estado de São Paulo*, February 25. Retrieved January 31, 2009 (http://clippingmp.planejamento.gov.br/cadastros/noticias/2005/2/25/noticia.180337/?searchterm=Argentina%20AIDS).

Fortunak, Joseph, and Otavio Antunes. 2006. *The ARV Production in Brazil—An Evaluation*. Rio de Janeiro: MSF/ABIA. Retrieved February 20, 2009 (www.abiaids.org.br/_img/media/ARV.pdf).

FSP. 2005. "Saúde: SP Raciona Entrega de Remédio Para Aids." *Folha de São Paulo*, March 14. Retrieved January 31, 2009 (http://sistemas.aids.gov.br/imprensa/Noticias.asp?NOTCod=63167).

Health GAP. 2005. "AIDS Activists Deliver Spine to Brazilian Embassy and Mission Urge Brazil to Show Leadership, Break Patent Monopolies on Costly HIV Medicines." Retrieved February 12, 2009 (www.healthgap.org/press_releases/05/051305_HGAP_PR_Brazil_CL_demo.html).

Kogan, Lawrence A. 2006. "Brazil's IP Opportunism Threatens U.S. Private Property Rights." *Inter-American Law Review* 38(1): 1–139.

Lages, Nicolau Pires. 2007. "Compras Governamentais Como Elemento Indutor Do Desenvolvimento Industrial E Tecnológico Do País." Retrieved January 30, 2009 (www.abifina.org.br/publicacoes.asp).

Leite, Fabiana. 2005. "Laboratórios Apontam Atraso de Repasses." *Folha de São Paulo*, February 24. Retrieved January 31, 2009 (www1.folha.uol.com.br/folha/cotidiano/ult95u106036.shtml).

Marques, Felipe, and Lia Hasenclever. 2006. "Política de Compra Governamentais: O Caso Das Compras de Anti-Retrovirais E Seus Efeitos Nocivos À Indústria Nacional." Rio de Janeiro: UFRJ.

Ministry of Health, Departamento de Assistência Farmacêutica e Insumos Estratégicos. 2008. "Investment and Production in Public Labs." Brasilia: Ministry of Health.

New York Times. 2005. "Brazil's Right to Save Lives." *The New York Times*, June 23. Retrieved February 12, 2009 (www.nytimes.com/2005/06/23/opinion/23thu3.html).

Nunn, Amy. 2008. *The Politics and History of AIDS Treatment in Brazil*. New York: Springer.

Nunn, Amy, Elize Fonseca, Francisco Bastos, Sofia Gruskin, and Joshua Salomon. 2007. "Evolution of Antiretroviral Costs in Brazil in the Context of Free and Universal Access to AIDS Treatment." *PLos Med* 4(11): 1804–17.

Oliveira, Maria Auxiliadora, Gabriela Chaves, and Ruth Epsztejn. 2004. "Brazilian Intellectual Property Legislation." Pp. 151–60 in *Intellectual Property in the Context of the WTO Trips Agreement: Challenges to Public Health*, edited by Jorge Bermudez and Maria Auxiliardora Oliveira. Rio de Janeiro: ENSP.

Palmedo, Mike. 2005. "3 More Members of Congress Write USTR on Brazilian Compulsory Licensing Dispute." Retrieved February 12, 2009 (http://lists.essential.org/pipermail/ip-health/2005-May/007950.html).

Possas, Cristina de Albuquerque. 2008. "Compulsory Licensing in the Real World: The Case of ARV Drugs in Brazil." Pp. 150–66 in *The Political Economy of HIV/AIDS in Developing Countries*, edited by Benjamin Coriat. Cheltenham: Edward Elgar Publishing.

Prada, Paulo. 2005. "Brazil Again Seeks to Cut Cost of AIDS Drug." *The New York Times*, August 19. Retrieved February 13, 2009 (www.nytimes.com/2005/08/19/

business/19abbott.html?scp=1&sq=19%20August%202005%20Brazil%20&st=cse).

Sell, Susan K. 2003. *Private Power, Public Law: The Globalization of Intellectual Property Rights*. Cambridge: Cambridge University Press.

Shadlen, Kenneth. 2009. "The Politics of Patents and Drugs in Brazil and Mexico: The Industrial Bases of Health Policies." *Comparative Politics* 41: 178–201.

UNDP. 2006. "Avaliação Da Capacidade de Produção de ARV Genéricos No Brasil." Geneva: UNDP.

US Embassy Brasilia. 2005. "Ambassador Meets with U.S. Pharmaceutical Firms Threatened with Licensing." June 3. (Diplomatic Cable). United States State Department. Retrieved February 13, 2009 (http://keionline.org/content/view/136/1).

Wilson, Joe. 2005. "Joe Wilson's Letter to USTR." Retrieved February 12, 2009 (www.cptech.org/ip/health/c/brazil/wilson05242005.pdf).

6 Consolidating the Pharmaceutical Alliance (2007–2013)

Few in Brazil have been as consistent and outspoken about the need for industrial policies to support domestic pharmaceutical companies than Nelson Brasil. While most other executives his age would have retired, he has become more energetic publishing editorials in newspapers, making presentations at conferences, and defending his ideas at seminars. In his position as vice-president of the Brazilian Association of Fine Chemical Industry (*Associação Brasileira da Indústria de Química Fina*—ABIFINA),[1] he witnessed the decline of, and struggled to defend, the country's pharmochemical industry. According to Brasil, the 1980s was the golden era for the industry when the government had a coherent set of policies that included tariff protection, the provision of credit through state development banks, technological support through state research institutes, and market guarantees. "The model was so important that it was adopted by India, which at the time was far behind Brazil. Brazil changed its rules and India kept theirs and now has become one of the biggest exporters of drugs," Brasil claimed.[2]

Since ABIFINA's creation in 1986, the industry association confronted drastic changes in the "rules of the game" that govern Brazil's pharmaceutical market. The boom years of the 1980s collapsed with the rapid adoption of neoliberal policies in the early 1990s. Trade liberalization combined with the strong appreciation of the Brazilian currency, the real, devastated the local pharmochemical sector. ABIFINA struggled to keep the industry from completely disappearing and failed to obtain government support from President Cardoso. "Even though he had a position favorable to development and against dependency of the 1970s, Cardoso did not reverse the economic opening but deepened the elements of globalization," asserted Brasil. Marginal improvements occurred under Cardoso's second term when José Serra became the Minister of Health. Serra defended the use of compulsory licenses and passed laws supporting the use of generic medicines. But Serra failed to understand the strategic role of active pharmaceutical ingredients (APIs). "When there is a patent, few concern themselves with formulation. The most important patents are in the synthesis, the API. This is what Serra lacked and what [Minister] Temporão is looking at," claimed

Consolidating the Pharmaceutical Alliance (2007–2013) 151

the vice-president of ABIFINA in his comparison of the two different health ministers.

For Nelson Brasil and many others, a coherent set of policies for governing the pharmaceutical sector finally crystalized during the tenure of José Gomes Temporão who served as Minister of Health from March 2007 to December 2010 under President Luis Inacio Lula de Silva. "Temporão does not represent a political party but that of a physician, a *sanitarista*, with a national program in line with all the ideas that ABIFINA has been defending," emphasized Brasil. Most Ministers of Health, such as Jose Serra, are life-long politicians, but a few, like Temporão, see the position as a top career achievement.[3] Temporão focused on implementing the ideas of the *sanitarista* movement, Brazil's health reform movement that criticized profit-based forms of health care and defended socialized medicine as a form of social justice. That a *sanitarista* like Temporão would find common cause with the for-profit fine chemical industry appears counterintuitive. But the context and available policy options shaped the growing ties between the state and local industrialists.

Haydu's methodological framework of recurrent problem solving to understand policy outcomes provides insight in the new collaborations between ideologically committed policymakers and local industrialists. According to the path dependent model, neoliberal policies, including the end of industrial policies, in the 1990s under Cardoso should have resulted in lock-in mechanisms that result in their continuance. Instead, the opposite occurred. As Chapter Five details, policymakers increasingly recognized the problematic links between patents and access to raw materials to make medicines. The treatment coalition needed additional partners to ensure the sustainability of the AIDS program. New industrial policies for the pharmaceutical sector secured the backing of the domestic private industry.

Treatment activists, inside and outside of government, and the local pharmochemical industry, wanted the same goal—to strengthen local production. But they viewed the topic of patents and medicines from distinct normative frameworks. While Brazilian health activists employed the discourse of health as a human right, local industrialists used developmentalist rhetoric and emphasized unfair trade rules. "The US on a daily basis even kidnaps intellectual property—not in the name of health but more so in the name of defense or economic abuse—and removes the concessions in name of anti-trust law," stated Brasil.[4] In his view, the US government operates under a double standard when it "breaks patents" in order to support the military industrial complex or to correct market abuses but denies developing countries to pursue similar objectives.

The period between 2007 and 2013 witnessed increasing pharmaceutical autonomy as Brazil developed programs to produce locally more raw materials used in medicines in the public health sector and included the local industry in its treatment alliance. This chapter explains why the state developed

152 *Consolidating the Pharmaceutical Alliance (2007–2013)*

industrial policies for the pharmaceutical sector but did not engage in direct production of raw materials. Instead, public-private partnerships between public labs and local pharmaceutical companies sought to nationalize the production of strategic medicines. These initiatives solidified the support of important sectors of the national bourgeoisie for the country's aggressive price negotiations with patent holders of important ARVs. In effect, a triple alliance of state, civil society, and industry assumed specific roles to support Brazil's universal treatment program. The cases of two ARVs, efavirenz and tenofovir, demonstrate the actions and relationships between these different groups to use of the flexibilities outlined by the Agreement on Trade-Related Aspects of Intellectual Property (TRIPS). In 2007, Brazil finally followed through with its threats and issued a compulsory license for efavirenz that demonstrated the power of Brazil's pharmaceutical alliance.

NEW INDUSTRIAL POLICIES FOR THE PHARMACEUTICAL SECTOR

Technological Transfer and Lead Up to Public-Private Partnerships

When developing countries signed on to TRIPS, they believed that the deal would include technology transfer.[5] However, attempts to create working groups and consultation systems at the intergovernmental level for resolving issues surrounding technological transfer only revealed the discrepancies between developed and developing countries (South Centre 2005). Brazil's experiences in requesting technology transfer of AIDS medicines from patent holders highlighted the strategic nature of pharmaceutical technology and different interests between transnational drug companies and developing countries.[6]

During price talks with transnational drug companies between 2000 and 2007, Brazilian negotiators requested voluntary licenses for patented ARVs. None of these negotiations resulted in a patent holder agreeing to transfer technology to Brazilian public or private labs under a voluntary license. Discussions advanced the furthest in the case of Merck's efavirenz, but Brazilian officials ultimately rejected company proposals. In the view of the Brazilians, Merck's proposal was unacceptable because the transfer was based on the condition that the API be provided by the company.[7] Only in recent years have health officials convinced proprietary companies to engage in technology transfer agreements.

Brazilian policymakers have taken a proactive approach towards acquiring technology and addressing the Achilles' heel of Brazilian local production—a weak pharmochemical sector. As detailed in Chapter Five, not only did patent holders restrict access to APIs, but on several occasions the poor quality of imported raw material increased costs and delayed

Consolidating the Pharmaceutical Alliance (2007–2013)   153

production, at times forcing the National AIDS Program to ration treatments. With the public labs monopolizing end-production of ARVs and the Ministry of Health establishing state enterprises in other product lines, why did the Brazilian government not also establish a state-owned pharmochemical company to produce APIs needed to produce the final dosage forms? A state-owned API factory would have sidestepped court injunctions that patent owners could issue in order to stop research and development of generic versions. Compared to the former administration of President Cardoso, the leftist Workers Party under President Lula had halted privatization plans and initiated some new state ventures. In the area of health, the government invested in a state company to produce blood-derived products[8] and a condom factory in the Amazon that uses natural latex collected from rubber tappers.

Current and former managers of public labs expressed the need for a stronger pharmochemical industry, but also had mixed opinions whether the government should enter the upstream industry. Eloan Pinheiro said she was against the idea of Farmanguinhos (FM) having its own API manufacturing plant due to public sector inefficiencies.[9] Nubia Boechat, who succeeded Pinheiro at the federal lab, had a different view. In fact, during her administration FM purchased a production facility from GlaxoSmithKline for R$18 million (about $9 million) to increase capacity to over 10 billion units. The purchase, however, did not include a pharmochemical division. Boechat advanced negotiations to acquire Microbiologica's old API factory, but the purchase never came to fruition.[10] Instead, policymakers opted for new industrial policies that include public-private partnerships to develop APIs and medicines for the public health sector. With India and China adhering to TRIPS in 2005, the need for developing local API capabilities became increasingly more important. In the view of policymakers, patent barriers could restrict the availability of both medicines and raw materials from Asian countries.

Industrial Policies for the Pharmaceutical Sector

Brazil's 2005 price dispute with Abbott revealed the need for a strong pharmaceutical base to support its AIDS treatment program, and the R$1 billion the Ministry of Health annually spent on ARV purchases attracted the interests of the privately owned local API makers. Nelson Brasil from ABIFINA had been fighting to obtain more government support for the sector. By the turn of the century, neoliberal ideology amongst policymakers began to give way towards a more interventionist attitude. Although economic policy making remained in the hands of orthodox economists like Pedro Malan, Health Minister Jose Serra favored state promotion of national development goals. He was instrumental in passing the Law of Generics in 1999, which stimulated the development of a national generic drug industry. Towards the end of Cardoso's presidency, new sector funds were set up to stimulate

154 *Consolidating the Pharmaceutical Alliance (2007–2013)*

technology in local industry, including the Health Sector Fund *(CT-Saúde)*. The Fund's objective was to encourage private investment in research and development for products destined for the public health sector.

The National AIDS Program also pushed the government to support the pharmaceutical sector to ensure the long-term sustainability of its treatment program and to improve its bargaining leverage in ARV price negotiations. By the time Alexander Grangeiro left the program in 2003, the link between compulsory licenses and industrial policies became apparent. But one had to come before the other. Contrary to claims by the transnational drug corporations that compulsory licenses were an illegal form of industrial policy, Brazil's AIDS officials involved in the use of compulsory licenses alleged that the legal instrument had become so political and exhausting that to base support for local industry on it was unreasonable. Rather, it was better to support local industry and technical capacity to better regulate the market.[11] Compulsory licenses, given their political and bureaucratic complexity, could never function as well-planned industrial policy.

With the arrival of Luiz Inacio 'Lula' da Silva to power in 2003, AIDS officials and local industrialists found a government interested in developing policies to support the pharmaceutical sector. The Workers' Party headed by Lula had been currying favor with Brazilian industrialists in the run up to the elections. The new administration now had a chance to deliver. While the new economic team promised not to rescind any previous economic commitments made during the Cardoso era,[12] key economic policymakers, such as economists Luciano Coutinho, Carlos Lessa, and Guido Manteiga, were more influenced by neostructuralist economic philosophies that favored more state intervention in the economy (Zanatta 2012).

Table 6.1 lists the major horizontal industrial policies that apply to the entire economy. The new administration first outlined their objectives in the *Guidelines for Industrial, Technological, and Trade Policies* (Brazil 2003), which envisioned more state support for strategic sectors of the domestic industry and created the Brazilian Agency of Industrial Development *(Agência Brasileira de Desenvolvimento Industrial)* in 2004 to guide and coordinate industrial policies. Specifically, the *Guidelines* chose the semiconductor, software, capital goods, and pharmaceutical industries as strategic sectors of the economy that required state support.

Lula's administration passed various horizontal policies that would impact several sectors of the economy. The "Innovation Act" (*Lei de Inovação*, Law 10.973/2004) and the "Good Act" (*Lei do Bem*, Law 11.196/2005) encouraged more collaboration between academic institutions and the private sector to create innovative products and services. Due to lackluster results from with the first round of policies, called Industrial, Technological and Foreign Trade Policy (*Política Industrial Tecnológica de Comércio Exterior*—PITCE), Lula's economic team then initiated the Productive Development Policy *(Política de Desenvolvimento Produtivo*—PDP) in 2008. This effort sought to increase competitiveness by achieving specific

Consolidating the Pharmaceutical Alliance (2007–2013)   155

Table 6.1   Horizontal Industrial Policies, 2004–2011

Year	Policy	Description
2004	Industrial, Technological, and Foreign Trade Policy (*Política Industrial Tecnológica de Comércio Exterior*—PITCE)	Promotes exports, stimulates innovation, and selects strategic industries (software, semiconductor, capital goods, and pharmaceuticals)
	Innovation Act (*Lei de Inovação*, 10.973)	Encourages research and scientific collaborations between private sector firms and universities
2005	The Good Act (*Lei do Bem*, 11.196)	Provides tax exemptions for private companies to invest in innovation and hire researchers
2008	Productive Development Policy (*Política de Desenvolvimento Produtivo*—PDP)	Establishes measurable goals to increase exports, investment, and R&D expenditures as a percentage of GDP
2010	Government Purchases Act (*Lei de Compras Governamentais*, 12.349)	Changed Public Procurement Act 8.666 so that state entities could give preferential treatment to local producers of goods and services at prices 25% higher relative to foreign offers
2011	Better Brazil Plan *(Plano Brasil Maior Decreto n° 7.540)*	Promotes export diversification, firm internationalization, human capital development, local production, and consumer access

targets in exports, investment, and R&D expenditures as a percentage of GDP. Importantly, the state changed some of the rules governing public procurement in order to overcome fiscal disadvantages faced by domestic producers. The Governmental Purchases Law *(Lei de Compras Governamentais 12.349/2010)* permits state entities to purchase products and services incorporating national technology from local producers at prices up to 25% higher than those offered by foreign suppliers. The legislation attempts to provide isonomy to local producers who face a higher tax burden when competing against imports from low-tax zones.

While horizontal policies applied to the entire economy, vertical industrial policies targeted specific industries. Given the industry's high levels of R&D, looming trade deficits, and tie-in to public health objectives, it is not surprising that policymakers chose the pharmaceutical sector for additional policies (Marques 2002; Ministry of Health 2003; Palmeira and Capanema 2004; Palmeira and Pan 2003). By 2008, the trade deficit in medicines reached US$4.6 billion (Almeida 2009). The first important public program for the pharmaceutical industry was Profarma, administered by Brazil's

156   *Consolidating the Pharmaceutical Alliance (2007–2013)*

National Development Bank for Economic and Social Development (*Banco Nacional de Desenvolvimento Econômico e Social*—BNDES). The extension of credit from the state development bank sought to strengthen local industry by allowing firms to upgrade facilities to stricter quality and regulatory standards (such as the Good Manufacturing Standards), expand their production portfolios, and stimulate domestic mergers and acquisitions.

Table 6.2 lists the vertical industrial policies specific to the health-related manufacturing industries, especially the pharmaceutical sector. Interestingly,

Table 6.2   Vertical Industrial Policies Specific to Health and Pharmaceuticals, 2000–2013

Year	Policy	Description
2000	Health Sector Fund *(CT-Saúde, Lei n° 10.168)*	Promotes technical capacity in areas related to the Unified Health System
2004	Profarma Program of the National Development Bank (*Banco Nacional de Desenvolvimento Econômico e Social*—BNDES)	Stimulates productive investment, capacity, and innovation of biotechnology sectors of the country's health industrial complex *(Programa de Apoio de Desenvolvimento da Cadeia Produtiva Farmacêutica)*
2007	More Health *(Mais Saúde)*	Establishes the Health Industrial Complex *(Complexo Industrial na Saúde)* as one of seven pillars of state action in the area of health
2008	Ministerial Directive 978 *(Portaria n° 978/ GM/MS)*	Lists strategic medicines used by SUS (List updated again in Ministerial Directive 1284/2010)
	Interministerial Directive 128 *(Portaria Interministerial n° 128/MPOG/MS/MCT/ MDIC)*	Establishes guidelines for the public procurement of medicines and drugs used by SUS
	Ministerial Directive 3.031 *(Portaria n° 3.031/GM/MS)*	Provides the criteria public labs will use to procure raw materials from national producers, including the use of public-private partnerships to produce medicines needed by SUS
2009	ANVISA Resolution 57 (RDC 57)	Requires all pharmochemical producers and importers to register active pharmaceutical ingredients with the regulatory agency
2012	Ministerial Directive 506 *(Portaria n° 506/GM/MS)*	Institutes the Program for the Development of the Health Industrial Complex (*Programa para o Desenvolvimento do Complexo Industrial da Saúde*—PROCIS)

Year	Policy	Description
	Ministerial Directive 837 (*Portaria n° 837/GM/MS*)	Defines guidelines and criteria for establishing productive development partnerships (*Parcerias para o Desenvolvimento Produtivo*—PDP)
	Law 12.715 (*Lei 12.715*)	Article 73 dispenses with tender process with contracts that involve technological transfer between public labs and private sector for strategic items used by SUS
2013	Innovate Health (*Inova Saúde*—Financing Agency for Studies and Projects Finep & Ministry of Health)	Provides R$1.2 billion in credit, subsidies, and equity stakes to develop technologies in biologics, medicines, and pharmochemicals.
	Ministerial Directive 80 (*Portaria n° 80/2013/INPI/MDIC*)	Gives priority to strategic medicines used by SUS in the examination of patent applications

the Ministry of Health assumed policies for supporting the pharmaceutical sector, instead of the Ministry of Development, Industry, and Foreign Trade (MDIC) that traditionally performed this role. Minister Temporão, who took command of the Ministry of Health in March 2007, centralized health-related industrial policies in the Secretariat of Science, Technology and Strategic Inputs under the rubric of the *Health Industrial Complex*. The Secretariat coordinated with other government agencies and programs to encourage import substitution and new innovations used in Brazil's Unified Health System (*Sistema Unica da Saude*—SUS).

The objectives of the Health Industrial Complex specifically mention the "structuring of public production and transfer of technology of strategic pharmo-chemicals to the country, including the nationalization of antiretrovirals" (Ministry of Health 2008: 47). Andre Porto, General Coordination for the Development of Pharmaceutical Production and Inputs, Ministry of Health, explains the goals of the industrial policies for the pharmochemical sector:

Verticalizing all the production of APIs here is nearly impossible today, but the more stages of synthesis done here, the better. What is most desirable is that the last steps of the API are done here. The problem with the entire route of synthesis is that the Chinese dominate the intermediate market. Setting up the entire intermediate industry here would be very expensive and involve lots of pollution.[13]

From 2008 onward, the Ministry of Health passed several directives designed to support the local drug and pharmochemical industries. For

158 *Consolidating the Pharmaceutical Alliance (2007–2013)*

example, Ministerial Directive 978 *(Portaria 978)* specifies a list of strategic medicines including, among others, all the ARVs used in the national treatment program.[14] ANVISA Resolution 57 (RDC 57), passed in 2009, requires all pharmochemical producers and importers to register APIs. Of the first 20 APIs, five are for ARVs.

The most important change affecting Brazil's pharmaceutical autonomy was the decision to establish partnerships between public labs and private API manufacturers for the production of active principals used in ARVs. When Eduardo Costa assumed command of the Health Ministry's public lab Farmanguinhos in February 2006, he introduced a new mode for acquiring APIs. Instead of carrying out auctions that awarded contracts to the lowest bidder and with little consideration for quality, the lab subcontracted out API production to prequalified domestic producers. The federal lab initiated "service contracts" for the procurement of pharmaceutical inputs. Importers took Farmanguinhos to court for allegedly contravening the country's rigid Law on Public Tenders *(Lei de Licitação 8.666)*. But the lab's lawyers made a convincing argument that the new modality for acquiring the API actually economizes resources since its technicians could monitor the production process and guarantee quality and technical specifications.[15] ARVs were the first product line to use the new modality.[16]

Later decrees formalized the "service contracts" initiated by Costa. Ministerial Directive 837 *(Portaria n° 837)* institutionalized the Partnerships for Productive Development *(Parcerias para o Desenvolvimento Produtivo*—PDPs) for producing strategic items for the Ministry of Health and transferring technology. The objectives included increasing national production of medicines, biologics, vaccines, medical equipment, diagnostic tools, and related items; lowering the costs SUS paid for acquiring innovative and essential items; and increasing the competitiveness of public and private institutions amidst dynamic technological change. Creating a PDP involves several steps. Health officials select a product and public laboratory and then chose a private company for the partnership. The Ministry of Health and the interministerial Executive Group of the Industrial Health Complex *(Grupo Executivo do Complexo Industrial da Saúde*—GECIS) give final approval to the executive plan. After the relationship is completed, the partners must register the product with ANVISA and make it available to SUS.

Between 2009 and 2013, the Ministry of Health has initiated 104 PDPs. Table 6.3 lists these public-private partnerships related to ARVs. Most of these partnerships involved local API makers like Cristalia, Nortec, and Globe. But in some cases they include a foreign producer like the Canadian drug company Apotex. In the case of PDPs involving patented products, there appear two modalities: first, in the case of Bristol Meyers Squibb (BMS), the patent holder agrees to transfer technology and the Ministry of Health sells their product for a determined amount of time at an agreed price until the transfer is complete (e.g. atazanavir and raltegravir); second,

Consolidating the Pharmaceutical Alliance (2007–2013)   159

Table 6.3   Public-Private Partnerships Involving Antiretroviral Medicines, 2007–2013

Year	Medicine	Public Labs	Private Companies
2007	Efavirenz	Farmanguinhos	Cristalia
2009	Tenofovir	Lafepe / Funed	Cristalia / Blumer / Nortec
2010	Heat-Stable Ritonavir	Lafepe	Cristalia
2011	Atazanavir*	Farmanguinhos	BMS / Nortec
	Raltegravir*	Lafepe	MSD / Nortec
2012	Lopinavir + Ritonavir* (Kaletra)	Farmanguinhos / Furp / Iquego	Cristalia
	Tenofovir + Lamivudine	Farmanguinhos / Funed / Lafepe	Cristalia / Blanver/ Globe Química / Cyg / Nortec
	Tenofovir + Lamivudine + Efavirenz	Farmanguinhos / Funed / Lafepe	Cristalia / Blanver / Globe Química / Cyg / Nortec
2013	Darunavir*	Farmanguinhos	Apotex / NT Pharm / Pharmchem / Globe

*Involves patented or patent-pending product.

Source: Ministry of Health (2014) and author.

a PDP is set up to complete development and registration of a product using the Bolar Exception in intellectual property legislation and sell the product once the patent expires (e.g. Kaletra and darunavir).

Brazil's industrial policies for the pharmaceutical sector represent a coup for ABIFINA. During Lula's government, the industry association achieved an important space in the policymaking process due to a shared interest with state elites in developing local capabilities to supply the growing demands of SUS. ABIFINA participates in GECIS, and Farmanguinhos, the federal lab responsible for producing most of the ARVs used by SUS, even gained a seat on the association's board of directors.

The normative frameworks regarding medicines, while still based on Constitutional guarantees concerning the right to health, now include issues of sovereignty and national development. BNDES officials Pedro Palmeiro and Luciana Capanema express their interests as a national concern over foreign dependency:

> Medicine is not the same as any other product. It is strategic. You can't remain exclusively in the hands of commercial relations. If there were a war for example between India and China, you must have capacity to produce locally . . . another possibility is if the US were to take action against India or China at the WTO for a certain product.[17]

Their scenarios are not without merit. In December 2008, Dutch customs officials confiscated a cargo of generic medicines in transit from

160 Consolidating the Pharmaceutical Alliance (2007–2013)

India to Brazil. The shipment included 570 kilos of losartan potassium, the active ingredient used to treat high blood pressure, capable of providing medicine to 300,000 people for one month. The product does not enjoy patent protection in either India or Brazil. After the cargo was released by Dutch authorities, it was shipped back to India. Both Brazil and India filed WTO dispute settlements against the European Union (Azevêdo 2009).

The distance between the Brazilian government and transnational drug companies, meanwhile, grew during Lula's second term in office. Jorge Raimundo, president of the consultative committee of INTERFARMA, which represented the interests of transnational drug companies, said that there was a close working relationship with Fernando Furlan, in charge of MDIC during Lula's first term, to encourage investments from foreign companies, protect intellectual property rights, encourage minimum state intervention, and provide a strong regulatory framework. "Now all has changed, and we have the Health Industrial Complex," he decried.[18] For Raimundo and other representatives of the foreign industry, the government should restrict its role to issues of access through targeted social policies and investments in the country's deteriorating hospitals. Accordingly, producing medicines should be left to the private sector and not based on economic nationalism. INTERFARMA has been particularly critical about the PDPs (INTERFARMA 2012). "What strategic means is different for different people. But what they say that is strategic is that Brazil can't be dependent on international sources of supply. Sometimes we see this as nationalistic," explained João Sanches, in charge of government affairs at the Brazilian division of Merck.[19]

Channels of communication regarding industrial policies reveal the new state-society relationships. When discussing industrial policies, INTERFARMA representatives played a minor role. In contrast, representatives from ABIFINA and ABIQUIF shaped policy design and define strategic objectives.[20] Civil society groups provided little input into designing programs but continued to support efforts for the national production of essential drugs. Through the National Health Council *(Conselho Nacional da Saúde),* the highest instance of society input into policies, activist organizations like ABIA defended local production of essential medicines. "For ABIA, it is a concern that being merely a country that consumes ARVs and not produces them could threaten Brazil's program since more and more resources will be needed. Thus, ABIA defends industrial policies in relation to medicines to ensure the country's autonomy," explained ABIA's director Veriano Terto.[21] Still, there are concerns that public health funds are diverted to promote industry (Vieira 2014). Institutionally, the Permanent Forum for Articulating with Civil Society, including several industry associations and consumer groups, formalized ties between state and civil society for coordinating government efforts carried out by GECIS.

SURPRISE COMPULSORY LICENSE AND DOMESTIC COALITIONS

The Decision to Issue a Compulsory License for Merck's Efavirenz

Industrial polices during the Lula administration enshrined the support of local industrialists. The Ministry of Health, headed by *sanitaristas* aligned with the government's renewed interest in state-supported industrial development, was at the center of constructing the triple alliance with advocacy groups on the one hand and the local bourgeoisie on the other. While early *sanitarista* ideology continued to be critical of the role of profit-based industry in the health system, the technological, regulatory, and political problems associated with patents and APIs informed their strategic pragmatism to foster ties with private API makers. Most importantly, the consolidation of the treatment alliance with local, private drug makers placed the state in a stronger position to confront foreign drug companies over prices.

In May 2007, Health Ministry Jose Temporão finally made good on Brazil's threats to "break the patents" of drugs used in its AIDS program. The minister said that US-based MerckSharpeDohme (MSD) failed to reduce the price of efavirenz to within the Ministry's budget parameters. Brazil asked MSD to reduce unit prices from $1.65 to $0.65—the same price the company sold in Thailand. Since Brazil purchases larger quantities of the AIDS medicine, Brazilian negotiators argued, they should receive at least a comparable price. At the time, there were 80,000 Brazilians using the ARV. MSD executives countered that its price for AIDS medicines is based on a country's level of development (measured by World Bank classifications of gross national income) and HIV prevalence rates, of which Thailand's is three times greater than Brazil's. During negotiations, MSD initially provided a discount of 5%, which increased to 30% in its last proposal, thus effectively reducing the unit price to $1.10. The company also offered to transfer technology to produce efavirenz. But for Brazilian officials the price discount was not steep enough and offers of technology transfer not in line with the country's strategic objectives to control pharmaceutical technology.

After nine rounds of negotiations and stocks of the medicine decreasing, Brazil's President Luiz Inacio 'Lula' da Silva, in a televised speech, announced the compulsory license on May 4, 2007. Ministerial Directive 886, declaring the medicine in the public interest, referred to numerous right to health justifications, including the International Declaration of Human Rights; the Convention on Economic, Social and Cultural Rights; Brazil's Constitution; and the *Doha Declaration*. Lula's discourse nonetheless went beyond human rights claims and to include more critical perspectives that questioned the social inequities embedded in the structure of

162 *Consolidating the Pharmaceutical Alliance (2007–2013)*

intellectual property: ". . . every discovery that interests humanity should be considered the patrimony of humanity; the inventor, the creator should have their benefits, make money, but this should still be for humanity. It is not possible that someone becomes rich on the misfortune of others" (Mundorama 2007).[22]

The compulsory license forced MSD to take a loss of US$40 million in 2007 for the patented drug efavirenz, but allowed the country to continue providing universal treatment to those in need—some 200,000 people in 2007. With a two-thirds price cut, AIDS officials estimated a total savings of US$104 million from 2007 through 2011 with annual government expenditures falling from US$40 million to US$12 million (see Viegas Neves da Silva, Hallal, and Guimarães 2012). The compulsory license had important knock-off effects in other negotiations, too. Brazil obtained price discounts in subsequent negotiations with Abbott for lopinavir/ritonavir and with Gilead Sciences for tenofovir.

A number of factors had changed in the run-up to the compulsory license compared to previous threats. First, the availability of WHO prequalified generic versions of the medicine was pivotal in providing an alternative supply of the strategic medicines in a short time horizon. In fact, initial purchases of the medicine came from three Indian companies prequalified by the World Health Organization, namely Cipla, Ranbaxy, and Aurobindo, for $0.45 per unit until public labs scaled up production. In the past, local producers—both government labs and private national companies—had provided input on costs. Knowing that Farmanguinhos provided support during the negotiations may have led patent holders to concede to government demands for a price discount in the past. On the one hand, the inability of Brazil's public labs to take advantage of the Bolar Exception (i.e. develop a drug and obtain regulatory approval for marketing before its patent expires) improved Merck's bargaining position. But on the other, the availability of generic alternatives certified by inter-governmental organizations weakened the firm's leverage and provided Brazilian health officials cover against criticism related to the quality of generic medicines.

A second important difference between previous threats and the compulsory license for efavirenz is that other sectors of the government backed the Ministry of Health. During the 2005 negotiations with Abbott, ministries related to trade and finance voiced concerns about the possible ramifications of trade sanctions were Brazil to issue a compulsory license for Kaletra. Two years later the situation had changed—all the other ministries supported the Ministry of Health.[23] One factor is the recent changes in ministers. João Sanches, Merck's communication's director, explained: "The problem was we had a new cabinet, a new Minister of Health and a new Minister of Commerce. And we, Merck, did not even have time to talk with these ministers because they had changed so quickly."[24] Merck officials did not have time to curry favor with strategically placed officials in the Lula government and entice them with prospective investment plans.

Consolidating the Pharmaceutical Alliance (2007–2013) 163

Third, there was less direct US pressure during negotiations. During previous contentious price negotiations, there had been parallel pressures of a trade panel at the World Trade Organization and threats of restricting US science and technological partnerships. In a review of US government documents related to the efavirenz compulsory license (obtained under the Freedom of Information Act request), US diplomats repeated the common theme of the importance of patents for generating new innovations. US officials did not make outright threats or present challenges at international bodies during the course of the efavirenz negotiations. If Brazil was going to "break" Merck's patent, the US ambassador only warned the Health Minister that there would be a "political storm" (Mazurkevich 2007). Brazilians involved in the negotiations also did not mention any US pressures. In fact, the US Trade Representative had removed Brazil from its Priority Watch list due to the country's efforts to protect intellectual property, although it continued to highlight concern over the use of compulsory licenses (USTR 2007). The US did not apply any trade sanctions nor initiate any out-of-cycle reviews of Brazil's intellectual property protection, despite pressures from the Pharmaceutical Research and Manufacturers of America (PhRMA).[25]

The industry and their supporters continued to stress the importance of strong patent laws. Certain groups such as USA for Innovation (2007) called on US Congress to fight Brazil and Thailand's "theft." But this language is not employed by the rest of the industry. Industry representatives, instead of invoking terms such as "theft" and "piracy," argued that Brazil's effective treatment program would not be possible without innovations carried out in the private sector that resulted from strong patent protection. A PhRMA representative said that the Brazilian government acted within the TRIPS agreement but "against the spirit of the law."[26] Representatives of the Brazil's pharmaceutical industry dispute the "public use" justification. Ciro Mortella, executive director of the Brazilian Pharmaceutical Industrial Federation (*Federação Brasileira da Indústria Farmacêutica*—Febrafarma), an umbrella organization that includes both foreign and domestic companies, argued that the compulsory license should not be used as means to economize resources and regulate drug prices. "Economic savings and public administration were not considered in the spirit of the law in intellectual property. When you talk of public interest in the law, you are talking about an exceptional situation, a situation outside the normal such as September 11th," he said.[27] In the view of foreign industry, compulsory licenses should only be used in times of a national emergency—a claim often repeated in the media. But TRIPS flexibilities also specify their use for government, non-commercial use.

Normative frameworks surrounding the compulsory licenses also tapped into the developmentalist discourse. While MSD viewed itself as the "victim" when efavirenz' market exclusivity was revoked, the company's discourse also invoked ideas of partnership in the country's economic development. Sanches from MSD questioned what defines the country's "public interest"

164 *Consolidating the Pharmaceutical Alliance (2007–2013)*

when issuing a public license: "What about the public's other interest in exports, R&D, jobs and bringing innovation to Brazil?"[28] The director said that, besides offers to transfer production and technology related to efavirenz, its CEO, Richard Clark had discussed with Brazil's President Lula the firm's investment plans for establishing an innovation hub in the biotech and life sciences in Brazil. But after the compulsory license, Tadeu Alves, the president of MSD's Latin American division, said that "the perception of Brazil will not be the same" and that the company is reviewing its investment plans in the country (Borsato 2007).

The firm's investment offers came too late and won too few supporters in the Brazilian state. Even Miguel Jorge, the head of Brazil's Ministry of Development, Industry and Trade at the time, acknowledged that Brazil was only saving a minor amount by relying on the compulsory license compared to the possible impact on future investment. Nonetheless, he said that MSD "precipitated this situation" and that other ministries supported the move (US Embassy Brasilia 2007). For Brazilian health authorities, MSD's actions, far from transferring technology to develop Brazil, have kept the country from developing important know-how. Eduardo Costa, Farmanguinhos' director, insisted that one of the factors that contributed to the government's decision to issue a compulsory was the company's court injunctions that limited access to the active principal ingredient of efavirenz.[29] Curtailing access to the key ingredient stymied the ability of public labs to research and development a generic version of the drug.

Government officials can relate the reasons and events leading up to the compulsory license. But fundamental in supporting the government's move has been the institutionalization of alliances made between civil servants at the Ministry of Health, civil society activists, and private domestic drug makers. The political coalition is important for weathering pressure from various corporate interests. In fact, policymakers witnessed pressures that Thailand faced when it became the first major developing country with local manufacturing capacity to issue compulsory licenses for public health reasons. Between November 2006 and January 2007, Thailand's military government issued compulsory licenses for two ARVs (efavirenz and the combination of lopinavir-ritonavir) and one antihypertension drug (clopidegrel) (see Ford et al. 2007).

The Consolidation of the Domestic Triple Alliance

Each time the government considered issuing a compulsory license and took the first step in the process by declaring a specific medicine in the "public interest" it created a political opportunity that resulted in increased societal mobilization. The two pillars of support for government initiatives for using TRIPS-related flexibilities are civil society organizations and the domestic pharmaceutical industry. The positive outcome of each failed attempt of using a compulsory license has been the establishment of

Consolidating the Pharmaceutical Alliance (2007–2013)   165

stronger relationships between the Ministry of Health and these two groups. The increasing politicization over the issue of patents gradually developed into a formidable triple alliance.

In the original formulation of this concept developed by Evans (1979), the triple alliance was a key component in explaining dependent development in the 1960s and 1970s. It was comprised of state bureaucrats, transnational capital, and local industry. While such a triple alliance in Brazil's pharmaceutical sector was never particularly strong, the unforeseen consequence of globalization thirty years later is the increasing distance between TNCs with the state and local industry, on the one hand, and the increasing incorporation of civil society groups tied into transnational networks of activists, on the other. In the case of Brazil, activist bureaucrats, acting as social movement insiders, in the Ministry of Health have been at the center of constructing this triple alliance between the state, civil society, and local industry.

By the time Brazil finally issued a compulsory license in 2007, the various actors in the triple alliance—the state, civil society and industry—had achieved concrete roles. In fact, several observers were surprised by the decree. Representatives from the domestic pharmochemical industry said that previous health ministers had always consulted with the makers of active principal ingredients when confronting TNCs, but Temporão did not. They never lobbied for a compulsory license and believed that it would have a marginal impact on the sector's development. Still, Nelson Brasil and others defended the use of compulsory licenses in terms of defending the country's sovereignty and health sector's needs.

Had the country's pharmaceutical sector been more fully integrated into global circuits of capital through trade relations or mergers and acquisitions with larger TNCs, their position would likely be different. When comparing the evolution of intellectual property laws between Mexico and Brazil, Shadlen (2009) correctly argues that Mexico incorporated fewer TRIPS flexibilities since Mexico's generic pharmaceutical industry is more closely tied to the US market and enjoys higher levels of foreign ownership. In contrast, Brazil incorporated more TRIPS flexibilities because of the interests of a nationally owned pharmaceutical base. Shadlen (2009) highlights the role of industry association ABIFINA in promoting more flexible intellectual property legislation. What is missing in his analysis of the Brazil case is the strategic role played by proactive public health officials to promote changes in intellectual property laws and industrial policies. In Brazil, the Ministry of Health, through its many affiliated organizations, has pushed for industrial policies to develop the country's pharmaceutical industry. The most important policy for obtaining the support of national capital was Farmanguinhos' decision to subcontract API production to domestic producers instead of holding tenders. The new public-private partnership, along with several industrial policies, solidified the support of the domestic pharmaceutical industry, especially the weakest link in the production chain—the pharmochemical producers.

166 *Consolidating the Pharmaceutical Alliance (2007–2013)*

The relationships between the Ministry of Health and civil society organizations developed along a different trajectory. The key intersection between the ministry and social movements has been the National AIDS Program. Other scholars have detailed how the body responsible for developing and implementing policies to deal with the epidemic recruited from activist NGOs (Bastos 1999; Nunn 2008; Rich 2013). This mobilizing structure continued in relation to the issue of intellectual property and access to medicines. During the 1990s, public health reformers failed to stop the passage of intellectual property legislation that would affect access to medicines, due in part to their weak links to strategic allies in civil society. At the time, the pharmaceutical sector, especially pharmochemical makers, were grappling with neoliberal reforms resulting in the removal of protectionist barriers and the scrapping of industrial policies. AIDS NGOs were not cognizant of the impact patent laws would have on drug prices until the use of patented ARVs became more widespread and the confrontation with the US occurred during a WTO panel. With the increasing salience of patents, the National AIDS Program has recruited from the Brazilian Interdisciplinary AIDS Association (*Associação Brasileira Interdisciplinar de AIDS*—ABIA).

While AIDS activists have been pivotal since the 1990s in pressuring government officials to confront TNCs and "break patents," more interesting from a resource mobilization perspective was the need for increasing technical competence in the area of pharmaceuticals and intellectual property law. Advocacy civil society groups such as Intellectual Property Working Group (*Grupo de Trabalho sobre Propriedade Intellectual*—GTPI) have become increasingly professionalized and organized in order to act as interlocutors with the government and explain the complex issues of pharmaceutical science and intellectual property rights to a wider audience.[30] These activists do not play a direct role in price negotiations between government and industry but maintain pressure on the state through formal organizations like the National Health Council *(Conselho Nacional da Saude)* and through informal channels of communication, especially with the National AIDS Program.

The weakest link in the *triple alliance* is the relationship between AIDS NGOs and the domestic pharmaceutical industry. There have never been formal channels of communication and mutual support between the two groups. Activists do not want to be viewed as pawns of private sector interests.[31] And the industry typically does not view activists as necessary allies to press for government policies. Nonetheless, during the 2005 Kaletra negotiations, NGOs sponsored studies detailing the capacities of Brazilian industry. Mario Scheffer from Grupo Pella Vida explained:

> We never had direct dialogue with industry. Now we are coming to understand the position of private industry here. For example: their reluctance to invest in producing ARVs if preference is given to buying from public labs. This is the reality.[32]

Consolidating the Pharmaceutical Alliance (2007–2013) 167

In the past, Pedro Chequer, the director of National AIDS Program, is largely credited with reaching out to the country's pharmochemical sector and building bridges between activists and local industry. From the perspectives of local drug makers, NGOs often are against industry. Nonetheless, there have been times when communication increased in order to demonstrate the competency of local industry.

The Triple Alliance in Action: Efavirenz and Tenofovir

Each confrontation between Brazil's government and transnational pharmaceutical companies has strengthened the triple alliance between activist bureaucrats, civil society, and local industry. During the first threats of a compulsory license and the WTO dispute in 2000–2001, Paulo Teixeira, Brazil's AIDS director at the time, recalled how the National AIDS Program reached out to NGOs for support. Missing from this alliance, however, was the participation of domestic private-sector drug companies. Industrial policies under Lula's government starting in 2003 cemented the support from the fine chemicals sector. From 2007 onward, the roles of the triple alliance have become more defined.

Experiences with efavirenz and tenofovir, two crucial ARVs included in Brazil's therapeutic consensus, illustrate the crystallization of a pharmaceutical alliance. Brazilian health officials began to mobilize for a compulsory for efavirenz in January of 2007 after it appeared that Merck would not budge in its negotiating position. Between the start of the year and May 2007, when efavirenz was declared in the public interest, the first step in issuing a compulsory license, the National AIDS Program began to articulate with civil society activists, starting with ABIA and MSF. Passarelli explained: "We knew we could count on their support, but other sectors of the government did not know what type of political support could be obtained."[33] Treatment activists outside the state, nevertheless, remained cautious in backing the government's position. Protests, mobilizations, and even lawsuits failed to force the government to issue a compulsory license for Kaletra in 2005. Gabriela Chaves, a pharmacist who works at ABIA and the GTPI, explained that civil society contemplated how to support the measure given past disappointments, but when a compulsory license was finally issued, cautious support turned into defensive jubilation. She explained the position of the social movement:

Within the movement there was discussion on how to support it. We had to support the measure but not completely. We were already disappointed in the case of Kaletra. But we were there when [President] Lula signed and it was extremely emotional. And then the pressure from the media and industry began. Industry ended up attacking the measure with all sorts of arguments. ABIA mapped out all the arguments that industry made in the media against the compulsory license. . . . We said

168 *Consolidating the Pharmaceutical Alliance (2007–2013)*

this is an important step for the country. In that way, we supported the government's measure and did them a favor. We tried to gain a space in the public opinion and were able to do so.[34]

Activists thus played an important role not only by voicing their political support to the government, but also, and perhaps more importantly, explaining the implications of the compulsory for the lives of patients. In the face of corporate-sponsored allegations concerning the quality of generic alternatives, the legality of compulsory licenses, and threats to continued supplies and future innovation, the clarifications provided by civil society campaigners helped ally public doubt and concern about their current and future sources of medicine.

The role of local industry is to assist in the local production of the drug. During the negotiations, Health Minister Alvares said that he received verbal confirmation from Eduardo Costa, Farmanguinhos' director, and from Costa's boss, Paulo Buss, the director of the FioCruz Foundation, that the Health Ministry's lab could have efavirenz ready in one year.[35] But the Ministry of Health and the federal lab only signed an agreement to produce the medicine after the government decreed the compulsory license. Pernambuco's public lab Lafepe was also selected to develop efavirenz since it had already developed a 200mg formulation of the drug and its experience could be leveraged in developing the 600mg dose currently in treatment protocols. Farmanguinhos, under the new modality of subcontracting out production of the API, selected three Brazilian pharmochemical companies to produce the raw material—Cristalia, Nortec, and Globe.

Despite the original one-year timeframe to have efavirenz ready for distribution in the public health system, scaling up production for 80,000 HIV patients posed a challenge for local labs and tested their relationships with AIDS activists. In fact, Farmanguinhos only delivered the first batch of production on February 2009—twenty-one months after the compulsory license. Indian generic drug makers supplied the medicine in the meantime. Civil society activists decried the lab's lack of transparency and delays in launching new ARVs. The establishment of a consultative council by Farmanguinhos in January 2008 to incorporate the voices of civil society representatives only increased this pressure.

Farmanguinhos director Eduardo Costa blamed patent owners for the delays in production. The federal lab tried to import the API prior to the compulsory license, but faced legal injunctions by the patent owner. "If we consider that pilot batches could only be carried out after the production of the API, we can see that the task was almost impossible," he defended.[36] Production of efavirenz also encountered technical problems when Farmanguinhos' formulation failed bioavailability tests in May 2008. Costa admitted the public lab's error in not demanding that Merck provide all the technical details of its reference drug—as determined by the

Consolidating the Pharmaceutical Alliance (2007–2013)   169

compulsory license decree—so that the generic copy would be identical (Cimieri 2008).

While the production of generic versions of efavirenz revealed the continued obstacles posed by patents and issues related to the internal organization of public labs, the case of tenofovir, marketed by US-based Gilead Sciences, demonstrated a different set of the tactics by the triple alliance to address patent issues related to high-priced medicines. By 2007, there were close to 31,000 patients using tenofovir. Per capita annual cost in that year stood at R$3,121, equal to R$89.8 million in expenditures for the drug, or about a tenth of overall ARV purchases. Brazil's negotiators obtained a deep discount for 2007 purchases after the compulsory license with Merck, but costs for the patented medicine remained high.

Local civil society analysts, working with public labs and international partners, noticed that Gilead's patent for tenofovir contained several questionable elements. In 2005, Wanise Barreto, a patent lawyer at Farmanguinhos, filed a pre-grant opposition to Gilead's patent application for tenofovir with Brazil's National Institute of Intellectual Property (*Instituto Nacional da Propriedade Intellectual*—INPI). She argued that Gilead's patent submission lacked an inventive step—a necessary requirement for obtaining a patent.[37] GTPI obtained Barreto's pre-grant opposition and, combining its information with its analysis and information provided by partners in India, undertook a supplementary review of Gilead's patent request for the drug. GTPI then sent its review to the National AIDS Program and to the INPI. Although Gilead filed for a patent in 1997, the patent office had not ruled on the company's patent application. With its patent pending, Gilead enjoyed a de facto monopoly. Civil society activists lobbied the National AIDS Program to declare tenofovir in the "public interest." The public interest declaration in this case would not be used for the purpose of a compulsory license but instead to speed up the patent office's decision.[38] A patent denial could then allow for the local production of the drug or to source it from alternative suppliers in Asia.

AIDS officials eventually convinced Brazil's Minister of Health, Jose Temporão, to declare tenofovir in the public interest, forcing INPI to rule on the drug's patentability. In 2009, Brazil's patent office denied Gilead's patent, thus opening up the possibility for alternative suppliers and local production. Up to that point, the only producer registered to sell the drug in Brazil was Gilead, but there were WHO-prequalified generic producers of the tenofovir in India. To avoid possible patent restrictions on Indian producers, ABIA teamed up with the Indian activists to file a pre-grant opposition to Gilead's patent of tenofovir in India, too. For local production, following the new modality of public-private partnerships, the Ministry of Health chose Farmanguinhos and Minas Gerais State public lab Funed to develop and produce tenofovir in collaboration with national API makers Globe, Nortec, and Blanver (Ministry of Health 2009).

170 *Consolidating the Pharmaceutical Alliance (2007–2013)*

THE FATE OF BRAZIL'S TRIPLE ALLIANCE AND CORPORATE POWER

The State

The post-TRIPS era poses challenges and opportunities to sustaining access to essential medicines under patent. In the future, health officials may not have readily available alternatives from generic drug makers in India and China when contemplating a compulsory license. The situation may create another opportunity for Brazil's public labs. Whereas many private pharmaceutical firms in developing countries may be constrained from developing generic versions of patented medicines due to strategic alliances or licensing agreements with originator companies, Brazil's public labs remain under the control of public health authorities. Two key challenges remain: successful public-private partnerships and foresight when taking advantage of the Bolar Exception, i.e. the legal provision that permits the lawful development and registration of a patented drug but not commercialization until its patent expires. Employing public labs to regulate prices of strategic medicines, ensuring the sustainability of the country's treatment program, and stimulating local development requires state management that combines bureaucratic agility with technological perspicacity. State managers must have foresight into the new medicines on the horizon that will become the future standards for treatment and mobilize resources for their early production. The process entails financial risks that even public labs seek to avoid. Since the process of reverse engineering can take one to three years to complete (some 21 months in the case of generic efavirenz), funds must be made available for research partners to develop promising new drugs on the horizon.

PDPs demonstrate a new strategy to control pharmaceutical technology, and even include novel fixed-dose combinations (FDC). In other countries, one-a-day FDCs, such as the combination of efavirenz/emtricitabine/tenofovir, have become standard treatment. In early 2014, FM registered tenofovir/lamivudine and tenofovir/lamivudine/efavirenz using the PDP modality. Since none of the individual ARVs are patent protected, it is easier to develop these formulas. Still, the success of the PDP model remains to be seen. The current timeframe to bring a new drug to market under the arrangement is between two to four years. And civil society activists are demanding more transparency regarding these arrangements.

Since the efavirenz episode in 2007, the Ministry of Health has not threatened any additional compulsory licenses. Instead, current strategies use technical criteria when negotiating high-priced medicines like ARVs (discussed in more detail in the next chapter) and PDPs to obtain voluntary licenses. To date, the only originator companies to have agreed to transfer pharmaceutical technology are BMS for atazanavir and MSD for raltegravir. In the case of the atazanavir deal signed in 2011, the patent holder will transfer all the technology, both the formula and API, by 2015 to Farmanguinhos and Nortec. In the meantime, BMS will be the sole supplier of the drug in Brazil's treatment program. Health officials claim the PDP will result in savings of R$81 million and maintain access to the 40,000 Brazilians using the drug (Isaude.net 2012). But civil society groups criticize the high price paid for the drug at US$1.67 per pill, quadruple the cheapest generic prices on the international market; limits on making innovations such as combinations with other drugs; and restrictions on sales abroad (GTPI 2013a). Still, Graph 6.1 shows progressive decline in the prices of the least expensive ARV combinations across treatment categories over the past six years.

New treatment protocols will test the government's strategy. In 2013, the National AIDS Program announced that ARV treatment should be made available as soon as someone tests positive for HIV, instead of previous guidelines that recommended treatment initiation when CD4 counts fall below 500 per cubic milliliter of blood (see Appendix Six).[39] With the new test-and-treat policy, the number of people who will enter the treatment program is likely to jump by 100,000, on top of the 353,000 in the treatment program as of 2013. Meanwhile, more individuals are migrating to more expensive second- and third-line treatments under patent. Budgetary pressures and rising treatment enrollment will put Brazil in a similar situation that it faced in 2005 when the introduction of more high-cost ARVs threatened the sustainability of the program. For example, Graph 6.2 shows that, while government import substitution efforts appear successful in redirecting the proportion of funds spent on locally produced generics at the expense

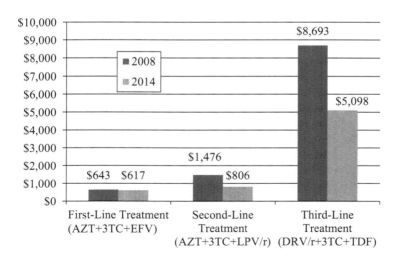

Graph 6.1 Least Expensive First-, Second-, and Third-Line Treatment Costs Per Person Per Year in US$, 2008 vs. 2014

Source: Author's Calculations, based on data from the Department of STDs, HIV, and Viral Hepatitis.

of foreign-produced ARVs, overall expenditures continue to rise and topped $380 million in 2012.

At the international level, Brazilian health officials in collaboration with civil society partners remain active in defending human rights and access to essential medicines. At the WHO, Brazilians defended generic medicines from being categorized as counterfeit drugs by the International Medical Products Anti-Counterfeiting Taskforce (IMPACT) and in the plurilateral agreement Anti-Counterfeiting Trade Agreement (ACTA). Created in 2006 to fight the growing sophistication of counterfeit methods of medical products as a public health threat, IMPACT has teamed up with international law enforcement agencies like INTERPOL to police medicines. ACTA seeks to establish new international standards for the enforcement of intellectual property rights. Critics say both IMPACT and ACTA conflate the notion of "counterfeit" drugs (related to trademarks) with "substandard" medicines (a legitimate public health threat). These enforcement efforts could restrict the supply of legitimate generic medicines (see Flynn 2013).

Brazil also continues to establish more South-South alliances. AIDS officials spearheaded the International Network in Technological Cooperation in HIV/AIDS. The network, including China, Ukraine, Brazil, Argentina, Thailand, and Cuba, focuses research efforts on developing technology used

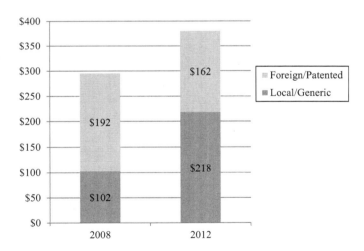

Graph 6.2 Estimated Expenditures on Foreign/Patented vs. Locally Produced/Generic ARVs Acquisitions in US$ millions, 2008 vs. 2012

Source: Author's Calculations, based on data from the Department of STDs, HIV, and Viral Hepatitis.

for softgel capsules of ritonavir as well as quality control of diagnostic kits.[40] In addition, the Ministry of Health has donated ARVs and technical support to other AIDS programs in South America and Portuguese-speaking Africa. In one instance, Brazil donated pharmaceutical technology from Farmanguinhos so that Mozambique can establish its own ARV factory. Lastly, Brazil assisted in the creation of the Drugs for Neglected Diseases Initiative that seeks to find treatments for diseases concentrated in the "bottom billion" of the world's population (see Flynn 2013).

Civil Society

The most enduring legacy of Brazil's experience with contentious AIDS policies is the state-civil society treatment coalition. The confrontation with the United States over the WTO panel crystalized these alliances and internationalized them to involve NGOs from abroad. Brazilian social movement organizations continue establishing more South-South links with activists in other countries. As patent laws spread and continue to impact prices throughout the world, these alliances and mutual support will also likely expand. These transnational networks prove crucial in uncovering weak patents, improving regulatory systems, and seeking cheaper generic alternatives than the current prices the Ministry of Health pays for ARVs.

On the domestic front, activists have continued to support public labs, explain the impact of patents on medicines to the public, and lobby the government for more transparency and better price contracts. The strongest link is the one between the social movement organizations and the National AIDS Program. Informal contacts and the revolving door between the two sides provide key channels for information and expertise. But with the rest of the government and the rest of the Ministry of Health, access to information and transparency remains problematic. GPTI, for example, has filed various official complaints to the Ministry of Health about the lack of transparency in awarding procurement contracts with both public labs and the PDPs. Instead of public-private partnerships based on voluntary licenses that policymakers have chosen, they have fought for compulsory licenses in order to accelerate the development of strategic medicines (GTPI 2013b). In relation with industry, civil society groups have taken an interest in their capabilities to ensure that alternative supplies enter the market in order to reduce prices. Still, they remain suspicious of public health funds used for industrial policies and profiteering by the private sector.

One key area civil society continues to apply pressures involves the regulatory environment concerning patents. First, activists have targeted pipeline patents. GTPI and the National Federal of Pharmacists *(Federação Nacional de Farmacêuticos)* convinced the attorney general to file a suit in 2007 against the constitutionality of awarding pipeline patents based on the Industrial Property Law of 1996 *(Lei 9.279/96)*. The legislation allowed for

174 *Consolidating the Pharmaceutical Alliance (2007–2013)*

the immediate recognition of patents awarded in other countries for 565 drugs in substitution of an evaluation by INPI. Other countries like India, in contrast, permitted "mailbox" patents, in which patent offices would evaluate applications submitted by drug companies once patents come into force. Activists estimated that awarding pipeline patents incurred losses of $420 million to $519 million between 2001 and 2007 just in the case of five ARVs (lopinavir/ritonavir [Kaletra], abacavir, nelfinavir, lopinavir, and efavirenz) (Fonseca and Bastos 2013; GTPI n.d.). If estimates were to include other medicines, the costs to the public health sector would reach the billions.

Second, social movement organizations have promoted patent evaluation models oriented to the interests of public health. Two different models appear in opposition to each other. One is the public health perspective, as outlined by Correa (2006), which specifies high patentability standards to ensure that only truly innovative medicines received patents. These intellectual property standards, adopted by a few countries like India and Argentina, limit the practice of *ever-greening* that drug companies employ to extend their commercial monopoly on a drug. In this public health-driven model, drug polymorphs and secondary therapeutic uses of an existing drug are not awarded patents. The second model is driven by the European Patent Office, the Japanese Patent Office, and the United States Patent and Trademark Office (USPTO). These patent offices have achieved a hegemonic position in patent evaluations and incorporate developing countries into their system through what Drahos (2008) calls "technocratic trust." The concern is that developing countries will emulate the practices of these countries by awarding patents for trivial steps in the innovation process. To this end, Brazilian activists protested technical agreements like the "Patent Prosecution Highway" between INPI and the USPTO, a patent office widely known for applying loose patentability standards (GTPI 2011).

Brazil continues to debate how best to govern intellectual property, and there are competing bills passing through Congress. In these discussions, activists lobby Congressional representatives and disseminate information to the public about public health perspectives concerning patent laws. The bill receiving their support, PL5402/13, stipulates more flexibility when issuing compulsory licenses for the public interest; strict criteria for awarding patents; patent limits to a maximum of 20 years from date of a patent application; and pre-grant opposition not just from ANVISA but also from civil society organizations, private firms, and other branches of government (Souza 2014). Passing the law would represent a major victory for civil society organizations, culminating years of activism in promoting the public health perspective in intellectual property.

Without a doubt, Brazilian civil society organizations have had a major impact on Brazil's policy-making process. "Despite their local/national basis, Brazilian coalitions, such as the GTPI, have had an influence on public policies comparable to major transnational organizations, like Oxfam

Consolidating the Pharmaceutical Alliance (2007–2013) 175

International," conclude Fonseca and Bastos (2013). However, the future of advocacy groups remains in doubt. Foreign donors, including private foundations and World Bank funds, have shifted their focus away from Brazil to least developed countries. Civil society groups like ABIA have struggled to raise funds from new sources. And wealthy Brazilians prefer to make donations to global brands like Doctors without Borders instead of local organizations. The National AIDS Program has provided funds to create new AIDS NGOs in smaller towns throughout the country where the epidemic has spread in order to ensure the presence of civil partners in the fight against the disease (Rich 2013). The survival of activist groups that retain highly trained pharmacists and patent lawyers, nevertheless, remains a concern for maintaining pharmaceutical autonomy.

National Industry

Brazilian firms (whether public labs or private sector firms) are being squeezed by both patent monopolies from above and market pressures from below. Besides patent restrictions on the lawful copying of medicines, they face increasing competition from generic suppliers in Asia. To confront patent power and market power, Brazil's pharmaceutical sector continues to receive support from the government's new industrial policies. In fact, Lula's successor, President Dilma Rousseff, also from the PT, continues to implement industrial policies. The Greater Brazil Plan, *(Plano Brasil Maior),* started in August 2011, seeks to offset the global economic downturn through various tax exemptions and increased use of state procurement power. Innovate Health *(Inova Saúde),* announced the following year, allocates R$1.2 billion in credit, subsidies, and equity stakes to develop technologies in biologics, medicines, and pharmochemicals. Most important has been the continued support from the federal development bank BNDES. To date, its Profarma program stated that its entire portfolio of 97 projects have translated into R$5 billion in investments and R$3 billion in financing (BNDES 2013). Between 2003 and 2007, national drug makers increased their share of the medicines market by 14 percentage points to 47%, lending support that industrial policies were partially effective (Palmeira et al. 2012).

State support, however, still has not translated into a larger share of the domestic market for local API makers. The Brazilian pharmochemical industry has increased output from 730 tons per year to 1,318 tons per year between 2006 and 2011, but the amount is still less than 1% of the total market (Bermudez et al. 2013). The experiences of two companies that first began producing active principals for ARVs—Labogen and Microbiologica—demonstrate the challenges and opportunities the industry has faced. The former went into bankruptcy after Rio de Janeiro public lab Instituto Vital Brazil (IVB) failed to pay a back debt for Labogen's raw materials and also due to its inability to compete in international tenders,

176 *Consolidating the Pharmaceutical Alliance (2007–2013)*

according to Labogen's former director Campos de Machado Neto.[41] Microbiologica continues to work in some areas related to HIV treatments, but now survives as a contract research company producing small batches of ARVs under development by transnational drug companies and exporting high-end products used as references for biological testing in the US.[42] Lelio Maçaira, who left Microbiologica, now operates a contract manufacturing company, Laborvida, producing medicines for both originator and generic medicines. His firm even won a bid to manage IVB's outsourced production.[43]

Global integration in the private sector, meanwhile, continues apace. In April 2009, French company Sanofi-Aventis purchased Brazil's third largest generic drug maker, Medley, for R$1.5 billion (about $750 million). Historically, expansion of Brazil's privately owned drug companies have resulted in increased foreign penetration in the form of mergers and acquisitions. This route to financial success chosen by Medley's shareholders represents a challenge to policymakers at the BNDES who are contemplating sector policies to forge a domestic, privately owned mega-pharmaceutical company, capable of competing head-to-head on the global market (Agência Estado 2007). Past historical experiences show that when a Brazilian drug company becomes large and lucrative enough, foreign investors acquire control. Mergers and acquisitions do not only occur as a result of foreign investors scooping up Brazilian firms. Cristalia, one of the few vertically integrated drug makers owned by Brazilian capital, acquired Argentinian company Ima in 2010. The Brazilian company has also taken a strategic approach to intellectual property. On the one hand, Cristalia has obtained 71 patents by 2014, and, on the other, it has contested Abbott's patent for lopinavir/ritonavir in the courts. In the midst of the judicial dispute, the drug maker has signed a public-private partnership to develop and distribute the drug with the Ministry of Health.

Transnational Drug Companies

Foreign capital has played an increasingly marginal role in the development of Brazil's pharmaceutical policies and industrial deepening. In light of Brazilian attempts to become more self-sufficient in medicines and economize fiscal resources spent on ballooning health budgets, what strategies and tactics have worked best for foreign-based firms to pursue patent power and avoid compulsory licenses?

Bristol-Myers Squibb (BMS), for example, has had fewer problems with government negotiators compared to other firms. Unlike Merck, which lost about US$30 million in revenue when the compulsory license for efavirenz was issued in 2007, BMS has never had market exclusivity of one of its ARVs threatened by the government. Most drug companies use some form of tiered pricing set by global headquarters and based on a country's GDP per capita and HIV prevalence rate. But local officials at

Consolidating the Pharmaceutical Alliance (2007–2013)   177

BMS have been able to convince the corporate head office to provide them with increased autonomy to negotiate local prices in Brazil, according Antonio Salles, BMS executive in charge of government relations.[44] When the National AIDS Program began to distribute atazanavir in 2004, BMS deviated from its global price guidelines and gave Brazil a deeper discount. Salles explained that one of the reasons was to avoid conflicts over prices. BMS's strategy is to project its image as a partner instead of being viewed as an obstacle in Brazil's success. The company's decision to transfer atazanavir's technology follows this course.

Another strategy employed by BMS is to stay ahead in the technological curve, even at the level of formulations. After Brazilians began to produce didanosine, BMS introduced an enteric-coated formulation that includes an extended release mechanism so that only one tablet, as opposed to two, must be taken each day. The National AIDS Program began distribution of the new formula in 2002. In January 2008, Farmanguinhos announced a partnership with local firms Blanver and Globe to produce the enteric version of the ARV.[45] Despite the announcement, as of 2013, the federal lab has not registered the product with ANVISA.

Overall, the uniformity of intellectual property laws across the world has increased the structural power of transnational drug companies. While companies will unlikely obtain overt bilateral support from the US or European Union for isolated patent disputes and the use of compulsory licenses, diplomats from the advanced developed countries will continue to focus their attention on bilateral trade agreements and international treaties to strengthen patent power. Since the turn of the century, the USTR has finalized 11 bilateral accords, one regional free trade agreement (Central American countries plus the Dominican Republic), and one multilateral agreement (Anti-Counterfeiting Trade Agreement [ACTA]), all of which include, to varying degrees, new standards and enforcements and/or what are called TRIPS-plus measures (McManis 2009; Rossi 2006; Smith, Correa, and Oh 2009). As explained in Chapter Two, these include restrictions on the use of compulsory licenses, increased data exclusivity provisions, patent linkage to drug registrations, among others—all of which restrict competition, raise prices, and limit access. Currently, the USTR is negotiating another multilateral agreement, the Trans-Pacific Partnership, which continues to reproduce the relationship of corporate insiders' access in the design of trade rules related to intellectual property.

PHARMACEUTICAL AUTONOMY AND STATE-SOCIETY RELATIONS

The policy challenges of sustaining HIV treatments drove, in large part, many of the new industrial policies for the pharmaceutical sector. In comparison to the previous administration of President Cardoso, which considered industrial policies taboo, Lula's economic team embraced "new developmentalism" to support local industry. *Sanitaristas* and their civil society allies continued to frame access to medicines as a human right, but policymakers and managers of industrial policies also emphasized the "strategic" nature of high-cost and essential medicines in the country's public health system. Local production of medicines also meant reducing the country's trade deficit, supporting domestic technological production, and increasing the competitiveness of Brazilian firms.

There are two competing interpretations of Brazil's renewed involvement in industrial policies and formation of new state-society alliances. An optimistic tone by Arbix and Martin (2010) characterizes Lula's new approach as "inclusionary state activism without statism." A number of facets distinguish the "new developmental state" model compared to the past. First, democracy weakened the coercive power of the developmental state erected during the country's military dictatorship. Second, due to successful monetary stabilization implemented by Cardoso and continued by Lula, Brazil could enjoy sustainable growth with low inflation and balanced accounts. Three, the government abandoned *dirigiste* policies of the past that sought to direct private investment. Four, economic de-regulation and privatization had not completely dismembered Brazilian "coordinated capitalism" due to the continued presence of state-controlled banks and pensions funds. Lastly, macro-economic stabilization increased the state's capacity for taxation, spending, and investment. In sum, the new developmentalism uses industrial policies more to enable firms to operate effectively in markets than to dominate investment decisions. Moreover, the new state approach to industrial policies emphasizes innovation and high-level dialogue that, in the end, seeks to address social objectives (Arbix and Martin 2010).

A more pessimistic view of Brazil's "new developmentalism" claims that the country may repeat many of the problematic ties between the state and the private sector common in the country's past whereby weak state institutions provide for privileged access by commercial interests (Almeida 2009; Zanatta 2012). Writing at the time of Brazil's authoritarian government, Cardoso (1975) introduced the concept of "bureaucratic rings" that emphasized the horizontal links between public and private sectors, which are "more comprehensive (i.e., not restricted to the economic interests) and more heterogeneous in their composition (including officials, businessmen, military, etc.)" than just a lobby, and whose effectiveness is "centered around a specific office holder" (Cardoso 1975: 208). In Brazil's authoritarian past, these "rings" legitimized state policies in the public interest despite a weak, or even lack of, formal democracy. For Zanatta (2012: 15), Brazil must create new institutional designs and stringent monitoring mechanisms in order to avoid the creation of "bureaucratic rings" through which a "network of relationships with the business elite . . . drive industrial policy in the interests of major national economic actors, members of the traditional elite." Indeed, a cursory review of BNDES disbursements suggests more state support towards large Brazilian firms that operate in low-tech fields

Consolidating the Pharmaceutical Alliance (2007–2013)   179

and want to internationalize their operations than to stimulate innovation in local cutting-edge industries (Almeida 2009; Flynn 2007).

A more focused look at the pharmaceutical sector, arguably a high-tech industry, provides a more nuanced picture. The evidence presented so far appears to depict more "inclusionary state activism" than a continuance of "bureaucratic rings." First, Brazil enjoys democratic politics and an active civil society. As shown in the cases of the drugs efavirenz and tenofovir detailed in this chapter, a professionalized and mobilized civil society plays an important role in demanding transparency, sharing information, and providing political support. While the relationships between industry and civil society are not particularly strong, and the criteria and pricing contracts between the state and industry could be more transparent, there is a degree of social accountability. The Ministry of Health has formal venues, such as Health Councils, operating at the municipal, state, and federal levels, and has issued directives reaching out to civil society to propose and monitor programs. These institutional differences, while imperfect, represent important changes in accountability and inclusion than the "bureaucratic rings" of the past.

Second, the relationship between the state and local pharmaceutical industrialists diverges from past versions of "bureaucratic rings." In Cardoso's model, personal ties between individuals play a more important role than trade associations in policy formulation and implementation. The Permanent Joint Forum for Articulation with Civil Society *(Fórum Permanente de Articulação com a Sociedade Civil),* which coordinates public-private partnerships with GECIS, includes various trade associations. Moreover, the state has increasingly professionalized its management (Souza 2013). In the past, bureaucratic rings provided channels for civil servants to obtain opportunities in the private sector. But the professional trajectories of policymakers involved in the health industrial complex tend to remain in the public sector.

In sum, Brazil's industrial policies in health trend towards Evans' notion of embedded autonomy than patrimonial politics (Evans 1995). More importantly, Brazil's triple alliance between state, society, and industry exercises an important political role when contesting the interests of more powerful actors, both domestic and foreign, in order to achieve pharmaceutical autonomy. The compulsory license of efavirenz revealed the institutionalization of the triple alliance between the state, society, and industry. While political leaders have not issued additional compulsory licenses since 2007, the political alliances, technological development, and discursive justifications have been established.

NOTES

1. ABIFINA states that its mission is to work for the industrial and technological development of Brazil's fine chemical industry. Interestingly, the industry

180 *Consolidating the Pharmaceutical Alliance (2007–2013)*

association says that it does not discriminate between foreign and domestic firms as long as they are committed to local development, but none of its associated members are foreign-based (see www.ABIFINA.org.br/historico.asp).

2. The model he refers to is Interministerial Directive No. 4/84 that outlined support from the Brazilian Development Bank (BNDES) and research center Codetec *(Companhia de Desenvolvimento Tecnológico)*. Nelson Brasil. Interview with author. Rio de Janeiro, RJ. June 30, 2008. See also Bermudez (1995).

3. José Gomes Temporão studied at the National School of Public Health *(Escola Nacional de Saúde Pública Sergio Arouca*—ENSP) in the late 1970s, which at the time and to this day remains a center for the development of *sanitarista* ideas and activism. In fact, the school is named after famous *sanitarista* leader Sergio Arouca. Before becoming Minister, Temporão also headed the Instituto Nacional do Câncer and the Rio de Janeiro State public lab Instituto Vital Brasil.

4. Brasil interview.

5. Technology transfer is defined as "transfer of systematic knowledge for manufacture of a product, for the application of a process or for the rendering of a service" (Chapter 1: 1–2 of the *Draft International Code of Conduct on the Transfer of Technology*).

6. The Brazilian government and transnational drug companies have achieved a limited number of partnerships in developing health technologies, most notably in the area of vaccines. FioCruz has joint projects with GlaxoSmithKline, and the Butanta Institute, another government research institute, with Sanofi Pasteur.

7. Agenor Alvares. Interview with author. Brasilia, DF. July 12, 2008.

8. The Ministry of Health, seeing a gap in the local production of Factor 8 and 9 as well as immunoglobulin, decided in 2004 to invest US$60 million to create a company called Hemobrás, specializing in blood-derived products and purchased the requisite technology from French state-owned company *Laboratoire français du fractionnement et des biotechnologies* (LFB).

9. Eloan Pinheiro. Interview with author. Rio de Janeiro, RJ. June 4, 2008.

10. Nubia Boechat. Interview with author. Rio de Janeiro, RJ. April 2, 2008.

11. Alexandre Grangeiro. Interview with author. São Paulo, SP. May 7, 2008.

12. See Letter to the Brazilian People *(Carta ao Povo Brasileiro)*, available at www.iisg.nl/collections/carta_ao_povo_brasileiro.pdf.

13. Andre Porto. Interview with author. Brasilia, DF. August 7, 2008.

14. In 2010, the Ministry of Health listed additional strategic products with Ministerial Directive 1284 *(Portaria 1284)*. In that year, there are 187 items on the list.

15. Subcontracting production services of APIs also overcame another contradiction in Brazil's complex regulatory framework governing pharmaceuticals. The Law of Generics stipulates that drug makers must retain three API producers in order to obtain generic certification of their product. Since public labs had to award contracts to the lowest priced seller, typically on a yearly basis, they often had only one supplier of raw material, which could change from year to year. Consequently, their products retained the denomination of *similar* as opposed to *generic*. While a *similar* and *generic* may have the same API, quality assurance is greater for *generics* since they pass through bioequivalence and bioavailability tests.

16. Eduardo Costa. Interview with author. Rio de Janeiro, RJ. June 15, 2009.

17. Pedro Palmeiro and Luciana Capanema. Interview with author. Rio de Janeiro, RJ. August 14, 2005.

Consolidating the Pharmaceutical Alliance (2007–2013)   181

18. Interviews with author: Jorge Raimundo. Rio de Janeiro, RJ. June 20, 2008; and Christopher Singer. Washington, DC. August 5, 2007.
19. João Sanches. Interview with author. São Paulo, SP. April 1, 2008.
20. Brasil interview; and Porto interview.
21. Veriano Terto. Interview with author. Rio de Janeiro, RJ. July 4, 2005.
22. Author's translation of original: http://mundorama.net/2007/05/04/discurso-do-presidente-da-republica-luiz-inacio-lula-da-silva-na-cerimonia-de-assinatura-de-ato-de-licenciamento-compulsorio-do-medicamento-efavirenz-brasilia-04052007/.
23. Carlos Passarelli. Interview with author. Brasilia, DF. December 13, 2007.
24. João Sanches interview.
25. US actions in the Brazil case suggest that direct US support to industry in cases of compulsory license has waned since Thailand issued compulsory licenses for medicines in late 2006 and early 2007. Several international civil society organizations criticized the US for pressuring Thailand after the Asian country issued several compulsory licenses. But following that episode the US has not taken any explicit actions against countries that opted for CLs. Instead of applying pressure in specific cases, US efforts in stronger IP protection focus on trade talks and international treaties.
26. Christopher Singer interview.
27. Ciro Mortella. Interview with author. São Paulo, SP. September 3, 2008.
28. Sanches interview.
29. Costa interview.
30. Renata Reis. Interview with author. Rio de Janeiro, RJ. May 5, 2008.
31. In fact, many interviewees related cases in which a drug company sponsors a patient group to sue the government in order to purchase their medicines to treat an ailment.
32. Mario Scheffer. Interview with author. São Paulo, SP. April 4, 2008.
33. Passarelli interview.
34. Gabriela Chaves. Interview with author. Rio de Janeiro, RJ. March 27, 2008.
35. Alvares interview.
36. Costa interview.
37. Specifically, the GTPI's pre-grant opposition argued that Gilead's patent request (PI 9811045–4) failed the test of an inventive step because the various analogues and pro-drugs of the chemical composition of tenofovir, as well as chemical structure and creation of salts for bio-absorption, had already been part of the public domain and did not go beyond current scientific knowledge. A copy of the pre-grant opposition, describing the technical objections, is available at www.deolhonaspatentes.org.br/default.asp?site_Acao=MostraPagina&PaginaId=980.
38. Chaves interview.
39. Test-and-treat strategies will hopefully address the challenge of continued high HIV incidence rates and difficulties in expanding health services to serve the continuous stream of new HIV diagnoses (Fundação Oswaldo Cruz 2012).
40. To become a member, countries must meet three criteria: 1) committed to fight HIV/AIDS, 2) have a flexible approach to intellectual property; and 3) have technical capacity and scientific capability in the pharmochemical and/or pharmaceutical sectors.
41. Campos de Machado Neto. Interview with author. São Paulo. July 7, 2008.
42. Jaime Rabi. Interview with author. Rio de Janeiro, RJ. April 16, 2008.
43. Lelio Maçaira. Interview with author. Rio de Janeiro. November 28, 2007.
44. Antonio Salles. Interview with author. São Paulo, SP. May 8, 2008.
45. See the announcement here: www.fiocruz.br/ccs/cgi/cgilua.exe/sys/start.htm?infoid=1497&sid=9&tpl=printerview.

182 *Consolidating the Pharmaceutical Alliance (2007–2013)*

REFERENCES

Agência Estado. 2007. "BNDES Quer Criar Grande Grupo No Setor Farmacêutico." Retrieved January 11, 2010 (http://ultimosegundo.ig.com.br/economia/2007/11/06/bndes_quer_criar_grande_grupo_no_setor_farmac234utico_1071 468.html).

Almeida, Mansueto. 2009. *Desafios da real política industrial brasileira do século XXI.* Texto para Discussão, Instituto de Pesquisa Econômica Aplicada (IPEA). Retrieved July 24, 2014 (www.econstor.eu/handle/10419/90932).

Arbix, Glauco, and Scott Martin. 2010. "Beyond Developmentalism and Market Fundamentalism in Brazil: Inclusionary State Activism without Statism." Retrieved October 31, 2011 (www.arbix.pro.br/wp-content/uploads/arbix-martin-madison-march-20102.pdf).

Azevêdo, Roberto. 2009. "Statement by Brazil at TRIPS Council: Public Health Dimension of TRIPS Agreement." Retrieved September 23, 2010 (http://keion line.org/blogs/2009/03/04/brazilian-intervention-at-trips-council).

Bastos, Cristiana. 1999. *Global Responses to AIDS.* Bloomington and Indianapolis: Indiana University Press.

Bermudez, Jorge. 1995. *Industria Farmaceutica, Estado E Sociedade: Critica Da Politica de Medicamentos No Brasil.* São Paulo: Hucitec/Sobrevime.

Bermudez, Jorge et al. 2013. "Avaliação Do Setor Produtivo Farmoquímico Nacional: Capacitação Tecnológica E Produtiva." Retrieved December 7, 2013 (www.agencia.fiocruz.br/ . . . /Apresentacao%20Seminario%20Anvisa.PDF).

BNDES. 2013. "BNDES Renova O Profarma E Amplia Apoio À Biotecnologia—BNDES." Retrieved December 7, 2013 (www.bndes.gov.br/SiteBNDES/bndes/bndes_pt/Institucional/Sala_de_Imprensa/Noticias/2013/Todas/20130411_pro farma.html).

Borsato, Cintia. 2007. "O Brasil Criou Empregos Na Índia." *Veja*, May 16. Retrieved October 25, 2008. (http://veja.abril.com.br/160507/p_058.shtml).

Brazil. 2003. *Guidelines for Industrial, Technological and Trade Policies.* Rio de Janeiro: Paz e Terra.

Cardoso, Fernando Henrique. 1975. *Autoritarismo e democratização.* Rio de Janeiro: Paz e Terra.

Cimieri, Fabiana. 2008. "Falha Em Teste de Genérico Do Efavirenz Atrasa Produção." *Estado de São Paulo*, May 20. Retrieved March 30, 2009 (www.abi aids.org.br/busca/resultView.aspx?lang=pt&seq=12436&fg=Artigos%20e%20 Not%C3%ADcias&nc=it).

Correa, Carlos. 2006. *Guidelines for the Examination of Pharmaceutical Patents: Developing a Public Health Perspective.* Geneva: WHO/ICTSD/UNCTAD.

Drahos, Peter. 2008. "Trust Me: Patent Offices in Developing Countries." *American Journal of Law & Medicine* 34(2–3): 151–74.

Evans, Peter. 1979. *Dependent Development: The Alliance of Multinational, State, and Local Capital in Brazil.* Princeton: Princeton University Press.

Evans, Peter. 1995. *Embedded Autonomy: States and Industrial Transformation.* Princeton: Princeton University Press.

Flynn, Matthew. 2007. "Between Subimperialism and Globalization: The Internationalization of Brazilian Capital." *Latin American Perspectives* 34(6): 9–27.

Flynn, Matthew. 2013. "Brazilian Pharmaceutical Diplomacy: Social Democratic Principles Versus Soft Power Interests." *International Journal of Health Services* 43(1): 67–89.

Fonseca, Elize Massard da, and Francisco Bastos. 2013. "Brazil's Response to the HIV/AIDS Epidemic: Integrating Prevention and Treatment." Pp. 149–61 in *Policy Analysis in Brazil*, edited by Jeni Vaitsman, Lenaura Lobato, and Jose M. Ribeiro. Bristol: Policy Press.

Consolidating the Pharmaceutical Alliance (2007–2013) 183

Ford, Nathan, David Wilson, Gabriela Costa Chaves, Michel Lotrowska, and Kannikar Kijtiwatchakul. 2007. "Sustaining Access to Antiretroviral Therapy in the Less-Developed World: Lessons from Brazil and Thailand." *AIDS* 21(Suppl. 4): S21–S29.

Fundação Oswaldo Cruz. 2012. *A Saúde No Brasil Em 2030: Diretrizes Para a Prospecção Estratégica Do Sistema de Saúde Brasileiro*. Rio de Janerio: Fiocruz/Ipea/Ministério da Saúde/Secretaria de Assuntos Estratégicos da Presidência da República.

GTPI. n.d. "A Inconstitucionalidade Das Patentes Pipeline." *De Olho nas Patentes*. Retrieved August 10, 2014 (www.deolhonaspatentes.org.br/default.asp?site_Aca o=MostraPagina&PaginaId=866).

GTPI. 2011. "Acordo Brasil E Estados Unidos Sobre Patentes: Quem Ganha E Quem Perde?" *De Olho nas Patentes*. Retrieved August 10, 2014 (www.deol honaspatentes.org.br/default.asp?site_Acao=mostraPagina&paginaId=891&aca o=blog&blogId=201).

GTPI. 2013a. "Civil Society Demands a Response from the Government in Relation to the Contract of ARV Drug Atazanavir." Retrieved August 10, 2014 (www. deolhonaspatentes.org.br/media/file/notas%20GTPI%202013/release%20ata zanavir_final%20(english).pdf).

GTPI. 2013b. "Para Que a Nova Política de Tratamento Para AIDS Seja Sustentável: Velhos E Novos Desafios." Retrieved August 10, 2014 (www.deolhonaspatentes. org.br/media/file/GTPI%20-%20para%20que%20a%20politica%20de%20 AIDS%20seja%20sustentavel.pdf).

INTERFARMA. 2012. *Inventário Das PPPs Na Cadeia Farmacêutica*. São Paulo: INTERFARMA. Retrieved August 9, 2014 (www.interfarma.org.br/uploads/biblioteca/21-interdoc-v-26–07–2012.pdf).

Isaude.net. 2012. "Antirretroviral Atazanavir Vai Ter Distribuição Nacional a Partir de 2013." *Isaúde*. Retrieved August 9, 2014 (www.isaude.net/pt-BR/noticia/32420/geral/antirretroviral-atazanavir-vai-ter-distribuicao-nacional-a-partir-de-2013).

Marques, Marília Bernandes. 2002. *Acessibilidade Aos Medicamentos: O Desafio de Vincular Ciência, Tecnologia, Inovação E Saúde No Brasil*. Brasilia: Centro de Gestão e Estudos Estratégicos.

Mazurkevich, Dorian. 2007. "GoB Breaks Merck Patents." (US Government Email Correspondence).

McManis, Charles R. 2009. "The Proposed Anti-Counterfeiting Trade Agreement (ACTA): Two Tales of a Treaty." *Houston Law Review* 46: 1235–56.

Ministry of Health. 2003. *Acesso Aos Medicamentos, Compras Governamentais E Inclusão Social*. Brasília: Ministry of Health.

Ministry of Health. 2008. "Mais Saude: Direito de Todos, 2008–2011." Retrieved April 30, 2009 (http://bvsms.saude.gov.br/bvs/pacsaude/pdf/mais_saude_direito_todos_2ed_p1.pdf).

Ministry of Health. 2009. "Parcerias Público-Privadas Viabilizam Produção Nacional de 24 Fármacos." Retrieved April 3, 2009 (http://portal.saude.gov.br/portal/aplicacoes/noticias/default.cfm?pg=dspDetalhes&id_area=124&CO_NOTICIA=10058).

Ministry of Health. 2014. "Parceria Para O Desenvolvimento Produtivo—PDP." *Portal da Saúde—Ministério da Saúde—www.saude.gov.br*. Retrieved August 8, 2014 (http://portalsaude.saude.gov.br/index.php/o-ministerio/principal/leia-mais-o-ministerio/581-sctie-raiz/deciis/l2-deciis/12090-parceria-para-o-desenvolvi mento-produtivo-pdp).

Mundorama.net. 2007. "Discurso Do Presidente Da República, Luiz Inácio Lula Da Silva, Na Cerimônia de Assinatura de Ato de Licenciamento Compulsório Do Medicamento Efavirenz." *Mundorama*. Retrieved August 9, 2014 (http://mundorama.net/2007/05/04/discurso-do-presidente-da-republica-luiz-ina cio-lula-da-silva-na-cerimonia-de-assinatura-de-ato-de-licenciamento-compul sorio-do-medicamento-efavirenz-brasilia-04052007/).

184 *Consolidating the Pharmaceutical Alliance (2007–2013)*

Nunn, Amy. 2008. *The Politics and History of AIDS Treatment in Brazil.* New York: Springer.

Palmeira, Pedro, and Luciana X. Capanema. 2004. "A Cadeia Farmacêutica E a Política Industrial: Uma Proposta de Inserção Do BNDES." *BNDES Setorial* 19(March): 23–48.

Palmeira, Pedro, and Simon Shi Koo Pan. 2003. "Cadeia Farmacêutica No Brasil: Avaliação Preliminar E Perspectivas." *BNDES Setorial* 18(September): 3–22

Palmeira, Pedro, Joao Paulo Pieroni, Adelaide Antunes, and Jose Vitor Bomtempo. 2012. "O Desafio Do Financiamento À Inovação Farmacêutica No Brasil: A Experiência Do BNDES Profarma." *Revista do BNDES* 37(June): 67–90.

Rich, Jessica. 2013. "Grassroots Bureaucracy: Intergovernmental Relations and Popular Mobilization in Brazil's AIDS Policy Sector." *Latin American Politics and Society* 55(2): 1–25.

Rossi, Francisco. 2006. "Free Trade Agreements and TRIPS-plus Measures." *International Journal of Intellectual Property Management* 1(1–2): 150–72.

Shadlen, Kenneth. 2009. "The Politics of Patents and Drugs in Brazil and Mexico: The Industrial Bases of Health Policies." *Comparative Politics* 41: 178–201.

Smith, Richard D., Carlos Correa, and Cecilia Oh. 2009. "Trade, TRIPS, and Pharmaceuticals." *Lancet* 373(9664): 684–91.

South Centre. 2005. "The Agenda for Transfer of Technology: The Working Group of the WTO on Trade and Transfer of Technology." Retrieved April 27, 2009 (www.southcentre.org/index.php?option=com_content&task=view&id=91).

Souza, Celina. 2013. "Modernisation of the State and Bureaucratic Capacity-Building in Brazilian Federal Government." Pp. 39–52 in *Policy Analysis in Brazil*, edited by Jeni Vaitsman, Lenaura Lobato, and Jose M. Ribeiro. Bristol: Policy Press.

Souza, Murilo. 2014. "Portal Da Câmara Dos Deputados." *Câmara Notícias.* Brasilia: Câmara Dos Deputados.

USA for Innovation. 2007. "Letter from Ambassador Ken Adleman, Executive Director, USA for Innovation, to Ambassador Condoleezza Rice, Secretary of State, Carlos M. Guierrez, Secretary of Commerce, Michael O. Leavitt, Secretary of Health and Human Services, Ambassador Susan Schwab, US Trade Representative." Retrieved October 25, 2008. (www.usaforinnovation.org/news/050907_USAFI_Adelman%20Letter.pdf.).

US Embassy Brasilia. 2007. "US Companies Press Trade Minister on Compulsory Licensing, Taxes, and Infrastructure." (Diplomatic Cable). United States State Deparment.

USTR. 2007. *2007 Special 301 Report.* Washington, DC: United States Trade Representative. Retrieved October 25, 2008 (http://www.ustr.gov/sites/default/files/asset_upload_file230_11122.pdf.).

Viegas Neves da Silva, Francisco, Ronaldo Hallal, and André Guimarães. 2012. "Compulsory License and Access to Medicines: Economics Savings of Efavirenz in Brazil." Retrieved July 28, 2014 (http://pag.aids2012.org/PAGMaterial/PPT/940_3379/cl%20efv%20final.pptx).

Vieira, Marcela. 2014. "Current Challenges on IP and Access to Medicines in Brazil: Views and Strategy from Civil Society." Rio de Janeiro: ABIA/GTPI. Retrieved July 28, 2014 (www.deolhonaspatentes.org.br/media/file/eventos/apresenta%C3%A7%C3%A3o%20marcela%20evento%20fiocruz.pdf).

Zanatta, Rafael A. F. 2012. *The Risk of the New Developmentalism: "Brasil Maior" Plan and Bureaucratic Rings.* Rochester: Social Science Research Network. Retrieved December 5, 2013 (http://papers.ssrn.com/abstract=2120002).

Conclusion

In June 2013, Brazilians returned to the street to protest against the large public expenditures being spent in preparation for the World Cup. Fare increases in public transportation sparked the demonstrations, but as the movement grew from a few thousand in São Paulo to millions in several cities throughout Brazil, the number and variety of demands also multiplied. People directed their anger at rising consumer prices, corruption, and career politicians. Of course, one important issue was the country's health care system. Protestors carried placards with slogans stating: "I don't care about the World Cup. I want money for health and education." And "We want FIFA-standard hospitals." Brazil spent approximately US$13.5 billion (approximately double the initial outlays) to build world-class soccer stadiums. Protestors felt enraged by the enormous amounts of money spent on the sports infrastructure while the country's health system continued to lag behind First World levels. The recent upsurge in citizens' anger and demands show that many similar social forces touched upon in this book continue to play out in the Brazilian society.

One is the country's interaction with an international organization and incursions on the nation's sovereignty. Just as the World Trade Organization (WTO) panels threatened Brazil's AIDS program in the past, Brazilians felt unjustly pressured by the Fédération Internationale de Football Association (FIFA). "The *Lei da Copa* (World Cup General Law), passed by the Brazilian Congress in 2012 under threat from FIFA, undermines the nation's sovereignty, humiliates its authorities, and violates other national legislation," wrote anthropologist Jaimes Amparo Alves (2013). Another factor is the social composition of the protestors. According to Singer (2014), middle-class participants comprised the majority protestors who took to the streets in the June 2013 protests. In the case of AIDS, middle-class activists also led civil society actions against stigma, prevention policies, and treatment access.

The June 2013 protests reveal that access to high quality and affordable health care continues as persistent social demand. Brazil has made important advances towards achieving the goals of the *sanitarista* movement, but many challenges remain. In their report *Twenty Years of Health System*

186   *Conclusion*

Reform in Brazil, Couttolenc, Gragnolati, and Lindelow (2013) provide a comprehensive picture of the changes to Brazil's Unified Health System (*Sistema Única da Saúde*—SUS) and some of the origins of social discontent. Their review of recent polls provides a mixed picture. Two polls found that about two-thirds of the population consider the public health system as "bad" or "terrible" and a growing number of people see health as one of the main problems facing the country. Another survey found an equal number of positive versus negative assessments of the public health system, with the Family Health Program (*Programa Saúde da Familia*—PSF), which focuses on primary and preventative care targeted towards lower socio-economic groups, receiving the most favorable assessments. In all surveys, most complaints highlighted long wait times, lack of doctors, and problematic referral services. Compared to other countries at comparable levels of development, Brazilians tend to have more negative attitudes towards their health system.

Are Brazilian attitudes towards the health system warranted? Couttolenc, Gragnolati, and Lindelow (2013) conclude that Brazil's past health reforms have achieved spectacular results in some metrics but not in others. Unmet needs and share of households reporting lack of money as reasons for not obtaining care has declined significantly. In fact, Brazil reports some of the lowest rates of "catastrophic spending" in health compared to other Latin America countries. Avoidable death, or declines in mortality due to timely and adequate access to the health system, has also fallen. The PSF, in particular, has led to reductions in infant mortality, diarrhea in children, hospitalizations from strokes, and declines in acute respiratory infections between 1990 and 2002. McGuire (2010) echoes the sentiment that Brazil has become a leader in primary health care. More problematic, however, are obstacles to treatments for more complex health conditions. Due to problems in referrals, diagnostic procedures, and access to specialty care, 60% of cancer patients received a diagnosis at a very late stage—limiting treatment options and curtailing survival rates. In fact, median waiting times in 2010 range from 76 to 113 days, depending on the type of treatment (Couttolenc, Gragnolati, and Lindelow 2013).

Twenty Years of Health System Reform in Brazil also shows mixed outcomes concerning the population's access to prescription drugs. Monthly household spending on drugs has declined from R$79 to R$59 between 1995 and 2008 in real terms. For households visited by PSF teams, SUS provides free distribution to 70% of all the drugs consumed. Still, problems persist. About 40% of the drugs prescribed in primary care settings were not available and nearly half of the prescription medicines were not provided for free. Additionally, surveys reveal large household expenditures on medicines not listed on SUS formularies, lots of prescriptions from non-SUS doctors, and products for self-medication, raising questions about to what degree prescription drug use is rational. Lastly, many drug prices in Brazil appear high in international terms, with mean prices 65% and 74% higher

Conclusion 187

for originator and generic brands, respectively, according to one study in the south of Brazil (Bertoldi et al. 2012).

Brazil has initiated a number of policies to address the costs of high-priced medicines (PAHO 2009). In 2003, the Medicines Market Regulatory Body (*Câmara de Regulação do Mercado de Medicamentos*—CMED) replaced the previous government initiatives to govern prices. For new medicines, analysts first decide if the drug provides a therapeutic advantage compared to existing treatments on the market. If so, the price is set at the lowest price practiced in Australia, Canada, Spain, the US, France, Greece, Italy, New Zealand, Portugal, or the exporter country. If the drug does not present a therapeutic advantage, about 80% of new registrations, then the price must be the same or lower than comparable treatment on the market and not more than any price in the aforementioned countries.[1] In addition, CMED applies an additional discount, called the Price Adequacy Coefficient *(Coeficiente de Adequação de Preços)*, which in 2008 was 24.92%, that applies to purchases made by the public sector. Along with the new price controls, Brazil has increased spending on high-cost medicines by 347%. Between 2003 and 2008, federal expenditures for 220 high-cost drugs that benefit some 730,000 people has risen from R$516 million to R$2.3 billion over the period (PAHO 2009). Still, civil society groups note that Brazil still is paying too high for several medicines. For example, SUS spent US$1,239 for the cancer drug rituximbabe (500mg) and US$82 for the tuberculosis drug linezolide (600mg) versus US$0.65 and US$2.50 for generic versions of the same drugs on the international market (Vieira 2014).

Another challenge is deciding which medicines should be included in SUS and thus paid through the public purse. To evaluate new technologies, the Ministry of Health created in 2011 the National Commission for the Incorporation of New Technologies (*Comissão Nacional de Incorporação de Tecnologias no SUS*—CONITEC).[2] Similar to the United Kingdom's National Institute for Health and Care Excellence (NICE), the body conducts cost-benefit evaluations of new health technologies and makes decisions on which items to include in the public health system. In the first nine months of its existence, 70% of the total 134 new requests related to medicines (Laranjeira 2012).

Court cases have played a major role in the government's efforts to better regulate the incorporation of new health technologies. Following the example of people with HIV, many other individuals and groups with different diseases have used the court system and the Constitutional right to health in order to obtain access to high-cost medicines and other procedures. Ferraz (2011) estimates that most of the cases involved access to patented drugs, of which 75% related to cancer.[3] Use of the court system to obtain access to high-cost medicines skyrocketed from 387 in 2005 to 2,174 in 2009 and costs jumping from R$2.4 million (US$1.2 million) to R$53 million (US$26.5 million). These are claims against the federal government. State governments, in Brazil's decentralized health system, appear

188 *Conclusion*

to bear the brunt of the costs. São Paulo State reported R$400 million on health-related litigation in 2008. Concerning the content of the claims, most lawsuits centered on medicines not included on government formularies because they are not cost effective compared to alternative therapies (Ferraz 2011). Indeed, health officials say they have received reports that commercial interests drive some of the lawsuits.[4]

Most lawsuits come from middle-class citizens who know their rights, have the capacity to use the legal system, and the means to hire lawyers (Ferraz 2011; Gauri and Brinks 2010). Since the judges tend to be sympathetic, spending on high-cost medicines resulting from court orders reached R$10,600 (US$5,300) per person, nearly quadruple the per capita amount spent on high-cost drugs that have been incorporated into SUS (Ferraz 2011). Health officials have reached out to judges and prosecutors to explain SUS's efforts to provide prescription drugs and why not all requests should be granted. Moreover, the increasing judicialization of health by middle-class individuals for high-cost drugs may divert public resources that could have a higher impact for a larger number of people at a lower socio-economic level.

The last issue raised by the protests and similar efforts to provide expensive AIDS medicines concerns the availability of resources to fund the public health system. Public spending on health has increased 111%, or from R$339 to R$714 per capita, between the first half of the 1980s to 2010 (Couttolenc, Gragnolati, and Lindelow 2013). During the same time, the government has rapidly expanded service capacity and number of services. Nonetheless, government spending on health at just under 4% of GDP is far lower than spending in wealthy countries and even less than some middle-income peers. Consequently, many Brazilians see access to private health insurance as a means to obtain faster access to care, although private insurance does not cover prescription medicines (Couttolenc, Gragnolati, and Lindelow 2013). *Sanitaristas*, however, continue to hold the view that "health is not for sale" and criticize the private sector for competing for resources through public health plans and service contracts with SUS (CEBES 2014).

With steady economic growth and huge oil deposits, Brazil may be better placed to increase funding to its health sector. Although lawmakers rejected proposals for a new "health tax" *(Contribuição Social da Saúde)* to provide additional funds for SUS, they did approve the "Oil Royalties Law" *(Lei dos Royalties do Petróleo)* that slated 25% of the revenue from the extraction of the huge pre-salt oil deposits off of Brazil's southeastern seaboard, estimated at R$112 billion over the next decade, to the health sector (Câmara dos Deputados 2013; Globo 2013). The influx of resources should address some of the current challenges faced by SUS and boost the country's pharmaceutical autonomy—the ability to provide for the prescription drug needs of the country in the face of new structural constraints.

Conclusion 189

PHARMACEUTICAL AUTONOMY IN A GLOBALIZING WORLD

Brazil's AIDS treatment program demonstrates both the limits and successful strategies of achieving "FIFA-standard levels of care" throughout the rest of its health system. As of 2013, the AIDS Program provided 23 different ARVs to over 352,000 people without copay or out-of-pocket expense. Achieving this feat was not easy. For the past 20 years, the government could not rely on windfall oil revenues and instead faced significant fiscal constraints. Policymakers thus drove down costs by facing down powerful commercial interests and political pressures. Brazil's experience providing AIDS medicines brings into sharp relief many of the battles of pharmaceutical autonomy in the brave new world of patents and is a useful lens for understanding the impact of contemporary global power structures on equity and policy space. An analysis of the 20-year period from 1990 to 2010 shows the swings between pharmaceutical autonomy and dependency.

From 1990 to 2001, Brazil demonstrated the ability to rapidly reverse engineer antiretroviral medicines and reduce per capita costs R$6,223 in 1998 to R$4,158 in 2002 while more than doubling the number of people in treatment (Grangeiro et al. 2006). When a United States-sponsored World Trade Organization panel threatened the country's program, Brazil's treatment coalition reached out to additional allies in the global civil society under the rubric of human rights. Brazilian diplomats and health officials sponsored rights-based resolutions in organizations affiliated with the United Nations while activists engaged in protests in front of the US Embassy and organized campaigns to shame transnational drug corporations. The period demonstrates increasing pharmaceutical autonomy as the US backed off and drug companies conceded to Brazilian price demands, but the structural impact of new patents started to be felt.

The years from 2002 to 2006 witnessed increasing pharmaceutical dependency with the incorporation of more patent-protected medicines into the country's treatment protocols and the migration of treatment-experienced individuals to these newer ARVs. Compared to other developing countries and the WHO's minimalist treatment guidelines, Brazil offers a comprehensive array of ARVs. Not surprisingly, treatment costs jumped to nearly R$1 billion (US$500 million) in 2005. Yet efforts to control costs through the use of compulsory licenses and increased local production faltered due to the patent thickets and court injunctions foreign companies used to limit Brazilian public labs' access to raw material. Not even civil society efforts through the National Health Council, lawsuits in the courts, or protests could force the government to take a more aggressive position.

Due to the obstacles in developing new, patent-protected medicines and the need to enlist additional allies to sustain the country's universal treatment program, the government initiated new industrial policies for the pharmaceutical sector. Public-private partnerships targeted the country's

190   *Conclusion*

pharmochemical sector to produce active pharmaceutical ingredients used in the antiretroviral medicines (ARVs). In effect, a triple alliance comprised of the state, society, and industry formed to defend the country's pharmaceutical autonomy between 2007 to the present. A compulsory license for Merck's efavirenz in May 2007 demonstrated the political force of this new treatment coalition to defend the country's sovereignty and support local technological development.

These episodes demonstrate the importance of three important factors: control over technologies, institutionalization of political coalitions, and normative frameworks based on human rights. Tracing the development of these factors over a longer duration of time also informs our understanding of current structures of dependency and strategies to expand the government's policy space. Compared to past depictions of dependent development, today's globalizing world presents new constraints and opportunities.

Technology

Despite complaints from patent holders and the defenders of a strong intellectual property system that Brazil's threats and compulsory licensing is a form of "piracy" threatening future innovation, transnational drug companies have profited handsomely from the country's universal AIDS program. According to data provided by the National AIDS Program, the Brazilian government spent a total of US$2.71 billion on ARVs between 1996 and 2007. Of this amount, foreign firms received US$1.85 billion, or 68% of the total.[5] Had Brazil waited until 2005 to adhere to the TRIPS accord or outlawed patents on medicines as many civil society activists demanded, total expenditures would have been less and local firms (both public and private) could have legally reverse engineered and produced more of the medicines.[6] Additionally, if Brazil had continued a coherent set of industrial policies since the 1980s without the abrupt trade liberalization in the early 1990s, local firms could have become global players similar to Indian firms.

In this case, patent power appears to have "kicked the ladder away," as articulated by Chang (2002), in that Brazil can no longer use strategies employed by other late-developing countries to freely copy and adapt existing technologies. Still, the ability of transnational corporations (TNCs) to control the spread of technology is more tenuous than before. In the past, dependent development rested upon the physical control of manufacturing operations to achieve high profit margins. Nowadays, TNCs require a robust global regulatory framework, or what Robinson (2004) calls a "transnational state," to secure surplus gains. In today's knowledge economy, legal rigor runs up against the nonstop diffusion of technological know-how and skills throughout the world. The contradiction between securing intellectual property rights based on state power and the potential of generic firms to copy medicines increases the political stakes in the game and presents a complicated policy terrain for health officials.

Brazil's experience shows that policymakers face a Catch-22 when considering the use of humanitarian flexibilities outlined in TRIPS and clarified in the *Doha Declaration*. Generic firms will not develop and produce a medicine until there are definitive market prospects, while policymakers will hesitate to use a compulsory license (CL) unless alternative drug supplies are readily available. Due to previous patent restrictions on active pharmaceutical ingredients (APIs), Farmanguinhos took 21 months after the CL was issued to produce efavirenz—time users of the drug cannot go without. In the meantime, Brazil had to import the drug from India using the Pan American Health Organization (PAHO) as an intermediary. The Paragraph 6 Decision of the *Doha Declaration*, regarding the use of CLs for countries that do not have manufacturing capabilities, affects countries like Brazil that can produce medicines locally. The situation will become more acute as new medicines receive patent protection in India, which, up to now, has been an important alternative supplier. For the time being, Brazilian health officials have opted for a limited number of technological transfer agreements but have not resorted to additional use of the CL beyond the case of efavirenz.

Transnational drug companies, meanwhile, continue to divide up the world market through conditions placed on voluntary licenses. These agreements between patent holders and local drug makers typically include geographical restrictions. According to these accords, licensees can sell to the local market or sub-Saharan Africa but not export production to middle-income countries. In August 2012, Bristol-Myers Squibb (BMS) filed a breach of contract suit against Indian generic drug maker Mylan Labs for exporting atazanavir via PAHO to Venezuela, despite the fact that neither country has yet to award a patent for the medicine. BMS helped Mylan to develop the drug on the condition that it sells the drug only in India and sub-Saharan Africa. A US federal judge ruled against BMS but stated the company could still pursue claims against the Indian generics company based on patent infringement, which it has attempted in India (Overley 2013; Pharmabiz.com 2014).

Political Alliances

Given increased political stakes over the control of knowledge-based technologies, political alliances play an increasingly significant role to secure pharmaceutical autonomy. Past models of dependent development conceived of these ties either as a triple alliance between transnational corporations (TNCs), the state, and local industrialists (Evans 1979), or in terms of "bureaucratic rings" that tie a technocratic class with commercial interests (Cardoso 1975). Nowadays, theorists of global capitalism posit a declining role of the state as a result of neoliberal policies and increasing class ties between foreign and domestic capitalists (Robinson 2004; Sklair 1995, 2001). Neither depiction appears in the case of Brazil's AIDS treatment

192 *Conclusion*

program. Instead, a powerful treatment coalition included state actors, civil society, and local industry. Admittedly, the Brazilian experience in local production of ARVs and patent confrontations is exceptional and unique, but still a case that can provide important theoretical insights.

Various social transformations inform the evolution of state-society relations over the past five decades. First, the nature of the state has changed. The Brazilian state has increasingly professionalized and improved its ability to implement complex social programs. While public administration still falls short of the ideals of a Weberian bureaucracy, nor is it free from corruption, the Brazilian state cannot be reduced to patrimonial politics common in the past (see Roett 1992). Previously, clientelism and personal connections to power brokers determined access to state-controlled resources, including health care. Now democratic institutions, a more educated and urban electorate, and a new generation of committed politicians reduced, but did not eliminate, patron-client relations. Since 2000, competitive recruitment in Brazil's federal government has increased the professionalism and qualifications of public servants, thereby limiting previous clientelistic criteria for recruitment and job advancement (Souza 2013).

A democratic regime affects the second important change—a more mobilized civil society. Today, activists are more adept at using the court system, competent in sharing experiences and information, and professional in their operations and discussions with specialized government agencies. In the past, social movements acted through corporatist institutions or faced outright repression from the authorities. Local social movement organizations are also increasingly networked with transnational advocacy networks. The social movement that has mushroomed in relation to IP, HIV/AIDS, and access to medicines has played and will continue to play a key role in defending a more flexible intellectual property regime. While it is difficult to assess the impact of activist pressures on intellectual property accords and patent battles (see Matthews 2011), the Brazilian experience demonstrates their crucial role in channeling information to policymakers, gaining media attention to important issues, and explaining complex issues to the wider public.

A third transformation focuses on the powerful links between the state and civil society. Evans' concept of synergy encompasses the "mutually reinforcing relations between government and groups of engaged citizens" (Evans 1996: 1119). In the case of Brazil's AIDS program, synergy is heavily politicized and involves an ideologically committed state actors, or what Santoro and McGuire (1997) call "social movement insiders." Where civil society has been absent, Rich (2013) notes these "bureaucratic activists" from Brazil's National AIDS program have attempted to fund and create progressive civil society organizations to promote the rights of those with HIV. When social movements capture a portion of the state, the institutional position provides a space for activists to lobby for progressive policies, develop coalitions within government and society, and publicize suspect deals. Such collaborations across the state-society divide will likely

Conclusion   193

determine the evolving domestic and international framework governing intellectual property rights and medicines.

Normative Framing

Another important difference between dependent development and contemporary strategies for achieving broad development outcomes is the use of a human rights framework. In the past, markets, goods, and economic growth were viewed predominantly through a utilitarian lens and often intertwined with nationalism. While nationalist rhetoric continues, rights-based discourses have achieved a hegemonic position. Brazil's success in achieving pharmaceutical autonomy is intertwined with the dissemination of rights-based norms at both the national and global levels.

Moyn (2010) argues that the human rights frame represents a "last utopia" not only because they made social struggles more pragmatic but also because of their moral purity. "The disavowal of earlier utopias took place in part out of the aspiration to achieve through a moral critique of politics the sense of a pure cause that had once been sought in politics itself" (2010: 171). But Moyn's critique focuses too narrowly on the international human rights crowd and their use of the courts and international human rights system to restorative or distributive justice. While Brazilian activists and officials employed the courts and pushed norms that framed essential medicines as a right to health, they did not avoid politics. They targeted the "moral purity" of their discourse at the commercial interests and foreign diplomats to foment "public stigmatization" against perceived enemies of the treatment program. Human rights have acted more as a mobilizing frame for coalition building and a discourse to contend powerful interests. It is one of the few counter-systems available for evaluating and critiquing large-scale organizations that dominate global capitalism (Sjoberg, Gill, and Williams 2001; Sjoberg 2009).

The human rights framework still has limitations. In the Brazil case, most policymakers viewed human rights as a means to balance the rights and obligations of intellectual property holders, not to deny outright their property claims as more critical frameworks assert. Jose Serra, Brazil's Minister of Health during the first conflicts over patented medicines, best asserted this view:

> Our position as government was not aimed at proposing the abolition of intellectual property protection, but rather to suggest and defend a position stating that patent rules must make it possible to achieve a balance between the objectives of the private and public interests.
>
> (Serra 2004: 10)

Such a discourse does not question the economic system that converts "creations of the mind" into forms of property. Instead, it just attempts to

194   *Conclusion*

trump one set of norms—the right to health—over another set of norms—the right to intellectual property.

The right to health framework also remains issue specific to access to medicines and rooted in a biomedical approach towards disease. While treatment activists included a number of actors from diverse political persuasions, what binds middle-class NGOs, global health experts, and activist bureaucrats into a formidable political coalition is their shared belief in the curative dimension of medicines. The deeper socio-economic structures that affect the equitable distribution of healthy life within and across countries, or what Freeman (2009) calls "health justice," remains elusive. Even in Brazil's AIDS program, discussions about historic levels of social inequality and marginality subsided as AIDS treatments were scaled up (Bastos 1999; Biehl 2007). While international treaties and some national Constitutions (including Brazil's) stipulate social determinants as part of the right to health, there has been less rights-based mobilization around health injustices related to persistent racism, growing classism, and endemic poverty.

Technologies, political alliances, and normative frameworks contribute towards achieving pharmaceutical autonomy. They reveal a new institutional configuration at the international level compared to the past situations of dependent development. During the period of national development efforts of the 1960s and 1970s, developing countries formed a New International Economic Order (NIEO) that called for a redistribution of economic power throughout the world. Such efforts failed to achieve any significant gains. The situation of the current phase of globalization is different.

Direct bilateral pressures typified the relations between the Global North and Global South in the past. While the USTR's Priority Watch Lists and threat of punitive sanctions persist, there are more options for developing countries to find redress. For example, the dispute resolution mechanism of the World Trade Organization, despite all its problems, creates a more even global playing field compared to the pressures that one country can impose on another. In 2009, Brazil won a WTO panel against trade-distorting US cotton subsidies and received the right to impose counter measures of $829 million annually on US imports and intellectual property rights owned by US companies until the US changes its policies. Treatment activists lobbied trade officials to take retaliatory measures on patented or patent-pending ARVs lopinavir/ritonavir (brand name Kaletra), darunavir, and etravirine, along with cancer drugs erlotinibe and trastuzumabe, and entecavir used to treat Hepatitis B. All the medications significantly impact SUS's budget (GTPI 2014).[7]

The rise of the so-called BRICS (Brazil, Russia, India, China, and South Africa) also demonstrates that the traditional rule-makers of the global economy—the United States, Europe, and Japan—must also take into account these large emerging markets. But this new multipolar arrangement has proposed few alternatives to the Bretton Woods institutions and, at best, proved more successful in blocking proposals that go against their

Conclusion 195

interests than proposing new initiatives, except for a new BRICS bank to rival the World Bank. Still, Brazil and other countries are no longer dependent on just trading with the United States or Europe, as more South-South trade networks increase. One concern is the rise of a new dominant economic power. Brazilian manufacturers have difficulty in competing against low-cost Chinese products.

BRAZIL'S EXPERIENCE IN COMPARATIVE PERSPECTIVE

While case studies have inherent limitations, they still provide useful idiographic analysis of the various factors tied to a specific outcome. Such an approach allows scholars to evaluate theories at multiple points of time and identify new factors for explaining historical processes. Dependency and global capitalist theories highlight the connections between the international political economy and the policy space countries have to achieve broad development objectives. State theory and social movement perspectives reveal the relationship between state structures and civil society. And normative frameworks draw attention to definitions, moral codes, and frames of competing actors.

Tracing these processes using Haydu's methodological approach of "recurrent problem solving" may provide useful comparisons between Brazil's experience providing treatment and those other middle-income countries with serious HIV epidemics. Table 7.1 compares the socio-economic conditions, epidemiologic situations, and government policies of Brazil with Thailand, South Africa, and India. What immediately stands out is Brazil's success in achieving a nearly 95% level of ARV coverage for those with CD4 counts below 200mm^3. Also striking is the enormity of the epidemic facing South Africa with prevalence rates reaching 17.8% of the population. Only in 2008 with a change of political leadership did the government scale up treatment, and now South Africa has the largest population of ARVs in the world. Why did the government change course? A path dependency model for understanding the South African case would have difficulty understanding this policy removal. According to this framework, would not Prime Minister Thabo Mbeki's decision in the early 2000s not to roll out treatment result in powerful lock-in mechanisms that make changing course or adopting a new policy increasingly difficult? Instead, the opposite occurred. Reform-minded politicians, allied with the social movement organizations like Treatment Action Campaign, forced intransigent political leaders and health officials to provide medicines (Forbath 2008).

Thailand also presents an interesting comparison to Brazil since both countries initiated early efforts to fight AIDS. Thailand's heath reformer and activist Mechai Viravaidya, who resembles many of the characteristics of a *sanitarista*, initiated the first prevention campaigns to fight the disease. In fact, his nickname is "Mr. Condom," and his name, "mechai," also refers

Table 7.1 Four Middle-Income Countries with Serious HIV/AIDS Epidemics

	Brazil	South Africa	Thailand	India
Population (2010 in millions)	195	50	69	1,171
GDP (2010 in current billions USD)	$2,087	$363	$319	$1,727
GDP per capita, PPP (2010)	$11,210	$9,477	$7,673	$3,214
Inequality (Gini)	53.9 (2009)	67.4 (2006)	42.5 (2004)	36.8 (2005)
Population below poverty line (poverty headcount)	21.4% (2009)	23% (2005)	8.1% (2009)	27.5% (2005)
HIV/AIDS adult prevalence rate (2009 est.)*	0.5%	17.8%	1.3%	0.3%
People living with HIV/AIDS (2009 est.)*	460,000–810,000	5,600,000 [5,400,000–5,900,000]	530,000 [420,000–660,000]	2,400,000 [2,100,000–2,800,000]
No. of people currently taking ARVs	201,279 (2010)**	919,923 (2009)*	65,481 (2009)*	428,638 (2011)***
% of PLWHA on ARVs (T-CD4 < 200/mm³)	94.8% (2006 est.)**	56% (2009 est.)*	62.4% (2009 est.)*	33.2% (2010 est.)***
Percent of GDP (public & private) spent on health (2009)	9%	8.5%	4.3%	2.4%
Year recognized product patents on pharmaceuticals	1997	1978	1992	2005

*UNAIDS; **Brazil's AIDS Program "MonitorAIDS"; ***India's National AIDS Control Organization (n.d.) and author's calculations.

Source: World Bank Indicators and World Health Organization National Health Accounts.

Conclusion   197

to a condom. Thailand also has a federal public lab, the Government Pharmaceutical Organization (GPO), responsible for producing medicines used in the public health system. The GPO has played an important role reverse engineering ARVs and lobbying for compulsory licenses, yet similar to Brazil's public labs, it does not produce the critical APIs used to make drugs. Thailand was also the first middle-income country to make extensive use of CLs for public health objectives. But in contrast to Brazil's democratic policies, compulsory licensing occurred under military rule.

Lastly, India has become the global powerhouse in the production of inexpensive and generic ARVs, but only a third of its population requiring treatment has access to the life-saving medicines. HIV-related social stigma, in part, explains India's failure to take aggressive approaches towards the disease (Akhavi 2008). Policymakers in India and South Africa appear more susceptible to conservative sexual mores compared to those in Brazil and Thailand. Another factor is the decentralized nature of the country's health system and programs. While both Brazil and India are federal entities with numerous states, Brazil centralized AIDS prevention and treatment programs. In relation to pharmaceutical patents, however, India waited until 2005 to adjust its intellectual property laws in compliance with the final TRIPS deadline while Brazil adjusted its national legislation in 1996. Having an economy less integrated into world trade made India less vulnerable to bilateral sanctions relative to Brazil, and its more politically powerful pharmaceutical industry contributed to its decision to delay TRIPS compliance. Compared to other countries, India's drug firms have been the main protagonists for compulsory licenses. For example, Natco lobbied and obtained a compulsory license for Bayer's cancer drug sorafenib. India also has strict criteria for awarding patents. Despite appeals to India's Supreme Court, Novartis could not overturn the Indian patent office's ruling on its cancer drug imatinib. Evaluators rejected the patent on the grounds that it was a minor modification on a known substance and thus failed the tests of novelty and an inventive step.

Generalizing findings beyond HIV/AIDS to other disease categories has inherent limitations. Indeed, HIV is quite unique. The idea of HIV exceptionalism refers to the novel approaches to fight the epidemic compared to other diseases. Policy experimentation, respect for human rights, and efforts to address stigma have influenced diverse initiatives to fight the disease across the world. The same exceptionalism and innovativeness also marks treatment rollout, not only in the Brazil, but around the world. In fact, HIV/AIDS can be considered one of the first diseases associated with contemporary globalization. By using a global lens we can truly understand the implications the disease has for global society (Altman 1999). As Brazilian journalist and founder of AIDS News Agency *(Agência de Notícias da Aids)* Rosali Tardelli sums up: "AIDS requires a different logic. AIDS has come to change the world and has a pedagogical role."[8] One area that the pandemic has affected is the access to medicines in a globalizing world.

198 *Conclusion*

ACCESS TO MEDICINES: GLOBAL CHALLENGES AND SOLUTIONS

While AIDS is the first global disease to truly illustrate the contradictions between patent-based business models and public health concerns, the subject of pharmaceutical autonomy extends beyond the pandemic. Increasingly, developing countries, home to 5.8 billion people, are experiencing an epidemiological transition. Higher incomes, changing diets, and improved living conditions are allowing people in the developing world to live longer, healthier lives. Although neglected tropical diseases continue to pose a problem for the poorest of the poor, the disease profile of the developing world increasingly resembles that of the developed world. Communicable diseases such as polio, yellow fever, and cholera are receding, while non-communicable diseases (NCDs) such as cancer, heart disease, and diabetes become more prevalent. According to the WHO (2011), NCDs are the leading killers in the world today, accounting for 63% of total deaths, or 36 million of the 57 million deaths that occurred throughout the world in 2008. Around 80% of all these deaths from NCDs occur in the developing world. However, access to medicines to treat NCDs remains limited and drug prices high in most middle- and low-income countries (WHO 2011).

Do global policies to provide AIDS medicines offer a useful blueprint for other disease categories? Regardless of a person's nationality or citizenship status, if she or he is HIV positive numerous multilateral and bilateral efforts including PEPFAR, UNITAID, and the Global Fund exist to fund treatment. In their book *AIDS Drugs for All*, Kapstein and Busby (2013) highlight the important factors that led to what is the first global prescription drug regime in the world. Along with studies demonstrating the efficacy and feasibility of treatment in low-resource settings, the cost of medicines must fall to a threshold level at which global funders do not balk at the cost. In the view of policymakers during the 1990s, patented ARVs costing in the thousands made providing life-saving drugs to the poor unthinkable. But, when Indian generic manufacturers began offering the same drugs for under US$200 per person per year, "AIDS drugs for all" became a foreseeable reality. Equally important is the content of activists' demands based on achievable objectives versus utopic or vague goals. "If transnational social movements are to be successful in shaping the political and economic agendas of governments and firms, they must fuse both rational/analytical and emotive/normative appeals into a single 'ask,'" write Kapstein and Busby (2013: 21). For this reason, rolling out AIDS medicines and malaria treatments are more likely to succeed than calls for universal education and reduction in carbon emissions. More focused demands, reduced costs, and a stronger institutional footing are required for success.

The problem with replicating the previous successes of the global ARV treatment regime, as outlined by Kapstein and Busby, is that it is predicated on segmented markets by firms that charge high prices for medicines in the

Conclusion 199

high-income countries used to fund R&D, while offering cheaper prices in low-income countries. But, access to medicines is not only a problem that affects the developing world, especially amidst growing inequality and fiscal crises. In Europe, where most citizens rely on national health insurance schemes to pay for medicines, governments are pressuring companies to lower their prices as part of fiscal austerity measures. One of the worst countries affected by the Eurozone crisis is Greece, whose government decreed a 25% reduction in the price of medicines purchased by its public health sector. Drug companies Novo Nordisk, Leo Pharma and Merck KGaA responded to Greek demands by removing their products from the market (Brabant 2010a, 2010b; Reuters 2012). Concerned about revenues and the domino effect of price controls, pharmaceutical companies exit markets when conditions are not favorable. Cases such as Greece's demonstrate the contradictions between a patent-driven business model and human need with serious consequences for individuals and public health.

In the US, where patented drugs cost double the price than in Europe, drug companies do not exit the market, consumers do. Individuals simply forego or cease taking medicines due to exorbitant prices. Even with health insurance, one in six people under 65 years old report problems paying for a medicine; for the uninsured, the number is one in three (Light 2009). As a result of the Great Recession, people cut back further on prescription drugs. With skyrocketing drug prices, more US citizens are searching elsewhere for affordable treatment, oftentimes to the border towns along Canada and Mexico. In the US, the prices for AIDS medicines are some of the highest in the world. Even with the Affordable Care Act guaranteeing a variety of essential health benefits, including prescription drug benefits, insurers still have flexibility to determine tiers of coverage. People with HIV who have new health plans have no problem accessing cheap off-patent generic ARVs but face significant obstacles when attempting to access more expensive treatments.

Another challenge is addressing the disease burdens common only to low-income countries. A global treatment program for AIDS worked because AIDS affects both the developed and developing world. There is no market incentive for pharmaceutical firms to invest in treatments for malaria, helminths, schistosomiasis, and many other diseases that affect only the poor. The lack of R&D expenditures on neglected tropical diseases (NTDs) is particularly acute. Of the US$240 billion spent on health R&D in 2010 (both private and public), only about 1% focused on these diseases that affect the most socially marginalized populations in the developing world (Røttingen et al. 2013). In 2011, total R&D funding worldwide for NTDs reached $3.05 billion (G-Finder 2012).

In multilateral venues, especially the World Health Organization (WHO), there is increasing debate about how to resolve the contradictions between access and innovation. In 2003 the WHO established the Commission on Intellectual Property Rights, Innovation and Public Health, which highlighted

200 Conclusion

the paucity of investments in developing health technologies for addressing the disease burdens in developing countries. A subsequent commission, the WHO Intergovernmental Working Group on Innovation, Intellectual Property, and Public Health (IGWG), met from 2006 to 2008 to consider innovative policies to encourage research into public health problems affecting the developing world. IGWG concluded its activities with the 2008 WHA resolution *Global Strategy on Public Health, Innovation and Intellectual Property* that aims to delink the costs of research and development from the prices of essential medicines. Not only could more research funding be directed to address the health needs of the "bottom billion" throughout the world, but eventually people in high- and middle-income countries might eventually benefit from more accessible prices.

The Expert Working Group on R&D Financing was established in November 2008 to examine current financing and R&D coordination efforts, as well as proposals for new and innovative sources of funding to stimulate research into diseases that affect the developing world. In their submission to the Group, Brazilian health officials suggested taxing the repatriated profits of transnational drug companies in order to raise resources for prizes and new investments in health technologies. Needless to say, many of Brazil's initiatives addressing intellectual property to problems of access to essential medicines have been resisted by developed countries. But other countries have allied with Brazil's position (see Flynn 2013). Thailand has been vocal about pharmaceutical companies profiteering from acquiring patents on disease specimens provided by developing countries affected by contagious outbreaks of Avian flu, H1N1, among others. In a statement to the WHO, the Thai government stated, "The costs in human terms associated with collective health insecurity clearly outweigh any gains or considerations in protecting intellectual property" (quoted in Labonte and Gagnon 2010: 9).

The WHO's Consultative Expert Working Group in May 2010 has recommended a Medical R&D Treaty, milestone prizes, and a percentage of government-funded research as potential mechanisms for securing resources for investing in health research to address the needs of those in developing countries (WHO 2012). CEWG also called for a Global Health R&D Observatory to monitor financial flows and to identify gaps in the development of existing and new therapeutic tools (WHO 2012). At the 2014 World Health Assembly, the WHO's governing body, delegates from member states approved resolutions to implement innovative R&D demonstration projects and a pooled funding mechanism for R&D focused on the health needs in middle- and low-income countries. The decision effectively creates a multilateral mechanism that backs delinking R&D costs from prices and open access to research data. While the resolution does not go as far as a Medical R&D Treaty that pegs country contributions to GDP levels, it represents an important advance in promoting a research agenda that addresses the health needs of the socially excluded while also seeking to

Conclusion 201

improve access. These achievements would not have been possible without the collaborative efforts of activists in both the public and private spheres.

NOTES

1. These 80% of new drug registrations that represent no therapeutic value over existing treatments reveal that they are *me-too* drugs, which means that they are structurally similar to known medications with minor modifications.
2. This body replaces the previous entity Technologies Incorporation Commission (*Comissão de Incorporação de Tecnologias*—CITEC) created in 2008.
3. Examples, according to Ferraz (2011), include etanercept and adalimumab (for rheumatoid arthritis), indursulfase (for mucopolissacaridosis II, or Hunter syndrome), human insulin analogs (for diabetes), sildenafil (for pulmonary hypertension), and peginterferon alfa and ribavirin (for hepatitis C).
4. Agenor Alvares. Interview with author. Brasilia, DF. July 12, 2008.
5. Author's calculation based on information from the National AIDS Program.
6. What would a more equitable distribution of benefits look like? One way to consider this question is to consider royalty rates when compulsory licenses are issued. The UNDP suggests a 4% rate of the generic price, which can rise or fall an additional 2% depending on additional factors such as innovativeness. Love (2005) favors a tiered royalty rate based on the price in the exporting country like the United Stated adjusted by per capita income or national income per person needing treatment. Royalty rates thus vary according to a country's income levels. When Brazil issued a compulsory license for Merck's efavirenz in 2007, the government stipulated a royalty rate of 1.5%. Based on total expenditures of US$72.1 million (Veigas Neves 2012) for the medicine between 2007 and 2011, Merck still received US$1.1 million. Based on Love's tiered royalty rate, this amount would have increased to US$4.6 million. Still, this amount is less than the average net return on sales of 17% to 18.5% the pharmaceutical industry averages, which is far higher than the median of 3.3% of all other industries in the Fortune 400 (Angell 2004). Given the estimated $40 million in lost revenue as a result of the compulsory license, we can estimated that the US$35 million could be seen as surplus gains.
7. The bilateral provisional accord between Brazil and the US included annual payments of US$147 million from the US government to the Brazil's the Brazilian Cotton Institute *(Instituto Brasileiro do Algodão)*. The two sides reportedly resolved the trade dispute in 2014.
8. Rosali Tardelli. Interview with author. São Paulo, SP. July 8, 2008.

REFERENCES

Akhavi, Negar, ed. 2008. *AIDS Sutra*. New York: Random House.
Altman, Dennis. 1999. "Globalization, Political Economy, and HIV/AIDS." *Theory and Society* 28: 559–84.
Angell, Marcia. 2004. *The Truth about the Drug Companies*. New York: Random House.
Bastos, Cristiana. 1999. *Global Responses to AIDS*. Bloomington and Indianapolis: Indiana University Press.
Bertoldi, Andrea Damaso, Ana Paula Helfer, Aline L. Camargo, Noemia U. L. Tavares, and Panos Kanavos. 2012. "Is the Brazilian Pharmaceutical Policy Ensuring

202 Conclusion

Population Access to Essential Medicines?" *Globalization and Health* 8(6). Retrieved July 28, 2014 (www.globalizationandhealth.com/content/8/1/6).

Biehl, João. 2007. "Pharmaceuticalization: AIDS Treatment and Global Health Politics." *Anthropological Quarterly* 80(4): 1083–1126.

Brabant, Malcolm. 2010a. "Second Company Pulls Greece Drugs." *BBC*, May 30. Retrieved February 11, 2011 (www.bbc.co.uk/news/10193799).

Brabant, Malcom. 2010b. "Drug Giant's Move Angers Greeks." *BBC*, May 29. Retrieved February 11, 2011 (www.bbc.co.uk/news/10189367).

Câmara dos Deputados. 2013. "Comissão Rejeita Contribuição Social Para a Saúde Nos Moldes Da CPMF." *Câmara Notícias*, November 12. Retrieved July 29, 2014 (www2.camara.leg.br/camaranoticias/noticias/SAUDE/456979-COMISSAO-REJEITA-CONTRIBUICAO-SOCIAL-PARA-A-SAUDE-NOS-MOLDES-DA-CPMF.html).

Cardoso, Fernando Henrique. 1975. *Autoritarismo e democratização*. Rio de Janeiro: Paz e Terra.

CEBES. 2014. "Cebes: Em Defesa Do Direito Universal À Saúde: Saúde É Direito E Não Negócio." *Cebes*. Retrieved August 6, 2014 (http://cebes.com.br/2014/08/em-defesa-do-direito-universal-a-saude-saude-e-direito-e-nao-negocio/).

Chang, Ha-Joon. 2002. *Kicking Away the Ladder—Development Strategy in Historical Perspective*. London: Anthem Press.

Couttolenc, Bernard, Michele Gragnolati, and Magnus Lindelow. 2013. *Twenty Years of Health System Reform in Brazil: An Assessment of the Sistema Unico de Saude*. The World Bank. Retrieved July 28, 2014 (http://documents. worldbank.org/curated/en/2013/01/17899895/twenty-years-health-system-reform-brazil-assessment-sistema-unico-de-saude).

Evans, Peter. 1979. *Dependent Development: The Alliance of Multinational, State, and Local Capital in Brazil*. Princeton: Princeton University Press.

Evans, Peter. 1996. "Government Action, Social Capital and Development: Reviewing the Evidence on Synergy." *World Development* 24(6): 1119–32.

Ferraz, Octavio Luiz Mo. 2011. "Health Inequalities, Rights, and Courts: The Social Impact of the Judicialization of Health." Pp. 76–100 in *Litigating Health Rights: Can Courts Bring More Justice to Health?* edited by Alicia Ely Yamin. Boston: Harvard University Press.

Flynn, Matthew. 2013. "Brazilian Pharmaceutical Diplomacy: Social Democratic Principles Versus Soft Power Interests." *International Journal of Health Services* 43(1): 67–89.

Forbath, William E. 2008. "Realizing a Constitutional Social Right—Cultural Transformation, Deep Institutional Reform, and the Roles of Advocacy and Adjudication." *U of Texas Law, Public Law Research Paper* 149. Retrieved August 15, 2011 (http://papers.ssrn.com/sol3/papers.cfm?abstract_id=1292879).

Freeman, Michael. 2009. "Right to Health." Pp. 44–67 in *Intepreting Human Rights—Social Science Perspective*, edited by Rhiannon Morgan and Bryan Turner. Hoboken: Routledge.

Gauri, Varun, and Daniel M. Brinks. 2010. *Courting Social Justice: Judicial Enforcement of Social and Economic Rights in the Developing World*. Cambridge: Cambridge University Press.

G-Finder. 2012. *Neglected Disease Research and Development: A Five Year Review*. Sydney: G-Finder. Retrieved February 5, 2014 (www.policycures.org/g-finder2012.html).

Globo. 2013. "Governo Publica Lei Dos Royalties Do Petróleo." *Política*. Retrieved July 29, 2014 (http://g1.globo.com/politica/noticia/2013/09/governo-publica-lei-dos-royalties-do-petroleo.html).

Grangeiro, Alexandre, Luciana Teixeira, Francisco I. Bastos, and Paulo Teixeira. 2006. "Sustainability of Brazilian Policy for Access to Antiretroviral Drugs." *Revista Saúde Púbica* 40(Suppl.): 1–9.

Conclusion 203

GTPI. 2014. "GTPI Participa de Consulta Sobre Retaliação Cruzada." *De Olho nas Patentes*. Retrieved July 29, 2014 (www.deolhonaspatentes.org.br/default. asp?site_Acao=mostraPagina&paginaId=891&acao=blog&blogId=455).

Jaime, Amparo Alves. 2013. "Beyond Samba and Football: The Brazilian Protests in Context." *openDemocracy*. Retrieved July 28, 2014 (www.opendemocracy.net/ jaime-amparo-alves/beyond-samba-and-football-brazilian-protests-in-context).

Kapstein, Ethan B., and Josh Busby. 2013. *AIDS Drugs for All*. Cambridge: Cambridge University Press.

Labonte, Ronald, and Michelle Gagnon. 2010. "Framing Health and Foreign Policy: Lessons for Global Health Diplomacy." *Globalization and Health* 6(14). Retrieved September 21, 2010 (www.globalizationandhealth.com/content/6/1/14).

Laranjeira, Fernanda. 2012. "Incorporação de Tecnologias No SUS." Retrieved July 28, 2014 (www.saude.sp.gov.br/resources/instituto-de-saude/homepage/ pdfs/seminario-de-inovacao-material/dra._fernanda_laranjeira.pdf?attach=true).

Light, Donald W. 2009. *The Risks of Prescription Drugs*. New York: Columbia University Press.

Love, Jaime. 2005. *Remuneration Guidelines for Non-Voluntary Use of a Patent on Medical Technologies*. Geneva: World Health Organization. Retrieved July 28, 2014 (www.who.int/hiv/amds/WHOTCM2005.1_OMS.pdf).

Matthews, Duncan. 2011. *Intellectual Property, Human Rights and Development: The Role of NGOs and Social Movements*. Cheltenham: Edward Elgar Publishing.

McGuire, James W. 2010. "From Laggard to Leader in Basic Health Services." Pp. 149–180 in *Wealth, Health, and Democracy in East Asia and Latin America*, edited by James McGuire. New York: Cambridge University Press.

Moyn, Samuel. 2010. *The Last Utopia: Human Rights in History*. Cambridge: Belknap Press of Harvard University Press.

National AIDS Control Organisation. n.d. "Directory of HIV Data." Retrieved November 11, 2011 (http://nacoonline.org/Quick_Links/Directory_of_HIV_Data/).

Overley, Jeff. 2013. "Mylan Ducks $15M Bristol-Myers Contract Suit Over HIV Drug—Law360." *Law360*. Retrieved July 30, 2014 (www.law360.com/ articles/464318/mylan-ducks-15m-bristol-myers-contract-suit-over-hiv-drug).

PAHO. 2009. *O Accesso Aos Medicamentos de Alto Custo Nas Américas: Contexto, Desafios E Perspetivas*. Brasilia: Pan American Health Organization, Brazil Ministry of Health, Brazil Ministry of Foreign Affairs. Retrieved October 21, 2010 (http://new.paho.org/bra/index2.php?option=com_docman&task=doc_view& gid=1082&Itemid=423).

Pharmabiz.com. 2014. "Trial Court Denies Injunction to BMS against Mylan from Blocking Access to Generic HIV Drug in Venezuela." *Pharmabiz.com*, September 30. Retrieved October 13, 2014 (www.pharmabiz.com/NewsDetails.aspx?aid= 84329&sid=2).

Reuters. 2012. "Germany's Merck Halts Supply of Cancer Drug to Greek Hospitals." *Reuters*, November 3. Retrieved November 4, 2012 (www.reuters.com/ article/2012/11/03/us-greece-drugs-idUSBRE8A205Z20121103).

Rich, Jessica. 2013. "Grassroots Bureaucracy: Intergovernmental Relations and Popular Mobilization in Brazil's AIDS Policy Sector." *Latin American Politics and Society* 55(2): 1–25.

Robinson, William I. 2004. *A Theory of Global Capitalism*. Baltimore and London: Johns Hopkins University Press.

Roett, Riordan. 1992. *Brazil: Politics in a Patrimonial Society*. Westport: Praeger.

Røttingen, John-Arne et al. 2013. "Mapping of Available Health Research and Development Data: What's There, What's Missing, and What Role Is There for a Global Observatory?" *The Lancet* 382(9900): 1286–1307.

Santoro, Wayne A., and Gail M. McGuire. 1997. "Social Movement Insiders: The Impact of Institutional Activists on Affirmative Action and Comparable Worth Policies." *Social Problems* 44(4): 503–19.

204 *Conclusion*

Serra, José. 2004. "The Political Economy of the Brazilian Struggle against AIDS." *An Institute for Advanced Study Friends Forum.* Retrieved October 25, 2008 (www.sss.ias.edu/files/papers/paper17.pdf).

Singer, André. 2014. "Rebellion in Brazil." *New Left Review* (85): 19–37.

Sjoberg, Gideon. 2009. "Corporations and Human Rights." Pp. 157–76 in *Interpreting Human Rights—Social Science Perspective*, edited by Rhiannon Morgan and Bryan Turner. Hoboken: Routledge.

Sjoberg, Gideon, Elizabeth A. Gill, and Norma Williams. 2001. "A Sociology of Human Rights." *Social Problems* 48(1): 11–47.

Sklair, Leslie. 1995. *Sociology of the Global System.* Baltimore: Johns Hopkins University Press.

Sklair, Leslie. 2001. *The Transnational Capitalist Class.* Oxford: Basil Blackwell.

Souza, Celina. 2013. "Modernisation of the State and Bureaucratic Capacity-Building in Brazilian Federal Government." Pp. 39–52 in *Policy Analysis in Brazil,* edited by Jeni Vaitsman, Lenaura Lobato, and Jose M. Ribeiro. Bristol: Policy Press.

Viegas Neves da Silva, Francisco, Ronaldo Hallal, and André Guimarães. 2012. "Compulsory License and Access to Medicines: Economics Savings of Efavirenz in Brazil." Presented at the International AIDS Conference, Washington, DC. Retrieved July 28, 2014 (http://pag.aids2012.org/PAGMaterial/PPT/940_3379/cl%20efv%20final.pptx).

Vieira, Marcela. 2014. "Current Challenges on IP and Access to Medicines in Brazil: Views and Strategy from Civil Society." Rio de Janeiro: ABIA/GTPI. Retrieved July 28, 2014 (www.deolhonaspatentes.org.br/media/file/eventos/apresenta%C3%A7%C3%A3o%20marcela%20evento%20fiocruz.pdf).

WHO. 2011. *Global Status Report on Noncommunicable Diseases 2010.* Geneva: World Health Organization.

WHO. 2012. *Research and Development to Meet Health Needs in Developing Countries: Strengthening Financing and Coordination, Final Report of the Consultative Expert Working Group on Research and Development: Financing and Coordination (CEWG).* Geneva: World Health Organization. Retrieved April 29, 2014 (www.who.int/phi/CEWG_Report_5_April_2012.pdf.).

Appendix One
Number of People in Brazil's National AIDS Treatment Program, 1998–2013

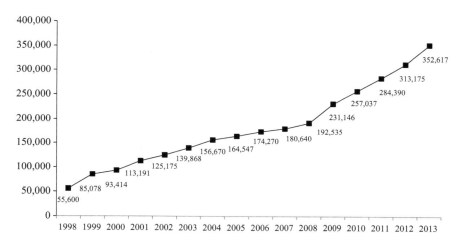

Source: Department of STDs, HIV, and Viral Hepatitis

Appendix Two
Generic Competition and Drug Prices

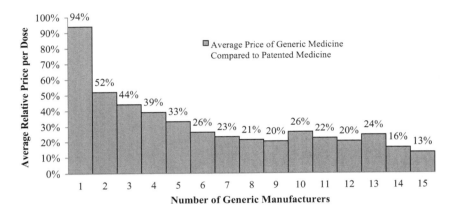

Source: Adopted from FDA (2010)

Appendix Three
TRIPS Flexibilities Concerning Pharmaceuticals and Related Brazilian Legislation Governing Intellectual Property Rights

Trips Flexibility	Brazilian Legislation
(1) **Transition Period:** The deadline that member countries have for making domestic laws compliant with TRIPS varies depending on their level of development. High-income countries had until 1996 to change their laws; middle-income countries, including Brazil and India, 2005; and least developed countries have until 2016 (Art. 65 and 66).	Brazil approved Industrial Property Law #9.279 in 1996 and implemented it the following year, several years before the 2005 deadline.
(2) **Patentability Criteria:** Exclude patentability of diagnostic, therapeutic, and surgical methods; human DNA; restrict "ever-greening" (Art. 27).	Industrial Property Law #9.279.
(3) **'Bolar' Early Working Exception:** Third parties may carry out all the necessary tests and procedures required for the registration of generic medicines before their patent expires (Art. 30).	Law #10.196 passed in 2001 amends articles 43 in Law #9.279 to provide for this exception.
(4) **International Exhaustion of Rights to Allow for Parallel Importing:** Without the consent of the patent holder on the domestic market, a product may be resold or imported from another country where the patent holder has authorized it to be placed on the market (Art. 6).	Decree #4.830 of 2003 amends Decree #3.201 to allow parallel importing of patented products when a compulsory license is issued.
(5) **Compulsory License:** The main legal instrument for correcting abuses by patent holders is the compulsory license (CL), which allows for the exploitation of a patent by third parties without the consent of the patent	Industrial Property Law #9.279 states a CL can be issued for the following reasons: failure to exploit patent; public interest; national emergency; remedy for anti-competitive practices; and

(Continued)

208 *Appendix Three*

Trips Flexibility	Brazilian Legislation
holder. Use of a CL is permitted in six instances: a. refusal to deal; b. cases of emergency or extreme urgency; c. to remedy anti-competitive practices; d. failure to obtain voluntary license under reasonable terms; e. public non-commercial use; and f. dependent patents for innovations requiring patented inputs. Before issuing a CL, a government must first attempt to reach a negotiated settlement with the patent holder, who, in the case of the CL, still has the right to receive royalties. There are two exceptions. First, prior negotiations are not required in cases of a national emergency and public, non-commercial use. Second, royalty payments may not be necessary when a CL is issued to correct anti-competitive practices (Art. 31).	failure to produce locally and dependent patents. Decree #3.201 of 1999 specifies the criteria for issuing a compulsory licensing in cases of national emergency and public interest. Decree #4.830 of 2003 amends Decree #3.201 to allow parallel importing of patented products when a compulsory license is issued.
(6) **Pro-Competitive Measures:** Permits countries to take measures to limit market abuses through licensing conditions and practices (Art. 4).	Industrial Property Law #9.279 of 1996 allows for pro-competitive measures but there is weak enforcement.
(7) **Pre- and Post-Grant Opposition and Revocation:** Countries can determine the appropriate method of implementing the provisions of TRIPS within their legal system; consequently, domestic legislation may allow other government agencies or members of society to participate in patent application process and contest patent claims (Art. 1.1).	Law #10.196 of 2001 amends article 229 in Law #9.279 stating that National Health Surveillance Agency (ANVISA) must give prior consent before patents are granted on all pharmaceutical products and processes.
(8) **Pipeline versus Mailbox:** A pipeline patent is a form of retroactive protection for drugs already patented in other countries, but not marketed at the time TRIPS comes into force. Otherwise, a mailbox system allows applications for patents for pharmaceutical product inventions to be filed but not examined until the end of the transition period (Art. 70.8).	Industrial Property Law #9.279 of 1996 allows for pipeline patents instead of a mailbox system.

Appendix Three 209

Trips Flexibility	Brazilian Legislation
(9) **Data Exclusivity Requirements:** Grants protection for undisclosed data drug firms provide to regulatory officials in order to obtain marketing approval. Extending the timeframe for protecting undisclosed data, a TRIPS-plus measure, restricts competition from generic drugs makers that could lower prices (Art. 31).	Law #10.603 of 2002 provides protection for up to 10 years for drugs that include new chemical entities and 5 years for all other drugs for undisclosed test data drug firms provide to ANVISA.
* Additional TRIPS flexibilities include **Prior Use:** If a person uses an invention before a patent is filed for the product, s/he may be granted the right to continue using the invention despite the granting of the patent (Art. 30); and **Experimental Exception:** The patent will not prohibit the experimental use of an invention by third parties for scientific purposes.	Included in Industrial Property Law #9.279.

Source: Flynn (2011)

Appendix Four
Antiretrovirals Distributed in Brazil's AIDS Treatment Program and Patent Situation, 2014

Generic Name-Symbol (Brand Name / Originator Company)	Year Distribution Began	No. of Patent Applications	Patent Protection**
Nucleoside/Nucleotide Reverse Transcriptase Inhibitor (NRTI)			
Abacavir-ABC (Ziagen / GlaxoSmithKline)*	2001	N/A	Yes
Didanosine-DDL (Videx / Bristol-Meyers Squibb)	1993	3	No
Lamivudine-3TC (Epivir / GlaxoSmithKline)	1999	1	No
Stavudine-D4T (Zerit / Bristol-Meyers Squibb)	1997	1	No
Tenofovir-TDF (Viread / Gilead Sciences)	2003	5	*Denied in 2009*
Zidovudine-AZT (Retrovir / GlaxoSmithKline)	1991	0	No
Non-nucleoside Reverse Transcriptase Inhibitor (NNRTI)			
Efavirenz-EFZ (Sustiva / Bristol-Meyers Squibb licensed to Merck & Co. in Brazil)*	1998	3	*Compulsory License in 2007*
Etravirine-ETR (Intelence / Tibotec)	2010	4	Yes
Nevirapine-NVP (Viramune / Boehringer Ingelheim)	2001	3	No
Protease Inhibitors (PI)			
Atazanavir-ATV (Reyatez / Bristol-Meyers Squibb)	2004	4	Yes

Appendix Four 211

Generic Name-Symbol (Brand Name / Originator Company)	Year Distribution Began	No. of Patent Applications	Patent Protection**
Darunavir-DRV (Previzta / Tibotec)	2007	11	Yes
Fosamprenavir-FPV (Telzir / GlaxoSmithKline)	2007	2	No
Indinavir-IDV (Crixivan / Merck)	1997	3	No
Nelfinavir-NFV (Viracept / Agouron licensed to Roche in Brazil)*	1997	N/A	Yes
Ritonavir-RTV (Norvir / Abbott)	1996	2	No
Saquinavir-SQV (Invirase / Roche)	1996	5	No
Tipranavir-TPV (Elodius / Boehringer-Ingelheim)	2011	6	Yes
Entry Inhibitor (EI)			
Enfuvirtide-T-20 (Fuzeon / Hoffman-La Roche)	2005	2	Yes
Integrase Inhibitor (II)			
Raltegravir-RAL (Isentress / Merck)	2008	2	Yes
Fixed-Dose Combinations (FDCs)			
Lamivudine + Zidovudine (Combivir / GlaxoSmithKline)	1999	1	No
Lopinavir + Ritonavir (Kaletra / Abbott) *	2001	12	Yes
Tenofovir + Lamivudine	2014	N/A	No***
Tenofovir + Lamivudine + Efavirenz	2014	N/A	No***

Note: ARVs removed from therapeutic consensus: zalcitabine, amprenavir, and delavirdine.
*ARVs patented through the pipeline. **Patent protection either through patent approval or patent pending. ***ARV developed by Brazil's Ministry of Health's Farmanguinhos

Source: Adopted from Villardi (2012), with data from INPI, National AIDS Program, and ANVISA.

Appendix Five
Antiretrovirals in Brazil's AIDS Treatment Program and Registered Producers, 2014

Antiretroviral (Originator Brand Name / Originator Company)	Start of Public Production	Public Labs with ANVISA Registration	Private Labs with ANVISA Registration
Nucleoside/Nucleotide Reverse Transcriptase Inhibitor (NRTI)			
Abacavir-ABC (Ziagen / GSK)			GSK
Didanosine-DDL (Videx / BMS)	1998	Farmanguinhos (FM), Iquego, IVB, FURP, Lafepe, LFM, Lifal, Laqfa	Teuto, União Química, Ranbaxy, Serono, Solvay, Cristalia, Neoquimica, Cellofarm, Eurofarma, UCI, Medapi, Blausiegel, De Mayo, Bergamo, BMS, Prodotti, Germed, Aspen, Greenpharma
Lamivudine-3TC (Epivir / GSK)	1998	Lafepe, FURP, Iquego, IVB, Funed, FM, Laqfa	GSK, Medapi, Prodotti, Cristalia, Eurofarma, Ranbaxy, Cellofarm, Blausiegal, Theraskin, Aspen
Stavudine-D4T (Zerit / BMS)	1998	FM, FURP, IVB, Lqfa, Iquego	União Química, Aurobindo, Ranbaxy, BMS, Eurofarma, Cellofarm, Cristalia, Aspen

Appendix Five 213

Antiretroviral (Originator Brand Name / Originator Company)	Start of Public Production	Public Labs with ANVISA Registration	Private Labs with ANVISA Registration
Tenofovir-TDF (Viread / Gilead Sciences)	2013	Funed, Lafepe	Gilead (via United Medical), Cristalia, Blanver
Zidovudine-AZT (Retrovir / GSK)	1994	FM, Funed, FURP, LFM, Iquego, Lafepe, Lifal	GSK, Cellofarm, União Química, Prodotti, Blausiegel, Cristalia, Teuto, Eurofarma, Medapi, Ranbaxy, Ibfarma, Theraskin, Greenpharma, Casi Quimica, Aspen
Non-nucleoside Reverse Transcriptase Inhibitor (NNRTI)			
Efavirenz-EFZ (Stocrin / BMS)	2009	Lafepe, FM	Cristalia, Cellofarm, MSD, Aspen
Etravirine-ETR (Intelence / Tibotec)			Janssen Cilag
Nevirapine-NVP (Viramune / Boehringer Ingelheim)	2000	FM, Iquego, Lifal, Funed	Cellofarm, Medapi, Boehringer Ingelheim, Ranbaxy Eurofarma, Aurobindo, Cristalia, Aspen
Protease Inhibitors (PI)			
Atazanavir-ATV (Reyatez / BMS)		FM*	BMS
Darunavir-DRV (Previzta / Tibotec)			Janssen Cilag
Fosamprenavir-FPV (Telzir/ GSK)			GSK
Indinavir-IDV (Crixivan / Merck)	2000	FM, FURP, Iquego, Lafepe, Lifal	MSD, Cristalia, Eurofarma, Medapi, Ranbaxy, Cellofarm, Germed, Aspen

(Continued)

214 *Appendix Five*

Antiretroviral (Originator Brand Name / Originator Company)	Start of Public Production	Public Labs with ANVISA Registration	Private Labs with ANVISA Registration
Nelfinavir-NFV (Viracept / Roche)		Iquego	Roche, Medapi, Cristalia, Cellofarm
Ritonavir-RTV (Norvir / Abbott)	2002	Lafepe	Abbott, Cristalia, Merck S/A, Neo Quimica
Saquinavir-SQV (Invirase / Roche)			Roche, Merck S/A, União Química, Cristalia
Tipranavir-TPV (Elodius / Boehringer-Ingelheim)			Boehringer Ingelheim
Entry Inhibitor (EI)			
Enfuvirtide-T-20 (Fuzeon / Hoffman-La Roche)			Roche
Integrase Inhibitor (II)			
Raltegravir-RAL (Isentress / Merck)			MSD
Fixed-Dose Combinations			
Lamivudine + Zidovudine (Combivir / GSK)	1999	FM, Lafepe, Funed, FURP, Iquego	União Química, GSK, Medapi, Prodotti
Lopinavir + Ritonavir (Kaletra / Abbott)			Abbott
Tenofovir + Lamivudine	2014	FM	Blanver
Tenofovir + Lamivudine + Efavirenz	2014	FM	

*Farmanguinhos (FM) registered to distribute BMS's product in 2014 but will only start local production in 2015.

Source: Adopted from Hasenclever (2004) and Villardi (2012), with data from INPI, National AIDS Program, and ANVISA.

Appendix Six
2014 Therapeutic Consensus for Seropositive Adults

First-line Treatment
tenofovir (or zidovudine) + lamivudine + efavirenz
Second-line Treatment
IRTN (e.g. lamivudine/zidovudine) + lopinavir/ritonavir (or atazanavir)
Third-line Treatment
darunavir/ritonavir (or tripranavir/ritonavir, raltegravir, etravirine, maraviroc, enfuvirtide) + other antiretrovirals (e.g. lamivudine + tenofovir)

Source: Department of STDs, AIDS, and Viral Hepatitis (2014).

Appendix Seven
Data Sources

Primary data sources combined government documents, news reports, and websites with various field research techniques. Past news reports came from the archives housed at the Brazilian Interdisciplinary AIDS Association (*Associação Brasileira Interdisciplinar de AIDS*—ABIA). Additional new reports came from searches on the Internet. Various Brazilian and foreign newspapers have searchable databases. Also crucial are the listserves, news aggregations, and blog postings from advocacy organizations and industry associations. Particularly useful has been the websites of Knowledge Ecology International (KEI) (keionline.org) and the Working Group on Intellectual Property (deolhonaspatentes.org.br). I also made Freedom of Information Act requests to obtain copies of diplomatic cables sent between US government officials concerning price negotiations and use of compulsory licenses.

The following industry associations provided both news updates and quantitative data about the pharmaceutical sector: the Brazilian Fine Chemicals Association (*Associação Brasileira da Indústria de Química Fina, Biotecnologia e suas Especialidades*—ABIFINA), the Brazilian Association of Generic Medicines Industries (*Associação Brasileira das Indústrias de Medicamentos Genéricos*—Pro-Generics) (www.progenericos.org.br), the Research-Based Pharmaceutical Association (*Associação da Indústria Farmacêutica de Pesquisa*—INTERFARMA) (www.interfarma.org.br), and the São Paulo State Pharmaceutical Industry Union (*Sindicato da Indústria de Produtos Farmacêuticos no Estado de São Paulo*—Sindusfarma) (www.sindusfarma.org.br).

Data on the prices and volumes of antiretroviral medicines (ARVs) came from a variety of sources. In my meetings with people from the National AIDS Program and other branches of the Ministry of Health, civil servants have been gracious enough to provide spreadsheets with purchase information. These sources include *la Biblía*, which has detailed price information from 2005 to 2008; the Health Price Bank *(Banco de Preços em Saúde)*, available at http://portalsaude.saude.gov.br/; and spreadsheets for drug purchases from 1996 to 2013.

Some of the most important information I gathered came from in-depth interviews with key informants. These interviews are listed below. In total,

Appendix Seven 217

I interviewed 60 people from various sectors of society. These unstructured interviews allowed me to reconstitute events, understand the relationships between groups, delve into the different strategies the various social actors pursued, and appreciate the underlying normative frameworks motivating different people. When interviewing managers or directors at pharmaceutical labs, I was often granted a tour of their operations. These site visits provided additional information about the pharmaceutical production process and crucial learning experiences for an outsider. While in the field, I also attended various conferences by the pharmaceutical industry and people involved in AIDS. Beyond the formal interviews, I have had innumerable informal conversations with industry professionals, activists, and medicines experts.

Interviewee	Professional Title or Relevance to Research	Date(s) Interviewed
	NGOs/Activists	
Jorge Beloqui	Grupo de Incentivo À Vida	11 Jul 08
Gabriela Chaves	Pharmacist, ABIA/MSF Coordinator	27 Mar 08
Michel Lowtroska	MSF Representative of Access to Essential Medicines Campaign	25 Mar 08 and 30 Jun 05
Renata Reis	ABIA Intellectual Property Coordinator	5 May 08
Mario Scheffer	Grupo Pella Vida/São Paulo	4 Apr 08
Rodrigo de Souza Pinheiro	Fórum de ONGs/AIDS do Estado de São Paulo	2 Jun 09
Veriano Terto	ABIA, Coordinator	4 Jul 05
	Outside Experts	
Octavio Antunes	Chemist, Federal University of Rio de Janeiro	29 May 08
Hayne Felipe	Farmanguinhos/Popular Pharmacy Program	17 Jun 05 and 22 Sep 08
James Fitzgerald	Pan-American Health Organization	20 Oct 08
Lia Hasenclever	Economist, Federal University of Rio de Janeiro	16 Jul 08
Luis Felipe M. Lima	Former ANVISA Director	12 Jul 05 and 28 Nov 07
Leo Palma	Deputy Director at Advisory Centre on WTO Law	11 Jun 06
Rosali Tardelia	Editor, Agencia AIDS News Service	8 Jul 08

(*Continued*)

218 *Appendix Seven*

Interviewee	Professional Title or Relevance to Research	Date(s) Interviewed
Public Labs		
Nubia Boechat	Former Director, Farmanguinhos (2002–2005)	Jul 05 and 29 Mar 08
Josiana Gomes Chaves	Funed, Assistant to the President	30 Jul 05
Eduardo Costa	Director, Farmanguinhos (2006–2009)	15 Jun 09
Andre Daher	Manager, Clinical Testing, Farmanguinhos (2002–Present)	17 Jul 08
Carlos Alberto Pereira Gomes	Ministry of Health (1998–2001), Director of Funed & ALFOB	25 Aug 08
Ricardo Oliva	Director FURP and President of ALFOB	17 Dec 08
Eloan Pinheiro	Director Farmanguinhos (1994–2001)	25 May 06
Cida Rodrigues and Gleide Gloria Silva	Head of Production and Assistant to the President, Iquego	14 Dec 07
Tuyoshi Ninomya	FURP, Technical Assistant	17 Jul 05
Leduar Guedes	Superintendent Director, Lafepe	23 Jul 08
Pedro Rolim	Former Director of Production and R&D, Lafepe	24 Jul 08
Private National Industry		
Vera Valente	Director, Pro-Genericos	18 Aug 05
Edson Lima	Director, API Manufacturing Division, Cristalia	6 May 08
Lelio Maçaira	Former Director Microbiologica, Director Laborvida	28 Nov 07 and 19 May 09
Otavio Pacheco	President, Cristalia	8 Jul 08
Jaime Rabi	Director, Microbiologica	16 Mar 08
Marcos Soalheiro	Director of Development, Nortec	17 Jun 08
Jose Machado de Campos Neto	Former Director, Labogen	7 Jul 08
Ciro Mortella	President, Brazilian Pharmaceutical Industry Federation (Febrafarma)	3 Sep 08
Nelson Brasil	Vice President, Brazilian Association of the Fine Chemical Industry (ABIFINA)	30 Jun 08

Appendix Seven 219

Interviewee	Professional Title or Relevance to Research	Date(s) Interviewed
	Brazilian Civil Servants	
Agenor Alvares	ANVISA Director, Present; Minister of Health, 2006–2007	12 Jul 08
Jarbas Barbosa	Director, Health Surveillance, Ministry of Health under Costa	23 Oct 08
Pedro Chequer	Director, National AIDS Program, 1996–2000, 2004–2006	12 Jul 08
Fernando Cardenas	Ministry of Health, 1999–2002; National AIDS Program, 2002–2003	10 Jul 08
Norberto Rech	Director, Pharmaceutical Assistance, under Costa	10 Sep 08
Humberto Costa	Minister of Health, 2002–2005	22 Jul 08
Saraiva Felipe	Minister of Health, 2005–2006	12 Dec 07
Alexander Grangeiro	Director, National AIDS Program 2003–2004	7 May 08
Liane Lage	Director, Drug Patent Review Office, National Intellectual Property Institute	15 Jul 08
Luiz Carlos Wanderley Lima	ANVISA, Intellectual Property Coordination (COOPI)	27 May 08
Pedro Palmeiro and Luciana Xavier de Lemos Capanema	BNDES, Manager and Engineer of Chemicals for Health Division	14 Aug 05
Carlos Passarelli	International Programs Coordinator, National AIDS Program	13 Dec 07
Andre Luiz de Abreu Porto	General Coordination for the Development of Pharmaceutical Production and Inputs, Ministry of Health	7 Aug 08
Rubens Ricupero	Brazilian Diplomat to GATT Negotiations and Former President of UNCTAD	15 Oct 07
Paulo Teixeira	Director, National AIDS Program, 2000–2003	7 May 08
Ana Paula Telles	General Coordination of Logistic Resources, Ministry of Health	11 Dec 07
Marco Antonio Vitoria	Medical Advisor, National AIDS Program, World Health Organization	15 Aug 06

(*Continued*)

220 *Appendix Seven*

Interviewee	Professional Title or Relevance to Research	Date(s) Interviewed
Leandro Luiz Viegas	Head of Division on Multilateral Themes, Office for Advisory on International Affairs, Ministry of Foreign Affairs	7 Jun 2010
Juliana Vallini	Lawyer, International Coordination Advisory, National STD/AIDS Program, Ministry of Health	22 Jun 2010
Transnational Drug Industry		
Jorge Raimundo	Former Director, GlaxoSmithKline; Currently at INTERFARMA	20 Jun 08
Antonio Salles	Director of Government Corporate Relations, Bristol-Myers Squibb	8 May 08
Paul Singer	Vice President, Pharmaceutical Research Manufacturers of America (PhRMA)	5 Aug 07
Joao Sanches	Merck Dohme & Sharp (MSD), Communications Director	1 Mar 08
Joao Carlos Ferreira	Director of Institutional Relations and Legal Affairs, Roche	11 Jul 08
US Officials		
Tim Hall	US Diplomat, Economics Section, US Embassy in Brasilia	11 Dec 07

Institutions/Facilities Visited	Location
Cristalia	São Paulo, SP
Farmanguinhos	Rio de Janeiro, RJ
Funed	Belo Horizonte, MG
FURP	São Paulo, SP
Hospital Emilio Ribas	São Paulo, SP
Lafepe	Recife, Pernambuco
Ministry of Health	Brasilia, DF
National AIDS Program	Brasilia, DF
Nortec	Rio de Janeiro, RJ

Appendix Seven 221

Conferences Attended	Location	Date
1° ENI-FarMed—Encontro Nacional de Inovação em Fármacos e Medicamentos	São Paulo	21 Nov 07
Seminário sobre o Complexo Econômico-Industrial da Saúde	Rio de Janeiro	19–20 May 08
Seminário Internacional Patentes, Inovação e Desenvolvimento	Rio de Janeiro	19–20 Jun 08
VII Congresso da SBDST e III Congresso Brasileiro de Aids	Goiania	7–10 Sep 08
Seminário Ano da França no Brasil— O Acesso aos Anti-Retrovirais nos Países do Sul: 20 anos após a introdução da Terapia Anti-Retroviral	Rio de Janeiro	11–12 May 09

REFERENCES

Department of STDs, AIDS, and Viral Hepatitis. 2014. *Protocolo Clínico e Diretrizes Terapêuticas para Manejo da Infecção pelo HIV em Adultos*. Brasilia: Ministry of Health. Retrieved August 5, 2014 (www.aids.gov.br/pcdt/sumario).

FDA. 2010. "Generic Competition and Drug Prices." Retrieved November 11, 2014 (http://www.fda.gov/AboutFDA/CentersOffices/OfficeofMedicalProductsandTobacco/CDER/ucm129385.htm).

Flynn, Matthew. 2011. "Corporate Power and State Resistance: Brazil's Use of TRIPS Flexibilities for Its National AIDS Program." Pp. 149–77 in *Intellectual Property, Pharmaceuticals, and Public Health: Access to Drugs in Developing Countries*, edited by Kenneth C. Shadlen. Cheltenham: Edward Elgar Publishing.

Hasenclever, Lia. 2004. *A Dinâmica Do Programa Brasileiro de Combate à AIDS e as Condições de Demanda de Medicamentos Anti-Retrovirais*. Rio de Janeiro: UFRJ.

Villardi, Pedro. 2012. *Panorama Do Status Patentário E Registro Sanitário Dos Medicamentos Antiretrovirais No Brasil*. Rio de Janeiro: ABIA.

Index

Note: Page numbers followed by *f* indicate a figure on the corresponding page.
Page numbers followed by *t* indicate a table on the corresponding page.

abacavir (ARV drug) 174
Abbott Pharmaceuticals 32, 54, 138–43, 162
Access to Medication in the Context of Pandemics such as HIV/AIDS resolution 113
acquired immune deficiency syndrome (AIDS): citizenship rights 85; countries with serious epidemics 196*t*; introduction 1–5; mother-to-child transmission of 4; prescription drugs 60; treatment activism 85–90; universal treatment for 21
active pharmaceutical ingredients (APIs): patent restrictions on 191; pharmaceutical technology 72, 73–4, 77–8; pharmochemical companies and 34–5; process for obtaining 105, 129; production of 30, 32–3, 189–90; triple alliances and 170–1
Advisory Committee on Trade Policy and Negotiations (ACTPN) 43
Affordable Care Act 199
AIDS Coalition to Unleash Power (ACT UP) 97
AIDS cocktail 1–3, 125 (see also "antiretroviral medicines")
AIDS Drug Assistance Programs (ADAPs) 2
AIDS Drugs for All (Kapstein, Busby) 198–9
AIDS News Agency *(Agência de Notícias da Aids)* 197

AIDS Prevention Support Group *(Grupo de Apoio à Prevenção à Aids*-GAPA) 3
Albuquerque, Carlos 89
Alvares, Agenor 141, 168
Alves, Jaimes Amparo 185
Anti-Counterfeiting Trade Agreement (ACTA) 172, 177
antiretroviral autonomy: compulsory licenses and 125, 164; development and raw materials 105–8; global demand for 129; government production 102–5, 128–9; overview 95–7; price conflicts over patents 108–17, 152; public labs, first initiatives 101–2; public-private partnerships with 159*t*; purchasing without a contract 133; research and development 135–8; state monopolization 101–8; technology transfer of 152
antiretroviral medicines (ARVs): access to 4, 11–12, 87, 198–201; availability of 171–3, 195; early days of treatment with 33; generic versions of 128, 144–5; new trials 31; overview 1–2; prices of 96; production in Brazil 21–2, 77, 84, 95; reluctance to offer 60; scientific findings concerning 89; zidovudine 97–101; *see also* generic drug alternatives; specific drugs/ medicines

224 Index

anti-tuberculosis drugs 50
ANVISA administration 110, 142, 145
Arouca, Sergio 79
Assistance Fund for Rural
Workers/*Fundo de Assistência
ao Trabalhador Rural*
(FUNRURAL) 79
atazanavir (ARV drug) 135, 137, 158,
170, 177, 191
Avian flu 200

Bale, Harvey 38
Barbosa, Jarbas 142
Barreto, Wanise 169
Bayh-Dole Act (1980) 59
Bermudez, Jorge 112
Betinho *see* José de Sousa, Herbert
biopharmaceutical intellectual property
(IP) protections 53
biopiracy 50
Boechat, Nubia 106
Bolar Exception 110, 111, 135, 137
"boomerang" model of transnational
activism 118
Boston Consulting Group 28
Brasil, Nelson 75, 151, 153
Brazil: bureaucratic capabilities 16;
conservative sexual mores in
197; development of health
system 67–8; HIV prevalence
rates 2; intellectual property
and trade agreements 43;
perspective on experience
195–7, 196t; pharmerging in
35–6; production technologies
14; Public Procurement Act 107;
semi-developmental state of 76;
sustainable growth in 178, 188;
see also National AIDS Program
Brazilian Agency of Industrial
Development *(Agência Brasileira
de Desenvolvimento Industrial)*
154
Brazilian Communist party *(Partido
Communista Brasileira)* 79
Brazilian Fine Chemical Industry
Association/*Associação
Brasileiro das Indústrias de
Química Fina, Biotecnologia e
suas Especialidades* (ABIFINA)
143, 150, 153, 159–60, 165
Brazilian Institute of Social and
Economic Analysis/*Instituto
Brasileiro de Analises Sociais e
Economicas* (IBASE) 124

Brazilian Interdisciplinary AIDS
Association/*Associação
Brasileira Interdisciplinar de
AIDS* (ABIA) 124, 143, 160,
166
Brazilian National Development
Bank/*Banco Nacional do
Desenvolvimento Econômico e
Social* (BNDES) 100, 178–9
Brazilian Network for the Integration
of the Peoples/*Rede Brasileira
pela Integração dos Povos*
(REBRIP) 139
Brazilian Official Pharmaceutical
Lab Association/*Associação
Brasileira de Laboratórios
Oficiais do Brasil* (ALFOB) 104,
128, 131
Brazilian Pharmaceutical Industrial
Federation/*Federação Brasileira
da Indústria Farmacêutica*
(Febrafarma) 163
Brazilian Social Democratic
Party/*Partido Social
Democratico Brasiliero* (PSDB)
103
Bretton Woods institutions 194
BRICS (Brazil, Russia, India, China,
and South Africa) 194–5
Bristol Meyers Squibb (BMS) 132–3,
158, 170–1, 176–7
bureaucratic activists 192
Burroughs Wellcome company 97–9
Bush, George W. 2

Campos Neto, Machado de 103
Capanema, Luciana 159
capitalism: global capitalism 13–18,
20, 191, 193, 195; intellectual
property and 58
Cardoso, Fernando Henrique: access
to AIDS treatment 89–90;
democracy arguments 16–17;
HIV program funding 18, 117;
intellectual property legislation
74; multipolar worldview 14;
overview 7–8; Sarney's Law 88;
sustainable growth in Brazil 178
Center for Responsive Politics 38
Central Medicines Agency/*Central de
Medicamentos* (CEME): closing
of 76; creation of 72–3; essential
medicines list 81–2; funding
from 98
Chaves, Gabriela 167–8

Index 225

Chequer, Pedro: essential medicines 4, 89; importation of medicines 132; legal actions by NGOs 143; negotiations by 167; state production of strategic goods 103, 104

China: exports to 130–1; pharmerging in 35; production technologies 14; reverse engineering of product 143; rise in medicine production 37; TRIPS accord adoption by 134

citizenship rights with HIV/AIDS 85

Clark, Richard 164

Clinton, Bill 114

Cohen, Abraham 43

Collor, Fernando 73–4, 100

Commission on Intellectual Property Rights Innovation and Public Health 40, 55, 199–200

Committee on Economic, Social and Cultural Rights (CESCR) 55–6

compulsory licenses (CL): backing away from 133–43; harm from 141; introduction 4–5; issuance of 110–11; negotiation strategy changes 133–5; policymaker hesitancy over 191; problems with 154; recent uses 45–7, 45*f*; triple alliance impact from 164–7; *see also* specific drugs/ medicines

Consultative Mechanism 114

Consumer Project on Technology (CPTech) 113

Convention on Economic, Social and Cultural Rights 161

Cordeiro, Hesio 79

Costa, Eduardo 158, 168

Costa, Humberto 126, 138

Daiichi Sankyo 38

Daley, William 111

da Silva, Luiz Inacio "Lula" 126, 133–5, 161, 178

Declaration of Commitment on HIV/ AIDS resolution 113

Declaration of Fundamental Rights of People with HIV (Declaração dos Direitos Fundamentais da Pessoa Portadora do Vírus da Aids) 86, 125

Defenders of Property Rights 139

democracy *vs.* neoliberalism: AIDS treatment activism 85–90;

neoliberalism alternatives 68–71; overview 67–8; pharmaceutical technology 71–8; social democratic health care reforms 78–85

Department of Pharmaceutical Assistance 126–7

dependency theory: defined 7; historical-structural analysis of 15; normative framing 18; past versions of 17; structural-historical lens of 8; technology and 12–13

deregulation 68, 69, 73, 78, 82

Dispute Settlement Panel 140 (see also WTO)

Doctors without Borders (MSF) 95, 113

Doha Declaration (2001) 45, 115–16, 144, 161, 191

Drugs for Neglected Diseases Initiative 173

Duda, Rubens 133

efavirenz (ARV drug): availability of 168; chemical process of 116; compulsory license for 23, 109, 142, 161–4, 176, 179, 190–1; expenditures on 144; formulations 136–8; generic versions of 134, 169, 170; improvements to 33; introduction 2, 5; patents for 174; triple alliances and 167, 170; TRIPS flexibilities 152

embedded autonomy 16, 179

epilepsy treatment 50

epistemic communities 17–18

European Patent Office 174

ever-greening process 46, 53, 174

Executive Group of the Industrial Health Complex/*Grupo Executivo do Complexo Industrial da Saúde* (GECIS) 158, 160

Expert Working Group on R&D Financing 200

Family Health Program/*Programa Saúde da Familia* (PSF) 186

Farmanguinhos Institute in Medicines Technology/*Farmanguinhos Instituto de Tecnologia em Fármacos* (FM): administrative changes 135–7; allocation of ARVs 128; API manufacturing

226 Index

plant 153; command of 158; enteric versions of ARVs 177; financing concerns 102; introduction 4–5 102; manufacturing medicines 105–7; medicine delivery by 168; patent medicine production 116
Federal Health Law 80–1
Fédération Internationale de Football Association (FIFA) 185
feedback loops 10
Felipe, José Saraiva 138, 141–2
Financing Agency for Studies and Projects/*Financiadora de Estudos e Projetos* (FINEP) 99, 108
Fine Chemical and Pharmochemical Trade Association/*Associaçao Brasileira das Indústrias de Química Fina e suas Especialidades* (ABIFINA) 75
FioCruz Foundation 137
fiscal discipline 69, 155
fixed-dose combinations (FDC) 170
foreign dependency 22, 118, 128, 159
frame analysis 19
Franco, Itamar 75
Freedom of Information Act (FOIA) 140, 141
Fundação para o Remédio Popular (FURP) 104, 136
Furlan, Fernando 141, 160

General Agreement on Tariffs and Trade (GATT) 41, 75
generic drug alternatives: antiretroviral medicines (ARVs) 128, 144–5; cost of 50; efavirenz 134, 169, 170; justification for 48; nelfinavir 134; World Health Organization and 172
Generics Law 104
Gilead Sciences 59, 133, 169
GlaxoSmithKline (GSK) 28, 35–6
Global AIDS Alliance 139
global capitalism 13–18, 20, 191, 193, 195
Global Fund for AIDS, Tuberculosis, and Malaria 3, 34, 129
globalization: current phase of 194; deepening elements of 150; diseases associated with 197; Industrial Property Law 74; neoliberal globalization 145;

new ideas about 13; production chains and workers 131; raw materials sourcing and 129; unforeseen consequence of 165
global pharmaceutical power: access to medicines 198–201; industry overview 34–8, 36*t*; intellectual property rights, normative frameworks 49–60; normative framing 193–5; overview 28–9, 189–90; pharmaceutical production cycle 29–34, 30*f*; political alliances 191–3; political power 38–48; technology 190–1; *see also* democracy *vs.* neoliberalism
Global Strategy on Public Health, Innovation and Intellectual Property resolution 200
Good Act (2005) 154
Good Manufacturing Practice (cGMP) 34
Governmental Purchases Law *(Lei de Compras Governamentais)* 155
Government Pharmaceutical Organization (GPO) 197
Grangeiro, Alexander 154
grassroots activism: coordinate actions of 112; lack of 80, 84; outside support 118; *sanitaristas* links 67, 85, 90
Greater Brazil Plan, *(Plano Brasil Maior)* 175
Great Recession 2, 199
Greece 187, 199
Grupo Pella Vida 166
Guarda Chuva Project (Umbrella Project) 104

Health Action International (HAI) 113
health care reforms 78–85
Health Industrial Complex 157, 160
health injustice 57, 194
Health Surveillance Agency/*Agência Nacional de Vigilância Sanitária* (ANVISA) 83, 104, 107
high-blood pressure treatment 50
Hirschman, Albert 15
H1N1 flu 200
human immunodeficiency virus (HIV): citizenship rights 85; countries with serious epidemics 196*t*; exceptionalism idea 197; infection with 1; monotherapy

for 88; prescription drugs for 60; stigma from 67; universal treatment for 21
humanitarian safeguards 4–5, 48, 113
human rights claims 55–8

import substitution industrialization (ISI) 71, 73
IMS Health 35
India: conservative sexual mores in 197; intellectual property and trade agreements 43; pharmerging in 35; production technologies 14; reverse engineering of product 143; rise in medicine production 37; TRIPS accord adoption by 134
Industrial Policies: horizontal policies 155–6, 155t; vertical industrial policies 156t–157t
Industrial, Technological and Foreign Trade Policy/*Política Industrial Tecnológica de Comércio Exterior* (PITCE) 154
Industrial Property Law/Act (1996) 72–5, 110–11, 145, 173–4
Innovate Health *(Inova Saúde)* 175
Innovation Act (2004) 154
Instituto Vital Brazil (IVB) 175
intellectual property rights (IPRs): critical views 58–60; human rights claims 55–8; impact of 112; improvements to trade 74; introduction 21; legislation for 111; natural rights perspective 49–51; normative frameworks 49–60; protection 41, 47–8; utilitarian arguments 51–5, 54f
Intellectual Property Working Group/*Grupo de Trabalho sobre Propriedade Intellectual* (GTPI) 166
INTERFARMA association 83, 160
Intergovernmental Working Group on Innovation, Intellectual Property, and Public Health (IGWG) 200
Interiorization of Health and Sanitation Program/*Programa de Interiorização das Ações de Saúde e Saneamento* (PIASS) 80
International Chamber of Commerce 13
International Declaration of Human Rights 161
International Federation of Pharmaceutical Manufacturers & Associations (IFPMA) 38–9
International Medical Products Anti-Counterfeiting Taskforce (IMPACT) 172
International Network in Technological Cooperation in HIV/AIDS 172
International Trade Commission 42
Investigational New Drug Application 31

Japan 41, 43–4, 52, 194
Japanese Patent Office 174
Joint Forum for Articulation with Civil Society *(Fórum Permanente de Articulação com a Sociedade Civil)* 179
Joint United Nations Programme on HIV/AIDS (UNAIDS) 129
Jorge, Miquel 164
José de Sousa, Herbert 124–5

Labogen company 103, 105
Lampreia, Luis Felipe 75
Law of Generics (1999) 153
Lazarus Drug 1
Lei da Copa (World Cup General Law) 185
Leo Pharma 199
leprosy 67
Long, Norman 19
lopinavir (ARV drug): compulsory license for 142, 164; development of 137–8; expense of 144; patents for 174, 176, 194; price discounts 162

Maçaira, Lelio 98–9, 131, 176
Machado Neto, Campos de 130, 176
Malan, Pedro 99
Manteiga, Guido 154
market power: defined 14, 34–5; development of 29; economies of scale and 34–5; exploitation of 48; globalization and 131; of low-cost producers 22, 126; of new arrivals 60, 108; pharmaceutical production process 21; raw materials and 37; shifting counters of 38; sourcing of foreign APIs 129; support for 175

228 *Index*

Martin, John C. 59
Marzulla, Nancie 139
Mbeki, Thabo 60, 195
Medical R&D Treaty 200
Medicare Prescription Act (2003) 38
Medicines Market Regulatory
  Body/*Câmara de Regulação
  do Mercado de Medicamentos*
  (CMED) 187
Merck: compulsory licenses
  negotiations 23, 111;
  formulation changes by 136;
  overview 28, 35–6; price
  discounts 125; revenue losses
  176
Merck KGaA 199
Merck Sharpe & Dohme (MSD) 4–5,
  161, 162, 170
Mexico 12, 35, 165, 199
Microbiologica (MB) 98–100, 103, 176
Minas Gerais 169
Ministry of Development, Industry, and
  Foreign Trade (MDIC) 157
monotherapy for HIV 88
mother-to-child transmission of AIDS 4
Movimento Sanitário 67–8, 79

National AIDS Program (Brazil):
  analysis of 8–12; ARV
  treatment availability 171–3;
  bureaucratic activists 192;
  civil society support 144,
  167; community consultants
  87–8; drug development 137;
  establishment of 68, 85; free
  distribution of AZT 98, 118;
  government support 154; HIV
  testing labs 89; human rights
  framework of 20; introduction
  3; key processes affecting 11–12;
  negotiated settlement with
  116; NGO community and 87,
  175; public interest declaration
  169; rationing of treatments
  153; state interaction 112–13;
  stavudine usage 137; supply
  problems 132–3
National Commission for the
  Incorporation of New
  Technologies/*Comissão Nacional
  de Incorporação de Tecnologias
  no SUS* (CONITEC) 187
National Development Bank
  for Economic and Social

Development/*Banco Nacional de
  Desenvolvimento Econômico e
  Social* (BNDES) 156
National Federal of Pharmacists
  (*Federação Nacional de
  Farmacêuticos*) 173
National Health Council/*Conselho
  Nacional da Saúde* (CNS)
  141–2, 160, 166, 189
National Institute for Health and Care
  Excellence (NICE) 187
National Institute for Patent Protection 72
National Institute of Health (NIH) 31,
  59, 72
National Institute of Industrial
  Property/*Instituto Nacional da
  Propriedade Industrial* (INPI)
  83, 167
National Sanitary Surveillance
  Agency/*Agencia Nacional de
  Vigilância Sanitária* (ANVISA)
  127
National Social Security Medical
  Assistance Institute/*Instituto
  Nacional de Assistência Médica
  da Previdência Social* (INAMPS)
  79
neglected tropical diseases (NTDs) 199
negotiation strategy changes 133–5
nelfinavir (ARV drug) 116, 134, 174
new developmentalism 178
New International Economic Order
  (NIEO) 194
New Medicines Policy 82, 104
New York Times 142
non-communicable diseases (NCDs)
  198
nongovernmental organizations
  (NGOs) 166, 175, 194
normative framing 18–20, 193–5
Nortec Química company 106
Novo Nordisk 199

Oil Royalties Law *(Lei dos Royalties do
  Petróleo)* 188
Oliva, Ricardo 136
Omnibus Trade and Competitiveness
  Act (1998) 42
Oswaldo Cruz Foundation 72, 96
Oxfam International 112, 174–5

Palmeiro, Pedro 159
Pan American Health Organization
  (PAHO) 138, 191

Paris Convention for the Protection of Industrial Property (1883) 41, 44
Partnerships for Productive Development/*Parcerias para o Desenvolvimento Produtivo* (PDPs) 158, 170–1
Patent Act (1836) 39
patent-based business models 4, 28, 29, 55, 198
patent power 39, 48, 190
patents: deadlines 8; efavirenz 174; impact on medicine 112; lead-ups to TRIPS 39–43, 52; lopinavir 174, 176, 194; medicine production 116; restrictions on APIs 191; ritonavir 53–4, 54*f*, 176, 194; TRIPS and 143; unpatented medicines 143; World Health Organization and 40; *see also* price conflicts over patents; treatment activism autonomy
path dependency models 9–10, 151, 195
Pedrosa, Stalin 88
Pereira Gomes, Carlos Alberto 129, 132
Permanent Forum for Articulating with Civil Society 160
Pfizer 28, 36
pharmaceutical alliance: compulsory licenses and domestic coalitions 161–9; industrial policies for 152–60; overview 150–2; technological transfer 152–3
pharmaceutical autonomy: analytical framework for understanding 8–12, 11*f*; in globalizing world 189–95; normative framing 18–20; overview 7–8; political alliances 15–18; state-society relations 177–9; technological capabilities 12–15; transnational corporations and 13, 14; *see also* treatment activism autonomy
pharmaceutical dependency 9, 22, 129, 143–5, 189
Pharmaceutical Research and Manufacturers of America (PhRMA) 28, 42, 163
pharmaceutical technology 71–8
pharmochemical producers: ARV production 100, 105, 131, 190; Brazilian currency impact 150; competition concerns 130; defined 34; demand horizons and 32–3; domestic partnerships 145, 165, 167; increased output of 175; industrial policies for 157; local production 151, 152–3, 157–8; national partnerships 136; neoliberal reforms 166; raw material production 168; synthetic chemical processes 116
Phase III drug tests 31–2
Pinheiro, Eloan 95–6, 104, 112, 116, 135–6
Pisani, Elisabeth 88
political alliances: creation of 1, 21, 60, 96, 179; entrenchment of 10; expansion of government action 97; maintenance of 12; overview 15–20, 191–3; pharmaceutical autonomy and 194; *sanitaristas* 118; transnational drug companies and 49
Porto, Andre 157
Presidential Directive *(Medida Provisória)* 83
Presidential Emergency Plan for AIDS Relief (PEPFAR) 2
Price Adequacy Coefficient *(Coeficiente de Adequação de Preços)* 187
price conflicts over patents: *Doha Declaration* 115–16; local working and 111–14; negotiated settlements 116–17; overview 108–10; views on 193
Priority Watch Lists 140, 194
Public Citizen group 50
public-private partnerships with ARVs 159*t*
Public Procurement Act 107

Rabi, Jaime 98, 99
Rech, Norberto 127, 128
reiterated problem solving 9, 10, 21
research and development of ARVs 135–8
Ricupero, Rubens 75
ritonavir (ARV drug): compulsory license for 142; development and supply 107, 138, 173; expenditures of 144; FDA approval 32; patents for 53–4, 54*f*, 176, 194; price discounts 162

230 *Index*

Roche company 125, 134
Rolim, Pedro 131, 137
rotavirus vaccines 31, 50
Rousseff, Dilma 175
Russia 35, 194

Salk, Jonas 58
Salles, Antonio 132
sanitarista movement: civil society allies 178; grassroots activism links 67, 85, 90; patent impact on medicine 112; pharmaceutical policies 103; political alliances 118; private sector criticism by 188; profit-based ideology 161; restructuring of the health system 80
Sanofi-Aventis 176
Sarney's Law 88–9, 101–2
scale economies 8, 15
Scaling Up the Response to HIV/AIDS resolution 114
Scheffer, Mario 112, 166
Scientific and Technological Development Support Program/*Programa de Apoio ao Desenvolvimento Científico e Tecnológico* (PADCT) 99
Serra, José: AIDS medicines costs 20; compulsory licenses 109; conflicts over patented medicines 193; election loss 126; essential medicines and 89; local production of medicines 108, 116–17; pharmaceutical reforms 82; politics of 103–4, 110, 115, 117–18; state promotion of national development 153
Singer, Christopher 28
Sjoberg, Gideon 57
social democratic health care reforms 78–85
social movement organizations 19, 195
sorafenib (cancer drug) 197
South Africa 2, 195, 197
South Korea 35–6, 131
state-society relations 177–9

Tardelli, Rosali 197
Tariff and Trade Act (1930) 42
technology: antiretroviral autonomy 152; control by transnational corporations 190; democracy *vs.*

neoliberalism 71–8; dependency theory 12–13; global pharmaceutical power 190–1; pharmaceutical alliance 152–3; pharmaceutical autonomy 12–15; pharmaceutical technology 72, 73–4, 77–8; production technologies 14
Teixeira, Paulo 67, 112
Temporão, Jose 161, 169
tenofovir (ARV drug): compulsory license for 142; development of 138; expenditures on 144; supplier of 132; treatment protocols 33, 135; triple alliances and 167, 170; TRIPS flexibilities 152
Terto, Jr., Veriano 125
Thailand 195, 197
Trade Act (1974) 43
Trade-Related Aspects of Intellectual Property (TRIPS): compliance with 106, 190; compulsory licenses 141; flexibilities in 75, 133, 152, 164; humanitarian safeguards 113; implementation and consequences 47–8; local working in 111; middle-income countries, adherence to 74; origins and implications of 21; overview 28, 39; patents 39–43, 143; safeguards outlined in 110; TRIPS-plus measures 177; WTO and 43–7, 45*t*, 69
transnational corporations (TNCs): economies of scale advantages 34; exports by 78; government conflict with 22; low-tax regions and 37; mergers and acquisitions with 165; pharmaceutical autonomy and 13, 14; strategy of 71–3; technology control by 190; triple alliance and 176–7, 191
Trans-Pacific Partnership 177
Treatment Action Campaign 195
treatment activism: Abbott negotiations 138–43; National AIDS Program supply problems 132–3; overview 124–6; pharmaceutical dependency 143–5, 144*f*; restructuring production of AIDS medicines 126–33, 127*t*
Trilateral Commission 13

Index 231

triple alliances: actions by 167–9; civil society 173–5; impact 164–7; national industry 175–6; the state 170–3, 171*f*, 172*f*; state-society relations 177–9; transnational drug companies 176–7, 191
TRIPS *see* Trade-Related Aspects of Intellectual Property
Tufts Center for Drug Development 50
Turkey 35
Twenty Years of Health System Reform in Brazil (Couttolenc, Gragnolati, Lindelow) 185–7

The Umbrella Project *(Projeto Guarda Chuva)* 127
UNESCO (United Nations Educational, Scientific, and Cultural Organization) 87
UN General Assembly Special Session on HIV/AIDS (UNGASS) 113
Unified Health System/*Sistema Única da Saúde* (SUS) 80–1, 87, 157, 186
United Nations (UN) 3, 189
United Nations Commission on Human Rights (UNCHR) 56, 113
United Nations Conference on Trade and Development (UNCTAD) 43
United Nations Development Program (UNDP) 143
United States (US) AIDS medicines 2–3, 199
United States Food and Drug Administration (FDA) 31, 83, 106
United States Patent and Trademark Office (USPTO) 174
United States Trade Representative (USTR): intellectual property rights 138–9; "local working" clause 111; political power and 38–9, 42; Priority Watch Lists 194; TRIPS-plus measures 177
University of Chicago 68
unpatented medicines 143
UN Special Rapporteur on Human Rights 56
US Embassy Brasilia 140

US President's Emergency Plan for AIDS Relief (PEPFAR) 129
utilitarian arguments for IPRs 51–5, 54*f*

Viravaidya, Mechai 195, 197
Vitoria, Marco Antonio 85–6

Washington Consensus 69
WHO Medicines Strategy 114
Workers' Party/*Partido dos Trabalhadores* (PT) 96, 126–7, 154
Working Group on Intellectual Property/*Grupo de Trabalho sobre Propriedade Intelectual* (GTPI) 139–40
World AIDS Day 142–3
World Economic Forum 13
World Health Assembly 113–14, 200
World Health Organization (WHO): access to AIDS medication 113, 129, 199; consultative status of 39; generic medicines 172; motions passed by 56; non-communicable diseases, prevalence 198; patents and 40; prequalification by 162; programmatic efforts to fight AIDS 86
World Intellectual Property Organization (WIPO) 43, 53
World Trade Organization (WTO): agreements 69; compulsory licenses dispute 167; control over technology 14; creation of 42; dispute resolution mechanism of 194; Dispute Settlement Panel 140; drug patent deadlines 8; establishment of 4–5, 13; intellectual property laws and 22, 97, 125; local working and 111–16; patent-based business model 29; prequalification program 34; price negotiations 163; threats to Brazil's AIDS program 185, 189; TRIPS and 43–7, 45*t*; UN relations with 39

zidovudine (ARV drug) 32, 87, 97–102, 108

Printed by PGSTL